COMPUTER PROGRAMMING IN FORTRAN 90 AND 95

V. RAJARAMAN
Emeritus Professor
Supercomputer Education and Research Centre
Indian Institute of Science, Bangalore

PHI Learning Private Limited
Delhi-110092
2026

*In fond memory of **Shri Asoke K. Ghosh** (October 1942 – February 2024), Founder Chairman and Managing Director of PHI Learning, whose vision endlessly inspires.*

The Legacy Continues. . . .

Published by Pushpita Ghosh, PHI Learning Private Limited, Rimjhim House, 111, Patparganj Industrial Estate, Delhi-110092 and Printed by Syndicate Binders, A-20, Hosiery Complex, Noida, Phase-II Extension, Noida-201305 (N.C.R. Delhi).

₹750.00

COMPUTER PROGRAMMING IN FORTRAN 90 AND 95
by V. Rajaraman

ISBN-978-81-203-1181-7 (Print Book)
ISBN-978-93-90669-86-8 (e-Book)

The export rights of the book are vested solely with the publisher.

Contents

Preface

This book introduces computer programming using Fortran 90 language. Fortran is the oldest high level programming language which was introduced in 1957 primarily as a language for use by scientists and engineers. Over the last 40 years Fortran evolved from Fortran II to Fortran IV to Fortran 77, to the current standard Fortran 90. Fortran 77 has been used extensively during the past 20 years. One of the main merits of Fortran 77 is its simplicity and the efficiency of compilers which give a good object code.

During the last twenty years a number of developments have taken place in computing and one has seen the emergence of many new languages such as Pascal, C and C++. The users of Fortran 77 wanted improvements in Fortran so that it is on par with the new languages for writing programs for a variety of applications. It took around 10 years to reach a consensus on a new standard for Fortran which is Fortran 90. This standard was published by the International Standards Organization in 1991 and accepted by the American National Standards Institute (ANSI) in 1992. Many vendors started writing compilers for Fortran 90 in 1993 and it is now available in all Workstations and Personal Computers.

Fortran 90 has many new features compared to Fortran 77. Even though the standard specifies that all Fortran 77 programs should be executable by Fortran 90 compilers without any change, Fortran 90 differs substantially from Fortran 77. Thus the author felt that it will be advisable to write an entirely new book on Fortran 90 conforming to the standard to capture its spirit rather than revising his existing Fortran 77 book. This book is appropriate for those who want to learn and develop programs in Fortran 90.

This book has 21 chapters. After an introductory chapter which traces the evolution of Fortran, the second chapter explains how one could write small Fortran 90 programs. This chapter gives a reader the flavour of the language. Syntax rules for writing constants, variables and expressions are presented in Chapters 3 and 4. This is followed by 4 chapters which together are sufficient to write interesting Fortran 90 programs. In Chapter 9 we explain how to write functions and subroutines using the language features presented till then. Using arrays and strings in programming are explained in Chapters 10 and 12. To enable students to start programming early, format free input/output statements have been used upto Chapter 10. In Chapter 11 we introduce format statement and explain its use. In Chapter 13 we explain how to develop complete Fortran programs to do reasonably interesting tasks. Chapters 14 to 20 introduce the new features of Fortran 90. Specifically we discuss the use of MODULES, defining data structures in Fortran 90 using derived types, operations on entire arrays, defining new operators and overloading existing operators. Fortran 90 allows recursion. We explain this feature and develop some recursive programs. A new data type called pointer has been introduced in Fortran 90. This is particularly useful to create list data structure and tree data structure which we explain with examples. We consolidate applications of MODULES in Chapter 19. Chapter 20 is a small chapter discussing miscellaneous features of Fortran 90. In October 1996 a new standard on Fortran, called Fortran 95, was announced. Compilers are not yet available for Fortran 95. We have given in Chapter 21 the major additional features of Fortran 95. It should be noted that Fortran 95 has introduced only small additions to Fortran 90. In an appendix we have given an exhaustive list of intrinsic functions available in Fortran 90. In fact the richness and variety of these intrinsic functions, which operate on scalars, arrays and strings, has made programming complex applications in Fortran 90 very easy.

One of the main merits of the book is the large number of complete Fortran 90 programs which have been carefully selected and written. Every concept in the language has been illustrated with an appropriate example program. This approach makes the book eminently suitable for self-study.

A book of this type naturally gained a number of ideas from previous books on this subject. The author expresses his thanks to all these authors, too numerous to acknowledge individually. Special thanks are due to Prof. C.N.R. Rao, President, Jawaharlal Nehru Centre for Advanced Scientific Research, Bangalore, for evincing keen interest in the author's endeavours and for continued encouragement.

The author acknowledges the financial support provided by the Curriculum Development Cell of the Centre for Continuing Education, Indian Institute of Science, Bangalore. The author thanks Prof. T. S. Mruthyunjaya, Chairman of the Centre for Continuing Education, for promptly providing the funds requested by the author.

The author would like to thank Ms. T. Mallika for an excellent job of word processing the manuscript. Thanks are due to Mr. N. Karthik and Miss. S. Kalaiselvi for keying in the programs given in this book and assistance in editing and debugging. The author thanks Mr. R. Krishnamurthy for numerous valuable discussions on Fortran 90 and providing some useful literature on the subject. Thanks are due to Dr. V. Kamakoti for reading the manuscript and giving valuable suggestions.

Thanks are due to Dr. S.K. Ghoshal for reading the book and for many useful suggestions. Dr. Daniel Rudolph who read the book to learn Fortran 90 sent me many valuable suggestions including a list of typographical errors in the first printing of the book. I thank him for his effort. I will be grateful to readers if they send me their suggestions and point out any inadvertant errors in the book. I may be reached by email at the address *rajaram@serc.iisc.ernet.in* or suggestions may be sent to me by post.

Finally the author would like to express his heartfelt appreciation to his wife Dharma who read the proofs, assisted in preparing the index and cheerfully devoted herself to this project.

Bangalore **V. Rajaraman**
October, 1999

1. Evolution of Fortran

In this book we will describe how to write programs in the new Fortran standard language known as FORTRAN 90. FORTRAN is the oldest high level language which was introduced in 1957 primarily as a language for use by scientists and engineers.

John Backus and his team working at IBM took the first initiative in 1954 with a report entitled "Preliminary Report, specification for the IBM Mathematical FORmula TRANslating System, FORTRAN". In 1957 the first FORTRAN compiler was released for the IBM 704. Based on user feedback it was improved and called FORTRAN II in 1958. FORTRAN became a very popular language and many versions started appearing. One of the popular ones in early 60s was FORGO which was a "load and go" FORTRAN for IBM 1620 and was widely used in Universities. The proliferation of different versions of FORTRAN made it difficult to port FORTRAN programs from one machine to another and thus pressure built up to standardize FORTRAN. American Standards Association standardized FORTRAN in 1966 which was known as FORTRAN IV. This standard was widely used for over a decade. In the meanwhile, users sought introduction of new data types such as characters, available in other languages. Users also wanted simpler input/output statements, which were introduced in a version of FORTRAN developed at the University of Waterloo, Canada called WATFOR. Many of these improvements were accepted as useful and the American National Standards Institute (ANSI) released a new standard for FORTRAN in 1978 named FORTRAN 77. This standard has been very popular and is being used widely. The ANSI standard was also adopted by International Standards Organization (ISO) in 1980.

FORTRAN has been the language of choice for Scientists and Engineers. A large number of applications and library programs have been written in FORTRAN which have withstood the test of time. One of the main merits of FORTRAN 77 is the efficiency of compilers, written to translate it which gave good object codes.

1.1 EVOLUTION OF FORTRAN 90

In the meanwhile Computer Scientists have been seriously concerned about good programming practices which promote development of reliable programs. FORTRAN being an old language could not be drastically changed to accommodate newer ideas in programming languages primarily because it had to be "upward compatible". In other words programs written in an earlier version of FORTRAN are required to execute without change when compiled using a later version of FORTRAN. Thus all the old language constructs had to be retained in the new version. It was also realized that to ease programming of many applications, organization of data elements into data structures would be essential. For example, a data structure called a record is necessary to write programs which process files. List and tree data structures are useful in many non-numeric applications. Character string and string manipulation instructions are useful in word processing applications.

Other desirable features which were introduced in other programming languages such as Pascal, C and C++ during the last decade were sought by FORTRAN programmers. These features mainly enhance

- Readability of code by using meaningful variable names, better control structures (DO, DO WHILE etc.), operations on arrays, and recursion.
- Reliability of programs by better management of global variables and parameters of subroutines.
- Reuse of existing code by introducing features which help development of programs with reusable modules.

It took a long time, over ten years, to reach a consensus between vendors of computers, professionals who use FORTRAN and standards organizations, on what should be the future FORTRAN. The main problems were

- How to keep the new standard compatible with FORTRAN 77 so that old programs can be executed with the new compiler.
- How many new features should be introduced without making the language difficult to learn and compilers inefficient.

Finally a compromise was reached and a standard called FORTRAN 90 was published by the International Standards Organization in 1991. This standard was also accepted by the American National Standards Institute (ANSI) in 1992. (ANSI X3.198—1992). Soon vendors started providing FORTRAN 90 on their new machines and compilers are now available on almost all Workstations and Personal Computers.

FORTRAN is an evolving language. After the announcement of FORTRAN 90, there has been further discussions on improving it. In October 1996 a new standard known as FORTRAN 95 was announced by ISO as a standard. FORTRAN 95 has introduced only a few minor changes. We have discussed these at the end of the book. As compilers for FORTRAN 95 are not yet widely available we cannot effectively test FORTRAN 95 programs now.

FORTRAN 90 has many new features compared to FORTRAN 77 and is thus more versatile. FORTRAN 77, however, is simple to use and good compilers producing very efficient codes are widely available. Thus FORTRAN 77 will continue to be used for sometime. In the long run, however, FORTRAN 90 and its successors will become the standard language for numerical computing. Thus it is necessary for all practising engineers and scientists to learn this language. The purpose of this book is to teach FORTRAN 90 programming and its recent extension, FORTRAN 95. We do not assume that a reader knows FORTRAN. We do, however, assume that a reader knows the basics of algorithms, computers and how algorithms are executed by computers. Those who do not know this are referred to the book "Computer Programming in FORTRAN 77" by the author of this book. Knowledge of a language such as BASIC, C or PASCAL will be useful but not essential.

2. Simple Fortran 90 Programs

Learning Objectives

In this chapter we will learn:

1. The structure of a Fortran 90 Program
2. How to develop small programs in Fortran 90
3. How to input data and print results of Fortran 90 Programs

---

In this chapter we will write some programs in Fortran 90 and by studying these programs learn some of the syntax and semantic rules of the language.

2.1 WRITING A PROGRAM

We will consider as the first example a program to find the area and perimeter of a rectangle whose sides are p and q. The area is given by:

area = pq

and the perimeter by

perimeter = 2(p+q)

We have written the formulae above as we would normally do in algebra. In algebra, when we write pq where p and q are variables it is implied that p is multiplied by q. When we write an instruction for a computer, however we have to explicitly specify that multiplication is to be performed. The formula is thus written in Fortran 90 as:

area = p*q

which is called a statement. p, q and area are called *variable names*. The symbol * is the *multiplication operator.* p*q is an *arithmetic expression.* The symbol = is the *assignment operator.* The semantics or meaning of the above statement is:

"Read the contents of the memory box whose label or name is p and multiply it by the contents of another memory box named q. Store the result in a memory box named area".

Figure 2.1 illustrates this. (Notice that we have used a different font to represent variable names and other symbols used in programs to distinguish them from the rest of the text.)

Observe that the contents of p and q are copied and used. They are not destroyed. The formula for perimeter is written as:

perimeter = 2*(p+q)

in the above statement, 2 is an *integer constant.* As before p, q and perimeter are variable names. 2*(p+q) is an arithmetic expression. The semantics of the statement is:

"Add the contents of the memory box named p to that of the memory box named q. Store

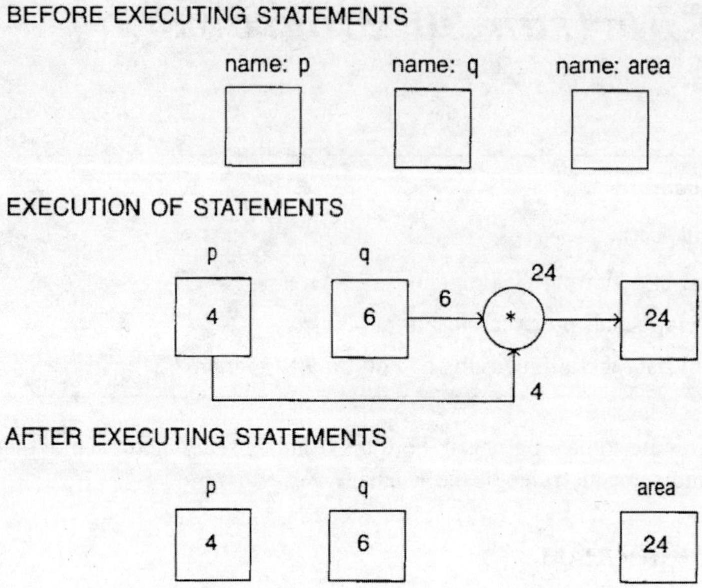

Fig. 2.1 Execution of statement area = p * q.

the result temporarily in a register of the CPU. Multiply this result by 2. Store the answer in the memory box named perimeter".

Figure 2.2 illustrates this. We have seen in this simple example the need for constants, variable names and operators. Example Program 2.1 is a Fortran 90 program to solve this problem.

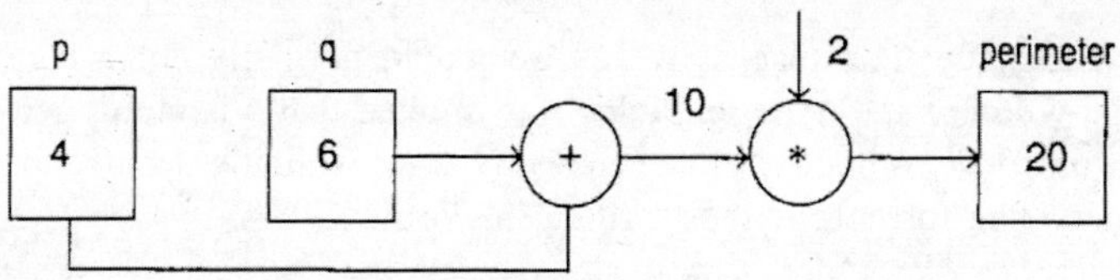

Fig. 2.2 Calculation of perimeter. Observe that the constant 2 is supplied by the compiler.

Example Program 2.1 Area and perimeter of a rectangle—Version 1

```
!PROGRAM 2.1
  !This program finds area and perimeter of a rectangle
  PROGRAM area_perimeter
    INTEGER:: p,q ,area, perimeter
    p=4
    q=6
    area=p*q
    perimeter=2*(p+q)
    PRINT *, "Area = ",area ," Perimeter=",perimeter
  END PROGRAM area_perimeter
```

We will now explain this program. The first line in the program starts with ! (An exclamation mark). Any line starting with ! is called a *comment*. Comments are useful to the programmer to read and understand a program. All comments are ignored by a compiler. If a comment is written in two lines each line must start with !. For example:

```
! This program finds the area and
! the perimeter of a rectangle
```

is a 2 line comment. A program may have any number of comments written anywhere. It is a good practice to include comments in a program which will help in understanding the program.

Observe the first line of the program following the comments:

```
PROGRAM area_perimeter
```

It is a statement which normally appears as the first line of all Fortran 90 programs. It consists of the keyword PROGRAM followed by a name given to the program by a programmer. The name can be upto 31 characters long. The first character must be a letter, that is, any one of the English letters, A, B, C, D ... Z, a, b, c, d ... z. In Fortran 90 no distinction is made between upper and lower case letters. In other words A and a, B and b ... Z and z are synonymous. The other characters may be any letter or a digit 0, 1, 2 ... or 9 or an underscore character _. A name is chosen which describes the program. In this case we named the program area_ perimeter.

In this program the next statement is:

```
INTEGER:: p, q, area, perimeter
```

This statement is called a *declaration.* It informs the compiler that p, q, area and perimeter are variable names and that individual boxes must be reserved for them in the memory of the computer. Further it tells that the data to be stored in the memory boxes named p, q, area and perimeter are integers, namely, whole numbers without a fractional part (e.g., 0, 1, 2, ...). These can be either positive or negative. The statement is said to define p, q, area and perimeter as of type INTEGER. The effect of this statement is shown in Fig. 2.3. Observe that 4 locations are reserved and named as: p, q, area and perimeter respectively.

Fig. 2.3 Effect of defining p, q, area and perimeter as integer variable names.

In this statement INTEGER is a *keyword.* In this book we will use capital letters to represent all keywords and small letters to represent *names,* also known as *identifiers,* used by us. In Fortran 90 blanks or white spaces are significant. Thus we should not write INTEG ER with an embedded blank as shown. There should also be no embedded blanks in variable names. For instance, perimeter should not be written as peri meter with embedded blanks. Blanks are, however, allowed as a separator to improve readability. For example, we can write

```
INTEGER :: p, q, area, perimeter
```

Observe that double colons are used to separate the keyword INTEGER and the variable names being declared as integer. A statement in Fortran 90 is written one per line. If it is a short statement, more than one statement may be accommodated in a single line. In such a case the statements are separated by a semicolon (;). For example we could have written

```
p = 4 ; q = 6
```

in Example Program 2.1. A line can have upto 132 characters. If a statement cannot be accommodated in a line then an ampersand symbol & is used to continue the statement on the next line.

The statement p = 4 is an *assignment statement.* It commands that the integer 4 be stored in the memory box named p. When the statement is executed, the integer 4 will be stored in the memory box named p as shown in Fig. 2.4.

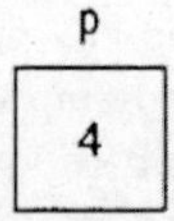

Fig. 2.4 Effect of statement p = 4.

More briefly we can state that this statement *assigns* a value 4 to the variable name p. The next statement q = 6 assigns 6 to q. Following this statement is the statement:

```
area = p * q
```

This is an *arithmetic statement.* It commands that the numbers stored in memory boxes p and q should be *copied* into the CPU. The original contents of p and q remain in their respective boxes. These numbers are multiplied by the CPU and the product is stored in the box named area. After executing this statement the box named area will contain 24 as shown in Fig. 2.1.

The next statement perimeter = 2 * (p + q) is also an arithmetic statement. We have already explained how this statement is interpreted. After this statement is executed the number stored in memory box named perimeter should be 20.

The next statement in the program is a command to *print* (or display) the contents of memory boxes named area and perimeter respectively. (In a briefer form we can say that the statement is a command to print the values of area and perimeter). The statement:

```
PRINT *, "Area = ", area, " Perimeter = ", perimeter
```

is called a *list-directed* print statement. It is called list-directed as a list of variables whose values are to be displayed is specified. The compiler normally uses a video display unit (VDU) to display the answers. The VDU is called the *default output device* as it is used by the compiler when no specification is given regarding the output device. There are other PRINT statements in FORTRAN which can be used to store the results in a file or print it on a printer. We will describe them later in this book.

When the PRINT statement

```
PRINT *, "Area = ", area, "  Perimeter = ", perimeter
```

is executed the following happens:

i. The string of characters enclosed within the double quote marks, namely, area = is displayed.
ii. The value stored in area is displayed. The number of columns used to display the value of area is decided by the compiler. It may not be the same for all compilers.
iii. On the same line the string two blanks followed by Perimeter = is displayed. Observe that we intentionally put two blank spaces in front of the string Perimeter to improve readability. Observe also that blank spaces within a character string are significant.
iv. Following this the value of perimeter is displayed. In this case the display will be as shown below:

```
Area = 24 Perimeter = 20
```

The last statement of the program is:

```
END PROGRAM area_perimeter
```

which tells the compiler that the *physical end* of the program has been reached and there are no more statements following this statement. We could have written this in either of the two forms shown below:

```
END PROGRAM
END
```

We, however, recommend the form

END PROGRAM *name of program*

as this form enhances the readability of the program.

2.2 INPUT STATEMENT

In Example Program 2.1 the variables p and q are assigned values in the program text. If we want to find the area and perimeter of another rectangle with sides 8 and 10, for instance, we have to replace the statements p = 4 and q = 6 by p = 8 and q = 10 respectively. We have to then recompile the program and run it again. This is not a good idea. We should actually have a facility to assign any desired values to p and q by feeding the data through an input unit. (Usually the keyboard of a Video Display Unit). This is possible if we can use an *input statement.* The input statement in Fortran 90 is:

```
READ *, p, q
```

This is called a *list-directed input statement.* The list of variables whose value is to be read is normally keyed in on a VDU's keyboard. This is the normal input device. If 8 is to be stored in p and 10 in q the input may be presented either as

8 10

with one or more blanks separating 8 and 10 or as

8, 10

with a comma separating 8 and 10. The value of p must be typed first followed by the value of q.

Example Program 2.2 Area and perimeter of a rectangle—Version 2

```
    !PROGRAM 2.2
    !This program finds area and perimeter of a rectangle
    !version2 using an input statement

    PROGRAM area_perimeter
       INTEGER:: p,q ,area,perimeter
       READ *,p,q
    area=p*q
    perimetor=2*(p+q)
    PRINT *, "Area = ",area ," Perimeter=",perimeter
 END PROGRAM area_perimeter
```

This program is written as Example Program 2.2. To compile and execute this program we have to use the commands appropriate to the operating system of the computer being used. The student should get this information from the users' manuals. We will write some more simple programs in the next section.

If you actually write this program, compile it and try to execute it, the computer will wait to get the values of p and q which are to be typed by you using the keyboard. A message to you to type the values of p and q is useful. We have done this in Example Program 2.3. Observe that before the READ statement we have written PRINT statement:

```
PRINT *, "Type values of p and q"
```

which will print the message: Type values of p and q.

Following this we have written:

PRINT*, "Use comma or blank to separate values" which displays:

```
Use comma or blank to separate values
```

As soon as you type the values of p and q the program will calculate the area and perimeter and display them.

Example Program 2.3

```
!PROGRAM 2.3
!This program finds area and perimeter of a rectangle
!version3 using prompt for input

PROGRAM area_perimeter
   INTEGER:: p,q ,area,perimeter
   PRINT *, "Type values of p and q"
   PRINT *, "Use comma or blank to separate values "
   READ *,p,q
   area=p*q
   perimeter=2*(p+q)
   PRINT *, "Area = ",area ,"  Perimeter=",perimeter
END PROGRAM area_perimeter
```

2.3 SOME FORTRAN 90 PROGRAM EXAMPLES

In this section we will write a few simple programs in Fortran 90. This is intended to let a student start programming quickly. Detailed rules of syntax of the language will be given later.

Example 2.1

As the first example we will write a program to convert a temperature given in Celsius to Fahrenheit. The formula for conversion is:

$$F = 1.8C + 32 \tag{2.1}$$

where C is the temperature in Celsius and F is the temperature in Fahrenheit. The program is given as Example Program 2.4.

Example Program 2.4 Conversion from celsius to fahrenheit

```
!PROGRAM 2.4
!THIS PROGRAM CONVERTS A CELSIUS TEMPERATURE
!TO FAHRENHEIT

PROGRAM temp_conversion
   IMPLICIT NONE
   REAL :: fahrenheit,celsius
   PRINT *, " Type value of celsius "
   READ *,celsius
   PRINT *,celsius
   fahrenheit=1.8*celsius+32.0
   PRINT *," fahrenheit= ",fahrenheit
END PROGRAM temp_conversion
```

The statement IMPLICIT NONE following the PROGRAM statement needs an explanation. It is placed there for historical reasons. In all early Fortran compilers including FORTRAN 77 it was not mandatory to declare variables. It was implicitly assumed that any variable name starting with I, J, K, L, M, N was an integer variable and a variable name starting with any of the other letters of the alphabet real. By experience it was found that not requiring the declaration of variables before their use was a source of serious logical errors in Fortran. It was thus decided in Fortran 90 that all variables have to be explicitly declared. However, as all FORTRAN 77 programs have to be accepted by Fortran 90 compilers to ensure compatibility, if a variable is by mistake, not declared in a Fortran 90 program then the compiler will not detect it as it will assume implicit typing rules. To ensure that this is not done by the Fortran 90 compiler it is a good practice to write the statement

```
IMPLICIT NONE
```

at the beginning of *every* Fortran 90 program. Then if a variable is undeclared it will be detected by the compiler and an error message will be displayed.

Observe that we have used more descriptive names for variable names rather than just F and C. Using such variable names makes the program more readable. Also observe that when we write the term 1.8C in Equation 2.1 the multiplication operator is implied. In a computer program such operators should be explicitly specified. The declaration:

```
REAL :: fahrenheit, celsius
```

informs the compiler that fahrenheit and celsius are variable names in which real numbers will be stored. By real number we mean a number with a fractional part, for example, 14.456 (We will describe later in detail the representation of real numbers in a computer). The following statement:

```
READ *, celsius
```

is a command to read a real number and store it in variable name celsius. We follow this with a statement to print the value read. This is done to find out whether the program read the input correctly. If the printed value differs from the value read it will immediately signal an error. This method of printing values of variables as soon as they are read is a good programming practice and is known as *echo check* of input.

The next statement is an arithmetic statement. Contents of celsius is multiplied by 1.8 and added to 32.0 and stored in fahrenheit. Observe that the number 32 is written with a decimal point to indicate that it is a real number. The last statement is to print the answer.

We will now consider an example of summing a small series. The use of intermediate variables simplifies the program and reduces the number of arithmetic operations performed by a computer.

Example 2.2

Required to calculate

$$sum = 1 - x^2/2! + x^4/4! - x^6/6! + x^8/8! - x^{10}/10!$$

A program to calculate the sum is given as Example Program 2.5. We will present a more concise program later in the book. Observe that after calculating x^2 and storing it in x2 the value stored in x2 is used to calculate x^4, x^6 etc. The sum is finally calculated and printed.

Example Program 2.5 Summing series

```
!PROGRAM 2.5
!PROGRAM TO SUM SERIES

PROGRAM sum_series
   IMPLICIT NONE
   REAL :: x,x2,x3,x4,x6,x8,x10,sum
   PRINT *, "Type value of x"
   READ *,x
   PRINT *," x = ", x
   x2=x*x
   x4=x2*x2/24.0
   x6=x4*x2/30.0
   x8=x6*x2/56.0
   x10=x8*x2/90.0
   sum=1.0-.5*x2+x4-x6+x8-x10
   PRINT *,"Value of x = ",x,"  Sum = ",sum
END PROGRAM sum_series
```

EXERCISES

2.1 Write a program to convert fahrenheit temperature to celsius.

2.2 Read the following program and explain what it does. Trace it with yard = 20

```
PROGRAM yard-feet
   IMPLICIT NONE
   INTEGER :: yard, feet, inch
   READ *, yard
   feet = 3* yard
   inch = 12 * feet
   PRINT *, "feet = " , feet, "  inches = ", inch
END PROGRAM yard-feet
```

2.3 Write a program to convert pounds to kilograms.

2.4 Write a program to read the radius of a circle and compute its area and circumference.

2.5 Write a program to express a length x given in millimeters in meters, centimeters and millimeters.

3. Numeric Constants and Variables

Learning Objectives

In this chapter we will learn:

1. Different types of numeric constants which are used in Fortran 90
2. Types of numeric variables in Fortran 90 and how they are declared and initialized
3. How constants may be given symbolic names
4. Specification of syntax rules for numeric constants and variables

---

In the last chapter we saw how small programs are written in Fortran 90. Before we write larger programs it is necessary to learn the rules of syntax of the language in some detail. We will give the rules for specifying constants and variable names in this chapter.

3.1 CONSTANTS

An entity which does not change during the execution of a program is called a constant. Constants may be classified as:

i. integer constants,
ii. real constants.

Integer constants

Integer constants are whole numbers without any fractional part. Real constants (also known as Floating point constants), on the other hand, may have fractional parts.

The allowed digits in a decimal constant are 0, 1, 2, 3, 4, 5, 6, 7, 8, 9.

Rule

A decimal integer constant must have at least one digit and must be written without a decimal point. It may have either sign + or –. If either sign does not precede the constant it is assumed to be positive.

Examples

The following are valid decimal integer constants:

i. 12345
ii. – 3469
iii. + 04013

The following are invalid decimal integer constants:

i. 11. (Decimal point not allowed)
ii. 45,256 (Comma not allowed)

iii. $ 125 (Currency Symbol not allowed)
iv. 2 5 (Embedded blank not allowed)
v. x248 (First symbol not a digit)

The range of values of an integer depends on the word size of a machine. In a 32-bit machine it has a range + $(2^{31} - 1)$ to $- 2^{31}$; which is + 217483647 to − 217483648.

Real constants

A real constant may be written in one or two forms called fractional form or the exponent form. The rules for writing a real constant in these two forms are given below:

Rule

A real constant in a fractional form must have at least one digit and must be written with a decimal point. It may have either the + or the − sign preceding it. If a sign does not precede it then it is assumed to be positive.

Examples

The following are valid real constants:

i. 1.0
ii. − 0.5678
iii. 5800000.0
iv. − 0.0000156

The following are invalid:

i.	1	(Decimal point missing)
ii.	− 1/2	(Symbol/illegal)
iii.	58,678.94	(Comma not allowed)
iv.	25_68.5	(Underscore not allowed)

In the examples above even though 5800000.0 and − 0.0000156 are valid real constants it is more convenient to write them as 0.58×10^7 and $- 0.156 \times 10^{-4}$ respectively. (× is multiplication symbol). The exponent notation for writing real constants provides this facility. In this notation these two numbers may be written as:

i. 0.58E7
ii. − 0.156E − 4

In the above examples E7 and E − 4 are used to represent 10^7 and 10^{-4} respectively.

In this notation a real constant is represented in two parts: a mantissa part (the part appearing before E) and an exponent part (the part following E). Thus 0.58 and − 0.156 are the respective mantissas and 7 and − 4 the exponents. We will now give the formal rule for writing real constants in the exponent form.

Rule

A real constant in the exponent form consists of a mantissa and an exponent. The mantissa must have at least one digit. It may have a sign. If a sign is omitted it is assumed to be positive. The mantissa is followed by the letter E or e and the exponent. The exponent must be an integer (without a decimal point) and must have at least one digit. A sign for the exponent is optional.

The actual number of digits in the mantissa and the exponent depends on the computer being used. The mantissa may have upto seven digits and the exponent may be between –38 and +38 in a 32-bit machine.

Examples

The following are valid real constants in the exponent form:

i. (a) 152E08 (b) 152.0E8 (c) 152E + 08 (d) 1520E7
ii. – 0.148E-5
iii. 152.859E25
iv. 0.01540E05

Observe that in (i) above four equivalent ways of writing the same constant are given:
The following are invalid:

i.	152.AE8	(Letter A in mantissa incorrect)
ii.	125 * E9	(* not allowed)
iii.	+ 145.8E	(No digit specified for exponent)
iv.	– 125.9E5.5	(Exponent cannot be a fraction)
v.	0.158E + 954	(Exponent too large)
vi.	125,458.25E – 5	(Comma not allowed in mantissa)
vii.	0.15E8.	(Decimal point in exponent not allowed)

3.2 SCALAR VARIABLES

A quantity which may vary during program execution is called a variable. Each variable has a specific storage location in memory where its numerical value is stored. The variable is given a name and the variable name is the "name tag" for the storage location. The value of the variable at any instant during the execution of a program is equal to the number stored in the storage location identified by the name of the variable. Figure 3.1 illustrates this. The variable name in Fig. 3.1 is total and its contents is 2.8.

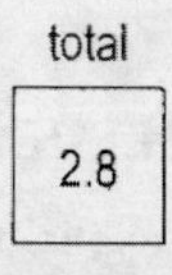

Fig. 3.1 A variable name and its contents.

When a variable name can contain only one number it is called a *scalar* variable. In Fortran 90 the word *identifier* is used as the general terminology for names given to variables, functions, constants, derived types, etc.

As variable names are name tags of memory locations where numbers are stored, and numbers are of two types, integer and real, one has to define a variable name as being of type real or type integer. A number stored in memory location with variable name of type integer is an integer (with the restrictions given while discussing integer constants) and one stored in a location with a variable name of type real may have a fractional part (with restrictions discussed in the last section). We will now give the rules for writing identifiers which are used as variable names.

Rule

An identifier is any combination of one or more letters (upper or lower case) or digits. The first character in the identifier must be a letter. It must not contain any character other than letters or digits. The underscore_ is taken as a letter. Identifier may be upto 31 characters long.

Both upper and lower case letters (i.e. capital and small letters) may be used for writing an identifier. Upper and lower case letters are treated as identical. In other words temp and Temp are not two different identifiers. The convention we will follow in this book is to use only lower case letters for variable names. No blanks may be embedded in a variable name.

Examples

The following are valid identifiers which may be used to name variables:

i. nA
ii. theta
iii. amin
iv. min50
v. temp_x
vi. absolute
vii. PROGRAM

The following are invalid identifiers:

i.	$count	(First character $ invalid)
ii.	roll#	(Character # not allowed)
iii.	no.	(Character . invalid)
iv.	2nd	(First character digit not allowed)
v.	ROLL No.	(No blanks allowed in a name)

We stated above that PROGRAM is a legal variable name even though it is a keyword. A set of keywords are used in Fortran 90 for special purpose and it is not advisable to use them as identifiers. In this book we will use capital letters for all keywords.

3.3 DECLARING VARIABLE NAMES

Identifiers used as variable names are explicitly typed as REAL or INTEGER by the following declaration which should appear at the beginning of a program before the variable names are used

type_name :: variable name, ..., variable name

We have used italics for *type_name* to emphasize that it is a keyword. The *type_name* available for variable names storing numbers are INTEGER for integers and REAL for real numbers. An example of valid declaration is given below:

```
INTEGER :: n, height, count, digit
REAL :: average, x_coordinate, p
```

Rule

All numerical variables in Fortran 90 should be declared as either INTEGER or REAL before they are used in a program. The declaration consists of the keyword INTEGER or REAL followed by :: (two colons without an embedded blank) and the list of variable names. The variable names are separated by commas.

When a variable name is declared, a memory location is identified and given this name. In Fig. 3.2 we illustrate this.

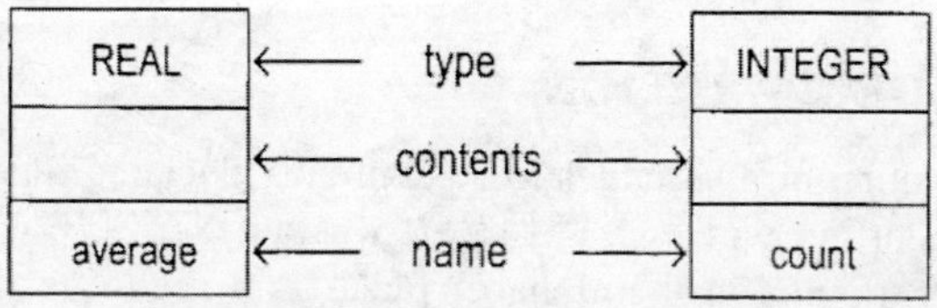

Fig. 3.2 Declaring a variable name reserves a memory box of appropriate type.

The following declarations of variables are invalid:

```
REAL, a, b, c (comma after REAL not valid)
INTEGER: x (: after INTEGER invalid)
INT :: x, y (INT is not the correct type-name)
```

Note that an enormous number of variable names may be defined using the rules to form identifiers. It is good practice to exploit this enormous choice in naming variables in programs by using meaningful identifiers. Thus, for example, if one is calculating temperature, pressure and the life of a catalyst in a chemical process, the corresponding variables in programs may be named temperature, pressure, catalyst_life respectively. Contrast this with the names t, p and cl which one may have given. These latter names are not meaningful and thus provide no help in understanding the role of a variable name in a program.

In Fortran 90 a value can be assigned to a variable name when it is declared. It is the initial value of the variable. For example we can write:

```
INTEGER :: x = 2, p = – 2842, val = 3492
REAL :: y, z = 2.5678E – 5, q = – 3.8469E3
```

In the above declaration y is not assigned any value. The other variables are assigned initial values specified.

When a variable is declared real the number of significant digits is around 7 and the exponent range is ± 38. These values are based on adoption of a standard prescribed by the Institution of Electrical and Electronic Engineers (called IEEE/ANSI standard). In many numerical computations 7 significant digits are found insufficient. Thus, Fortran 90 allows one to declare some variables as *double precision* which doubles the number of significant digits. The declaration used in this case is:

```
REAL(KIND = 2) :: a, b, x
```

The variable a, b, x are assigned sufficient storage in the computer to store double precision numbers. The numbers of mantissa and exponent digits to be assigned to double precision reals is specified in IEEE floating point standard which allows 15 mantissa digits and exponent range of ±310. We discuss this again in Section 20.1.

Besides reals, Fortran 90 also allows declaration of variable names as COMPLEX. The declaration

```
COMPLEX :: p
```

specifies that the variable name p stores a tuple: (real part of p, imaginary part of p) which may be, for example, (2.856, 3.5E1). Complex constants may also be defined in Fortran 90. For example, (2.85E2, – 3.56) is a complex constant where the first number is the real part and the second the imaginary part. We discuss the definition and use of complex quantities in greater detail in Section 20.3.

3.4 IMPLICIT DECLARATION

FORTRAN 77 did not require variables to be explicitly declared. It was implicitly assumed that any variable name starting with I, J, K, L, M, N was an INTEGER and a variable name starting with any of the other letters in the alphabet REAL. Not requiring the declaration of variables before their use led to serious errors in FORTRAN 77 programs which were difficult to detect. Thus FORTRAN 90 designers wanted declaration of variables to be compulsory as in other languages such as C and Pascal. But this was not enforced as old FORTRAN 77 programs had to be accepted by Fortran 90 compilers. In other words, it was decided that FORTRAN 77 should be a subset of Fortran 90. Thus old syntax rules had to be honoured.

Thus if by mistake a Fortran 90 programmer forgot to declare a variable, the compiler will not detect it and give it a default type based on the first letter of the name. To ensure that this mistake does not happen it is advised that all Fortran 90 programs must have the statement

```
IMPLICIT NONE
```

before declaring variables. In this book we will put IMPLICIT NONE at the beginning of every program before variables are declared.

The statement

```
IMPLICIT NONE
```

informs the compiler that no variable name has a default type. Thus it is compulsory to declare the type of each variable used in the program. If it is not done, the Fortran 90 compiler will signal a syntax error.

3.5 NAMED CONSTANTS

A constant appearing as it is in a program does not convey any meaning regarding its purpose or role to a programmer. It is attractive to associate an identifier or a name with the constant and use this name instead of the numerical constant. For example, if the constant π appears in many places in a program it is better to call it pi rather than use its value 3.1415926 everywhere. Another situation where it is preferable to use a name rather than a value is when a quantity such as min_balance is given a value which does not change in the program. Suppose it is, say, 500 then if the constant 500 is used everywhere its meaning will not be obvious to a person who reads the program. Further if the value is changed for some reason to say 750 one has to change 500 to 750 at all places where it occurs. There is a possibility of missing some and this will lead to an incorrect program. The statement used to name a constant is:

```
REAL, PARAMETER :: pi = 3.1415926
INTEGER, PARAMETER :: min_balance = 500
```

where the constant π is to be used we use the name pi and wherever minimum balance of 500 is to be used we use the name min_balance. If the value of min_balance is to be changed to 750 then the PARAMETER statement is changed to

```
INTEGER, PARAMETER :: min_balance = 750
```

This will automatically assign 750 to min_balance wherever it occurs.

A value cannot be assigned to the name used to represent a constant in a program. This will defeat the very purpose of naming a constant. The compiler will signal an error if an attempt is made to assign a value to it.

To summarize we use a PARAMETER statement to give a name to a constant when

- the constant is used in many places in a program
- a meaningful name for a constant would aid in understanding the program.

Example 3.1

We conclude this chapter with a simple example. A cylindrical tub of diameter d has water filled upto a height of 0.2 meters. If a tap is opened to fill it and water flows at the rate of 2 litres per minute, find the height to which it will be filled after 5 minutes.

Volume of a tub of diameter d and height h is

$$\pi d^2\ h/4$$

If f is the volume of water flowing per minute into the tub then, the height filled after time t can be calculated from the formula

$$f * t = \pi\ d^2\ h/4$$

$$\text{or } h = 4\ f * t/\pi\ d^2$$

Example Program 3.1 is written to solve this problem:

Example Program 3.1 Height to which a tub is filled

```
!PROGRAM 3.1
!TO FIND THE HEIGHT TO WHICH WATER IS FILLED
!IN A CYLINDRICAL TUB
PROGRAM fill_tub
  IMPLICIT NONE
  REAL, PARAMETER :: pi = 3.14159265
  REAL :: height, flow, diameter, time, init_height
  PRINT *, "Type values of init_height, flow, time, diameter"
  READ *, init_height, flow, time, diameter
  PRINT *, "init_height = ", init_height, "  flow = ", flow
  PRINT *, "time = ", time, "  diameter = ", diameter
  height = init_height + (4.0 * flow * time)/(pi * diameter * diameter)
  PRINT *, "height after", time, "  minutes = ", height
END PROGRAM fill_tub
```

Observe in the program the declaration of pi as a constant PARAMETER. Observe that in the declaration

```
REAL :: height, flow, diameter, time, init_height
```

We did not initialize init_height to 0.2. We instead read the value from the input. This is a better approach as init_height may change and if we had initialized it inside the program, the program has to be changed and recompiled. In this case we do not change the program; we only change the input data.

SUMMARY

1. An entity which does not change during the execution of a program is called a constant and one which may vary during program execution is called a variable.
2. In Fortran 90 numeric constants are of two types; integer and real. Integers are whole numbers without fractional parts and reals have fractional parts.
3. An integer constant is written without a decimal point and may range between ± 217483647 in computers with 32-bit words such as IBM PC.
4. Real constants may be written either using a fractional notation, for example, 252.68 or using a mantissa and exponent notation, for example, 0.25268E3.
5. Real constants may have upto 7 digit mantissa and exponent range of ± 38.
6. A variable name is a label of a location in a computer's memory where a number may be stored.
7. A variable name may be upto 31 characters long. The characters may be upper or lower case letters or underscore character. The first character must be a letter.
8. A variable name must be declared as REAL or INTEGER depending on whether it is intended to store a real value or an integer.
9. A variable name may be declared REAL (KIND = 2) if we want to specify that it is to store a double precision number (i.e. a number with 15 digit mantissa).
10. A variable name may be declared COMPLEX which will allocate storage to store the real and imaginary parts of a complex number.
11. It is possible to associate a name with a constant and use this name instead of the numerical constant. For example, if we write

    ```
    REAL, PARAMETER:: pi = 3.1415926
    ```

    then we can use the name pi instead of using the number 3.1415926 wherever the constant π is to be used.

EXERCISES

3.1 Pick the incorrect decimal integer constants from the following list. Explain why they are incorrect:

i. – 4689
ii. + – 785
iii. 4.25, 325
iv. 1/4
v. 62 – 34.86
vi. 0234
vii. 2A45
viii. Ox234

3.2 Pick the incorrect type declarations from the following list. Explain why they are incorrect:

```
REAL, servo, mass, iota
INTEGER :: servo, digit, count
INTEGER :: rs, ps, unsigned
REAL :: real, root, big
```

3.3 Pick the incorrect floating point constants from the following list. Explain why they are incorrect:

i. 40,943.65
ii. 425E2.5
iii. .0045E + 6
iv. 1/2.2
v. 465
vi. 43

3.4 Pick the incorrect identifiers from the following list. Explain why they are incorrect:.

i. constant
ii. variable
iii. integer
iv. Rs-ps
v. roll. no
vi. lambda
vii. lab man
viii. parameter

3.5 Pick the incorrect statement from the following:

```
REAL PARAMETER :: e = 2.31
INTEGER :: PARAMETER :: max_value = 250
INTEGER, PARAMETER :: min_value = 10
REAL, PARAMETER :: epsilon = 0.5 E–7
```

4. *Arithmetic Expressions*

Learning Objectives

In this chapter we will learn:

1. How to form arithmetic expressions using integer variables, real variables and constants
2. Various arithmetic operators, their precedence when they operate on variables, and rules of associativity among operators of equal precedence
3. The assignment operator, assignment statement, and their use

---

An arithmetic expression is a series of variable names and constants connected by arithmetic operation symbols, namely, addition, subtraction, multiplication, division and exponentiation. During the execution of the program the actual numerical values stored in variable names are used together with the operation symbols, to calculate the value of the expression. In this chapter we will discuss the syntax rules for writing arithmetic expressions and the rules followed by Fortran 90 to evaluate them.

4.1 ARITHMETIC OPERATORS AND MODES OF EXPRESSIONS

The arithmetic operation symbols used in Fortran 90 and their meanings are given in Table 4.1. In Table 4.1 the symbol – is used for both unary minus and subtraction. In the expression – a + b the – symbol is a unary minus, that is, it indicates that the negative of a is to be taken. In the expression a – b, however, the – symbol indicates a binary – or subtraction. Thus in this case b is to be subtracted from a.

Table 4.1 Arithmetic Operator Symbols

Operator symbol	*Arithmetic operation*
+	Addition
–	Subtraction or unary minus
*	Multiplication
/	Division
**	Exponentiation

The / operation for integers gives the integer quotient after division. Thus if we write 7/3 the answer would be 2. Observe in integer division the result is an integer. The remainder after division is ignored.

4.2 INTEGER EXPRESSIONS

Integer expressions are formed by connecting constants or variable names declared as integer or integer constant identifiers with similar quantities. For example, the following are integer expressions:

```
    INTEGER, PARAMETER :: max = 20
    INTEGER :: a, b, c, d, k, p, m
  i. - a + b
 ii. p/m + max
iii. - a + b * m ** 4
 iv. (k/m*8)
  v. a + c * 6 + max
```

The following are incorrect integer expressions:

```
INTEGER :: a, b, c, d, k, p, m
   i. a - b + j          (j not declared integer)
  ii. a - 4.0            (4.0 not an integer)
 iii. a ++ b + c         (++ occur together)
  iv. a/b * - c          (Two operator symbols, namely, * and - occur together)
   v. a (b + c)          (Operator missing after a)
  vi. a ** b + m * - k   (Two operator symbols namely * and - occur together)
 vii. (p * (m + k)       (One right parenthesis missing)
viii. k /*m              (Two operators / and * occur next to one another)
```

4.3 REAL EXPRESSIONS

Real expressions are formed by connecting (using arithmetic operators) variable names declared as real variables or real constant identifiers. The following are a list of real expressions:

```
REAL PARAMETER :: a = 3.145
REAL :: x, y, z, p, d, j
  i.  - x + y
 ii.  n/z + a
iii.  - z + p + n * z
 iv.  (x/y - j) * (p/j * 6.0)
  v.  x * p - 8.5 + p/0.8435E- 2/j + a
 vi.  z**3
```

In example (vi) above a real variable is raised to an integer power. This is allowed. In this case z is multiplied by itself 3 times.

The following are incorrect real expressions:

```
REAL :: x, y, z, n, p, j
  i.  x - z + d          (d not declared REAL)
 ii.  (x + y)(p + z)     (Missing operator. Should be written as (x + y) * (p + z) if that is intended)
iii.  z/* n              (* follows another operator /)
 iv.  n . j              (. not an arithmetic operator)
  v.  x/+p               (Two operators / and + occur together)
 vi.  (x + (j - p)       (Right parenthesis missing)
vii.  z p * n            (Missing operator between variables)
```

Fortran 90 allows mixing integers and reals in an expression. Such a facility is useful, particularly as an error such as writing 2 * a when 2.0 * a was intended is common and earlier Fortran compilers would reject it. This facility of mixing real and integer modes should be used carefully and is not recommended to beginners. Later in this chapter we will discuss rules applicable to mixed mode expressions.

4.4 PRECEDENCE OF OPERATIONS IN EXPRESSIONS

In a program the value of any expression is calculated by executing one arithmetic operation at a time. The order in which the arithmetic operations are executed in an expression is based on the rules of precedence of operators. The precedence of operators is: unary minus (–) FIRST, exponentiation (**) SECOND, multiplication (*) and Division (/) THIRD, Addition (+) and Subtraction (–) LAST. This is shown in Table 4.2.

Table 4.2 Precedence of Arithmetic Operators

Operator	*Precedence*
Unary –	FIRST
**	SECOND
* , /	THIRD
+ , –	LAST

For example, in the integer expression – a * b/c + d the unary – is done first, the result – a is multiplied by b, the product is divided by c (integer division) and d is added to it. The answer is thus:

$$\frac{-ab}{c} + d$$

All expressions are evaluated from left to right. All the unary negations are done first. After completing this the expression is scanned again from left to right; now all * and / operations are executed in the order of their appearance. Finally all the additions and subtractions are done starting again from the left of the expression.

For example, in the expression:

```
- a * b/c + d/k - m/d * k + c
```

the computer would evaluate – a in the first left to right scan. In the second scan

$$\frac{-ab}{c}, d/k \text{ and } \frac{m}{d}k$$

would be evaluated. In the last scan the expression evaluated would be:

$$\frac{-ab}{c} + \frac{d}{k} - \frac{m}{d}k + c$$

In the following expression:

```
a ** b/c + d ** e * f - h/p * r + q
```

The compiler will evaluate in the first left to right scan

$$a^b \text{ and } d^e$$

In the next left to right scan it will evaluate

$$\frac{a^b}{c}, d^e * f, \frac{h}{p} * r$$

In the last left to right scan it will evaluate

$$\frac{a^b}{c} + d^e * f - \frac{h}{p} * r + q$$

In the expression

$$x * y + z/n + p + j/z$$

in the first scan

$$xy, \; z/n \quad \text{and} \quad j/z$$

are evaluated. In the second scan the expression evaluated is:

$$xy + \frac{z}{n} + p + \frac{j}{z}$$

Use of Parentheses

Parentheses are used if the order of operations governed by the precedence rules are to be overridden.

In an expression with a single pair of parentheses the expression inside the parentheses is evaluated FIRST. Within the parentheses the evaluation is governed by the precedence rules.

For example, in the expression:

$$a * b/(c + d ** k/m + k) + a$$

the expression within the parentheses is evaluated first giving:

$$c + \frac{d^k}{m} + k$$

After this, the expression is evaluated from left to right using again the rules of precedence giving:

$$\frac{ab}{c + \frac{d^k}{m} + k} + a$$

If an expression has many pairs of parentheses then the expression in the innermost pair of parentheses is evaluated first, the next innermost next and so on till all parentheses are removed. After this the operator precedence rules are used in evaluating the rest of the expression.

For example, in the real expression:

$$((x * y) + z/(n * p + j) + x)/y + z$$

xy, np + j will be evaluated first.

In the next scan

$$xy + \frac{z}{np + j} + x$$

will be evaluated. In the final scan the expression evaluated would be:

$$\frac{xy + \frac{z}{np + j} + x}{y} + z$$

4.5 EXAMPLES OF ARITHMETIC EXPRESSIONS

In this section we will consider some expressions which occur frequently in practice and are improperly translated into Fortran 90 expressions by beginners.

Example 4.1

Consider the expression:

$$\frac{1}{1 + x}$$

where x is a real variable.

A beginner might write the expression as 1/1 + x. This expression is syntactically correct. It does not, however, mean what the programmer intended it to mean. The computer will evaluate it using the hierarchy rules as (1/1) + x. Observe that this mistake in writing is an error in logic rather than in syntax and the computer cannot detect this error. It will go ahead and compute wrongly resulting in a wrong answer. The correct way (logically and syntactically) of translating the expression is 1/(1 + x). The parentheses enclosing the denominator expression are essential.

In the expression (1+x) the constant 1 is an integer and x is declared REAL. An expression such as this which mixes an integer with real is called a *mixed mode expression*. Fortran 90 allows this. It automatically converts the integer to real before adding. In general a "narrower type" is converted to a "broader type" to avoid losing information. Beginners should avoid mixing types as the "automatic conversion" may lead to errors which are difficult to locate. We will discuss this in greater detail later in the chapter.

Example 4.2

Consider the expression:

$$\frac{a + b}{a - b}$$

where a and b are real. A translation of this which is syntactically correct, might be a + b/a – b.

This will be evaluated as:

$$a + \frac{b}{a} - b$$

which is not what the programmer intended. The expression a+b/(a–b) is also a wrong translation as the expression evaluated would be:

$$a + \frac{b}{a - b}$$

The correct expression is (a + b)/(a – b)

The above examples illustrate the need for parentheses. In practice a good rule to follow is: "if in doubt use parentheses".

Example 4.3

Consider the expression $a^2 + b^2 - 2ab$. A careless programmer might translate this into a ** 2 + b ** 2 – 2a * b. This has a syntax error. The expression 2a * b has no meaning syntactically. It is to be written as 2 * a * b. An operator is required, it is not implied. After this correction the expression is syntactically correct and does what the programmer intended it to do. The expression is:

```
a ** 2 + b ** 2 - 2 * a * b
```

Observe that exponentiation may be done with an integer. This is in fact more efficient from the point of view of computer arithmetic. If the exponent is in integer mode the computer evaluates the expression a**2 by multiplying a by a. If the exponent is real (even if it is a whole number for example a ** 2.0) the computer evaluates it by using the formula $a^b = e^{b \ln a}$ where ln a is natural logarithm of a. Compared to successive multiplications, evaluation using exponential and logarithmic functions is much slower and gives a larger rounding error. If a is negative use of logarithmic function is not valid. Thus if a is negative a ** 2.0 will give an error message whereas a ** 2 will give the correct answer.

Example 4.4

Consider a polynomial expression: $5x^4 + 3x^3 + 2x^2 + x + 10$.

A correct syntactic translation of this expression is:

```
5 * x ** 4 + 3 * x ** 3 + 2 * x ** 2 + x + 10
```

This, however, is an inefficient way of writing a polynomial for computer evaluation as it involves a total of 4 addition operations and 9 multiplication operations (verify this). Another technique of writing the polynomial requires a far lesser number of arithmetic operations and is given below:

$$\begin{aligned} 5x^4 + 3x^3 + 2x^2 + x + 10 &= 10 + x + 2x^2 + 3x^3 + 5x^4 \\ &= 10 + x(1 + 2x + 3x^2 + 5x^3) \\ &= 10 + x(1 + x(2 + 3x + 5x^2)) \\ &= 10 + x(1 + x(2 + x(3 + 5x))) \end{aligned}$$

Translated into Fortran 90 this is:

```
10 + x * (1 + x * (2 + x * (3 + 5 * x)))
```

The above expression requires only four multiplications and four additions. Even though this expression is efficient it is less readable. Further, errors could be made in parenthesizing. Whenever there are a large number of parentheses in an expression one check is to separately count the number of left and right parentheses. These counts should be equal.

Example 4.5

Consider the expression

$$x^{1/3} - y^{-2}$$

A careless translation of this to Fortran 90 is:

```
x ** (1/3) - y ** - 2
```

The above expression is syntactically incorrect as in y ** – 2 two operators ,** and – follow one another. After correction we get

```
x ** (1/3) - y ** (- 2)
```

This still has an error. In the term x ** (1/3) the division 1/3 is integer division of 1 by 3. As the result of an integer operation can only be an integer, 1/3 gives an integer answer 0.

A correct translation is

```
x ** (1.0/3.0) – y ** (– 2)
```

Example 4.6

Consider the expression:

$$(-1)^i x^{2i+1}/2y$$

A careless translation of this would be

```
INTEGER :: i; REAL :: x, y
– 1 ** i * x ** 2i + 1/2 * y
```

This has a syntax error. 2i has an operator missing. If we correct it and write

```
– 1 ** i * x ** 2 * i + 1/2 * y
```

This will be evaluated as

$$(-1)^i * x^2 * i + 0 * y$$

when we do a left to right evaluation and use rules of operator precedence. The correct expression should use appropriate parentheses. It is shown below:

```
– 1 ** i * x ** (2 * i + 1)/(2.0 * y)
```

Example 4.7

Consider the expression:

$$a\left(\frac{x+y}{z}\right)^{3.5}$$

A careless translation of this is

```
a (x + y/z) ** 3.5
```

This has a syntax error. Multiplication operator is missing after a. If we correct it and write it as:

```
a * (x + y/z) ** 3.5
```

the expression evaluated will be

$$a * \left(x + \frac{y}{z}\right) ** 3.5$$

The correct expression is:

```
a * ((x + y)/z) ** 3.5
```

Example 4.8

Consider the following expression:

$$\frac{mv^2}{2.5} + \frac{gh}{4d}$$

A careless programmer may translate this as:

```
m * v * v/2.5 + gh/4.d
```

In the second term gh is written as it appears in the formula and is wrong. 4d is translated as 4.d which is also wrong. They should be written as g * h and 4 * d respectively. After making these corrections the expression is:

```
m * v * v/2.5 + g * h/4 * d
```

which is syntactically correct. There is still one error left. g * h/4 * d will be evaluated as:

$$\frac{gh}{4} * d$$

The correct way of writing this would be:

```
m * v * v/2.5 + (g * h)/(4 * d)
```

Example 4.9

Consider the expression 2^{k^n}. Note that $(2^k)^n$ is not the same as $2^{(k^n)}$. If the expression is written in Fortran 90 as

```
2 ** k ** n
```

without parentheses it is ambiguous and some processors may not accept it. It should be written as (2 ** k) ** n if you want to evaluate $(2^k)^n$ or as 2 ** (k ** n) if you want to evaluate $2^{(k^n)}$.

A note on integer division

When an integer is divided by another integer the answer may have a fractional part. All fractions are, however, discarded during calculation with the / operator. Thus 3/4 will give an answer 0 and 5/4 an answer 1. When expressions are evaluated using hierarchy rules, whenever division is performed, the truncated numbers are the ones which are used in the final evaluation. Thus i/10 * 10 and 10 * i/10, even though they seem equivalent, give different answers. If i = 35, the first expression gives:

35/10 * 10 = 3 * 10 = 30

The second expression gives:

10 * 35/10 = 350/10 = 35

4.6 ASSIGNMENT STATEMENTS

An assignment statement has the following form:

Variable name = *expression*

For example,

```
total_pay = gross_pay – deduction + allowance and
rate = gross_rate – discount
```

are assignment statements.

```
Total_pay + deduction = gross_pay + allowance
```

is not an assignment statement as this has expressions on both sides of the assignment operator =.

When an assignment statement is executed, the expression on the right of the assignment operator is first *evaluated* and the *number* obtained is stored in the storage location named by the variable name appearing on the left of the assignment operator.

Thus when an expression is assigned to a variable the previous value of the variable is *replaced by* the value calculated using the expression. For example, in the assignment statement b = b + 3 the integer 3 is added to the number stored in variable name b and this new value replaces the old value stored in b.

The equal sign must thus be interpreted as "is to be replaced by" rather than "is equal to" (A more appropriate symbol would have been ← instead of =).

Type conversion in statements

In the examples given in the last section the variable type used in the expression on the right hand side of the = sign was the same as the variable type on the left. This need not be so.

Rule

A variable declared REAL can be set equal to an integer expression and vice-versa.

If an integer expression is assigned to a real variable name then the value of the integer expression is converted to a REAL number and is stored in the REAL variable name.

For example, consider the following statements:

```
INTEGER :: j , k
REAL :: a
a = j/k
```

If j = 3 and k = 2 then j/k = 1 and the variable a will be assigned the value 1.0.

If a real expression is assigned to an integer variable the value of the real expression is "truncated" and stored in the integer variable name. In other words the fractional part of the real number obtained by evaluating the expression is chopped off (not rounded!) and the integer part is stored in the integer variable name.

For example, consider the following statements:

```
REAL :: a, b
INTEGER :: p
p = a/b
```

If a = 7.2 and b = 2.0 then a/b = 3.6. When 3.6 is assigned to p it will be truncated to 3 (as p is declared INTEGER) and stored in p.

4.7 DEFINING VARIABLES

A variable is said to be *defined* if a value has been assigned to it. In other words, a variable is defined if a number has been stored in the storage location corresponding to its name.

Unless a variable is defined it cannot be used in an arithmetic expression. Values may be assigned to variables when they are declared in a program.

They may also be defined by the statement:

Variable name = Constant

For example, x = 4.5 defines the variable x by storing 4.5 in the memory location corresponding to x.

If all the variables appearing on the right of the assignment operator in an assignment statement are defined then the variable on the left is also defined. It follows from the fact that when an assignment statement is executed the numerical value of the expression on the right of the assignment operator is evaluated and stored in a memory location corresponding to the variable on the left.

For example, the statement b = a * d + e – f defines the variable b if a, d, e and f are already defined.

4.8 SOME PROBLEMS DUE TO ROUNDING OF REAL NUMBERS

Real numbers are stored in a computer's memory with a finite number of mantissa and exponent digits. Usually most computers have around 8 mantissa digits and 2 exponent digits. Thus answers cannot have more than 8 significant digits. Thus for example 1.0/3.0 will be truncated after 8 digits and will be approximated by 0.33333333. Thus if we write

```
x = 1.0/3.0
y = x + x + x
```

the variable y will contain 0.99999999 and not 1.0.

If k is an integer variable name and we write k = y, k will contain 0 as y will be truncated.

Example 4.10

Rounding of real numbers has other effects which a Fortran 90 programmer should know. For example, assuming that a computer can store eight significant digits, if we write:

```
w = x + y – z
```

With x = 0.5, y = 0.25434678E9 and z = 0.25434677E9, the operator precedence rules of Fortran 90 will add y to x first and subtract z from it. Thus

x + y = 0.5E0 + 0.25434678E9 = 0.25434678E9

As only 8 digits can be stored in the mantissa of a real variable, x is ignored. If we now subtract z from this result we get w = 0.1E2. If we write w as w = x + (y – z) then (y – z) is computed first giving 0.1E2. When this is added to x = 0.5E0 we get 0.1E2 + 0.005E2 = 0.105E2 or 10.5 which is the correct result.

Example 4.11

Consider the expression

```
((a + b) ** 2 – 2.0 * a * b – b ** 2)/a ** 2
```

Let a = 0.1E0, b = 0.1E4

The numerator computed to eight significant digits is:

(0.10001E4) ** 2 – 0.2E3 – 0.1E7
= 0.10002E7 – 0.2E3 – 0.1E7
= 0.1E7 – 0.1E7 = 0

The denominator is a ** 2 = 0.1E – 1
The expression evaluates to 0 whereas the answer algebraically should be

$$(a^2 + b^2 + 2ab - 2ab - b^2)/a^2 = 1.0$$

Example 4.12

Consider the statement:

w = x * y/z

with x = 0.5E – 30, y = 0.5E – 20 and z = 0.25E – 25
The arithmetic expression x * y/z will be evaluated using the operator precedence rules as:

0.5E–30 * 0.5 E–20 = 0.25 E–50

This exponent is smaller than – 38 which is the smallest exponent that can be stored in a 32-bit computer. The compiler will signal an arithmetic *underflow error* and halt. If we had written the expression as:

x * (y/z)

it will evaluate y/z first giving 0.2E6 which will be multiplied by x = 0.5E – 30 giving 0.1E – 24 which is the correct answer.

Example 4.13

Consider the expression

w = x * y/z

with x = 0.5E30, y = 0.5E30, z = 0.25E30. Evaluating x * y again as per precedence we get 0.25E60. The exponent is now larger than +38 the largest exponent that can be stored in a 32-bit computer. The compiler will signal an arithmetic *overflow error* and halt. If we compute x * (y/z) we get (y/z) = 0.2E1 and multiplying by x we get 0.1E31 which is the correct answer.

The main point brought out by these examples is that the asssociative law of algebra, namely,

xy/z = (xy)/z = x (y/z)

is not valid when limited precision floating point arithmetic is carried out on a computer. The order of carrying out operations is important primarily because of rounding of real numbers (due to limited precision) and the limited range of real numbers that may be stored in a computer. The reader should not be unduly alarmed by these observations as in most problems such situations may not occur. A Fortran 90 programmer should, however, be aware of these problems and look carefully in situations where very large or very small numbers occur.

4.9 MIXED MODE EXPRESSIONS

Fortran 90 allows mixing of reals with integers in expressions. In such a case integers are converted to reals before computation. However, if there is an integer sub-expression in the expression, it is computed using integer arithmetic. This feature is often overlooked by programmers and leads to unexpected errors. Consider the expression:

(1 + x)/(1 – x)

In the above expression 1 is converted to real and the expression is correctly computed. If we want to write an expression for $ix^2/2$ where i is an integer and x is real and write (i/2) * x * x then (i/2) is computed using integer arithmetic. Thus if i = 1 the expression will be zero which is wrong.

Consider the expression:

```
INTEGER :: k
REAL :: x, y
y = x * k/4 with x = 8, k = 3
```

If we write y = x * (k/4) then y will be equal to 8. * (3/4) = 8. * 0 = 0. If we write y = (x * k)/4 then k is converted to real first giving 24.0 for the numerator. The denominator integer 4 is converted to real and 24.0 is divided by 4.0 giving 6.0.

Thus whenever integer division is seen in a sub-expression one should re-examine the expression carefully.

It has been observed in practice that mixing integers with reals can lead to mistakes which are difficult to locate. The conversion is so automatic that it is easy to overlook a problem. Thus it is better not to use this facility if you are a beginner.

Fortran 90 provides *explicit type conversion* functions using which a programmer can intentionally change the type of expressions in an arithmetic statement. The explicit type conversion functions are REAL and INT. For example, if we write:

REAL (*integer expression or variable name*)

then the integer expression or variable name is converted to real. If we write:

INT (*real expression or variable name*)

then the real expression or variable name is converted to integer. These functions are safer to use as the programmer intentionally uses them. Using this we can write the expression:

$(i/2)\ x^2$ as:
REAL (i)/2 * x * x

The expression xk/4 may be written as:

x * REAL (k)/4

These functions are simple to use as the programmer intentionally uses them. Using the type conversion we can write the expression:

$$\frac{i}{2} x^{2i+1}$$

as: REAL(i)/2 * x ** (2 * i + 1)

4.10 INTRINSIC FUNCTIONS

Besides the simple arithmetic operations on variables a number of useful built-in functions, also known as intrinsic functions, are available in Fortran 90. The method of using a function is to write:

Function name (*variable name or expression*)

The argument of a function may be either in real mode or integer mode depending upon the function being evaluated. The argument should be enclosed in parentheses. If a function has more than one argument the arguments are separated by commas.

Some of the intrinsic functions available in Fortran with their description and the number and mode of their arguments are listed in Table 4.3. An extensive list of functions is given in Appendix A.

Table 4.3 List of Some Instrinsic Functions in Fortran

Function	*Name*	*Definition*	*No. of arguments*	*Type of arg*	*Type of f(arg)*
Integer to real conversion	REAL	Integer expn.converted to real	1	Int.	Real
Real to integer conversion	NINT INT	Real expn.converted to nearest integer Result truncated	1	Real Real	Int. Int.
Absolute value	ABS IABS	|arg| |arg|	1 1	Real Int.	Real Int.
Remainder (2 arguments)	AMOD MOD	Remainder when arg 1 is divided by arg 2	2 2	Real Int.	Real Int.
Transfer of sign (2 arguments)	SIGN ISIGN	Sign (arg2) |arg1|	2 2	Real Int.	Real Int.
Positive difference (2 arguments)	DIM IDIM	arg2-min(arg1, arg2)	2 2	Real Int.	Real Int.
Mathematical Functions:					
Exponential	EXP	e^x	1	Real	Real
Logarithm	LOG LOG 10	ln x $\log_{10}x$	1 1	Real	Real
Square root	SQRT	$\sqrt{x}$	1	Real	Real
Sine	SIN	Sin x (x in radians)	1	Real	Real
Cosine	COS	Cos x (x in radians)	1	Real	Real
Hyperbolic Sine	SINH	Sinh x	1	Real	Real
Hyperbolic Cosine	COSH	Cosh x	1	Real	Real
Arc Sine	ASIN	$\text{Sin}^{-1}x$	1	Real	Real
Arc Cosine	ACOS	$\text{Cos}^{-1}x$	1	Real	Real
Arc Tangent	ATAN	$\text{Tan}^{-1}x$	1	Real	Real

A number of points should be noted while using functions:

1. A function may be used in arithmetic expressions in a way similar to a variable name.
2. A function may be used as the argument of a function. For example, Sin |x| may be written as:

```
SIN(ABS (x))
```

3. The mode of a function may be either integer or real as given in Table 4.3. The mode of the arguments and of the result of all mathematical functions, namely, exponential, sine, cosine, etc., are real. There is no automatic mode conversion of function arguments. Thus if k is an integer the expression EXP(k) is incorrect whereas EXP(REAL(k)) is correct.
4. While evaluating an arithmetic expression, any functions appearing in it have the highest precedence. They are thus evaluated first. Before evaluating a function its argument is evaluated.
5. The value evaluated for arguments of functions must lead to meaningful function evaluation. Thus negative argument value for SQRT, zero or negative argument value for LOG, zero argument value of arg2 in MOD are invalid.
6. In the Sine and Cosine functions the argument x is assumed to be in radians. Thus angles in degrees should be converted to radians before these functions are used.
7. The arctangent function returns only the principal value, namely, a value of the function between $\pm \pi/2$.

4.11 EXAMPLES OF USE OF FUNCTIONS

Example 4.14

This example illustrates rounding a real number to the nearest integer. For example, 1.5 should be rounded to 2, –1.5 to –2, 1.4 rounded to 1 and –1.4 to –1.

Rounding of a real number r to the nearest integer would be done by the function:

INT (ABS(r) + 0.5)

Observe ABS(r) which is necessary to round negative real numbers. If we had written INT(r + 0.5), –1.6 would have been rounded to –1. INT (ABS (r) + 0.5) rounds – 1.6 to +2. We thus have to restore the sign of r. This may be done using the sign function as follows:

ISIGN (INT(ABS(r) + 0.5), INT (r))

The ISIGN function takes the sign of the second argument and affixes it to the first argument.

Example 4.15

This example illustrates the use of MOD function to pick the least significant digit of an integer. For example, for an integer 5842 the least significant digit is 2. For an integer k the least significant digit is given by:

LSD = IABS(MOD(k,10))

The IABS value is taken as k may be negative, leading to a negative value for MOD (k, 10).

Example 4.16

A company charges Rs. 10/- minimum charges for electricity consumption upto 30 units and charges in addition to Rs. 10, Re. 0.25 per unit for consumption above 30 units. An expression is to be developed for charge calculation.

The function DIM gives the excess over a pre-assigned number and can be used to find consumption above 30 units. If we use the variable name consn to store the value of units consumed, then

```
DIM(consn, 30. 0)
```

equals zero if consn is less than or equal to 30 and equals (consn – 30.0) if consn is greater than 30. Thus the statement:

```
charge = 10.0 + 0.25 * DIM(consn, 30.0)
```

implements the requirement.

Observe that both arguments of DIM are in real mode.

Example 4.17

Some mathematical expressions and their Fortran equivalents are given below:

Expression

$$\frac{\alpha}{\sqrt{\alpha^2 + \omega^2}} \text{Cos}(\omega t + \phi)$$

Fortran equivalent

```
alpha * COS(omega * t + phi)/SQRT(alpha ** 2 + omega ** 2)
```

Example 4.18

Expression

$$\log_e \sqrt{\frac{x}{yz}}$$

```
LOG(SQRT(x/(y * z)))
```

Example 4.19

Expression

$$\frac{1 - e^{-\alpha\sqrt{x}}}{1 + xe^{-|x|}}$$

Fortran equivalent

```
(1.0 – EXP(– alpha * SQRT(x)))/(1.0 + x * EXP (– ABS (x)))
```

Example 4.20

Expression

$$a \text{ Cos } x + b \text{ Cos}^2 x + c \text{ Cos}^3 x$$

Fortran equivalent

```
a * COS(x) + b * COS(x) ** 2 + c * COS(x) ** 3
```

Even though the above translation is syntactically correct it wastes computer time as COS(x) is being evaluated thrice in the expression. It would instead be economical to write—

```
y = COS(x)
f = a * y + b * y ** 2 + c * y ** 3
```

Observe in the above example that we have split up one arithmetic statement into a sequence of two statements. If a series of statements are given the computer evaluates them one after the other in the order in which they are given. Thus if one writes

```
x = 2.0
b = x ** 2 + 4.5
c = b/x
```

x will be set equal to 2.0. With this value of x the value of b will be evaluated as (4. + 4.5) which equals 8.5. Finally the value of c will be evaluated as 8.5/2. = 4.25.

We will conclude this chapter by writing a few programs to illustrate some of the concepts studied in this chapter.

Example 4.21

Mangoes cost Rs. 62.80 per dozen. It is required to find the cost of mangoes to the nearest paisa and print the answer as rupees and paise. A program to do this is given as Example Program 4.1.

Example Program 4.1 Calculates cost of mangoes—Version 1

```
!PROGRAM 4.1
!THIS PROGRAM CALCULATES THE PRICE OF 28 MANGOES GIVEN THE
!PRICE OF DOZEN MANGOES
PROGRAM price_mangoes
   IMPLICIT NONE
   INTEGER :: rupees, paise, cost_of_28
   REAL :: cost_dozen, rcost_28
!READ COST OF 12 MANGOES
   PRINT *,"TYPE COST OF DOZEN MANGOES"
   READ *,cost_dozen
   PRINT *,"cost of dozen mangoes =",cost_dozen
!CALCULATE THE PRICE OF MANGOES IN PAISE
   rcost_28=((cost_dozen*100.0/12.0)*28.0)
!0.5 ADDED TO rcost_28 FOR ROUNDING.
   cost_of_28=rcost_28+0.5
   rupees=cost_of_28/100
   paise=cost_of_28-(rupees*100)
   PRINT *,"cost of 28 mangoes =", " Rs",rupees, " ps",paise
END PROGRAM price_mangoes
```

In this program the cost of a dozen mangoes is given and is read by the READ statement and immediately printed to ensure that the correct value was received. In the next statement the cost of 28 mangoes is computed in paise. We do this as it is required to output the price in rupees and paise. The variable rcost_28 is declared REAL and we store the cost of 28 mangoes in paise. The answer may have fractional paise. In the next statement we find the cost to the nearest integral paisa. This is done by adding 0.5 to rcost_28 and assigning this value to an integer variable cost_of_28. (Note that if x is real and x = 3.49 and i is an integer, then when we write i = x + 0.5 = 3.99, 3 is stored in i after truncation. If, on the other hand, x = 3.51, then i = x + 0.5 = 4.01 stores 4 in i. Thus adding 0.5 has the effect of rounding a real number to its nearest integer when it is stored in an integer variable name).

In the next statement rupees is obtained by using integer division. Having found the rupee part of cost_of_28 the paise part is computed in the next statement. Finally the cost_of_28 mangoes is printed in rupees and paise.

Example Program 4.1 is correct and will work for the given problem. It is, however, not general. If we want to calculate the price of 29 mangoes instead of 28 the program should be re-written. When a program is written it should be made as general as possible. We can easily generalize the program by keeping the quantity to be bought and cost per dozen as variables. This will enable us to use the same program for different quantities of mangoes and varying costs by changing only the data entered on a terminal. This generalized program is given as Example Program 4.2.

Example Program 4.2 Version 2 of Example Program 4.1

```
!PROGRAM 4.2
!THIS PROGRAM CALCULATES THE PRICE OF x MANGOES GIVEN THE
!PRICE OF DOZEN MANGOES
PROGRAM price_mangoes_general
   IMPLICIT NONE
   INTEGER :: rupees, paise, cost, quantity
   REAL :: cost_dozen
!READ COST OF 12 MANGOES
   PRINT *,"TYPE COST OF DOZEN MANGOES AND QUANTITY"
   READ *,cost_dozen, quantity
   PRINT *,"cost of dozen mangoes = ",cost_dozen
!CALCULATE THE PRICE OF MANGOES IN PAISE
   cost=NINT((cost_dozen*100.0/12.0)*quantity)
   rupees=cost/100
   paise=cost-(rupees*100)
   PRINT *," cost of",quantity,"  mangoes = ", " Rs", rupees, "  ps", paise
END PROGRAM price_mangoes_general
```

Observe the statement:

```
cost = NINT((cost_of_dozen (100.0/12.0) * quantity)
```

This statement uses the intrinsic function NINT which rounds the real argument to its nearest integer.

Example 4.22

Two sides of a triangle are of lengths a and b respectively. The angle included by these sides is θ in degrees. It is required to find the length of the third side and the area of the triangle.

The length of the third side is

$$(a^2 + b^2 - 2ab \text{ Cos}\theta)^{1/2}$$

and the area is

$$\text{area} = ab \text{ Sin}\theta/2$$

Example Program 4.3 Area of triangle—Version 1

```
!PROGRAM 4.3 INCORRECT PROGRAM
!PROGRAM CALCULATES AREA AND SIDE OF A TRIANGLE
!a AND b ARE LENGTH OF TWO SIDES
!theta IS THE ANGLE BETWEEN THESE SIDES IN DEGREES

PROGRAM triangle_1
   IMPLICIT NONE
   REAL :: a,b,c,theta,area
   PRINT *, "Type values of a, b, theta"
   READ *,a,b,theta
   PRINT *,"sides a=", a," b  =",b
   PRINT *,"included angle=",theta
   c=SQRT(a**2.0+b**2.0-2.0*a*b*cos(theta))
   area=a*b*SIN(theta)/2.0
   PRINT *,"side c=",c,"  area=",area
END PROGRAM triangle_1
```

A careless programmer might have written Example Program 4.3 to solve this problem. This program has the following defects:

i. The angle given in degrees has been directly used in computing cosine and sine. The argument of the cosine and sine function must be in radians.

ii. Division by 2.0 in the computation of area could be written as multiplication by 0.5. Multiplication is faster compared to division.

iii. a ** 2.0 and b ** 2.0 should be replaced by a ** 2 and b ** 2 respectively. Remember that a real variable may be raised to an integer power and it is more efficient to do so.

The modified program is given as Example Program 4.4.

Example Program 4.4 Area of triangle—Version 2

```
!PROGRAM 4.4
!MODIFIED PROGRAM 4.3
!theta GIVEN IN DEGREES

PROGRAM triangle_2
   IMPLICIT NONE
   REAL :: a,b,c,theta,area,rad_theta
   REAL, PARAMETER :: pi=3.14159265
   PRINT *, "Type values of a, b, theta"
   READ *, a,b,theta
   PRINT *, "sides a=", a," b=",b
   PRINT *, "included angle=", theta
   rad_theta=theta*pi/180.0
   c= SQRT(a**2+b**2-2*a*b*cos(rad_theta))
   area=0.5*a*b*SIN(rad_theta)
   PRINT *,"side c=",c,"  area=",area
END PROGRAM triangle_2
```

Example 4.23

A five digit positive integer is given. It is required to find the sum of individual digits. For example, if the given number is 96785 the required sum is 9 + 6 + 7 + 8 + 5 = 35. Finding the sum of digits of a number is used in data processing to validate numbers read in as data. A program to find the sum of digits of an integer is given as Example Program 4.5.

Example Program 4.5 Adding digits of a number

```
!PROGRAM 4.5
!THIS PROGRAM READS AN INTEGER WHICH IS 5 DIGITS LONG
!AND SUMS THE DIGITS IN IT

PROGRAM sum_digits
   IMPLICIT NONE
   INTEGER :: digit_1,digit_2,digit_3,digit_4,&
      digit_5,sum,n
   PRINT *, "Type a five digit number "
   READ *,n
   PRINT *,"Number=",n
!THE FOLLOWING STATEMENT FINDS THE LEAST SIGNIFICANT
!DIGIT OF n
   digit_1=n-(n/10)*10
   n=n/10
   digit_2=n-(n/10)*10
   n=n/10
   digit_3=n-(n/10)*10
   n=n/10
   digit_4=n-(n/10)*10
   n=n/10
   digit_5=n
   sum=digit_1+digit_2+digit_3+digit_4+digit_5
   PRINT *,"sum of digits = ",sum
END PROGRAM sum_digits
```

One method of checking whether the program is correct is to act as though we are a computer and execute each instruction as it is given in the program. This is known as *tracing the program*. Assume that the number read in is 96785. We now follow the instructions in the program.

After reading the number the program prints it. The values stored in the variables in each step is shown below:

```
n = 96785
digit_1 = n - (n/10) * 10
        = 96785 - 9678  * 10 = 5
n = n/10 = 9678
digit_2 = n - (n/10) * 10 = 9678 - 9670 = 8
n = n/10 = 9678 /10  = 967
digit_3 = n - (n/10) * 10 = 967 - 960 = 7
n = n/10 = 967/10 = 96
digit_4 = n - (n/10) * 10 = 96 - 90 = 6
n = n/10 = 96/10 = 9
digit_5 = 9
sum = digit_1 + digit_2 + digit_3 + digit_4 + digit_5
      = 5 + 8 + 7 + 6 + 9 = 35
```

Example Program 4.5 has the following defects:

i. The given number is read into variable name n by the READ statement. In subsequent statements the number stored in n is changed in order to find the individual digits. At the end of the program the original number read is not available in the computer's memory. In the above example the number read into n is 96785 and the one which is left in n at the end of the program is 96. It is advisable to write the program in such a way that the original number read into the memory is preserved.

ii. In order to find the least significant digit of a number we may use the MOD function. This makes the program easier to understand.

iii. If n happens to be negative the program will fail.

Rectifying these defects Example Program 4.5 is modified as Example Program 4.6. Observe that the data is read into a variable name number. The absolute value of this data is copied into a variable name n which is used in subsequent statements. At the end of the program the data read into number is still intact.

Example Program 4.6 Summing digits of a number—Version 2

```
!PROGRAM 4.6
!THIS IS A MODIFIED VERSION OF PROGRAM 4.5

PROGRAM sum_digits_mod
  IMPLICIT NONE
  INTEGER :: digit_1,digit_2,digit_3,digit_4,&
     digit_5,sum,n,number
  PRINT *, "Type a five digit number "
  READ *,number
  PRINT *,"Number = ",number
  n=IABS(number)
!THE MOD FUNCTION RETURNS LEAST SIGNIFICANT
!DIGIT OF n
  digit_1=MOD(n,10)
  n=n/10
  digit_2=MOD(n,10)
  n=n/10
  digit_3=MOD(n,10)
  n=n/10
  digit_4=MOD(n,10)
  n=n/10
  digit_5=n
  sum=digit_1+digit_2+digit_3+digit_4+digit_5
  PRINT *,"sum of digits = ",sum
END PROGRAM sum_digits_mod
```

Observe that there is a simple repetitive pattern in this program. A concise program may be written which employs this pattern. In order to do this we need some more instructions which will be discussed in the next chapter.

SUMMARY

We have introduced many concepts in this chapter. We will summarize them now.

1. Arithmetic expressions are formed by variable names and or constants operated on by arithmetic operators.
2. In Table 4.1 we have given all arithmetic operators and their meanings.
3. An expression is evaluated by scanning it from left to right. The order of application of operators is determined by rules of operator precedence. In Table 4.2 we summarize these rules.
4. An assignment expression is: x = (expression) the symbol = is an assignment operator. The expression is calculated and the result is stored in x.
5. The type of variable on the left hand side of an assignment operator need not match that of the expression on the right hand side. The value of the right hand expression is converted to the type of variable on the left hand side and stored in it.
6. Fortran 90 allows mixing of real and integers in arithmetic expressions. In such a case integers are converted to real before computation. Integer sub-expressions are computed using integer arithmetic rules. It is not a good practice to mix integers and reals. Explicit type conversion using built-in or intrinsic functions is a better solution.
7. There are a large number of built-in functions also known as intrinsic functions in Fortran 90. It is a good practice to use them wherever appropriate as they make programs reliable and readable.

EXERCISES

4.1 Write Fortran 90 expressions corresponding to the following:

Assume all quantities are of type real

i. $\dfrac{ax + b}{ax - b}$

ii. $\dfrac{2x + 3y}{x - 6}$

iii. $x^5 + 10x^4 + 8x^3 + 4x + 2$

iv. $(4x + 3)(2y + 2z - 4)$

v. $\dfrac{ax + b}{c} + \dfrac{dy + e}{2f} - \dfrac{a}{bd}$

vi. $\dfrac{a}{b(b - a)}$

4.2 What is the final value of b in the following sequence of statements?

```
REAL :: b
INTEGER :: i
b = 2.56
b = (b + 0.05) * 10
i = b
b = i
b = b/10.0
```

If b = 2.56 is replaced by b = 2.54 above, what is the final value of b?

4.3 What is the value of i calculated by each of the following statements?

```
INTEGER :: i, j = 3, k = 6
```

i. `i = j * 2/3 + k/4 + 6 – j * j * j/8`

ii. `REAL :: a = 1.5, b = 3.0 ; INTEGER :: i`
`i = b/2.0 + b * 4.0/ a – 8.0`

iii. `INTEGER :: i, j = 3`
`i = j/2 * 4 + 3/8 + j * j * MOD(j, 10)`

4.4 Write the final value of k in the following program

```
INTEGER :: k = 5, i = 3, j = 252, m
m = i * 1000 + j * 10
k = m/1000 + k
```

4.5 Evaluate the following expressions

```
REAL :: a = 2.5, b = 2.5
```

i. `a + 2.5/b + 4.5`
ii. `(a + 2.5)/b + 4.5`
iii. `(a + 2.5)/b + 4.5`
iv. `a/2.5/b`

4.6 Write Fortran 90 statement for each of the following expressions:

i. $\log_{10} x + \text{Cos } 32^0 + |x^2 + y^2| + 2\sqrt{xy}$

ii. $a\, e^{-kt}$

iii. $T + r\log_e (V_{cc} - k (V_d + V_e) + 1)$

iv. $\dfrac{1}{\alpha\sqrt{2\pi}}\, e^{\sqrt{2\sigma(x-m)^2}}$

4.7 Write a program to evaluate the following expressions:

$w = a/s(s - a);\ x = wa;\ t = x/s^{-a}$

4.8 Write a program to calculate T

$$T = 0.0092 * 2a\left[\log_{10}\frac{4a^2}{b} - \log_{10}\left(a\sqrt{2 - L}\right)\right] + 0.004\left[a\left(a\sqrt{2 - L}\right) + 0.45\, b\right]$$

given a = 15.2, b = 10.2, L = 1.2.

4.9 Given a five digit integer write a program which will reverse the digits and print it. (Suppose the given number is 46548 the reversed number printed should be 84564.)

4.10 The value of a, b, c, d, e and f to be read in are $-192.53 * 10^4$, $-1456.2 * 10^4$, .000042, 4234567.8, 4235.8492, –9942.3485. Write a program to calculate

$$g_1 = \frac{ab}{cd + e} + f, \quad g_2 = \frac{a}{bc} - d$$

4.11 i. Mr. Gupta deposits Rs. 1000 in bank A. The bank gives simple interest of 15 percent per annum. Write a program to determine the amount in Mr. Gupta's account at the end of 5 years.

ii. Mr. Agarwal deposits Rs. 1000 in bank B. The bank gives compound interest of 13 percent annually. Write a program to determine the amount in Mr. Agarwal's account at the end of 5 years.

iii. Mr. Bajaj deposits Rs. 1000 in bank C. The bank gives compound interest of 12 percent compounded every three months. Write a program to determine the amount in Mr. Bajaj's account at the end of 5 years.

The programs should be general so that if either the deposit or the interest rate changes the program need not be rewritten.

4.12 Write a program to convert Fahrenheit temperature to Centigrade.

4.13 Write a program to convert pounds to kilograms.

4.14 Write a program to convert an amount given in Pounds, Pence to Rupees and Paise (Assume One Pound = Rs. 47.85). Print the answer to the nearest paisa.

4.15 Write a program to express a quantity in millimeters in meters, centimeters and millimeters.

4.16 Write a program to read the radius of a circle in cms. and compute its circumference and area.

4.17 Given the sides of a triangle a, b, c, write a program to find its area. (Area = $\sqrt{s(s-a)(s-b)(s-c)}$ where $2s = a + b + c$).

4.18 Given the x, y coordinates of a point write a program to find its r, θ coordinates ($r = \sqrt{x^2 + y^2}$, $\theta = \tan^{-1}(y/x)$)

5. *Input-Output Statements*

Learning Objectives

In this chapter we will learn:

1. How to input data using list-directed READ statement
2. How to output results using list directed PRINT statement
3. How to display strings along with output results to make the results understandable

---

In order to solve a problem on a digital computer it is necessary to transfer the required data from one of its input units to its memory. This is done by input statements. Information may be transferred to the memory from one of several types of input units. We will, however, confine our discussions in this chapter to a statement which is used to read information typed using the default input unit which is normally the keyboard of a video display unit (VDU).

After a program is executed the results of the computation are to be transferred from the memory of the computer to one of several output units. This is achieved by output statements. We will consider in this chapter an output statement, called the PRINT statement. The PRINT statement commands the computer to display the results on the default output unit which is normally the screen of a video display unit.

As the two statements are duals we will discuss them together. Normally input-output statements consist of two parts: an executable part and a declarative part. The executable part commands certain items to be read into the memory or read out of it. The declarative part gives information on the exact form in which data will be typed or is to be displayed.

The declarative part is called the FORMAT to be specified. When format is not specified the input-output statement is called list directed or "format-free". With list-directed statements the input data can be typed in a flexible form and the output is displayed by the computer in a standard form. When data is typed in a special format or if output is to be displayed in a specified form then FORMAT statements should be used. This will be considered in a later chapter.

5.1 LIST-DIRECTED INPUT STATEMENTS

The general form of the input statement is:

READ *, *LIST*

The statement causes data to be read from a video terminal and assigned to the variables named in the list.

Examples

```
READ*, a, b, c, i, j
READ*, inval, x, height, weight
```

In the first example the list is a, b, c, i, j. In the second it is inval, x, height, weight.

The values to be assigned to the variables in the list of the READ statement are typed on successive columns of a line. The values are typed in the same sequence as in the list and are separated by a comma or one or more blanks. If some values remain they may be typed in the next line. A single value, however, should not be split between two lines. A blank column will be represented by the symbol □ in this book.

In the example above if the values to be assigned to a, b, c, i, j are respectively 5.847×10^{-3}, –.52589, 53.25, 342, 583 they should be typed on a line as shown below:

5.847E–3, –.52589, 53.25, 342, 583

We have assumed that a, b, c are REALs and i, j, INTEGERs. A READ statement commands the computer to read the first line from the input unit and assign the numbers in it between commas (or blanks) to successive variables in the list. If values for all the variables in a list are not found in one line then the next and succeeding lines are read until values are assigned to all the variables. Once a line is read by a READ statement it cannot be read again. Every time a READ statement is encountered in a program a new line is read. Thus if one writes the three statements shown below:

```
READ*, a
READ*, i
READ*, b
```

then three lines would be required, the first one containing the value of a, the second one the value of i and the third the value of b.

The following points should be remembered while typing input data:

1. The values should be typed in the same order as specified in the list. While typing a particular value no column should be left blank. For example the number .85935 is typed incorrectly in the following line.

Column →	1	2	3	4	5	6	7
	.	8	5		9	3	5

2. The numerical values should be within the allowed range of values of real and integer variables.

3. When an E is typed to assign an exponent at least one number should follow it. For example .85E is illegal.

4. No value should be split between two lines. For example the value .85935 should not be typed as shown below:

First line:

Column →	78	79	80
	.	8	5

Next line:

Column →	1	2	3
	9	3	5

5. If a number is not typed, that is two commas follow one another with a blank between them, no value is read. The old value in the variable, if any, remains unchanged. A blank between commas is *not* taken as 0.

For example, if the input for the statement:

READ *, a, b, c is 2.5, , 9.8

then no value is read into b. It retains its old value.

6. If an integer is typed as input meant for a real, it is converted into real and stored. If a number with a decimal point or an exponent is found in a field meant for an integer, it is an error and the compiler will give an error message.

7. If n identical values are to be read into n variables it is not necessary to type the value n times. Instead one may type n* *<value>*. For example, if a = b = c = d = 5.5 is to be read we may write:

READ*, a, b, c, d

and type in a data line

4 * 5.5

instead of 5.5, 5.5, 5.5, 5.5.

If no value follows * in the above form, null values are assumed for the variables. In other words their values remain unchanged. In Example Program 5.1 we have shown the input and output for a program to illustrate the points made in this section. Observe that the printed values of a and b do not exactly match the input values. This is due to errors in decimal to binary conversion and rounding. The consequences of this error was explained in Section 4.8 (p. 29).

Example Program 5.1 Illustrates how to input data

```
!PROGRAM 5.1
!PROGRAM ILLUSTRATES HOW TO INPUT DATA
PROGRAM input
  IMPLICIT NONE
  INTEGER :: i,j
  REAL :: a,b,c,d
  PRINT *, "Type 5.847E-3, -.52589, 53.25, 342, 583 "
  READ *, a,b,c,i,j
  PRINT *, " a = ", a, " b = ", b, " c = ", c
  PRINT *, " i = ", i, " j = ", j
  PRINT *, "Type 2.5, , 9.8"
  READ *, a,b,c
  PRINT *, " a = ", a, " b = ", b, " c = ", c
  PRINT *, " Type 4*5.5"
  READ *, a,b,c,d
  PRINT *, " a = ", a, " b = ", b, " c = ", c, " d = ",d
  PRINT *, " Type 25,3.5,9.8"
  READ *, a,i,b
  PRINT *, " a = ", a, " i = ", i, " b = ", b
END PROGRAM input
```

DISPLAYED OUTPUT

```
a = 0.5847000051E-02 b = -0.5258899927 c = 53.25000000
i = 342 j = 583
a = 2.500000000 b = -0.5258899927 c = 9.800000191
a = 5.500000000 b = 5.500000000 c = 5.500000000 d = 5.500000000
1525-097 A READ statement using decimal base input found the invalid digit '.' in the input file. The program will recover by assuming a zero in its place.
a = 25.00000000 i = 305 b = 9.800000191
```

5.2 LIST-DIRECTED OUTPUT STATEMENT

The general form of the PRINT statement is:

PRINT *, *List*

This statement causes the values of the variables specified in the list to be displayed.

Examples

```
PRINT*, x, y, i
PRINT*, mix, value1, sum, j
```

In the first example the list is x, y, i. In the second example it is mix, value1, sum, j.

The values of the variables in the list are displayed in the same order as specified in the list. Thus in the first example the value of x will be printed first followed by the values of y and i. The values of all the variables specified in the list are printed in one or more lines. Enough blank space is left between successive printed numbers for neatness and clarity. The exact form in which the data is printed when list directed print statement is used is not standardized and is dependent on the specific Fortran 90 processor.

It is often desirable to print strings of characters along with the output to enhance readability. We have been doing it in all the programming examples. We will now give some more examples.

Consider the statement

```
PRINT *, "The co-ordinates of point x are x1 = ", x1, " x2 = ", x2
```

When executed this statement will display

i. The string: The co-ordinates of the point x are x1 =
ii. The value of x1
iii. The string: x2 = Observe the blank before x2 to enhance readability. Blank is also displayed.
iv. The value of x2

Observe the commas preceding and following variable name x1. They are required. Similarly, following PRINT * a comma is required. Instead of quote mark used above we may also use apostrophe'. We may thus write:

```
PRINT *, 'Apostrophes are allowed to enclose strings'
```

If an apostrophe is itself in a string we can use a quote mark to enclose the string and apostrophe will be displayed. For example

```
PRINT *, "Shiva's Dhanush"
```

will be displayed as

Shiva's Dhanush

If we want to display the string

He said "I am fine"

We may either write

```
PRINT *, 'He said "I am fine"'
```

or

```
PRINT *, "He said ""I am fine"""
```

Observe that in the first form we use apostrophes (') to enclose the string. In the second form, as the string itself has quote marks ("), we use two consecutive quotes wherever a quote is part of a string. In FORTRAN 77 only quotes were allowed and we had to use this technique. In FORTRAN 90, however, as either quote marks or apostrophe may be used, when apostrophe is in a string quote marks are used to enclose it and vice-versa.

If a message is to be displayed in more than one line then two separate PRINT statements are used.

Example Program 5.2 Illustrates some output statements

```
!PROGRAM 5.2
!PROGRAM TO ILLUSTRATE HOW DATA IS DISPLAYED

PROGRAM in_out
   IMPLICIT NONE
   REAL :: a,b,c,x1,x2
   INTEGER :: d,f
   PRINT *, "Type values of a, b, c as follows:"
   PRINT *, " 26.48, -367.68, 40 "
   READ *, a,b,c
   PRINT *, "Type values of d, f as -30, -256"
   READ *, d,f
   PRINT *,"Displayed output "
   PRINT *,"————————— "
   PRINT *,a,b,c,d,f
   PRINT *,"a = ",a," b = ",b," c = ",c
   PRINT *,"d=",d," f=",f
   PRINT *," Type 2.5,3.5"
   READ *, x1, x2
   PRINT *," Coordinates of point x are: x1 = ", x1, " x2 = ", x2
   PRINT *,'Apostrophes are allowed to enclose strings'
   PRINT *,"Shiva's Dhanush"
   PRINT *, 'He said "I am fine"'
   PRINT *, "He said ""I am fine"""
   PRINT *, "End of display "
END PROGRAM in_out
   Displayed output
   —————————
   26.47999954 -367.6799927 40.00000000 -30 -256
   a = 26.47999954 b = -367.6799927 c = 40.00000000
   d= -30 f= -256
   Coordinates of point x are: x1 = 2.500000000 x2 = 3.500000000
   Apostrophes are allowed to enclose strings
   Shiva's Dhanush
   He said "I am fine"
   He said "I am fine"
   End of display
```

6. Conditional Statements

Learning Objectives

In this chapter we will learn:

1. The need for conditional statements and how they are expressed in Fortran 90
2. Relational Operators available in Fortran 90
3. The need to be careful in nesting conditional statements

The order in which the statements are written in a program is extremely important. Normally the statements are executed sequentially as written in the program. In other words when all the operations specified in a particular statement are executed, the statement appearing on the next line of the program is taken up for execution. This is known as normal flow of control. If one were restricted to this normal flow of control it would not be possible to perform alternate actions based on the result of testing a condition.

Example 6.1

Suppose we introduce in Example 4.21 (Chapter 4) a rule that a discount of 10 percent is given on purchases of mangoes greater than five dozens. To implement this rule we need a statement which will test the quantity purchased to determine if it is more than five dozens. Such a statement is called a *conditional statement*. Using this statement Example Program 4.2 is rewritten as Example Program 6.1.

Example Program 6.1 Cost of mangoes with discount

```
!PROGRAM 6.1
!COST OF MANGOES – DISCOUNTED CASE
PROGRAM mango_disc
   IMPLICIT NONE
   REAL :: cost_dozen,discount
   INTEGER :: rupees,paise,quantity,cost
   PRINT *, " Type cost of dozen mangoes and quantity "
   READ *,cost_dozen,quantity
   PRINT *,"cost of dozen mangoes =",cost_dozen," quantity =",quantity
   IF(quantity > 60) THEN
      discount=0.1
   ELSE
      discount=0.0
   ENDIF
```

```
  !THE FOLLOWING STATEMENT CALCULATES COST IN PAISE
    cost = NINT((cost_dozen*100.0/12.0)*REAL(quantity)*(1.0-discount))
    rupees=cost/100
    paise=cost-rupees*100
    PRINT *,"Number of mangoes = ",quantity
    PRINT *,"cost Rs = ",rupees," ps = ",paise
  END PROGRAM mango_disc
```

The new statement introduced is:

```
IF (quantity > 60) THEN
   discount = 0.1
ELSE
   discount = 0.0
ENDIF
```

The statement is interpreted as:

if quantity is greater than 60 then perform the statement discount = 0.1 (i.e., set discount = 0.1), otherwise perform the statement discount = 0.0.

Thus in Example Program 6.1 after the READ statement the IF statement sets discount to 0.1 if the quantity of the purchase is greater than 60 and sets it to 0 otherwise. The next statement computes the cost (in paise) with discount = 0.1 if quantity > 60 and discount = 0 otherwise.

In the IF statement we have used a relational operator >, which compares two quantities. We will discuss next the relational operators available in Fortran 90.

6.1 RELATIONAL OPERATORS

Table 6.1 lists all the relational operators available in Fortran 90.

Table 6.1 List of Relational Operators

Operator		*Meaning*
New form	Old form	
==	.EQ	Equal to
>	.GT.	Greater than
<	.LT.	Less than
>=	.GE.	Greater than or equal to
<=	.LE.	Less than or equal to
/=	.NE.	Not equal to

The old form for relational operators given in Table 6.1 was used in FORTRAN 77 as at that time some terminals did not have the mathematical symbols. For compatibility with old programs Fortran 90 still allows the old form. The new form is, however, clearer and we will use this form in all the programs in this book.

Two real or integer variables, constants or expressions connected by a relational operator returns a value which can be either *true* or *false*. For example, the expression n < k can be true or false. Similarly the expression index == 4 would be true if index has a value 4, else it will be false. The symbol == (two equal to symbols with no blank between them) is a relational operator used to compare the values of variables (or constants) whereas the symbol = is used to signify the operation of replacement. Thus a = b means replace a by b whereas a == b checks for the arithmetic equality of a and b and returns a value *true* or *false*.

An expression formed with relational operators is known as logical expression. Some valid logical expressions are given below:

i. a >= b
ii. k /= b
iii. (a + b/c) < (c + d + f)
iv. a == x
v. x <= 0.005

In general two integer or real expressions may be connected by a relational operator. Real and integers should not be mixed in a logical expression.

Some illegal logical expressions are given below:

i.	INTEGER:: k; 2.5 < k	(An integer cannot be compared with a real quantity)
ii.	(a + b) << (c + d)	(<< not a valid relational operator)
iii.	d = a	(= not legal. Should write ==)
iv.	a = < b	(=< is not a valid operator; <= is the correct operator)

6.2 THE BLOCK IF CONSTRUCT

The statement we discussed:

```
IF (quantity > 60) THEN
   discount = 0.1
ELSE
   discount = 0.0
ENDIF
```

is a particular case of general form of the IF construct. The forms of IF available in Fortran 90 are:

```
IF (logical expression) THEN
   block of statements-t
ELSE
   block of statements-f
ENDIF
```

By *block of statements-t* and *block of statements-f* we mean a sequence of one or more Fortran 90 statements. The number of statements in the block is arbitrary. This IF construct is interpreted as shown in the flowchart of Fig. 6.1. When the *logical expression* is *true* the *block of statements-t* is executed, else, *block of statements-f* is executed. Control then reaches the statement following ENDIF.

The other forms of logical IF construct are:

```
IF (logical expression) THEN
   block of statements-t
ENDIF
```

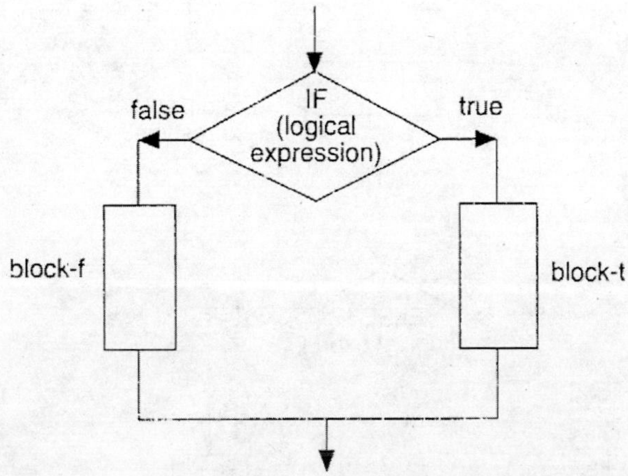

Fig. 6.1 Flowchart corresponding to an IF construct.

In this case, there are no statements in the ELSE branch. Thus if the logical expression is true then *block of statements-t* is executed, else, the statement following ENDIF is executed. This corresponds to the flowchart of Fig. 6.2.

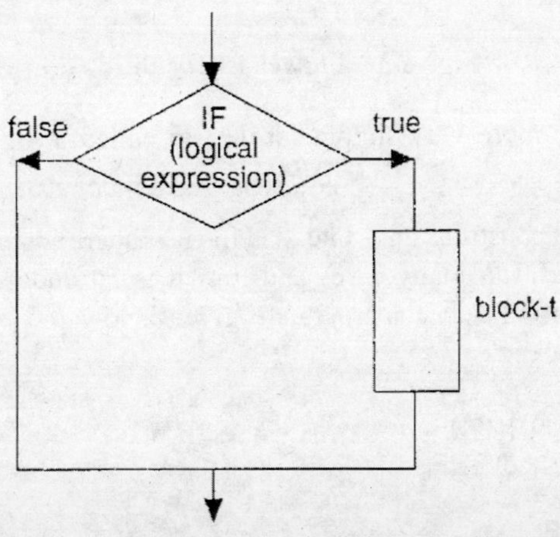

Fig. 6.2 Flowchart for second form of IF construct.

Another IF construct is:

```
IF (logical expression) THEN
   block of statements-1
ELSE IF (logical expression) THEN
   block of statements-2
ELSE
   block of statements-3
ENDIF
```

A flowchart corresponding to the above form is shown in Fig. 6.3. In general any number of ELSEIF or IF clauses can be nested but care must be taken to properly match them. The last statement must always be ENDIF.

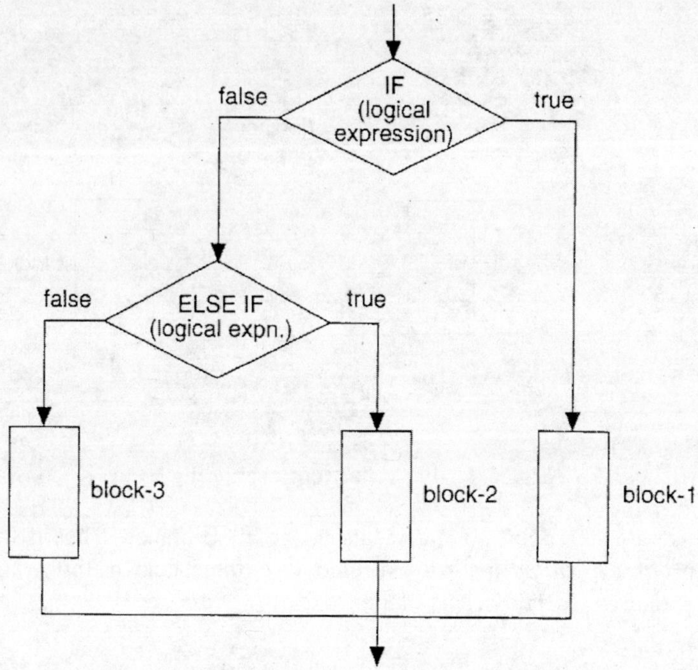

Fig. 6.3 Flowchart for third form of IF construct.

There is one more very simple form of IF called a logical IF statement. The form is:

IF (*logical expression*) *statement*

In the above construct only one statement is there instead of a block of statements. The simple form is useful in many cases and thus it is introduced in Fortran 90 language.

A number of valid IF constructs are given below:

Example 6.2

i.
```
IF (a > b) THEN
   IF (c > d) THEN
      x = y
   ELSE
      x = z
   ENDIF
ELSE IF (a == b) THEN
      x = w
ELSE
      x = p
ENDIF
```

Figure 6.4 is the flowchart equivalent of this group of statements:

ii.
```
IF (a/= b) THEN
   IF (k == l) THEN
      q = t + p
      r = s + g
   ENDIF
ENDIF
```

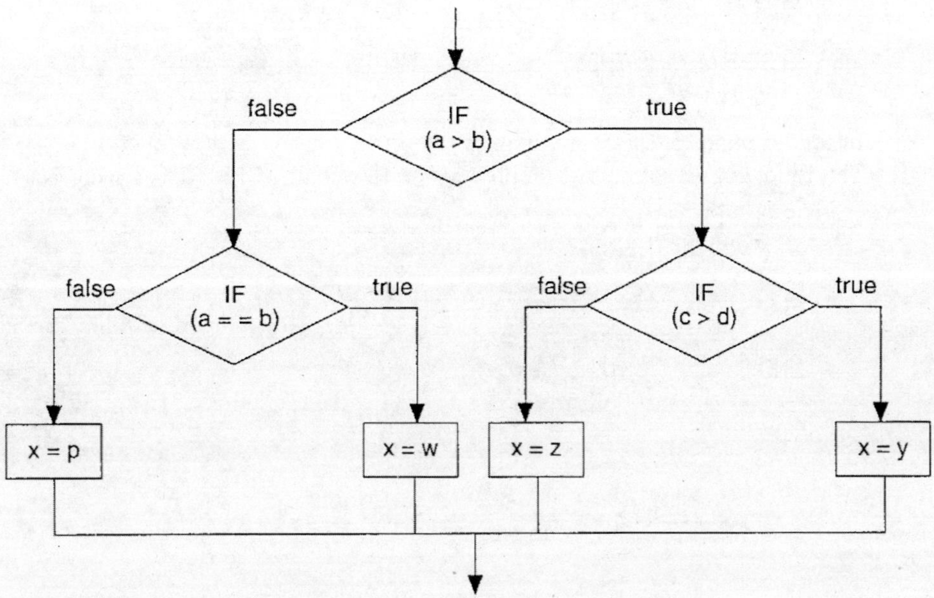

Fig. 6.4 Flowchart for Example 6.2(i).

iii.
```
IF (a > b) c = d
```

iv.
```
IF (a < b) THEN
    IF (p < q) c = d
ENDIF
```

Example 6.3

The following are incorrect IF constructs:

i.
```
IF (a >= b)
    THEN x = y + z
    ELSE x = y - z
ENDIF
```

Error: THEN must be in the first line. ELSE must be in a separate line. The correct form is:

ii.
```
IF (a >= b) x = y + z
ELSE
    x = y - z
ENDIF
```

iii.
```
IF (a >= b) THEN
    x = y + z
ELSE
    x = y - z
ENDIF
```

The first statement in (ii) above is a logical IF. It is however followed by an ELSE. THEN is missing. The correct form is (iii) given above.

iv.
```
IF (a >= b) THEN
    x = y + z
ELSEIF (a >= c) THEN
    x = y - z
```

In this example ENDIF is missing.

The following IF structure to represent the flowchart of Fig. 6.5 is incorrect:

v.
```
IF (a > b) THEN
    IF (c > d) THEN
        x = y
ELSE
        x = z
ENDIF
```

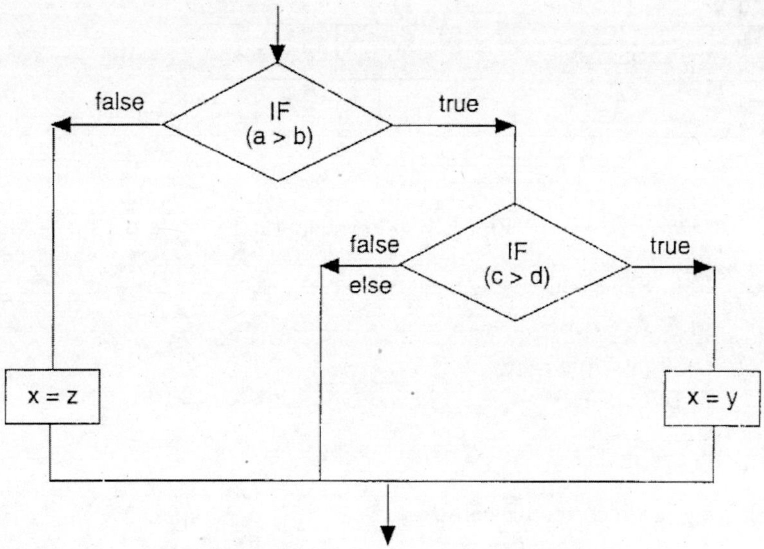

Fig. 6.5 Flowchart for Example 6.3(v).

The correct form is either vi or vii.

vi.
```
IF (a > b) THEN
    IF (c > d) THEN
        x = y
    ENDIF
ELSE
        x = z
ENDIF
```

or vii.
```
IF (a > b) THEN
    IF (c > d) x = y
ELSE
    x = z
ENDIF
```

6.3 EXAMPLE PROGRAMS USING IF STRUCTURES

Example 6.4

A flowchart to solve the problem of finding the largest of three numbers is given in Fig. 6.6. A program corresponding to this is given as Example Program 6.2.

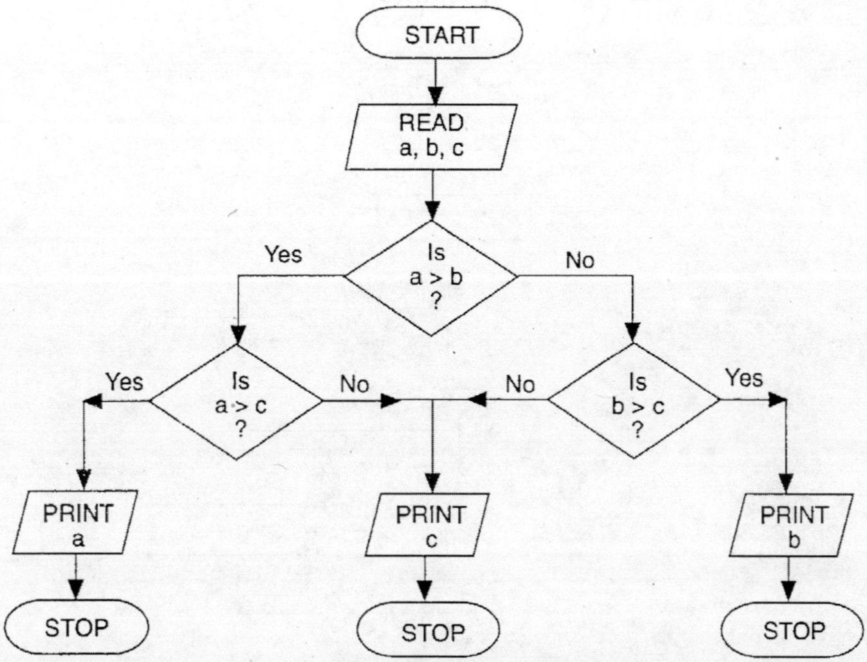

Fig. 6.6 Flowchart for finding the largest of three numbers

Example Program 6.2 Picking the largest of three numbers—Version 1

```
!PROGRAM 6.2
!PICKING LARGEST OF THREE NUMBERS

PROGRAM find_largest_1
   IMPLICIT NONE
   INTEGER :: a,b,c
   PRINT *, "Type values of a, b, c"
   READ *,a,b,c
   PRINT *,"a =",a," b =",b," c =",c
   IF(a>b) THEN
      IF(a>c) THEN
         PRINT *,"largest =",a
      ELSE
         PRINT *,"largest =",c
      ENDIF
   ELSE IF(b>c) THEN
      PRINT *,"largest =",b
   ELSE
      PRINT *,"largest =",c
   ENDIF
END PROGRAM find_largest_1
```

Example 6.5

An alternate strategy for solving the same problem of picking the largest of 3 numbers is given in flowchart of Fig. 6.7. A Fortran 90 program corresponding to this flowchart is given as

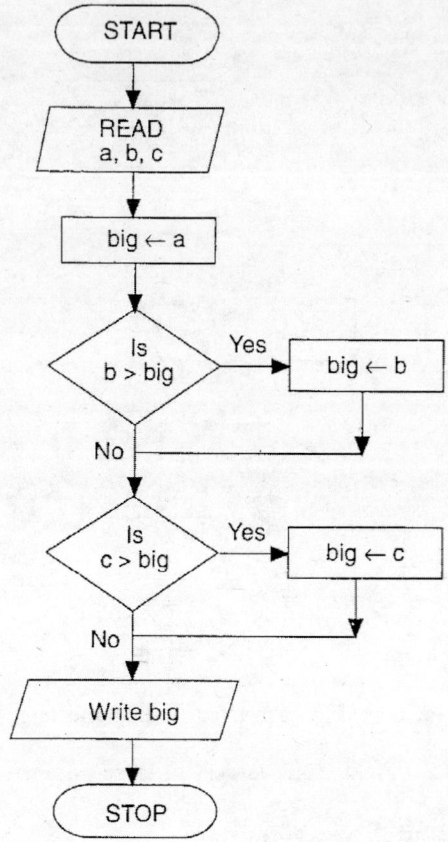

Fig. 6.7 Flowchart for picking the largest of three numbers—Version 2.

Example Program 6.3. Observe that this program is easier to understand. Further it can be easily generalized to pick the largest of an arbitrary set of numbers. We will do this in the next chapter.

Example Program 6.3 Picking the largest of three numbers—Version 2

```
!PROGRAM 6.3
!PICKING LARGEST OF THREE NUMBERS - VERSION2

PROGRAM find_largest_2
   IMPLICIT NONE
   INTEGER :: a,b,c,big
   PRINT *, "Type values of a, b, c"
   READ *,a,b,c
   PRINT *,"a =",a," b =",b," c =",c
   big = a
   IF(b>big) big=b
   IF(c>big) big=c
   PRINT *,"largest number =",big
END PROGRAM find_largest_2
```

Example 6.6

A program to find the roots of a quadratic equation will now be developed. Given a quadratic equation

$$ax^2 + bx + c = 0$$

the roots are given by the formula

$$x = \{-b \pm \sqrt{b^2 - 4ac}\}/2a$$

or

$$x = \{-b \pm (b^2 - 4ac)^{1/2}\}/2a$$

Assume that a is not equal to zero. We should consider three cases:

i. The discriminant $(b^2 - 4ac) < 0$ in which case there are two complex conjugate roots.

ii. The discriminant $(b^2 - 4ac) = 0$ in which case the two roots are real and equal. The roots are $-b/2a$.

If a, b, c are real then $b^2 - 4ac$ would normally not be exactly 0 due to rounding errors. Thus branching based on the equality of $b^2 - 4ac$ will often not succeed. We should define a small enough number epsilon which for all practical purposes can be considered as zero. It is reasonable to take the value 0.5E – 7 as epsilon for a 32-bit computer. Thus instead of checking if $b^2 - 4ac == 0$ we will check if $|b^2 - 4ac| \leq$ epsilon.

iii. The discriminant $(b^2 - 4ac) > 0$ in which case both the roots are real.

The algorithm may be expressed as given below:

```
Read a, b, c ;
discriminant = (b² – 4 ac) ;
if discriminant < 0)
  then
     {discriminant = – (discriminant);
        Imaginary part of root = (discriminant)^1/2/2a
        Real part of root = –b /2a;
        Write out the complex conjugate roots}
  else
        If (|discriminant| < = epsilon)
          then
             {root = –b/2a ;
                Write out repeated roots}
  else
        {root1 = – b + (discriminant) ^1/2/2a;
          root2 = – b – (discriminant) ^1/2/2a;
          Write out the two real roots}
  end of algorithm
```

The above algorithm is translated to Fortran 90 in Example Program 6.4. Observe the ease of translating the algorithm. Note the indentation of the if statement to aid program understanding.

Example Program 6.4 Roots of a quadratic equation

```
!PROGRAM 6.4
!FINDING SOLUTIONS OF A QUADRATIC EQUATION
!WE ASSUME a /=0

PROGRAM quadratic
  IMPLICIT NONE
  REAL,PARAMETER :: epsilon=0.5e-7
  REAL :: a,b,c,discr,xim1,xim2,xreal1,xreal2,sqrt_discr
  PRINT *, " Type values of a,b, c"
  READ *,a,b,c
  PRINT *,"a =",a," b =",b," c =",c
  discr=b*b-4*a*c
  IF(discr<0) THEN
    discr = -discr
    xim1 = 0.5*SQRT(discr)/a
    xim2 = -xim1
    xreal1 = -b*0.5/a
    PRINT *,"Complex conjugate root "
    PRINT *,"Real part = ",xreal1
    PRINT *,"Imaginary part = ",xim1,xim2
  ELSE IF(ABS(discr) < epsilon) THEN
    xreal1= -b*0.5/a
    PRINT *,"Repeated roots"
    PRINT *,"real roots =",xreal1
  ELSE
    sqrt_discr = SQRT(discr)
    xreal1 = (-b + sqrt_discr )*0.5/a
    xreal2 = (-b - sqrt_discr )*0.5/a
    PRINT *,"Real roots"
    PRINT *,"Root 1 =",xreal1," Root 2 =",xreal2
  ENDIF
END PROGRAM quadratic
```

Example 6.7

The income tax rates are given by the following rules:

i. No tax is chargeable on net taxable income <= 35,000
ii. 20% is charged on income above 35,000 but below 60,000
iii. 30% is charged on income above 60,000 but below 1,20,000
iv. On income above 1,20,000 the rate is 40%.

Example Program 6.5 Income tax calculation

```
!PROGRAM 6.5
!PROGRAM CALCULATES INCOMETAX GIVEN SLABS
PROGRAM tax_calc_1
  IMPLICIT NONE
  INTEGER :: income,tax
!READ NET TAXABLE INCOME
  PRINT *, " Type income "
  READ *,income
  PRINT *,"Net taxable income =",income
  IF(income <=35000) THEN
    tax = 0
```

```
   ELSE IF(income <=60000) THEN
   tax = ANINT((income-35000)*0.2)
   ELSE IF(income <=120000) THEN
   tax = 5000 + ANINT((income-60000)*0.3)
!ANINT ROUNDS THE TAX TO NEAREST RUPEE
   ELSE
   tax = 23000 + ANINT((income-120000)*0.4)
   ENDIF
   PRINT *,"Tax to be paid is Rs ",tax
END PROGRAM tax_calc_1
```

Given the net taxable income find the tax to be charged to the nearest rupee. A program to solve this problem is given as Example Program 6.5. Observe the use of IF, ELSE IF, ELSE IF, ELSE, ENDIF construct. We have calculated for the income above Rs. 60,000, the tax on Rs. 60,000 manually, which is equal to $(60{,}000 - 35{,}000) * 0.2 = 5000$ and added to it the tax for the income in the slab 60000 to 120000. Even though this program is correct for the given problem it is not a general program. Finance ministers change the slabs and rates regularly each year! It is thus a good idea to keep the rates and slabs as variables and rewrite the program. If the rates or slabs are changed we only have to feed the new data. A generalized program is given as Example Program 6.6. This will work as long as there are three rates and three slabs. If the number of slabs change this program has to be changed. Later in this book this possibility will also be taken into account in writing a program.

Example Program 6.6 Income tax calcuation—Version 2

```
!PROGRAM 6.6
!PROGRAM FOR TAX CALCULATION VERSION2
PROGRAM tax_calculation
   IMPLICIT NONE
   INTEGER :: income,slab_1,slab_2,slab_3,r_tax
   REAL :: rate_1,rate_2,rate_3,tax
!READ SLABS AND RATES
   PRINT *, " Type values of slab1, slab2 and slab3"
   READ *,slab_1,slab_2,slab_3
   PRINT *,"Slab_1 =",slab_1," Slab_2 =",slab_2," Slab_3 =",slab_3
   PRINT *, " Type values of rate1, rate2 and rate3"
   READ *,rate_1,rate_2,rate_3
   PRINT *,"Rate_1 =",rate_1," Rate_2 =",rate_2," Rate_3 =",rate_3
   PRINT *, "Type income "
   READ *,income !INCOME IS NET TAXABLE INCOME
   PRINT *,"Net income =",income
   IF(income < slab_1) THEN
      tax = 0
   ELSE IF(income < slab_2) THEN
         tax = (income - slab_1)*rate_1
   ELSE IF(income < slab_3) THEN
         tax = (income - slab_2)*rate_2 +(slab_2 - slab_1)*rate_1
   ELSE
         tax = (income - slab_3)*rate_3 +(slab_3 - slab_2)* rate_2 +(slab_2 -slab_1)*rate_1
   ENDIF
!CALCULATE TAX TO NEAREST RUPEE - ROUNDED TAX
   r_tax = ANINT(tax)
   PRINT *,"Net taxable income =",income
   PRINT *,"Tax to be paid =",r_tax
END PROGRAM tax_calculation
```

SUMMARY

1. An IF construct is used to take one of two alternate paths in a program based on whether a condition is true or false.
2. A condition is a logical variable which can be either true or false. Two real or integer variables, constants or expressions connected by a relational operator returns a value which is either true or false. For example, in the expression (a >= b) a, b are reals and >= is a relational operator. (a >= b) is a logical variable as the result of evaluating (a >= b) is either true or false.
3. The relational operators available in Fortran 90 are == (for equal to), > , < , >= , <= , /= (not equal to). Remember that = is an assignment operator whereas == is a relational operator to check equality.
4. There are many forms in which a logical IF construct may be written. These are:

   i. IF (*logical expression*) THEN
      block of statements
   ELSE
      block of statements
   ENDIF

   ii. IF (*logical expression*) THEN
      block of statements
   ENDIF

   iii. IF (*logical expression*) *statement*

   iv. IF (*logical expression*) THEN
      block of statements
   ELSE IF
      block of statements
   ELSE
      block of statements
   ENDIF

   In form (iv) any number of ELSE IFs are allowed between IF and ELSE. This is known as *nested* IF.
5. While writing complex logical constructs it is essential to do a proper indenting of statements for easy readability.

EXERCISES

6.1 Given a point (x, y) write a program to find out if it lies on the x-axis, y-axis or at the origin, namely, (0, 0).

6.2 Extend the program of Exercise 6.1 to find whether a point (x, y) lies in the first, second, third or fourth quadrant in x – y plane.

6.3 Given a point (x, y) write a program to find out whether it lies inside, outside or on a circle with unit radius and centre at (0, 0).

6.4 Given a 4 digit number representing a year write a program to find out whether it is a leap year.

6.5 Given the four sides of a rectangle write a program to find out whether its area is greater than its perimeter.

6.6 Given a triangle with sides a, b, c write a program to find whether it is an isosceles triangle.

6.7 Given three points (x_1, y_1), (x_2, y_2) and (x_3, y_3) write a program to find out whether they are collinear.

6.8 Given the numbers A, B and C write a program to print their values in an ascending order. For example if A = 10, B = 11 and C = 6 your program should print out:

Smallest number = 6
Next higher number = 10
Highest number = 11

6.9 Write a program to round a positive number greater than 1 but less than 2 with four significant digits to one with three significant digits. For example:

1.452 rounded would give 1.45
1.458 rounded would yield 1.46
1.455 rounded would be 1.46
1.445 rounded would be 1.44

6.10 A bank accepts deposits for one year or more and the policy it adopts on interest rate is as follows:

i. If a deposit is less than Rs. 10,000 and for 2 or more years the interest rate is 15 percent compounded annually.

ii. If a deposit is Rs. 10,000 or more but less than Rs. 15,000 and for 2 or more years the interest rate is 16 percent compounded annually.

iii. If a deposit is more than Rs. 15,000 and is for 1 year or more the interest is 17 percent compounded annually.

iv. On all deposits for 5 years or more interest is 18 percent compounded annually.

v. On all other deposits not covered by the above conditions the interest is 10 percent compounded annually.

At the time of withdrawal a customer data is given with the amount deposited and the number of years the money has been with the bank. Write a program to obtain the money in the customer's account and the interest credited at the time of withdrawal.

7. Implementing Loops in Programs

Learning Objectives

In this chapter we will learn:

1. The necessity of loop constructs in a programming language
2. How to set up block DO loops in Fortran 90
3. How to set up count controlled DO loops in Fortran 90

Consider Example Program 4.6 which is reproduced here as Example Program 7.1 for ready reference. We see a repetitive structure in this program. The statements:

```
digit_1 = MOD (n, 10)
      n = n/10
```

Example Program 7.1 Finding the sum of digits of a number

```
!PROGRAM 7.1
!THIS IS A COPY OF PROGRAM 4.6
PROGRAM sum_digits_mod
   IMPLICIT NONE
   INTEGER :: digit_1,digit_2,digit_3,digit_4,digit_5,sum,n,number
   PRINT *, "Type a five digit number "
   READ *,number
   PRINT *,"Number = ",number
   n=iABS(number)
!THE MOD FUNCTION RETURNS LEAST SIGNIFICANT
!DIGIT OF n
   digit_1=MOD(n,10)
   n=n/10
   digit_2=MOD(n,10)
   n=n/10
   digit_3=MOD(n,10)
   n=n/10
   digit_4=MOD(n,10)
   n=n/10
   digit_5=n
   sum=digit_1+digit_2+digit_3+digit_4+digit_5
   PRINT *,"sum of digits = ",sum
END PROGRAM sum_digits_mod
```

are executed again and again. The first statement finds the least significant digit of n and assigns it to digit_1. The second statement reduces the length of n by one digit by discarding its least significant digit. The same two operations are repeated four times till all digits in n are exhausted. It is thus clear that if we repeatedly execute these two statements while n /= 0 (i.e. as long as n /= 0) and add the digit obtained at each step to the sum of digits we would get the answer. This is shown in the flowchart of Fig. 7.1. Observe that the steps: digit = MOD (n, 10), sum = sum + digit and n = n/10 are carried out again and again using a program loop as long as n /= 0. When n becomes 0 control leaves the loop and executes the steps PRINT*, sum and STOP. Reformulating the strategy of finding the sum of digits using a program loop has made the program concise and at the same time it has been generalized. This method is general as it will add the digits of a number regardless of the number of digits in it.

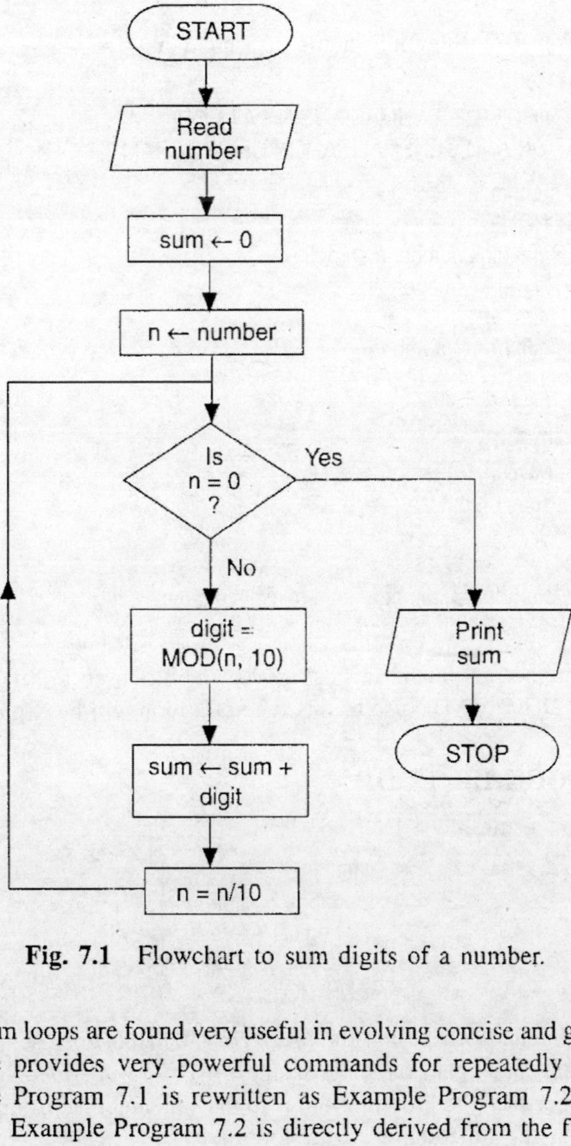

Fig. 7.1 Flowchart to sum digits of a number.

As such program loops are found very useful in evolving concise and generalized programs, Fortran 90 language provides very powerful commands for repeatedly performing a set of statements. Example Program 7.1 is rewritten as Example Program 7.2 using a Fortran 90 command called DO. Example Program 7.2 is directly derived from the flowchart of Fig. 7.1. The command:

```
DO
    block of statements
END DO
```

commands that the block of statements enclosed by DO and END DO be repeated again and again. Observe that in the above construct there is no way of leaving the loop! It will go on repeating the block of statements unless it is forcibly stopped by switching off the computer! We thus need an *exit condition* to leave the loop. This is provided by the statement:

```
IF (n == 0) EXIT
```

This statement commands that if n equals 0 then control should leave the DO loop and go to the statement following the END DO statement.

Example Program 7.2 Summing digits of a number

```
!PROGRAM 7.2
!SUMMING DIGITS OF A NUMBER USING A LOOP
!MODIFICATION AND GENERALISATION OF PROGRAM 7.1

PROGRAM sum_digits_loop
   IMPLICIT NONE
   INTEGER :: d,digit,number,n,sum=0
   PRINT *, "Type an integer "
   READ *, number
   PRINT *,"number =",number
   n = number
   DO
      IF(n==0) EXIT
      digit = MOD(n,10)
      sum = sum + digit
      n = n/10
   END DO
   PRINT *,"Number =",number," sum of digits =",sum
END PROGRAM sum_digits_loop
```

There is another command in Fortran 90 which is used to set up loops. This is called a *count controlled DO loop*. The use of this type of a loop will be explained later in this chapter.

7.1 THE BLOCK DO LOOP

The general form of the block DO loop is:

```
DO
   block of statements-1
IF (logical expression) EXIT
   block of statements-2
END DO
```

The DO command orders that the *block of* statements enclosed by DO and END DO is to be executed again and again as long as the *logical expression* is *false*. When the *logical expression* becomes *true* the program jumps to the statement next to END DO. The flowchart of Fig. 7.2 illustrates the functioning of the loop.

Even though the IF statement can be anywhere within the DO loop it will normally be the statement immediately following the DO statement. In this case the DO loop will be executed as long as the *logical expression* is *false*. The programmer should ensure that the logical expression will become *true* so that control leaves the loop.

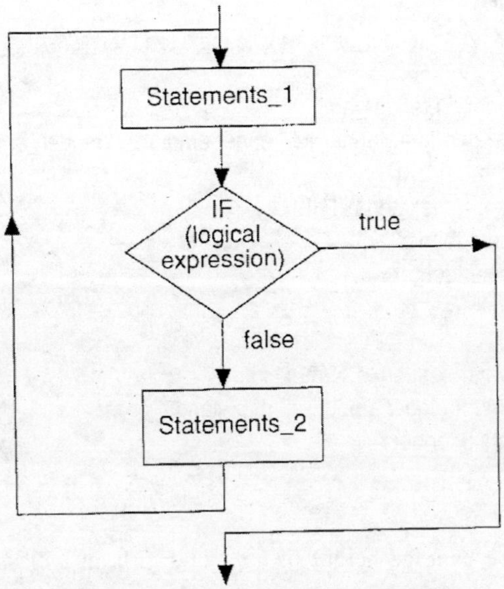

Fig. 7.2 Flowchart of block DO loop.

We will now give a few examples of using a DO loop.

Example 7.1

A procedure to pick the maximum tender among a group of tenders is given as Procedure 7.1.

Procedure 7.1 Procedure to pick the maximum tender among a set of tenders

Step 1: Read tender identity and tender amount
Step 2: max tender = tender amount;
max tender identity = tender identity
Step 3: Perform Steps 4 and 5 as long as the end of the list of tenders is not reached.
Step 4: Read tender identity and tender amount
Step 5: If tender amount > max tender
then {max tender = tender amount
max tender identity = tender identity}
Step 6: Write max tender identity , and max tender

In *Step 3* we have written that *Step 4* and *Step 5* are to be repeated as long as the end of list of tenders is not reached. We must have some method of signalling that the end of tenders is reached. We do this by using 0 as tender identity number. All valid tenders will have a tender identity number greater than 0 (i.e. positive).

Procedure 7.1 is converted into a Fortran 90 program and given as Example Program 7.3.

Example Program 7.3 Picking maximum tender

```
!PROGRAM 7.3
!PROGRAM TO PICK MAXIMUM TENDER
!A TENDER IDENTITY NUMBER 0 IS USED TO SIGNAL END OF TENDER
```

```
PROGRAM max_tender
  IMPLICIT NONE
  INTEGER :: tender_id,tender_amt,max_id,max_tend=0
  DO
    READ *,tender_id,tender_amt
    PRINT *,"Tender_id =",tender_id,"tender amount =",tender_amt
    IF(tender_id == 0) EXIT
    IF(tender_amt > max_tend) THEN
      max_tend = tender_amt
      max_id = tender_id
    ENDIF
  END DO
  PRINT *,"maximum tender_id =",max_id
  PRINT *,"Maximum tender amount =",max_tend
END PROGRAM max_tender
```

Example 7.2

A procedure to find the average height of boys and girls in a class is given as Procedure 7.2.

Procedure 7.2 Procedure to find the average height of boys and girls

Step 1: Initialize counters to accumulate total number of girls and boys and their respective heights.
Repeat Steps 2, 3, and 4

Step 2: Read an input line with the data (roll number, sex code, height)

Step 3: *If* roll number = 0 then go to Step 5. Otherwise continue

Step 4: *If* sex code = 1 then
  Sum of boys height = Sum of boys height + height
  Total boys = Total boys + 1
else if sex code = 2 then
  Sum of girls height = Sum of girls height + height
  Total girls = Total girls + 1
else signal error and goto *Step 2*

Step 5: Average boy height = Sum of boys height/Total boys

Step 6: Average girl height = Sum of girls height/Total girls

Step 7: Print Total boys, Average boy height,
  Total girls, Average girl height

This procedure is converted into a Fortran 90 program in Example Program 7.4. It is assumed that the data is presented in the following form:

Data

2345	1	115.5
2685	2	100.2
2742	3	100.8
2743	2	102.4
2746	1	104.3
000	0	0

Example Program 7.4 Average height of boys and girls

```
!PROGRAM 7.4
!PROGRAM TO FIND AVERAGE HEIGHT OF BOYS AND GIRLS IN A CLASS.
!THE END OF DATA IS SIGNALLED BY A DATA WITH 0 AS ROLL NUMBER

PROGRAM average_height
   IMPLICIT NONE
   INTEGER :: sex_code,total_girls=0,total_boys=0,roll_no,valid_data=0
   REAL :: height,total_girl_height=0,total_boy_height=0,av_girl_height,av_boy_height
   DO
      READ *,roll_no,sex_code,height
      PRINT *,"Roll no =",roll_no,"Sex code =",sex_code,"Height =",height
      IF(roll_no == 0) EXIT !EXIT FROM THE LOOP
      IF(sex_code == 1) THEN
         total_boy_height = total_boy_height + height
         total_boys = total_boys + 1
      ELSE IF(sex_code == 2) THEN
         total_girl_height = total_girl_height + height
         total_girls = total_girls +1
      ELSE
         PRINT *,"Error in sex code "
         PRINT *,"Roll no =",roll_no,"Sex code =",sex_code,"Height =", height
         CYCLE !RETURN TO FIRST STATEMENT FOLLOWING DO
      ENDIF
      valid_data = valid_data + 1
   END DO
   av_boy_height = total_boy_height /REAL(total_boys)
   av_girl_height = total_girl_height/REAL(total_girls)
   PRINT *,"Total boys = ",total_boys," average height of boys =", av_boy_height
   PRINT *,"Total girls =",total_girls," average height of girls =", av_girl_height
   PRINT *,"No.of valid data items =",valid_data
END PROGRAM average_height
```

The program should be general to accommodate any class size as we cannot assume a fixed number of students in a class. We should thus repeat computing total height of boys and girls as long as data remain to be read. We have used a data item with 0 in the roll number field to indicate the end of data. Observe also that if there is an error in the sex code of a data item that data item should not be used in computing. This is ensured in the Procedure.

In Example Program 7.4 observe the new statement CYCLE. The CYCLE statement is a command not to continue with sequential execution of other statements in the DO loop and return to the first statement following DO. In this example if sex code is neither 1 nor 2 it is an error in data. Thus it is not a valid data and should not be used to increase the count of valid data. CYCLE statement in this example achieves this as the updating of valid data is done after ENDIF and will not be executed as CYCLE would have taken control back to the READ statement.

7.2 COUNT CONTROLLED DO LOOP

Besides the block DO loop another construct called count controlled DO loop is available in Fortran 90. In fact in FORTRAN 77 the count controlled DO loop was the only one available.

The general form of the count controlled DO loop is:

DO *count* = *initial value, final value, increment*
    block of statements
END DO

where *count* is an integer variable name and *initial value, final value* and *increment* are integer variable names or integer expressions.

Another valid form for the DO loop is

DO *count* = *initial value, final value*
    block of statements
END DO

In the above form *increment* is assumed to be 1.

The execution of the DO loop is given in the flowchart in Fig. 7.3. We see that the *block of statements* between DO and END DO are executed first with *count* taking on the value *initial*

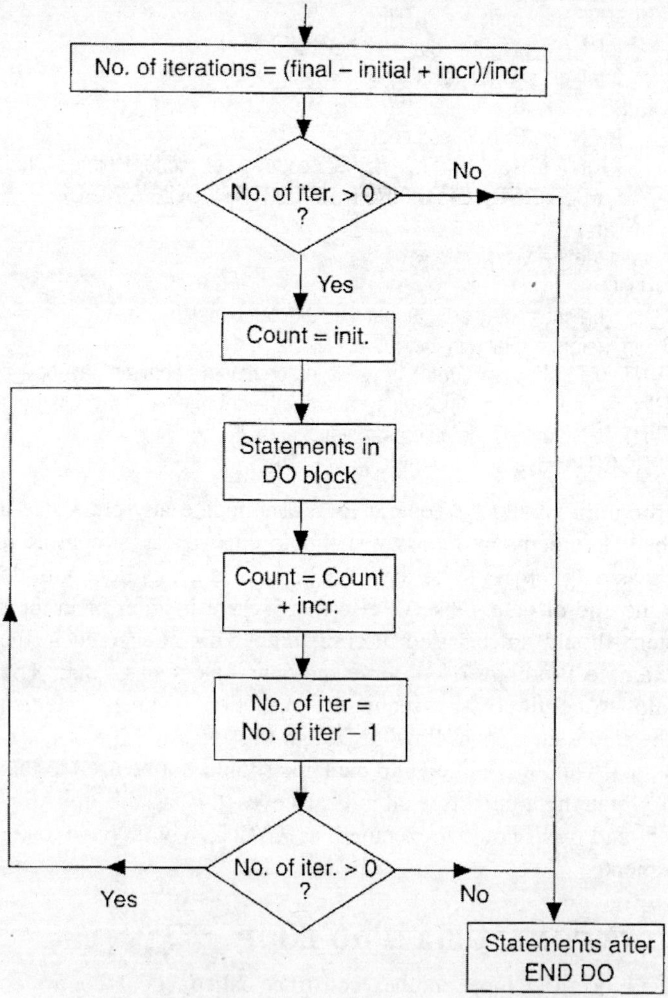

Fig. 7.3 Flowchart of a count controlled DO loop.

value; next with *count* = *count* + *increment* and so on, with *count* being increased by *increment* in each subsequent pass through the loop. The number of times the loop is to be executed is given by the formula:

Number of iterations = (*final value* – *initial value* + *increment*)/*increment*

where the division is integer division. If the number of iterations is found to be negative or zero, the block of statements is not executed.

In Table 7.1 we give a number of numerical examples of count controlled DO indices to clarify the above.

Table 7.1 Calculating Number of Iterations of DO Loop

DO Statement	*initial*	*final*	*increment*	*No. of iterations*
DO i = 1, 10	1	10	1	10
DO i = 2, 12, 3	2	11	3	4
DO i = 1, – 5	1	– 5	1	0
DO i = – 2, –11, – 2	– 2	– 11	– 2	5
DO i = – 10, 2	– 10	2	1	13

The following are valid DO statements:

i. DO j = k, m + p, n   Integer expressions are allowed as DO loop parameters
ii. DO j = 1, p + n, 3

The following are invalid DO statements

INTEGER :: i, j, k, m; REAL :: p, q, r
i. DO i = 5.10   (. incorrect)
ii. DO j =   (Parameters missing)
iii. DO p = q, r   (Reals not allowed as parameters)

Illustrative Examples

Example 7.3

Consider Example Program 2.3 which converts Celsius to Fahrenheit temperature. In that program only one Celsius temperature is read and is converted to Fahrenheit. Assume we want to convert Celsius to Fahrenheit for Celsius = – 100, – 99, – 98, ... 0, 1, 2, 3 ... 100. In other words, we want to tabulate Fahrenheit equivalent of Celsius temperatures of – 100 to + 100 in steps of 1 degree Celsius. Example Program 7.5 illustrates how a count controlled DO loop may be used to do this.

Observe in Program 7.5 that we declare celsius as INTEGER as the values for which it is to be converted are integers. Fahrenheit, however, is REAL as it could have a fractional part. After reading the initial value of celsius (– 100 in this example), the title for the table is printed. This is followed by the DO loop. In this loop fahrenheit is calculated. Observe that celsius is converted to REAL. This is not essential in Fortran 90 but is a good programming practice. After printing the converted values, celsius is incremented. The statements in the loop are repeatedly executed for celsius value upto and *including 100*. When celsius value reaches 101 the program leaves the loop and prints the line: End of conversion.

Example Program 7.5 Tabulating celsius fahrenheit equivalent

```
!PROGRAM 7.5
!USE OF COUNT CONTROLLED LOOP TO TABULATE CELSIUS TO
!FAHRENHEIT CONVERSION

PROGRAM temp_conv_1
  IMPLICIT NONE
  INTEGER :: initial_celsius,final_celsius,celsius
  REAL :: fahrenheit
  PRINT *, "Type initial and final celsius values "
  READ *,initial_celsius,final_celsius
  PRINT *,"Celsius    Fahrenheit"
  DO celsius=initial_celsius,final_celsius
    fahrenheit = 1.8*REAL(celsius) + 32.0
    PRINT *,celsius,"    ",fahrenheit
  END DO
  PRINT *,"End of conversion"
END PROGRAM temp_conv_1
```

Example 7.4

A list of 50 integers are arranged in serial order. It is required to print the serial number of those integers which are negative and count the number of negative numbers.

Example Program 7.6 does this. Observe the use of serial as an index of the DO loop. Observe that if a number is greater than or equal to zero the statement:

```
IF (number >= 0) CYCLE
```

transfers control to the DO statement. Thus the statements following IF upto END DO are not executed. This ensures that only negative numbers are counted and their serial numbers printed. The count of negative numbers is printed outside the DO loop.

Example Program 7.6 Finding negative integers

```
!PROGRAM 7.6
!DATA IS A LIST OF INTEGERS
!REQUIRED TO FIND SERIAL NO.OF NEGATIVE INTEGERS

PROGRAM find_negative
  IMPLICIT NONE
  INTEGER :: serial,number,k,count_negative=0
  PRINT *, "Type no. of integers "
  READ *,k
  DO serial=1,k
    PRINT *,"Type integer "
    READ *,number
    PRINT *,"Number =",number
    IF(number >= 0) CYCLE
    count_negative = count_negative + 1
    PRINT *,"Serial =",serial," ",number
  END DO
  PRINT *,"Number of negative numbers =",count_negative
  END PROGRAM find_negative
```

Example 7.5

Assume that the following series is to be summed:

$$\text{Sum} = x - x^3/3! + x^5/5! - x^7/7! + \ldots (-1)^n x^{2n-1}/(2n - 1)!$$

The first step in evolving a procedure is to obtain a *recurrence relation* which gives the technique of finding a term in a series from previous terms. By inspection of the series:

$$i^{th} \text{ term} = (-1)^{i-1} x^{2i-1}/(2i - 1)!$$

$$(i - 1)^{th} \text{ term} = (-1)^{i-2} x^{2i-3}/(2i - 3)!$$

$$\text{Thus } i^{th} \text{ term} = \{(-1)x^2/(2i - 2)(2i - 1)\} * (i - 1)^{th} \text{ term}$$

Example Program 7.7 uses this recurrence relation to sum the series. Observe that in the DO loop denominator is calculated as an integer. It is converted to REAL during division.

Example Program 7.7 Summing series with DO loop

```
!PROGRAM 7.7
!SUMMING OF SERIES WITH DO LOOP

PROGRAM sum_series
   IMPLICIT NONE
   REAL :: x,term,sum
   INTEGER :: i,n,denominator
   PRINT *, "Type values of x and n"
   READ *,x,n
   PRINT *,"x =",x," n =",n
   sum = x;term = x
   DO i=2,n
      denominator = (2*i-2)*(2*i-1)
      term = term*(-x)*(x)/REAL(denominator)
      sum=sum + term
   END DO
   PRINT *,"Sum =",sum
END PROGRAM sum_series
```

Example 7.6

Given a set of points $(x_1, y_1), (x_2, y_2), \ldots (x_n, y_n)$ it is required to fit a straight line $y = mx + c$ through these points which is the best approximation to these points. In other words, optimal values for m and c in the above equation for the straight line are to be found. A popular criterion is to find the values of m and c which minimize the sum of the squares of the error as given below:

$$(\text{Error})^2 = \Sigma [y_i - (mx_i + c)]^2$$

Σ is summation for $i = 1$ to n

The values of m and c determined using the above criterion are derived in elementary books in statistics and are reproduced below:

$$m = \frac{n\Sigma x_i y_i - \Sigma x_i \Sigma y_i}{n\Sigma x_i^2 - (\Sigma x_i)^2}$$

$$c = [\Sigma y_i - m\ \Sigma x_i]/n$$

Σ is summation for i = 1 to n.

A computer program which reads in n pairs of values (x, y) and computes m and c is easily written with DO loops as shown in Example Program 7.8.

Observe that in each pass through the DO loop a pair of values for x and y is read. The values of x and y are used to form Σx, Σy, Σxy and Σx^2. After all the n values are read and the totals accumulated, control passes out of the DO loop and the values of m and c are calculated using the formulae given above.

Example Program 7.8 Fitting a straight line

```
!PROGRAM 7.8
!THIS PROGRAM FITS A STRAIGHT LINE THROUGH n PAIRS OF
!x,y COORDINATES .THE STRAIGHT LINE IS y=mx+c
PROGRAM straight_line
  IMPLICIT NONE
  INTEGER :: i,n
  REAL :: sum_x=0,sum_y=0,sum_xy=0,sum_xsq=0,x,y,numerator,denominator,m,c
!READ THE NUMBER OF POINTS n
  PRINT *, "Type no. of points "
  READ *,n
  DO i=1,n
    PRINT *, "Type values of x and y "
    READ *,x,y
    PRINT *,"x =",x," y =",y
    sum_x = sum_x + x
    sum_y = sum_y + y
    sum_xy = sum_xy + x*y
    sum_xsq = sum_xsq + x*x
  END DO
  numerator = REAL(n)*sum_xy - sum_x*sum_y
  denominator = REAL(n)*sum_xsq - sum_x*sum_x
  m = numerator/denominator
  c = (sum_y - m*sum_x)/REAL(n)
  PRINT *,"Equation of straight line is "
  PRINT *,"y =",m,"x +",c
END PROGRAM straight_line
```

Example 7.7

It is required to tabulate the values of the function shown below for integer values of k from 0 to 15.

$$P(k) = e^{-a}\, a^k/k!$$

A program using a DO loop to tabulate the function is given as Example Program 7.9. Observe that the value of P(k) for k = 0 is calculated outside the DO loop to avoid division by

0. The function e^{-a} which is independent of k is computed outside the DO loop and only the terms dependent on k are computed inside the loop. The expression calculated within the DO loop is based on the relation:

$$P(k) = e^{-a} \frac{a}{k} \frac{a^{k-1}}{k\,(k-1)!} = \frac{a}{k} P(k-1)$$

Example Program 7.9 Tabulation of Poisson function

```
!PROGRAM 7.9
!POISSON FUNCTION TABULATION

PROGRAM poisson
  IMPLICIT NONE
  INTEGER :: k
  REAL :: a,pois
  PRINT *, " Type value of a"
  READ *,a
  PRINT *,"a= ",a
  pois = EXP(-a)
  k = 0
  PRINT *,"k    poisson(k)"
  PRINT *,k," ",pois
  DO k=1,15
    pois = pois*a/REAL(k)
    PRINT *,k,"     ",pois
  END DO
  END PROGRAM poisson
```

7.3 RULES TO BE FOLLOWED IN WRITING DO LOOPS

There are a number of rules which should be remembered in setting up DO loops. Some of these rules are the syntax of the DO st...ement. Most of them, however, are to ensure logical consistency of programs using DO loop.

Rule 1 : The DO loop indices should not be reals. Only integers are allowed.

For example the statement:

```
REAL :: x
DO x = 0.1, 1000.0, 0.1
```

is illegal in Fortran 90. Even though it seems that this loop will be executed 10,000 times if real arithmetic is used, due to rounding in the addition of real numbers, the loop may be executed more than 10,000 times.

Rule 2: Enclosed within a DO loop there may be other DO loops. That is, the DO to END DO blocks of latter DOs must be enclosed within the DO to END DO block of the first one. A set of DOs satisfying this rule is called nested DOs.

The configuration of DOs shown in Fig. 7.4(a) is logically correct whereas the one shown in Fig. 7.4(b) is not logically correct as the loops in Fig. 7.4(b) cross. To avoid such a logical error Fortran 90 allows labelling of DO loops.

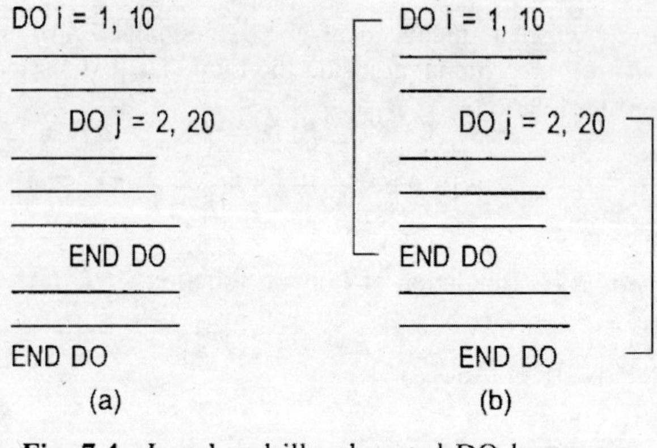

Fig. 7.4 Legal and illegal nested DO loops.

We can label a DO loop as shown below:

```
loop1 : DO i = 1, 10
          block of statements
        END DO loop1
```

The label is any Fortran 90 identifier. The label is followed by a colon : In case a DO is labelled the corresponding END DO must be appended by the same label as shown below. Nested loops with labelling are shown in Fig. 7.5.

```
outer_loop: DO i = 1, 10
   inner_loop: DO j = 2, 20
                  - - - - - - - -
                  - - - - - - - -
               END DO inner_loop
                  - - - - - - - -
                  - - - - - - - -
            END DO outer_loop
```

Fig. 7.5 Showing labelled nested DOs.

Whenever DO statements are nested it is recommended that the inner DO loops be indented as shown in Fig. 7.5. Each DO statement must have a corresponding END DO.

An example using nested DOs is given next.

Example 7.8

It is required to tabulate the following function for m = 0, k = 0 and for m = 1 to 5, k = 1 to 10.

$$P(m, k) = e^{-a}\, e^{-b}\, a^m\, b^k/m!k!$$

A program to do this is given as Example Program 7.10. After printing the value of P(0, 0), this program computes and prints P(m, k) for k ranging from 1 to 10. When the inner loop is completed control will reach the outer DO loop. This loop will set m = 2 and P(m, k) will be computed again for k from 1 to 10. The program will leave the loops only after calculating P(m, k) for m = 1 to 5 and for each m calculating P(m, k) for k = 1 to 10. Thus the block of statements enclosed by the inner DO loop will be executed 50 times.

Example Program 7.10 Two dimensional Poisson function

```
!PROGRAM 7.10
!TABULATING TWO DIMENSIONAL POISSON FUNCTION

PROGRAM poisson_2
   IMPLICIT NONE
   INTEGER :: k,m
   REAL :: poisson,a=0.1,b=0.1,poisson_x
!CALCULATE p(0,0)
   poisson = EXP(-a)*EXP(-b)
   k = 0;m = 0
   PRINT *,"k =",k," m=",m," poisson=",poisson
outer: DO m=1,5
   poisson = poisson * a/REAL(m)
   poisson_x = poisson
inner: DO k=1,10
         poisson_x = poisson_x*b/REAL(k)
         PRINT *,"k =",k," m=",m," poisson=",poisson_x
      END DO inner
      END DO outer
END PROGRAM poisson_2
```

Rule 3: The DO loop parameters *count, initial-value, final-value* and *increment* should not be redefined by statements within the DO loop block.

The program segment shown in Fig. 7.6 which tries to start computation of P(k) inside the DO loop from k = 0 is illegal.

```
                 !PROGRAM SEGMENT WITH ERROR - 1
                 READ *, a
                 poisson = exp(-a)
                 DO k = 1, 10
Error --->       k = k - 1
                 poisson = poisson * a/(REAL(k) + 1)
                 PRINT *, k, poisson
                 END DO
```

Fig. 7.6 An invalid attempt to change DO parameter.

The program segment given in Fig. 7.7 is also invalid as it redefines one of the DO loop parameters within the loop.

```
                 !PROGRAM SEGMENT WITH ERROR - 2
                    DO i = j, k, m
Error --->          k = k * m
                    -------
                    -------
                    END DO
```

Fig. 7.7 An attempt to change DO loop parameter.

As the DO loop parameters are controlled by the DO statement, any redefinition within the loop will upset the loop count and this is not allowed. We conclude the chapter with a simple example in which a block DO loop is used.

Example 7.9

The record of marks of a set of students is given in the following form: Roll Number, Marks. The last data is signalled by typing a negative number in the roll number field. It is required to find the number of students who get more than 90 marks and their roll numbers. It is also required to find the average marks of the class.

A program to do this is given as Example Program 7.11. Observe in this program that

i. Wherever counts or sums are to be accumulated the corresponding variables are initialized in the INTEGER declaration (outside the DO loop).

ii. Average marks are computed after the DO loop completes all its iterations.

iii. EXIT and CYCLE are used appropriately.

iv. Observe that the statement to print the title List of roll numbers with marks > 90 is placed before the DO loop. A common mistake is to place it inside the loop in which case the title will be printed every time the DO loop is executed.

Example Program 7.11 Counting high marks and finding average

```
!PROGRAM 7.11
!HIGH MARKS AND AVERAGE

PROGRAM marks_90
   IMPLICIT NONE
   INTEGER :: roll_no,marks,count=0,high_count=0,sum_marks=0,avg_marks
   PRINT *,"List of roll numbers with marks > 90"
   DO
      READ *,roll_no,marks
      IF(roll_no < 0) EXIT
      sum_marks = sum_marks + marks
      count = count +1
      IF(marks <=90) CYCLE
      PRINT *,"Roll no =",roll_no," marks =",marks
      high_count = high_count +1
   END DO
   avg_marks = sum_marks/count
   PRINT *,"No.of students with marks > 90 = ", high_count
   PRINT *,"Total no.of students =",count
   PRINT *,"Average marks =",avg_marks
END PROGRAM marks_90
```

SUMMARY

1. If a block of statements are to be executed repeatedly a DO loop is used.

2. There are two types of DO loops. One is called a block DO which is of the form

```
DO
   block of statements
END DO
```

In this case the block of statements are repeated endlessly. If the control is to leave the loop there must be a statement

IF (*logical expression*) EXIT

which will take control out of the loop when the logical expression becomes *true*. It is to be ensured by the programmer that this will happen to ensure exit from the loop.

3. A statement IF (*logical expression*) CYCLE within a DO loop takes control back to the beginning of the DO loop skipping statements following it when *logical expressions* becomes true. Thus in the loop

```
DO
   IF (logical expression – 1) EXIT
   s2
   s3
   IF (logical expression – 2) CYCLE
   s4
   s5
   s6
END DO
```

when *logical expression* – 2 becomes true, statements, *s4, s5, s6* are not executed and control returns to the first statement in the DO loop.

4. The other type of loop is a count controlled DO loop. The general form of a count controlled DO loop is

```
DO i = init, final, incr
   block of statements
END DO
```

where i is an integer variable name, init, final, incr are integers or integer expressions. The block of statements in the loop are executed. MAX ((final – init + incr)/incr, 0) times starting with i = init and incrementing it by incr after each execution of the loop.

5. Another form of count controlled DO loop is:

```
DO i = init, final
   block of statements
END DO
```

In this case incr is taken as 1.

6. DO loops may be *completely nested* within other loops. Loops cannot cross.

7. The values of loop parameters init, final, incr should not be changed inside the DO loop.

EXERCISES

7.1 Given an integer, write a program to reverse and print it. For example if the given integer is 12386 the number printed should be 68321.

7.2 Given a set of integers write a program to find those which are palindromes. For example, the number 123321 is a palindrome as it reads the same from left to right and from right to left.

7.3 Given an octal number (a number in base 8) of arbitrary length write a program to find its decimal equivalent. For example the decimal equivalent of the octal number 2673 is

$$2 * 8^3 + 6 * 8^2 + 7 * 8^1 + 3 * 8^0 = 1467$$

7.4 Given any decimal number write a program to find its octal equivalent. For example, the octal equivalent of 242 is 362.

7.5 Given values for a, b, c and d and a set of values for the variable x evaluate the function defined by

$$\begin{aligned} f(x) &= ax^2 + bx + c && \text{if } x < d \\ f(x) &= 0 && \text{if } x = d \\ f(x) &= -ax^2 + bx - c && \text{if } x > d \end{aligned}$$

for each value of x, and print the value of x and f(x). Write a program for an arbitrary number of x values.

7.6 A machine is purchased which will produce earnings of Rs. 1000 per year while it lasts. The machine costs Rs. 6000 and will have salvage value of Rs. 2000 when it is condemned. If 12 percent per annum can be earned on alternative investments what should be the minimum life of the machine to make it a more attractive investment compared to alternative investments?

7.7 The interest charged in instalments buying is to be calculated by a computer program. A tape recorder costs Rs. 2000. A shopkeeper sells it for Rs. 100 down and Rs. 100 for 21 more months. What is the monthly interest charged?

7.8 Write a program which will evaluate the function f for the set of values of x (.5, 1, 1.5, 2, 2.5, 3) and tabulate the results.

$$f = 1 + x^2/2! + x^4/4! - 50 \sin^2 x + (4 - x^2)^{1/2}$$

Caution: The answer may not be a real number.

7.9 Write a computer program to evaluate the following sum:

$$S = \Sigma(-1)^n x^{n/2}/n(n + 1) \text{ for } n = 1 \text{ to } 10$$

7.10 Tabulate the function

$$f(x, y) = (x^2 + y^2 + 2xy)/(x^2 + y^2 + 8xy)$$

for the following set of values of (x, y)

$$(x, y) = (0, -10), (2, -8), (4, -6), (6, -4), (8, -2), (10, 0) \text{ and } (12, 2).$$

7.11 Tabulate simple and compound interest for all combinations of the following deposits, interest rates and years of deposit.

Deposit	1000	2000	3000	4000	5000
Rate	12%	14%	16%		
Years	1	2	3		

7.12 Tabulate the following function using DO loops

$f(x) = (x^2 + 2x + 3)/(x - 20)$

for (i) x = −6, −5, −4, −3, −2, −1, 0, 1, 2, 3,
(ii) −6.5, −4.5, −2.5, −0.5, 1.5, 3.5

8. *Logical Expressions and More Control Statements*

Learning Objectives

In this chapter we will learn:

1. The use of logical operators
2. Precedence rules when logical, relational and arithmetic operators are combined in an expression
3. The use of CASE statement when one out of a set of alternate blocks of statements are to be executed

---

8.1 INTRODUCTION

We have seen in Chapter 6 that real or integer quantities may be connected by relational operators to yield an answer which is True or False. For example the expression

marks >= 60

would have an answer 'True' if marks is greater than or equal to 60. The result of the comparison marks >= 60 is called a logical quantity. Fortran 90 provides a facility to combine such logical quantities by *logical operators* to yield logical expressions. These *logical expressions* are very useful in translating intricate problem statements. This is illustrated by the following examples.

Example 8.1

A university has the following rules for a student to qualify for a degree with Physics as the main subject and Mathematics as the subsidiary subject:

1. He should get 50 percent or more in Physics and 40 percent or more in Mathematics.
2. If he gets less than 50 percent in Physics he should get 50 percent or more in Mathematics. However, he should get at least 40 percent in Physics.
3. If he gets less than 40 percent in Mathematics and 60 percent or more in Physics he is allowed to re-appear in an examination in Mathematics to qualify.
4. In all other cases he is declared to have failed.

These rules may be expressed as the following decision table (Table 8.1).

Table 8.1 A Decision Table for Examination Results

Physics Marks	> = 50	> = 40	> = 60	Else
Mathematics Marks	> = 40	> = 50	< 40	
Pass	X	X		
Repeat Mathematics			X	
Fail				X

The rules in Table 8.1 may be expressed by Example Program 8.1 which uses logical expressions.

Example Program 8.1 Examination result processing

```
!PROGRAM 8.1
!A PROGRAM FOR IMPLEMENTING RULES IN TABLE 8.1
PROGRAM exam_results
  IMPLICIT NONE
  INTEGER :: roll_no,phy_marks,maths_marks
!A roll_no OF ZERO INDICATES END OF DATA
  DO
    READ *,roll_no,phy_marks,maths_marks
    IF(roll_no == 0) EXIT
    IF((phy_marks >= 50 .AND. maths_marks >= 40) .OR. &
      (phy_marks >= 40 .AND. maths_marks >= 50)) THEN
    PRINT *,"roll no =",roll_no,"Physics marks =", &
      phy_marks," Maths marks =",maths_marks," PASSED"
    ELSE IF(phy_marks >= 60 .AND. maths_marks < 40) THEN
      PRINT *,"Roll no =",roll_no," Physics marks =", &
        phy_marks," Maths marks =",maths_marks,&
        "REPEAT MATHS"
    ELSE
      PRINT *,"Roll no =",roll_no," Physics marks =", &
        phy_marks,"Maths marks =",maths_marks,&
        "FAILED"
    ENDIF
  END DO
  PRINT *,"End of processing"
END PROGRAM exam_results
```

Observe the second logical IF statement in the program. It is equivalent to the English statement:

If Physics marks is greater than or equal to 50 *and* Mathematics marks is greater than or equal to 40 *or* if Physics marks is greater than or equal to 40 *and* Mathematics marks is greater than or equal to 50 then PRINT “PASSED”.

The connectives used, namely, *and*, *or* have well defined meaning when they operate on logical quantities. We will now give the rules of syntax for forming logical expressions and the precise nature of the operations *and*, *or* and *not*.

8.2 LOGICAL CONSTANTS, VARIABLES AND EXPRESSIONS

We saw in the last section that in addition to real and integer constants, variables and expressions, Fortran 90 has another category known as logical constants, variables and expressions. A logical variable is a two valued variable, it can assume one of two values TRUE or FALSE. A logical constant is thus either TRUE or FALSE.

A logical constant is written in one of the following forms:

```
.TRUE.
.FALSE.
```

Observe the dots before and after TRUE and FALSE. These dots are required punctuations.

The rules for writing a logical variable name are identical to those for real and integer variable names. The variable name, however, has to be declared LOGICAL by a Type declaration. Thus the statement:

```
LOGICAL :: game, mate, switch
```

will define the variable names game, mate and switch as logical and capable of assuming only .TRUE. or .FALSE. values.

Logical variable names and constants may be combined by logical operators to form logical expressions.

Fortran 90 has one unary logical operator .NOT. which is defined in Table 8.2. If a logical variable a is .TRUE., .NOT. a is .FALSE. and when a is .FALSE. then .NOT. a is .TRUE.

Table 8.2 Definition of Unary Logical Operator .NOT.

a	.NOT. a
.TRUE.	.FALSE.
.FALSE.	.TRUE.

There are four binary operations .AND., .OR., .EQV. and .NEQV. which are defined in Table 8.3. .EQV. is known as the equivalence operator. The expression a.EQV.b is .TRUE. when *both* a and b are .TRUE. or when both a and b are .FALSE. The operator .NEQV. is actually .NOT. of .EQV. The dots appearing before and after the logical operators are required punctuation.

Table 8.3 Definition of Binary Logical Operators

a	b	a.AND.b	a.OR.b	a.EQV.b	a.NEQV.b
.FALSE.	.FALSE.	.FALSE.	.FALSE.	.TRUE.	.FALSE.
.FALSE	.TRUE.	.FALSE.	.TRUE.	.FALSE.	.TRUE.
.TRUE.	.FALSE.	.FALSE.	.TRUE.	.FALSE.	.TRUE.
.TRUE.	.TRUE.	.TRUE.	.TRUE.	.TRUE.	.FALSE.

Example 8.2

A company has three shareholders, Agarwal, Bhatia and Chamanlal. Agarwal owns 50 shares, Bhatia 30 and Chamanlal 20 shares. For a measure to pass, it must be supported by shareholders the sum of whose holdings exceed 2/3 of the total shares. A program which will determine if a measure is successful or not and print an appropriate message will now be developed.

Example Program 8.2 Use of logical variables in a program

```
!PROGRAM 8.2
!ILLUSTRATES USE OF LOGICAL VARIABLES

PROGRAM voting
   IMPLICIT NONE
   LOGICAL :: agavot,bhavot,chavot,measure
   INTEGER :: serial
```

```
  DO
    READ *,serial,agavot,bhavot,chavot
    PRINT *,"Serial =",serial,agavot,bhavot,chavot
    IF(serial == 0) EXIT
    measure = (agavot .AND. bhavot) .OR. (agavot .AND. chavot)
    IF(measure) THEN
      PRINT *,"Serial no =",serial,"MEASURE PASSED"
    ELSE
      PRINT *,"Serial no =",serial,"MEASURE FAILED"
    ENDIF
  END DO
  PRINT *,"End of processing"
END PROGRAM voting
```

Let a 'yes' vote be represented by .TRUE. and a 'no' vote by .FALSE. Let the passage of the measure be indicated by .TRUE. and its failure by .FALSE. A logical variable name measure will be set .TRUE. by the program if the measure passes and .FALSE. if it fails. Example Program 8.2 is developed for this problem.

Observe the statement:

```
READ*, serial, agavot, bhavot, chavot
```

In this statement agavot, bhavot, chavot are logical quantities. The input data is prepared using T for *true* and F for *false*. Thus if all vote NO the data will be:

```
123, F, F, F
```

where 123 is the serial number.

In the statement:

```
measure = (agavot .AND. bhavot) .OR. (agavot .AND. chavot)
```

the expression on the right of equal sign will be .TRUE. if and only if agavot is .TRUE. *and* bhavot *or* chavot is .TRUE. It may thus be written also as:

```
measure = agavot .AND. (bhavot .OR. chavot)
```

The statement IF(measure) THEN is a logical IF statement. If the logical variable measure is .TRUE. then the message Measure passes is printed, else the message Measure fails is printed.

8.3 PRECEDENCE RULES FOR LOGICAL OPERATORS

The rules of precedence of operators in evaluating a logical expression are:

i. The expression is scanned from left to right and all .NOT. operations are performed.
ii. The expression is rescanned from left to right and all .AND. operations are executed next.
iii. In the next scan from left to right all .OR. operations are executed.
iv. If parentheses are present, the expression within the innermost pair of parentheses is evaluated first. Within the parentheses the rules of precedence as given above are followed. Parentheses are removed starting from the innermost to the outer.

The rules of precedence of logical operators is shown in Table 8.4.

Table 8.4 Precedence of Logical Operators

Operator	*Precedence*
.NOT.	Highest (Done first)
.AND.	
.OR.	↓
.EQV., .NEQV.	Lowest (Done last)

Some more examples of logical expressions are given below.

Example 8.3

1. a > b * 4.2 .AND. d == COS(x)
2. a + 5.2 > b * 4.8 .AND. c + 5.2 > d
3. a – 5.5 >= 9.5 .OR. c < d .AND. x >= y

In the above examples all three types of operators, namely arithmetic, relational and logical are present. Fortran has rules of operator precedence to be followed while evaluating such expressions. The rules are:

i. Scan the expression from left to right. Perform all function evaluations first and store the intermediate results.
ii. Rescan the expression from left to right. Perform all the arithmetic operations. The arithmetic operators have their own precedence namely ** first, * and / second, + and – last. Store intermediate results.
iii. Rescan the expression from left to right. Perform all the relational operations. The relational operators are all of equal rank. In other words the relational operations are performed in the order in which they appear. Store the logical or truth values obtained as a result of performing the relational operations.
iv. Rescan the expression from left to right and perform the logical operations. The logical operator precedence is .NOT. first, .AND. second, .OR. third, .EQV. and .NEQV. last. Thus the examples given above will be evaluated as follows:

Example 8.3(1)

a > b * 4.2 .AND. c == COS (x)

Evaluate	first	COS(x)
	next	b * 4.2
	next	a > b * 4.2, c == COS(x)
	last	(a > b * 4.2) .AND. (c == COS (x))

Example 8.3(2)

a + 5.2 > b * 4.8 .AND. c + 5.2 > d

Evaluate	first	a + 5.2, b * 4.8, c + 5.2
	next	(a + 5.2) > (b * 4.8), (c + 5.2) > d
	last	((a + 5.2) > (b * 4.8) .AND. ((c + 5.2) > d))

Example 8.3(3)

```
a – 5.5 >= 9.5 .OR. c < d .AND. x >= y
```

Evaluate	first	(a – 5.5)
	next	(a – 5.5) >= 9.5, c < d, x >= y
	next	(c < d) .AND. (x >= y)
	last	(a – 5.5 >= 9.5) .OR. ((c < d) .AND. (x >= y))

If a = 15.0, c = 6.0, d = 4.0, x = 3.0 and y = 4.0 the result will be

.TRUE. .OR. (.FALSE. .AND. .FALSE.) = .TRUE.

In Table 8.5 we summarize the rules of precedence when arithmetic, relational and logical operations are combined.

Table 8.5 Precedence of Combination of Operators

Operator	*Precedence*	
Function evaluation	Highest	(Done first)
unary + or –	↓	
**		
* or /		
binary + or –		
== , /= , < , <= , > , >=		
.NOT.		
.AND.		
.OR.		
.EQV., .NEQV.	Lowest	(Done last)

The rules of precedence may (as usual) be modified by the appropriate use of parentheses. As beginners may have problems remembering the exact order of precedence of operators it is always safe to use appropriate parentheses to clarify the order in which computations are to be performed.

8.4 SOME EXAMPLES OF USE OF LOGICAL EXPRESSIONS

Example 8.4

Another decision table for examination results processing is given as Table 8.6. It is to be expressed as a Fortran 90 program.

A program which corresponds to Table 8.6 is given as Example Program 8.3. In this program it is assumed that each line of input has the roll number of candidate and his/her marks in the main and ancillary subject. Status = 1 is used to indicate special status. End of students' data is reached when roll_no = 0 and this is used to exit from the loop. Observe the use of logical expressions and connectives in the program.

Table 8.6 A Decision Table for Declaring Results

Conditions	*Rules*					
Main Marks	≥ 50	≥ 40	≥ 60	≥ 40	≥ 40	ELSE
Anc. Marks	≥ 40	≥ 50	< 40	≥ 40	< 40	
Special Status	No	No	No	Yes	Yes	
Actions						
Pass	x	x	–	x	–	–
Repeat Anc.	–	–	x	–	x	–
Fail	–	–	–	–	–	x

Example Program 8.3 Examination results processing—2

```
!PROGRAM 8.3
!ILLUSTRATES THE USE OF LOGICAL VARIABLES
!SPECIAL STATUS INDICATED BY STATUS = 1
!ROLL NO = 0 INDICATES END OF DATA

PROGRAM results
  IMPLICIT NONE
  INTEGER :: status,roll_no,main_mks,anci_mks
  LOGICAL :: c1,c2,c3,c4,c5,pass,repeat
  DO
    READ *,roll_no,main_mks,anci_mks,status
  PRINT *,"Roll no =",roll_no,"Main marks =",main_mks,"Ancillary marks =", &
    anci_mks,"Status =",status
  IF(roll_no == 0) EXIT
  c1 = main_mks >= 50
  c2 = main_mks >= 40
  c3 = main_mks >= 60
  c4 = anci_mks >= 50
  c5 = anci_mks >=40
  pass = (c1 .AND. c5) .OR. (c2 .AND. c4) .OR. (c2 .AND. c5 .AND. (status == 1))
  repeat = (c3 .AND. .NOT. c5) .OR.(c2 .AND. .NOT. c5 .AND. (status == 1))
  IF(pass) THEN
    PRINT *,"Roll no =",roll_no,"PASS"
  ELSE IF(repeat) THEN
      PRINT *,"Roll no =",roll_no," REPEAT"
    ELSE
      PRINT *,"Roll no =",roll_no," FAIL"
  ENDIF
  END DO
  PRINT *,"End of processing"
END PROGRAM results
```

Example 8.5

A program is to be written to decide whether on a given date an employee in an organization has completed 1 year service. In order to do this a line is typed for each employee containing the data: employee number, day of joining, month of joining and year of joining. The form in which data is input is shown in Table 8.7.

Table 8.7 Data Input for Example 8.4

Data	Explanation
09 08 1992	Today's date
3452 08 09 1990	Employee's data
3462 09 08 1991	
3672 08 07 1991	
3792 10 08 1991	

A decision table to decide whether an employee has completed one year's service is given in Table 8.8.

Table 8.8 Decision Table to decide completion of one year's service

Diff. in year	> 1	= 1	= 1	E
Diff. in month	–	> 0	= 0	L
Diff. day	–	–	> 0	S
				E
One year service completed?	Yes	Yes	Yes	No

The conditions checked in Table 8.8 are:

1. Difference between today's year and the year an employee joined.
2. Difference between today's month and month an employee joined.
3. Difference between today's day and the day an employee joined.

The reader can convince himself about the correctness of the table by fixing today's date and trying a number of cases of joining dates.

A program which implements Table 8.8 is given as Example Program 8.4. The reader would notice the simplicity of writing a program corresponding to the decision table.

Example Program 8.4 Checking completion of one year service

```
!PROGRAM 8.4
!PROGRAM CHECKS COMPLETION OF ONE YEAR SERVICE
PROGRAM service
   IMPLICIT NONE
   INTEGER :: emp_no,day,month,year,today_day,today_month, &
      today_year,diff_year ,diff_month,diff_day
!emp_no = 0 INDICATES END OF DATA
   READ *,today_day,today_month,today_year
   PRINT *,"Today's date =",today_day,"Today_month =", &
      today_month,"Today_year =", today_year
   DO
      READ *,emp_no,day,month,year
      IF(emp_no == 0) EXIT
      PRINT *,"Emp no =",emp_no," Date joined =", &
         day,"/",month,"/",year
      diff_year = today_year - year
      diff_month = today_month - month
      diff_day = today_day - day
```

```
        IF((diff_year > 1) .OR. (( diff_year == 1) .AND. &
           (diff_month > 0)) .OR. (((diff_year == 1) .AND. &
           (diff_month == 0)) .AND. (diff_day >= 0))) THEN
           PRINT *,"Emp no =",emp_no," is Eligible"
        ELSE
           PRINT *,"Emp no =",emp_no," is not Eligible"
        ENDIF
     END DO
  END PROGRAM service
```

8.5 THE CASE STATEMENT

A control construct called the CASE construct is available in Fortran 90. It is useful when one out of a set of alternative actions is to be taken based on the value of an expression.

It is particularly useful when variable values are classified with codes. We will first illustrate the use of a CASE construct with an example.

Example 8.6

A company manufactures three products: engines, pumps and fans. It gives a discount of 10 percent on order for engines if the order is for Rs. 5,000 or more. The same discount of 10 percent is given on pump orders of value of Rs. 2,000 or more and on fan orders for Rs. 1,000 or more. On all other orders it does not give any discount. A program which implements this policy is given next.

Assume that the following codes are used to indicate the product:

Code 1 for engines
Code 2 for pumps
Code 3 for fans

A data is made up for each order with its serial number, the product code followed by the amount of order. For example if the order has serial number 2527 and is for pumps worth Rs. 2,500 the data will be shown as:

2527, 2, 2500.00

A decision table showing the above discount policy is given as Table 8.9.

Table 8.9 Decision Table for Discount Policy

Product Code Order Amount	1 ≥ = 5000	2 ≥ = 2000	3 ≥ = 1000	Else
Discount	10%	10%	10%	0

Example Program 8.5 Discount calculation using logical IF

```
!PROGRAM 8.5
!DISCOUNT CALCULATION EXAMPLE USING LOGICAL IF
!THE DECISION TABLE OF TABLE 8.9 IS USED
```

```
PROGRAM discount_1
   IMPLICIT NONE
   INTEGER :: serial_no,code
   REAL :: amount,discount,net_amount
   PRINT *,"Serial_no   Code   Discount   net_amount"
   DO
      READ *,serial_no,code,amount
      IF(serial_no == 0) EXIT
      discount = 0
      IF(code == 1) THEN
      IF(amount >= 5000.0) discount = 0.1
      ELSE IF(code == 2) THEN
         IF(amount >=2000.0) discount = 0.1
      ELSE IF(code ==3) THEN
         IF(amount >= 1000.0) discount =0.1
      ELSE IF((code < 1) .OR. (code > 3)) THEN
         PRINT *,"Error in code",serial_no," code =",code
      ENDIF
      net_amount = amount*(1.0 - discount)
      PRINT *,serial_no,code,discount,net_amount
   END DO
   PRINT *,"End of processing"
END PROGRAM discount_1
```

A computer program using only IF statements to implement the above decision table is given as Example Program 8.5. In Example Program 8.5 observe that a sequence of nested IF THEN ELSEIF statements are used. The nesting of IFs with ELSEs will make the program difficult to read and understand. As such nested IFs occur often in practice a control construct known as CASE is available in Fortran 90 which is useful to write such programs. The same problem is solved using a CASE statement in Example Program 8.6.

Example Program 8.6 Discount calculation using CASE

```
!PROGRAM 8.6
!DISCOUNT CALCULATION EXAMPLE WITH SELECT CASE
!THE DISCOUNT TABLE OF 8.7 IS USED
PROGRAM discount_2
   IMPLICIT NONE
   INTEGER :: serial_no,code
   REAL :: amount,discount,net_amount
   PRINT *, "Ser.   Code   Discount   Net amount"
   DO
      READ *,serial_no,code,amount
      IF(serial_no == 0) EXIT
      discount = 0.0
      SELECT CASE(code)
         CASE(1)
            IF(amount >= 5000.0) discount = 0.1
         CASE(2)
            IF(amount >= 2000.0) discount = 0.1
```

```
        CASE(3)
            IF(amount >= 1000.0) discount = 0.1
        CASE DEFAULT
            PRINT *,"Error in code ",serial_no,"Code =",code
        END SELECT
        net_amount = amount*(1.0 - discount)
        PRINT *,serial_no,code,discount,net_amount
    END DO
  PRINT *,"End of processing"
END PROGRAM discount_2
```

In this program the statement:

SELECT CASE(code)

will transfer control to CASE 1 if code == 1, to CASE 2 if code == 2 and to CASE 3 if code == 3. If code is less than 1 or greater than 3 then control will go to CASE DEFAULT. If code == 2, for example, then control will go to CASE 2. The statements following CASE 2 will be executed. In this case the statement IF (amount >= 2000.0) is *true* discount will be assigned the value 0.1. After executing this control goes to the statement following END SELECT statement, namely the statement:

net_amount = amount * (1.0 – discount)

We now explain the syntax and semantics of CASE construct. The general form of the CASE construct is:

```
SELECT CASE (case expression)
    CASE (case selector)
        block of statements
    CASE (case selector)
        block of statements
        .
        .
        .
    CASE DEFAULT
        block of statements
END SELECT
```

The *case expression* is either an integer expression or a logical expression and must evaluate to a single value. Real expression is not allowed as case expression.

Case-selector can be in one of the following five forms:

integer or *truth value* .TRUE. or .FALSE.
integer-1 : *integer*-2
integer-1 :
: *integer*-2
A list of integers

In a CASE statement *case expression* is evaluated (Assume it is an integer expression). The integer value of the expression is matched with each of the *case selectors* starting from the first one. As soon as it matches with a *case selector* the block of statements following CASE upto the next CASE are executed and control branches to the statement following END SELECT. If none of the *case selectors* match then the block of statements following CASE DEFAULT are executed. CASE DEFAULT is optional. Thus if there is no match with any *case selector* and no CASE DEFAULT is there then control goes to the statement following END SELECT.

This is shown in the flowchart of Fig. 8.1. We saw that the *case selector* can be in one of five forms. The first form is simple. Others need an explanation. If the case selector is in the second form, for example, it is 2:6 then if case expression evaluates to *any* value >= 2 and <= 6 the block of statements following it are executed. If it is, say, 5: then the block is executed for all values of case expression >= 5. If the expression is :4 then the block is evaluated for all the values of case expression <= 4. The *case selector* can also be of the type (1, 2, 7, 9, 15:) in which case the block is evaluated if the value of the *case expression* is 1, 2, 7, 9 or > = 15. The *case expression* should not evaluate to more than one *case selector*. If it does it is a logical error.

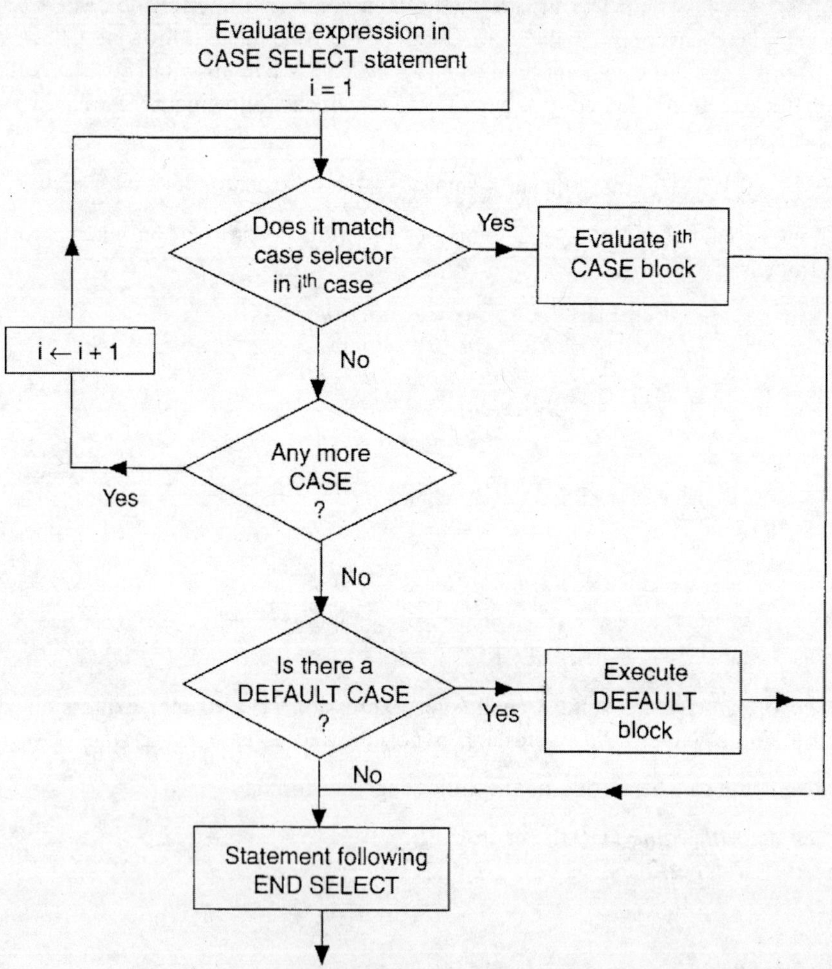

Fig. 8.1 Flowchart for CASE statement.

A few examples of CASE statements are given now:

Example 8.7

```
SELECT CASE (month)
   CASE (1, 3, 5, 7, 8, 10, 12)
      days = 31
   CASE (4, 6, 9, 11)
      days = 30
   CASE (2)
   IF (MOD(year, 100) = = 0) THEN
      IF (MOD (year, 400) = = 0) THEN
         days = 29
      ELSE
         days = 28
      ENDIF
   ELSE IF (MOD (year, 4) = = 0) THEN
      days = 29
      ELSE
      days = 28
   ENDIF
CASE DEFAULT
   PRINT *, "Error in month"
END SELECT
```

Example 8.8

The above can also be written as:

```
LOGICAL :: leap_year; INTEGER :: year, month, days
IF (MOD(year, 100) == 0) THEN
   IF (MOD (year, 400) == 0) THEN
      leap_year = .TRUE.
   ELSE
      leap_year = .FALSE.
ELSE IF (MOD(year, 4) == 0) THEN
      leap_year = .TRUE.
ELSE
      leap_year = .FALSE.
no days: SELECT CASE (month)
         CASE (1, 3, 5, 7, 8, 10, 12)
            days = 31
         CASE (4, 6, 9, 11)
            days = 30
         CASE (2)
         february : SELECT CASE (leap_year)
            CASE (.TRUE.)
               days = 29
            CASE (.FALSE.)
               days = 28
            END SELECT february
      CASE DEFAULT
         PRINT *,"Error in month"
END SELECT no_days
```

The second version shows that a CASE statement can be labelled for clarity. Further it shows that SELECT CASE can appear in a block of statements within CASE. It also shows the use of logical expression in CASE statement.

Example 8.9

```
INTEGER :: day_of_week
SELECT CASE (day_of_week)
   CASE (1:5)
      PRINT*, "Full day"
   CASE (6)
      PRINT *, "Half day"
   CASE (7)
      PRINT *, "Holiday"
END SELECT
```

Example 8.10

```
INTEGER :: temp_celsius
SELECT CASE (temp_celsius)
   CASE (:15)
      PRINT *, "Cold day"
   CASE (16:25)
      PRINT*, "Nice day"
   CASE (26:34)
      PRINT *, "Warm day"
   CASE (35:)
      PRINT *, "Hot day"
END SELECT
```

We conclude this section by developing two Example Programs.

Example 8.11

In Chapter 6 we gave a program (Example Program 6.4) to solve a quadratic equation:

$$ax^2 + bx + c = 0$$

We identified three cases, namely, the discriminant $(b^2 - 4ac) < 0$, $|b^2 - 4ac| \leq$ epsilon and $(b^2 - 4ac) > 0$. We used logical IF statements in that example to write the program. We now rewrite the program (as Example Program 8.7) using the SELECT CASE statement. We first assign a value 1, 2 or 3 to an index discr_code depending on the value of $(b^2 - 4ac)$. This index is used in a SELECT CASE statement to branch to the appropriate block. This program is clearer compared to Example Program 6.4. This program will work for any set of values of (a, b, c).

Example Program 8.7 Solution of quadratic equation

```
!PROGRAM 8.7
!SOLUTION OF QUADRATIC EQUATION

PROGRAM quadratic
   IMPLICIT NONE
   REAL ,PARAMETER :: eps = 0.5e-6
   INTEGER :: discr_code,serial
   REAL :: a,b,c,discr,xim_1,xim_2,xreal_1,xreal_2,temp
```

```
!EACH DATA SERIAL, VALUES OF a,b,c. serial = 0 IS END OF DATA
 DO
   READ *,serial,a,b,c
   IF(serial == 0) EXIT
   discr = b**2 - 4*a*c
   PRINT *,"a =",a,"b =",b," c =",c,"discriminant =",discr
   IF(discr < 0) THEN
     discr_code = 1
   ELSE IF (ABS(discr) <= eps) THEN
     discr_code = 2
   ELSE
     discr_code = 3
   ENDIF
   SELECT CASE(discr_code)
     CASE(1)
       discr = -discr
       xim_1 = 0.5*SQRT(discr)/a
       xim_2 = -xim_1
       xreal_1 = -0.5*b/a
       PRINT *,"Complex conjugate roots"
       PRINT *,"Roots =",xreal_1,"+ i ",xim_1
       PRINT *," ",xreal_1,"+ i ",xim_2
     CASE(2)
       xreal_1 = -0.5*b/a
       PRINT *,"Repeated roots"
       PRINT *,"Roots =",xreal_1
     CASE(3)
       temp = SQRT(discr)
       xreal_1 = (-b + temp)*0.5/a
       xreal_2 = (-b - temp)*0.5/a
       PRINT *,"Real roots"
       PRINT *,"Root 1=",xreal_1," Root 2=",xreal_2
   END SELECT
 END DO
 PRINT *,"End of processing"
END PROGRAM quadratic
```

Example 8.12

Suppose the rates of tax on gross income are as shown in Table 8.10.

Table 8.10 Table of Tax Rates

Income	*Tax*
<Rs. 10,000	Nil
Rs. 10,000 to Rs. 19,999	10 percent
Rs. 20,000 to Rs. 29,999	15 percent
Rs. 30,000 to Rs. 49,999	20 percent
≥ Rs. 50,000	25 percent

A program is required to compute the tax. A simple programming technique may be used to code the slab in which a particular income is to be placed. Suppose we divide the income by 10000 as shown below:

slab_code = income/10000
Then for Income < 10000, slab_code = 0

for 20000 > Income >= 10000, slab_code = 1
for 30000 > Income >= 20000, slab_code = 2
for 50000 > Income >= 30000, slab_code = 3 or 4
and for Income >= 50000, slab_code ≥ 5

Observe that if the income > 50000 then slab_code > 5. Thus if we want to use a SELECT CASE construct with slab_code as case index then we should map these values to one index. This is done in Example Program 8.8.

Example Program 8.8 Tax calculation—use of CASE

```
!PROGRAM 8.8
!ILLUSTRATES USE OF SELECT CASE
PROGRAM tax_calc
   IMPLICIT NONE
   INTEGER :: account_no,income,slab_code
   REAL :: tax_rate,tax
   PRINT *,"Ac.no    Net income    Tax "
   DO
      READ *,account_no,income
      IF(account_no == 0)EXIT
      slab_code = income/10000
      SELECT CASE(slab_code)
         CASE(0)
            tax_rate = 0.0
               PRINT *,account_no,income,tax
         CASE(1)
            tax_rate = 0.1
               tax = REAL(income - 10000)*tax_rate
               PRINT *,account_no,income,tax
         CASE(2)
            tax_rate = 0.15
               tax = 1000 + REAL(income - 20000)*tax_rate
               PRINT *,account_no,income,tax
         CASE(3,4)
            tax_rate = 0.2
               tax = 2500 + REAL(income - 30000)*tax_rate
               PRINT *,account_no,income,tax
         CASE(5:)
            tax_rate = 0.25
               tax = 6500 + REAL(income - 50000)*tax_rate
               PRINT *,account_no,income,tax
      END SELECT
   END DO
   PRINT *,"End of processing"
END PROGRAM tax_calc
```

Observe that the two cases slab_code = 3 and slab_code = 4 in which the action is identical can be put together and this is done in Example Program 8.8. Further all slab_codes ≥ 5 are encoded by CASE (5:).

SUMMARY

1. Fortran 90 supports logical variables which can be either *true* or *false.*
2. Logical variables are to be declared at the beginning of a program using the statement:

   LOGICAL :: *List of variable names*
3. Logical variables are combined using logical operators. Logical operators available in Fortran 90 are:

   .NOT., .AND., .OR., .EQV. and .NEQV.
4. A relational expression when evaluated has a value .TRUE. or .FALSE. Thus relational expressions may be connected by logical operators.
5. A logical expression may be formed using arithmetic, relational and logical operators. The precedence of operators must be observed while evaluating the expression. The rules of precedence are summarized in Table 8.5.
6. Fortran 90 supports a control construct known as SELECT CASE to branch to one out of a number of alternative blocks of statements. Use of SELECT CASE construct leads to readable programs.

EXERCISES

8.1 The policy followed by a company to process customer orders is given by the following rules:

   i. If a customer order is less than or equal to that in stock and his credit is OK supply his requirement.
   ii. If his credit is not OK do not supply. Send him an intimation.
   iii. If his credit is OK but the item in stock is less than his order, supply what is in stock. Intimate to him the date the balance will be shipped.

   Write a Fortran 90 program to implement the above rules. Use of a decision table is recommended.

8.2 Given the date an employee joined a job in the firm: Day/Month/Year and given today's date write a program to find out whether the given joining date of an employee is a legal date. For example, a date such as 10/14/81 is illegal as the month cannot exceed 12. If today's date is 17/5/82 an year of joining such as 95 or 30 would be illegal. Further depending on the month, the range of valid days should be determined.

8.3 A certain steel is graded according to the results of three tests. The tests are:

   i. Carbon content < 0.7 percent
   ii. Rockwell hardness > 50
   iii. Tensile strength > 30,000 kilos/cm

The steel is graded 10 if it passes all three tests, 9 if it passes only tests 1 and 2, 8 if it passes only test 1, and 7 if it passes none of the tests. Obtain a flowchart corresponding to this statement of the problem. Write a program corresponding to this flowchart.

Obtain a decision table corresponding to this problem. Is an action specified for all the eight possible rules corresponding to the outcomes of the three condition tests? Discuss the difference between the flowchart and decision table formulations. Write a Fortran 90 program corresponding to the decision table.

8.4 Obtain decision tables for simulating an automatic stamp vending machine with the following specifications:

i. It should dispense 25, 15 and 10 paise stamps
ii. It should accept 50, 25 and 5 paise coins
iii. It can accept not more than one coin for each transaction
iv. If more than one coin of the same denomination is to be returned as change after dispensing the stamp, the machine cannot do it. Instead the coin should be returned and a 'no change' signal turned on.

The machine should dispense the stamp and the right change and must indicate exceptional cases such as 'insufficient amount tendered', 'no stamp available', 'no change available', etc.

Write a program to simulate the machine. The input to the program are: Amount tendered and the stamp requested. The output of the program should be: whether stamp is dispensed or not, the value of the stamp dispensed, the denomination of the coins returned (if any) and no change signal if no change is returned and no stamp if the stamp is not available.

8.5 A set of rules in a government service for promotion are as follows:

The service has six salary points. Provided a candidate's conduct, diligence and efficiency are considered satisfactory, and he has spent one year as a Class I officer, and has passed satisfactorily the departmental test he advances to the next higher salary point from points 1 or 2. If he is at a higher salary point, then if his conduct, diligence and efficiency are considered satisfactory, and one year has elapsed since his last increment and he has satisfactorily completed a departmental course then he advances to the next higher salary point. Analyse the above statement and find out the input data necessary to decide whether a candidate is to be promoted or not. Write a program to implement the rules.

8.6 The offshore gas company bills its customers according to the following rate schedule:

First 50 cmeters Rs. 40 (flat rate)
Next 300 cmeters Rs. 1.25 per 10 cmeters
Next 3000 cmeters Rs. 1.20 per 10 cmeters
Next 2500 cmeters Rs. 1.10 per 10 cmeters
Next 2500 cmeters Rs. 0.90 per 10 cmeters
Above this Re. 0.80 per 10 cmeters

Given an input for each customer in the format:

Customer number, Previous meter reading, new meter reading

Write a program to output the following:

Customer number, Previous reading, New reading, Gas used, Total bill

8.7 An electricity company has three categories of customers: Industrial, Bulk industrial and domestic. The rates for these are tabulated below:

Industrial

Minimum upto 5000 units	Rs. 1500
Next 5000 units	Re. 1.25 per unit
Next 10000 units	Re. 1.23 per unit
Above this	Re. 1.20 per unit

Bulk Industrial

Minimum upto 5000	Rs. 1800
Next 5000 units	Re. 1.30 per unit
Next 10000 units	Re. 1.28 per unit
Above this	Rs. 1.25 per unit

Domestic

Minimum upto 100 units	Rs. 50
Next 100 units	Re. 1.50 per unit
Next 200 units	Re. 1.45 per unit
Above this	Re. 1.40 per unit

Given the customer number, category of customer, the previous meter reading and the current reading, write a program to output along with the input data, the charges for use of electricity.

9. *Functions and Subroutines—Basics*

Learning Objectives

In this chapter we will learn:

1. How to write and use user defined functions in Fortran 90
2. The difference between internal and external procedures
3. The concept of generic functions
4. How to write and use subroutines in Fortran 90
5. The concept of local and global variables
6. How to break up a problem into procedures and develop programs in a modular fashion

---

9.1 INTRODUCTION

In the Fortran language procedures are program segments which have an independent existence. In other words procedures may be developed separately and tested. They can then be used by other programs. There are two types of procedures in Fortran 90 known as functions and subroutines. We have already encountered in Chapter 4 some built-in functions, also known as *intrinsic* functions, such as SIN and EXP. Programs for evaluating such functions have already been written, tested and incorporated in the Fortran Processor by a professional programmer. When we write SIN(y) we invoke such a predefined function. Besides such predefined functions we may write programs for functions which we may need frequently but which are not in the library. In such a case it is a good idea to write a good efficient program for this, put it in our own "private library" and use it just like using a predefined function.

Another motivation for providing subroutines and functions in Fortran is to enable a Fortran user to use programs developed by others, when it satisfies his requirements. There are many good Fortran library programs available for the Fortran user. For example, a large number of efficient, well tested programs for common problems in matrix manipulation, algebraic equation solution, statistical computations etc., have been developed and leased by companies. Two well known subroutine libraries are known as IMSL (International Mathematical and Statistical Library) and NAG (Numerical Algorithm Group). Most computer manufacturers also supply libraries for mathematical and statistical work. Besides this, professional societies publish certified algorithms in a large variety of areas. For example, the Association for Computing Machinery (USA) publishes "Collected Algorithms".

A third motivation for providing subroutines and functions in Fortran is to enable breaking up a large computer programming job into a number of subtasks. These subtasks may be assigned to different programmers who can develop a subprogram for each subtask independently. The subprograms may then be linked together to do the job. The idea of dividing a large program into smaller manageable programs is useful even if the programs are to be developed by the same person. Such a methodology leads to more reliable, understandable programs.

In this chapter we will discuss the methods of defining and using functions and subroutines. Functions and subroutines may be classified as:

Predefined (built-in) or intrinsic functions
External functions or function subprograms
Generic functions
Subroutine subprograms

We have already encountered *intrinsic* functions such as SQRT, SIN, COS, MOD, etc. A table of functions available in Fortran 90 is given in Appendix A.

An *external function* or a function subprogram is defined by a group of statements. It is implicitly referenced by the appearance of its name in a program.

A *generic function* is a function which returns a value of the same type as that of its argument.

A *subroutine* subprogram is also defined by an independent group of statements. It is explicitly referenced by using a statement known as CALL in Fortran.

In the rest of this chapter we will explain how functions and subroutines are defined and used in Fortran.

9.2 FUNCTION SUBPROGRAMS

Example 9.1

Consider the function defined below:

$$\begin{aligned} S(x) &= 3 \qquad && x > 3 \\ S(x) &= x && 3 \geq x \geq -3 \\ S(x) &= -3 && x < -3 \end{aligned} \tag{9.1}$$

The above function may be defined by the Fortran program (Example Program 9.1).

Example Program 9.1 Program for function s(x)

```
!PROGRAM 9.1
!A PROGRAM DEFINING S(x)
!THE FUNCTION IS COMPUTED BELOW

PROGRAM fun_sx
   IMPLICIT NONE
   REAL :: S,x
   PRINT *, "Type value of x"
   READ *,x
   IF(x < -3.0) THEN
      S = -3.0
   ELSE IF(x > 3.0)THEN
      S = 3.0
   ELSE
      S = x
   ENDIF
   PRINT *,"S(x) =",S
END PROGRAM fun_sx
```

Observe that the independent variable of the function S(x) is x and it is read as an input. For a given value of x the program computes S(x) as defined by Eq. 9.1 and assigns the answer to the variable S. The variable S (the name of the function) is the output which is printed out by the program.

If S(x) is to be used to evaluate the expression of Eq. 9.2

$$z = (S(a) + S(b))/S(a + b) \tag{9.2}$$

it may be done somewhat inelegantly as shown in Example Program 9.2. Observe that the program to calculate the function S(x) is duplicated thrice; once to calculate S(a); second time to find S(b) and third time to find S(a + b). Before using the function the argument x is assigned the required value. The calculated value of the function stored in S is assigned to variables

Example Program 9.2 Computing S(a) + S(b)/S(a + b)

```
!PROGRAM 9.2
!REPEATED USE OF S(x) TO COMPUTE (S(a)+S(b))/S(a+b)
PROGRAM fun_sx_use
   IMPLICIT NONE
   REAL :: S,x,a,b,Sa,Sb,S_a_plus_b,z
   PRINT *, "Type value of a,b"
   PRINT *, " a+b should not be 0"
   READ *,a,b
!COMPUTE S(a)
   x = a
   IF(x < -3.0) THEN
      S = -3.0
   ELSE IF(x > 3.0) THEN
      S = 3.0
   ELSE
      S = x
   ENDIF
   Sa = S
!COMPUTE S(b)
   x = b
   IF(x < -3.0) THEN
      S = -3.0
   ELSE IF(x > 3.0) THEN
      S = 3.0
   ELSE
      S = x
   ENDIF
   Sb = S
!COMPUTE S(a+b)
   x = a+b
   IF(x < -3.0) THEN
      S = -3.0
   ELSE IF(x > 3.0) THEN
      S = 3.0
   ELSE
      S = x
   ENDIF
   S_a_plus_b = S
   z = (Sa + Sb)/S_a_plus_b
   PRINT *,"(S(a)+S(b))/S(a+b) =",z
END PROGRAM fun_sx_use
```

Sa, Sb, and S_a_plus_b respectively when x = a, x = b, and x = a + b. Fortran 90 provides a much more convenient method of defining and using functions which relieves the user from the chore of transmitting the parameter value to the function and duplicating the statements of the program every time the function is used. A program using this method is given as Example Program 9.3.

Example Program 9.3 Illustrating a function subprogram

```
!PROGRAM 9.3
!ILLUSTRATES USE OF FUNCTION SUB PROGRAM
!FUNCTION SUB PROGRAM IS GIVEN BELOW
REAL FUNCTION S(x)
   IMPLICIT NONE
   REAL,INTENT(IN) :: x
   IF( x < -3.0) THEN
      S = -3.0
   ELSE IF(x > 3.0) THEN
      S = 3.0
   ELSE
      S = x
   ENDIF
   END FUNCTION S

PROGRAM fun_s_use
   IMPLICIT NONE
   REAL :: a,b,S,z
   PRINT *, "Type a,b"
   READ *,a,b
!FUNCTION S(x) USED WITH APPROPRIATE ARGUMENTS
   z = (S(a) + S(b))/S(a+b)
   PRINT *,"(S(a)+S(b))/S(a+b) =",z
END PROGRAM fun_s_use
```

Observe the simplicity of the Example Program 9.3. In this program the statement:

REAL FUNCTION S(x)

informs the compiler that the program segment following it defines a function with an argument x which will return a value of type REAL. The statement END FUNCTION S returns control to the main program. In the statement

z = (S(a) + S(b))/S (a + b)

the appearance of S(a) informs the processor that a function with name S is to be used with argument a. Thus a is substituted for x and control is transferred to the first executable statement following the statement: REAL FUNCTION S(x). The function is evaluated and the END FUNCTION S statement returns control to the main program with the value of S(a). Then S(b) is similarly evaluated. Finally (a + b) is substituted for the argument and S(a + b) is evaluated. These values are then used to compute z.

The argument x used in the subprogram is to indicate the method of computation and is a dummy argument. The value used for x is given by the program which calls or uses the subprogram. The subprogram is called by the appearance of the function name S.

Observe the declaration of x in the REAL FUNCTION S(x)

REAL, INTENT(in) :: x

This declaration is to clearly specify that x is an independent variable which is intended as an input to the function. In other words given x, S(x) will be computed.

In Example Program 9.3 we considered a function with a single argument. In general functions may have many arguments. Consider for example the following problem.

Example 9.2

A bank gives simple interest at r percent per year if the balance in one's account is Rs. 500 or more. No interest is given for balance less than Rs. 500. It is required to find the balance in an account at the end of x years.

The independent variables, in this example, are interest rate, balance in one's account and the number of years of deposit. The quantity to be calculated based on these independent variables is the total interest amount.

Thus the function in this case is the interest and the arguments are interest rate, the balance in one's account and the number of years of deposit.

Example Program 9.4 Function to calculate interest

```
!PROGRAM 9.4
!ILLUSTRATES MULTIARGUMENT FUNCTION

REAL FUNCTION interest(rate,balance,years)
   IMPLICIT NONE
   REAL, INTENT(IN) :: rate,balance,years
   IF(balance > 500.0) THEN
      interest = years*balance*rate/100.0
   ELSE
      interest = 0
   ENDIF
END FUNCTION interest
```

A function subprogram which calculates the interest is given as Example Program 9.4. In fact this subprogram could be made more general if the minimum balance (to earn interest) is also taken as a variable. In that case the subprogram may be written as shown in Example Program 9.5. Keeping the arguments as variables generalizes the subprogram and makes it usable under varying conditions. As the purpose of a subprogram is to allow its flexible use by a class of users it is worthwhile to make it as general as possible.

Example Program 9.5 Function to calculate interest—generalized

```
!PROGRAM 9.5
!ILLUSTATES USE OF FUNCTION interest
!GENERALIZED CASE

PROGRAM balance_calculation
   IMPLICIT NONE
   REAL :: rate,bal,yrs,min,intr,interest
   INTEGER :: serial
```

```
DO
   READ*,serial,rate,bal,yrs,min
   IF(serial == 0) EXIT
   intr = interest(rate,bal,yrs,min)
   bal = bal + intr
   PRINT *,"Serial =",serial,"Balance =",bal," Interest =",intr
   END DO
END PROGRAM balance_calculation
!..................................................
!FUNCTION SUB PROGRAM TO COMPUTE INTEREST
REAL FUNCTION interest(rate,balance,years,min_bal)
   IMPLICIT NONE
   REAL,INTENT(IN) :: rate,balance,years,min_bal
   IF(balance > min_bal) THEN
      interest = years * balance * rate/100.0
   ELSE
      interest = 0.0
   ENDIF
END FUNCTION interest
```

9.3 SYNTAX RULES FOR FUNCTION SUBPROGRAMS

The general form of a function subprogram is:

TYPE FUNCTION *name* (a_1, a_2, ... a_n)

____

____

name = *expression* (a_1, a_2, ... a_n)

____

____

____

____

END FUNCTION *name*

The first statement in a function subprogram defines the name of the FUNCTION. It should be declared REAL FUNCTION or INTEGER FUNCTION or LOGICAL FUNCTION. The body of the subprogram follows the function declaration and specifies the computation to be performed on the arguments. The last statement in a subprogram is the END FUNCTION *name* statement which signifies the end of the subprogram. The value calculated in the function body is stored in *name* and returned to the calling program. A subprogram is a program in itself and may be separately compiled. The following rules must be remembered while defining functions:

i. The rule for writing a function name is the same as for variable names. The FUNCTION may be declared REAL, INTEGER or LOGICAL in a way analogous to that used for variable names.

ii. If the type of the FUNCTION is not declared in the FUNCTION statement then the type of the name of the FUNCTION must be declared at the start of the FUNCTION body. This type determines the type of value which will be returned by FUNCTION subprogram to the calling program.

iii. In the body of the subprogram the name of the function must appear at least once on the left hand side of a statement. A value is assigned to the name of the function in this statement.

iv. The arguments used in defining a FUNCTION subprogram may only be real or integer or logical variable names (This rule will be relaxed later).

v. The dummy arguments of the FUNCTION are to be assigned values when the FUNCTION is called. Thus it is a good idea to declare these arguments using one or more type statements.

type, INTENT(IN) :: $a_1, a_2, \ldots a_n$

Observe that the variables are declared with the qualification INTENT(IN) which says that $a_1, a_2 \ldots a_n$ will be given values by the calling program. This qualification is not essential. In other words we can omit it and the compiler will accept the statement. If a variable is declared with qualification INTENT(IN), any attempt to change its value within the function definition will be declared an error by the compiler. Thus it is a good practice to declare all input variables with this qualification.

vi. The *name* of the FUNCTION through which a value is returned to the calling program must be declared in an appropriate *type* declaration in the calling program. For instance, if the FUNCTION *name* is real then the *name* should be declared REAL in the calling program.

vii. The last statement of the FUNCTION subprogram must be an END statement signifying the END of the subprogram. The following three forms are allowed:

END
END FUNCTION
or
END FUNCTION *name*

We recommend the last form as it clearly defines the END of a specified FUNCTION. If the latter form is used the *name* must be the same as the *name* of the FUNCTION.

The function is called by a program by the appearance of the FUNCTION name in a statement. The rules to be remembered when calling a FUNCTION are listed below:

i. The arguments in the calling FUNCTION must agree in number, order and mode with those in the FUNCTION statement in the subprogram.

ii. The arguments in the calling program may be expressions, variable names or constants provided condition (i) is satisfied.

iii. A function may call other functions but cannot call itself directly or indirectly. If a function calls itself it is called a *recursive call.* Fortran 77 did not allow it. Fortran 90 allows it but we must use special techniques which will be discussed in a later chapter. For the present we will assume that recursive calls are not allowed. Some of the rules given above are relaxed in Fortran 90. We will discuss them in a later chapter.

iv. The name of the FUNCTION in which the computed value is returned must be declared in a type declaration in the calling program.

The concept of calling of a function program and the return of a value by the subprogram is summarized in Fig. 9.1. The subprogram is called by the appearance of the function name. The values of arguments specified in the call are taken as the values of the dummy arguments in the function subprogram and the value to be stored in name is computed. When the subprogram reaches its logical end, the value stored in name by the subprogram is accessed by the calling program. Thus the input to the function subprogram is through the variable list in the calling program and the output of the subprogram is the value stored in name. These variable names provide the connecting link between the calling and called program. Besides these the function subprogram may have other variables which it uses while computing the value of name. These variable names are private to the subprogram and are not accessible to the calling program. In fact the calling program does not even know that the subprogram uses these variable names. These variable names are *local* to the subprogram. The statement labels, if any, used by subprogram are also local to the subprogram. In other words statement labels and variable names appearing locally in a subprogram can be used by the calling program without any ambiguity.

Thus a subprogram can be written separately and kept in a library for use by a class of users. With this facility a large program may be divided into a number of subprograms and linked together.

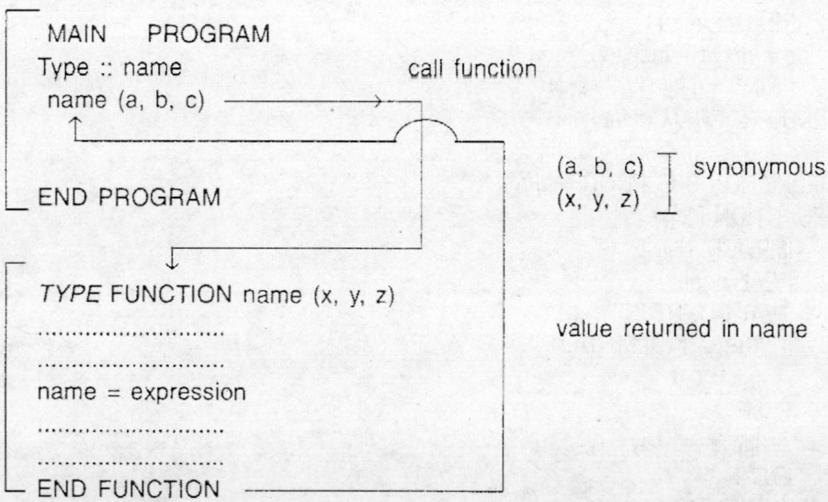

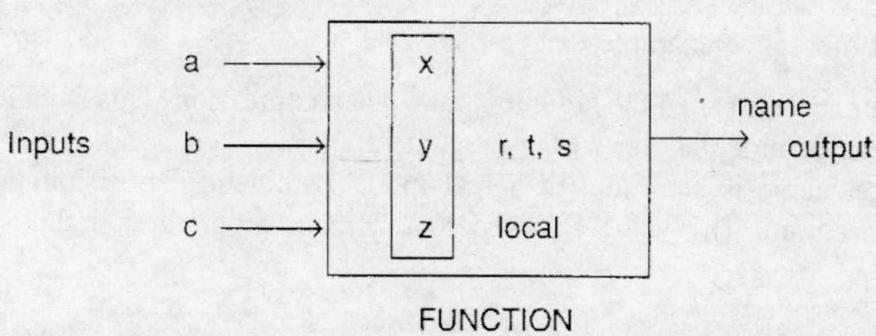

Fig 9.1 Illustrating calling of a function subprogram.

We will close this section with two examples in which function subprograms are used.

Example 9.3

Suppose the frictional force acting on a particle is given by the equations:

$$f(y) = 0 \text{ for } |y| \leq .5 \qquad (9.3)$$
$$= 2y^2 \; |y| > .5$$

It is required to use this function in Eq. (9.4)

$$g = (mv/t) - f(v^2) + at \qquad (9.4)$$

A small program to do this is written as Example Program 9.6.

Example Program 9.6 Defining function fric

```
!PROGRAM 9.6
!FUNCTION DEFINITION AND USE
PROGRAM g_formula
   IMPLICIT NONE
   REAL :: m,fric,v,a,t,g
   PRINT *, " Type values of m, v, a, t"
   READ *,m,v,a,t
   g = m*v/t - fric(v*v) + a*t
   PRINT *,g
END PROGRAM g_formula
!........................................
!FUNCTION SUB PROGRAM fric
FUNCTION fric(y)
   IMPLICIT NONE
   REAL :: fric
   REAL,INTENT(IN) :: y
   IF(ABS(y) <= 0.5) THEN
      fric = 0.0
   ELSE
      fric = 2.0 * y * y
   ENDIF
END FUNCTION fric
```

It is seen from the above example that

i. When the function is called the argument may be an expression. This is valid provided it is in the same mode as the dummy argument.
ii. The function name is set equal to a real mode arithmetic expression in the body of the subprogram. The value returned to the main program will thus be in real mode.

Example 9.4

We now write a function which reverses a given integer. For example, if an integer 45789 is its input, 98754 is its output. The function reverse-of is given in Example Program 9.7.

Example Program 9.7 Reversing an integer

```
!PROGRAM 9.7
!ILLUSTRATING USE OF FUNCTIONS

PROGRAM use_reverse
  IMPLICIT NONE
  INTEGER :: reverse_of,p,q
  PRINT *, " Type an integer "
  READ *,p
  q = reverse_of(p)
  PRINT *,"Reverse of ",p,"is",q
END PROGRAM use_reverse
INTEGER FUNCTION reverse_of(n)
  IMPLICIT NONE
  INTEGER :: digit,rev_of_n=0,no
  INTEGER,INTENT(IN) :: n
  no = n
  DO
    IF(no == 0) EXIT
    digit = MOD(no,10)
    rev_of_n = rev_of_n * 10 + digit
    no = no/10
  END DO
  reverse_of = rev_of_n
END FUNCTION reverse_of
```

9.4 GENERIC FUNCTIONS

The functions we discussed so far can return only one type of result for a given type of argument. In designing intrinsic functions it is inconvenient to have different names for the same function depending on the type of argument. For example, in Fortran 77, for finding the absolute value of a variable IABS(k) is used if k is an INTEGER variable and ABS(k) if k is REAL. Fortran 90 relaxes this rule and for many functions it allows use of the same name regardless of the type of argument and returns a value whose type is the same as that of the argument. Such functions are known as *generic functions*. For example, the function ABS can have either a REAL or an INTEGER argument and returns a value of the same type. Thus ABS is a generic function. It is also possible for users to define generic functions. The method of doing this will be discussed later in this book.

9.5 SUBROUTINES

A function subprogram returns a single value to the main program when it is called. If more than one value is to be returned to the main program then a subprogram called a SUBROUTINE is used. In cases where no value is returned to the main program but specific operations are performed like arranging a list of numbers in ascending order or transposing a matrix then also SUBROUTINES are used.

Consider, for example, a program which needs frequent solution of quadratic equations. In this case the procedure for obtaining the roots of the quadratic equation may be formulated separately and a program written. Such a program would return four values: the two real parts and the two imaginary parts of the roots. As a function subprogram cannot be used in such a case a subroutine is used instead. We give now a subroutine to find the roots of a quadratic equation (Example Program 9.8).

Example 9.5

A quadratic equation is

$$ax^2 + bx + c = 0 \tag{9.5}$$

If a = 0 then the equation is not really a quadratic and it is a linear equation with a single root

$$x\ real\ 1 = -\ c/b \tag{9.6}$$

If a is not equal to zero then we define a discriminant

$$discriminant = (b^2 - 4\ ac) \tag{9.7}$$

If the discriminant is greater than or equal to zero the roots are real and are given by

$$x\ real\ 1 = (-\ b + \sqrt{b^2 - 4\ ac})/2a \tag{9.8}$$

$$x\ real\ 2 = (-\ b - \sqrt{b^2 - 4\ ac})/2a \tag{9.9}$$

If the discriminant is less than zero then the roots have both real and imaginary parts and are given by:

$$x\ real\ 1 = x\ real\ 2 = -\ b/2a \tag{9.10}$$

$$x\ imaginary\ 1 = \sqrt{b^2 - 4\ ac}\ /2a \tag{9.11}$$

and

$$x\ imaginary\ 2 = -\ x\ imaginary\ 1 \tag{9.12}$$

When a subroutine is written to solve a quadratic it is essential to account for all the above cases and make it very general. The meaning and purpose of all the variables used as arguments of the subroutine must be given at the top of the subroutine.

Observe in Example Program 9.8 that the variable names that represent the values to be returned to the main program are included in the list of arguments. The name of the SUBROUTINE, namely roots does not and should not appear in the body of the subprogram. It is merely a title given to the SUBROUTINE so that the main program may refer to it.

The important points to remember while using a subroutine are:

i. The arguments on which the subroutine is to operate are to be transmitted to the subroutine from the calling program. The transmittal is achieved through the variables a, b and c in the above example and explicitly mentioned in the argument list of the subroutine. As subroutines are independent programs they may be separately written. The arguments in the list are dummies which indicate the number and type of arguments on which operations are performed by the subroutine.
ii. After the operations are performed the results are to be transmitted back to the calling program. This is also achieved through dummy arguments listed in the argument list of the subroutine.
iii. The arguments a, b, c are inputs from the calling program. They are declared in the body of the subroutine as REAL with qualifier INTENT(IN). The results computed by the subroutine to be returned to the calling program are x_real1, x_real2, x_imag1, x_imag2. They are declared as REAL with qualifier INTENT(OUT).

Example Program 9.8 Subroutine to find roots of a quadratic equation

```
!PROGRAM 9.8
!THE FOLLOWING SUBROUTINE roots COMPUTES THE ROOTS
!OF A QUADRATIC EQUATION a*x*x + b*x + c = 0
!GIVEN a,b,c THE SUBROUTINE RETURNS THE REAL PARTS OF
!THE ROOTS x_real1 AND x_real2 AND THE IMAGINARY PARTS
!x_imag1 AND x_imag2 (IF ANY). IF a = 0 ONLY x_real1
!IS RETURNED AND OTHER ROOTS ARE MADE ZERO. AN
!INTEGER i IS SET TO 1 IF a==0,TO 2
!IF DISCRIMINANT >=0(REAL ROOTS)
!AND TO 3 IF DISCRIMINANT < 0. i CAN BE USED BY THE
!CALLING PROGRAM TO GIVE CORRECT MESSAGES
SUBROUTINE roots(a,b,c,x_real1,x_real2,x_imag1,x_imag2,i)
  IMPLICIT NONE
  REAL :: discr,d ! LOCAL VARIABLES
  REAL,INTENT(IN) :: a,b,c
  REAL,INTENT(OUT):: x_real1,x_real2,x_imag1,x_imag2
  INTEGER,INTENT(OUT) :: i
  REAL,PARAMETER :: epsilon = 0.5e-6
!IF ABS(a) <= epsilon THEN a IS ASSUMED TO BE ZERO
  IF(ABS(a) <= epsilon) THEN
    x_real1 = -c/b;x_real2 = 0
    x_imag1 = 0;x_imag2 = 0
    i = 1
    RETURN
  ENDIF
  discr = b*b - 4*a*c
  IF(discr >= 0) THEN
    d = SQRT(discr);i = 2
    x_real1 = 0.5*(-b + d)/a
    x_real2 = 0.5*(-b - d)/a
    x_imag1 = 0;x_imag2 = 0
  ELSE
    d =SQRT(-discr) ; i =3
    x_real1 = -0.5*b/a;x_real2 = x_real1
    x_imag1 = 0.5*d/a ; x_imag2 = -x_imag1
  ENDIF
END SUBROUTINE roots
```

iv. It is important to use INTENT(IN) qualifier with variable intended as inputs. When this qualifier is used the compiler is informed that these values should **not** be changed by the subroutine. Any mistaken attempt to change these values is signalled as an error by the compiler and computation is stopped.

v. Variables can also be qualified as INTENT(INOUT). In such a case the variables can be changed by the subroutine.

vi. Besides variables which are needed for communication between the calling program and the called program some variables are needed within the subroutine for local use. In this example they are discr and d which are declared in this SUBROUTINE. They are called *local variables* and have no meaning outside the SUBROUTINE where they are declared.

vii. In this subroutine the integer variable i is returned to the calling program to indicate different cases which occur. This is extremely useful to the main program to print appropriate messages.

As a SUBROUTINE may return more than one value and in some cases may not return any value, a special statement is required in the calling program to call it. The general form of this statement is:

CALL *name (list of arguments)*

The name of the subroutine may be any valid Fortran 90 identifier. The list of arguments must agree in number, order and mode with the dummy arguments in the SUBROUTINE definition. For example, the SUBROUTINE roots (a, b, c, x_real1, x_real 2, x_imag 1, x_imag2, i) considered in Example Program 9.7 may be called by the statement:

CALL roots (p, q, r, x_r1, x_r2, x_i1, x_i2, flag)

The value p, q and r will be substituted in place of a, b and c in the SUBROUTINE and the values of roots calculated by the SUBROUTINE stored in x_r1, x_r2, x_i1, x_i2.

After the SUBROUTINE does its job, control returns to the statement following the CALL statement. Control returns normally when END SUBROUTINE statement is reached. If it is required to leave the SUBROUTINE and return to the calling program when an exceptional condition occurs then a statement RETURN is available in Fortran 90. In Example Program 9.8 when the equation is not really quadratic (case a < = epsilon) we have used a RETURN statement.

The concepts useful in understanding the linking of a subroutine with a main program are illustrated in Fig. 9.2. The dummy argument list in the SUBROUTINE consists of both input and

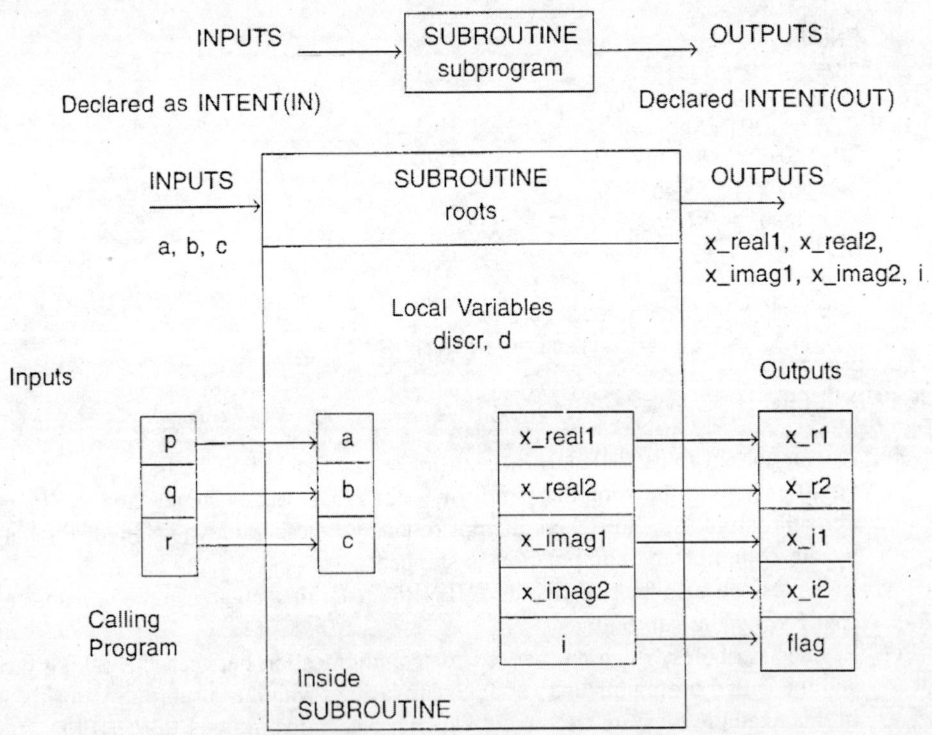

Fig. 9.2 Inputs and outputs of SUBROUTINE subprogram.

output variables. The corresponding arguments in the calling program have values stored in them when the CALL statement is executed. The dummy arguments are synonymous to those in the calling program and take on the appropriate values when the subroutine is executed. When control returns to the calling program the output arguments in the SUBROUTINE list are referred by the corresponding arguments of the calling program and thereby transferred to the calling program. In Example Program 9.9 we have illustrated how the SUBROUTINE written for solving quadratic equation can be called with different input values.

Example Program 9.9 Quadratic equation solution—using SUBROUTINE

```
!PROGRAM 9.9
!THIS PROGRAM CALLS SUBROUTINE ROOTS

PROGRAM use_roots
  IMPLICIT NONE
  INTEGER :: serial,flag
  REAL :: p,q,r,x_r1,x_r2,x_im1,x_im2
  DO
    READ *,serial,p,q,r
    IF(serial == 0) EXIT
    PRINT *,"Serial =",serial,"p =",p,"q =",q,"r =",r
    CALL roots(p,q,r,x_r1,x_r2,x_im1,x_im2,flag)
    SELECT CASE(flag)
    CASE(1)
      PRINT*,"Linear equation, only one root"
      PRINT *,"Root =",x_r1
    CASE(2)
      PRINT*,"Two real roots"
      PRINT*,"Root1 =",x_r1,"Root2 =",x_r2
    CASE(3)
      PRINT*,"Complex conjugate roots"
      PRINT*,"root 1 =",x_r1," + i",x_im1
      PRINT*,"root 2 =",x_r2," + i",x_im2
    END SELECT
  END DO
  PRINT*,"No more data"
END PROGRAM use_roots
```

We will now consider some examples of SUBROUTINE definition and calling, which will clarify some points.

Example 9.6

A SUBROUTINE may call another SUBROUTINE which may in turn call a third SUBROUTINE. The sequence of calls and returns are illustrated in Example Program 9.10.

Example Program 9.10 Illustrates sequence of CALLS and return in SUBROUTINE

```
!PROGRAM 9.10
!ILLUSTRATING CALLS AND RETURNS FROM SUBROUTINES

PROGRAM main
   PRINT *,"Output of Example Program 9.10"
   PRINT *,"Call to f from main"
   CALL f
   PRINT *,"Control has returned to main"
END PROGRAM main

SUBROUTINE f
   PRINT *,"Control now in f"
   PRINT *,"Call to g from f"
   CALL g
   PRINT *,"Control has returned to f"
END SUBROUTINE f

SUBROUTINE g
   PRINT *,"Control now in g"
   PRINT *,"Call to h from g"
   CALL h
   PRINT *,"Control has returned to g"
END SUBROUTINE g

SUBROUTINE h
   PRINT *,"Control now in h"
   PRINT *,"Return to calling program"
END SUBROUTINE h
```

```
Output of Example Program 9.10
Call to f from main
Control now in f
Call to g from f
Control now in g
Call to h from g
Control now in h
Return to calling program
Control has returned to g
Control has returned to f
Control has returned to main
```

Fig. 9.3 The Output of Example Program 9.10.

Observe that a subroutine may have no argument if it does not compute anything. Observe that when a SUBROUTINE f calls a SUBROUTINE g from f, g will do its task and return to statement following the statement calling g. The output of Example program 9.10. is shown as Fig. 9.3.

The student should examine the output of the program along with the program to understand the flow of control from calling SUBROUTINE to the called SUBROUTINE and back from the called to the calling SUBROUTINE.

Earlier versions of Fortran did not allow a SUBROUTINE to call itself either directly or indirectly. This restriction has been removed in Fortran 90. Such calls known as *recursive calls* are allowed in Fortran 90. We will discuss how this is done later in this book.

To conclude this section we note that subroutine subprograms receive inputs from a calling program, process them and return the processed results as outputs. Inputs to the subroutine should not be normally altered by the subroutine and this may be specified by declaring these variables with INTENT(IN) qualifier. The subroutines we discussed in this section are *external subprograms*. They are independent programs which can be separately compiled. The separately compiled programs should be combined or linked together to form one executable object program. The correspondences between variables used in the calling program and subprogram is implicitly specified by the requirement that the variables in the calling program must agree in number, order and mode with those in the called subprogram. This rule is sometimes too restrictive. We will see later in this book how this rule has been relaxed in Fortran 90 by using explicit interface specification between the calling and called programs.

Besides external subprograms Fortran 90 allows internal subprograms which are defined within a program and used. Such a method is useful for top down development of a program. We will explain this in the next section.

9.6 INTERNAL PROCEDURES

Consider the problem of processing the examination results of a group of students. It is specified that there are three subjects with 100 marks being the maximum in each subject. A student passes in first class if he/she gets 60 or more marks on the average, in the second class if the average is 50 or more, third class if 40 or more and fails otherwise. A procedure is given in English to solve this problem.

Repeat Steps 1 to 5 for all students records

Step 1	Read student record
Step 2	Edit record
Step 3	Reject records with errors
Step 4	Find average marks and class of a student
Step 5	Print results

Reading a record is simple requiring only one statement. We can combine Steps 2, 3 as procedure for editing and Step 4 as another procedure for finding average marks and class. With this we can define this procedure further as:

Repeat Steps 1 to 4 for all student records

Step 1	Read a student record
Step 2	CALL edit procedure
	IF error in record return to Step 1
Step 3	CALL process-record
Step 4	Print processed record

We can now write a Fortran 90 program for this problem as shown in Example Program 9.11. The structure of the program is shown below (in pseudo code).

```
PROGRAM student-result
   variable declarations
DO
   READ record
   IF (end of records) EXIT
   Count number of records
   CALL edit-record
   IF (error in record) CYCLE
   CALL process-record
   PRINT processed record
END DO
CONTAINS
   SUBROUTINE edit-record
     statements for editing
   END SUBROUTINE edit-record
   SUBROUTINE process-record
     statements for processing records
   END SUBROUTINE process-record
END PROGRAM student-result
```

Example Program 9.11 Processing students' records

```
!PROGRAM 9.11
!ILLUSTRATES USE OF INTERNAL SUBROUTINES
!TOP DOWN PROGRAM DEVELOPMENT
PROGRAM student_result
   INTEGER :: roll_no,marks_1,marks_2,marks_3,total,avg,class,bad_record = 0, no_records = 0
   LOGICAL :: error
   DO
      READ *,roll_no,marks_1,marks_2,marks_3
      IF(roll_no == 0) EXIT
      no_records = no_records + 1
      CALL edit_record
      IF(error) CYCLE
      CALL process_record
      PRINT *,"Roll no =", roll_no,"Marks 1=",marks_1,&
          "Marks 2=", marks_2,"marks 3=",marks_3, &
          "total =",total,"average=", avg,"class =",class
   END DO
   PRINT *,"No of records processed =",no_records
   PRINT *,"No of bad records =",bad_record
   CONTAINS
   SUBROUTINE edit_record
      error = .FALSE.
      IF((marks_1 > 100) .OR. (marks_1 < 0)) error = .TRUE.
      IF((marks_2 > 100) .OR. (marks_2 < 0)) error = .TRUE.
      IF((marks_3 > 100) .OR. (marks_3 < 0)) error = .TRUE.
      IF(error) THEN
         PRINT *,"Error in record with serial_no=",roll_no
         bad_record = bad_record+1
      ENDIF
   END SUBROUTINE edit_record
```

```
    SUBROUTINE process_record
       total = marks_1 + marks_2 + marks_3
!AVERAGE ROUNDED TO THE NEAREST INTEGER
       avg = REAL(total)/3.0 + 0.5
    IF(avg >= 60) THEN
          class = 1
    ELSE IF(avg >= 50) THEN
          class = 2
    ELSE IF(avg >= 40) THEN
          class = 3
    ELSE
          class = 0
    ENDIF
  END SUBROUTINE process_record
END PROGRAM student_result
```

Observe that the SUBROUTINEs are placed inside the PROGRAM. The keyword CONTAINS is used to indicate that the SUBROUTINEs following it are internal SUBROUTINEs. Observe in the above example that all variables are declared in main PROGRAM and they are global. They are available to all internal SUBROUTINEs contained in PROGRAM. This is the most common way in which internal SUBROUTINEs are used. The rules, however, are more general. There could be local variable names within the SUBROUTINEs which are entirely private to them. If the same name is used by PROGRAM and SUBROUTINE then they are not synonymous. They are each local to the procedures within which they are declared. The internal SUBROUTINEs may have a list of dummy variables just as external subroutines. They have a similar use. There are special *scoping rules* which specify the domain within which they are local and where they are global. We will discuss this later in this book.

SUMMARY

1. There are two types of procedures in Fortran 90 called functions or subroutines.
2. There are two types of functions—user defined or built-in. Built-in functions, known as intrinsic functions are part of the Fortran 90 language. User defined functions are specified as a program unit by a user and are normally separately compiled.
3. Separately compiled procedures in Fortran 90 are known as external procedures.
4. A function normally has one or more arguments and gives a single result which is returned via the name of the function.
5. A Fortran 90 program has a main program unit followed by any number of external procedures (functions or subroutines).
6. A function is called by the main program by the appearance of the function name along with input arguments.
7. The type of value returned is defined by the type of function name.
8. There are a class of functions called generic functions in which the same function name can be used regardless of argument type.
9. A subroutine receives one or more inputs via its arguments (normally defined with an INTENT (IN) qualifier) and returns one or more results via specified arguments (normally defined with an INTENT (OUT) qualifier). A subroutine may just perform some operations on inputs and not return any results.

10. A subroutine is called by a main program by a CALL statement.
11. Variables declared within a procedure are local to it. Communications with other procedures is only via the arguments.
12. Procedures may be contained entirely within a main program. Such procedures are known as internal procedures and are not separately compiled. A program is designed with internal procedures mainly to improve understandability of the program.
13. In this chapter we have assumed that the interface between a main program and external procedures are implicitly defined by ensuring that the arguments of the calling program and called program agree in number, order and type. This rule is relaxed in Fortran 90 by explicit INTERFACE specification which we will discuss later.

EXERCISES

9.1 Write a function subprogram for the function f(x) defined as follows:

$f(x) = 2x^2 + 3x + 4$ for $x < 2$
$f(x) = 0$ for $x = 2$
$f(x) = 2x^2 + 3x - 4$ for $x > 2$

9.2 Write a function to evaluate

$$f(x) = 1 + \frac{x^2}{2!} + \frac{x^4}{4!} + \frac{x^6}{6!} + \frac{x^8}{8!} + \frac{x^{10}}{10!}$$

9.3 Write a subroutine to find out whether three points (x_1, x_2), (x_3, x_4) and (x_5, x_6) are collinear. The inputs are the co-ordinates of the points, the output is a logical quantity which is set to true if the points are collinear and false otherwise. The main program should print an appropriate message.

9.4 Given a set of n integers evolve a program which will find

i. The total number of even integers in the set
ii. The total number of odd integers in the set
iii. The sum of all even integers
iv. The sum of all odd integers

Structure the program using subroutines.

9.5 Evolve a subprogram which will accept a pair of co-ordinates and return a code which will specify in which quadrant a point lies (for example (–3, 6) is in the second quadrant).

9.6 Given n sets of lengths and breadths of rectangles, obtain a subprogram to find those rectangles whose area is greater than their perimeter. Extend the subprogram to find the average of the areas of the rectangles.

9.7 Given a set of co-ordinates (x, y) of points write a function which will output all points which are inside the unit circle with its centre at (0, 0).

9.8 Given a 5 digit integer write a function which will return its modulus 11 check digit. Modulus 11 check digit is defined as follows:

Number = 34568. Modulus 11 check digit x satisfies the equality MOD $(x + 8 \times 2 + 6 \times 3 + 5 \times 4 + 4 \times 5 + 3 \times 6, 11) = 0$.

Observe that the check digit is multiplied by 1, the next digit by 2, and so on.

9.9 Write a function which calculates and returns the distance between any two points whose coordinates are (x_1, y_1), (x_2, y_2).

9.10 The force f due to gravity between two bodies of masses m_1, m_2, is given by:

$$f = Gm_1 m_2/r^2$$

where G = 6.673E – 11, r is the distance (in meters) between the two bodies and m_1, m_2 are in Kg. Write a REAL function to calculate f. G should be defined as a parameter.

9.11 A telephone company produces monthly statements for its customers with each statement having the following data:

i. The outstanding amount carried over
ii. The interest due on that amount for the month
iii. Any payment received during the month
iv. The total current amount due

Write a procedure which reads all the necessary data and prints a statement.

9.12 Write a program with two subroutines to find the mean and median of a set of n numbers. One subroutine finds the mean and the other the median. A mean of n numbers is the sum of the numbers divided by n. The median x of a set of numbers is a number such that the subset with values < x = subset with values > x. For example for the set 1, 3, 6, 3, 8, 9, 7, the mean is 37/7 = 5.2857 and the median is 6. Rewrite the program with two internal subroutines.

10. *Defining and Manipulating Arrays*

Learning Objectives

In this Chapter we will learn:

1. The use of a data structure called an array which may have one or more dimensions
2. How an array is declared
3. How data is read into an array
4. How data stored in arrays is processed
5. Operations on entire arrays available in Fortran 90

10.1 ARRAYS VARIABLE

The variables considered so far were single entities, that is, each variable name stores one number. There is another type of variable called an array variable. An array variable name refers to a group of quantities by a single name. Each member in the group is referred to by its position in the group. Suppose a shop stocks different wattages of bulbs and the stock of each wattage bulbs is to be represented. One way of representing this is to make a table:

Wattage	15	25	40	60	100
Stock	25	126	300	570	28

We can codify each wattage by a digit and represent the above table as:

Wattage Code:	1	2	3	4	5
Stock:	25	126	300	570	28

where 1 represents 15 watts, 2 : 25 watts, 3 : 40 watts, 4 : 60 watts and 5 : 100 watts.

We can now represent the stock of bulbs by:

(25 126 300 570 28)

with the wattage codes not being mentioned explicitly but implied. Stock is an array variable with 5 elements.

A particular element of the array is referenced by its position in the array, starting with first position.

Thus stock (1) = 25
stock (2) = 126
stock (3) = 300
stock (4) = 570
stock (5) = 28

In memory one location is reserved for each element of the array. The locations are contiguous:

Variable name	stock (1)	stock (2)	stock (3)	stock (4)	stock (5)
Contents	25	126	300	570	28

Assume that the cost of each wattage bulb is represented by an array cost as shown below:

cost (1) = 3.50; cost (2) = 6.50; cost (3) = 7.75; cost (4) = 8.50; cost (5) = 9.50

Referring to Example Program 10.1 the declarations:

```
INTEGER :: stock (5), watt_code
REAL :: cost (5), total_cost = 0
```

informs the compiler that stock is an array with 5 elements and each element is an integer. It also declares watt_code as an integer. The next declaration informs the compiler that cost (5) is a five element array of reals. It initializes total_cost to zero. In the DO loop the first statement reads the values of stock (1) and cost (1). The next statement computes the cost of the number of bulbs in stock with watt_code = 1 and adds it to the total_cost. The DO loop is repeated for all 5 values of watt_code and the total_cost is computed. Finally the total_cost is printed.

Example Program 10.1 Finding cost of bulbs

```
!PROGRAM 10.1
!CALCULATING TOTAL COST OF BULBS
!ILLUSTRATES USE OF ARRAYS

PROGRAM cost_bulbs
   IMPLICIT NONE
   INTEGER :: stock(5),watt_code
   REAL :: cost(5),total_cost=0
   DO watt_code = 1,5
      READ *,stock(watt_code),cost(watt_code)
      total_cost = total_cost+REAL(stock(watt_code))*cost(watt_code)
   END DO
   PRINT *,"TOTAL COST =",total_cost
END PROGRAM cost_bulbs
```

The declarations in this example may also be written as:

```
INTEGER, DIMENSION (5) :: stock
INTEGER :: watt_code
REAL, DIMENSION (5) :: cost
REAL :: total_cost = 0
```

The declaration of arrays with an explicit DIMENSION is preferred as it is more general. We now consider another example.

Example 10.1

There are fifty students in a class and the marks obtained by each student in an examination are typed on one or more lines. A computer program is required which will print out the highest and the second highest marks obtained in the examination. This problem is a variation of the problem of picking the largest from a set of numbers. In this problem after picking the largest number in the set it should be eliminated from further consideration and the remaining numbers searched for the largest. A program to do this is given as Example Program 10.2. The new statements used in this program will be explained below:

Example Program 10.2 Finding the highest and second highest marks

```
!PROGRAM 10.2
!PICKING FIRST AND SECOND MARKS
PROGRAM first_second
   IMPLICIT NONE
   INTEGER, DIMENSION(50) :: marks
   INTEGER :: first=0,second=0,i
   PRINT *, " Type 50 individual marks "
   READ *,(marks(i),i=1,50)
   DO i=1,50
      IF(marks(i) > first) first = marks(i)
   END DO
   DO i=1,50
      IF(marks(i) == first)CYCLE
      IF(marks(i) > second) second = marks(i)
   END DO
   PRINT *, "First mark=",first,"Second mark =",second
END PROGRAM first_second
```

The statement:

```
INTEGER, DIMENSION (50) :: marks
```

informs the compiler that marks is an array with 50 *elements* in which each element is of type INTEGER. The same information may also be written as:

```
INTEGER :: marks (50)
```

which defines marks to be an array of a size 50 (or dimension 50). This enables the compiler to reserve 50 locations in memory to store the 50 elements of the array marks.

Observe next the method of reading an array with an *implied DO loop* in the READ statement:

```
READ *, (marks (i), i = 1, 50)
```

which commands that first data item read is to be stored in marks (1), the second data in marks (2) and so on till the 50th data read is stored in marks (50). The data may be typed in one or more lines.

We could also have written

```
DO i = 1, 50
   READ *,  marks (i)
END DO
```

in which case the compiler will expect only one data item per line and will read 50 lines.

A third more concise statement is

```
READ *, marks
```

which will read 50 data items from one or more lines and store them in marks (1), marks (2), ..., marks (50). The declaration that marks is an array of 50 components is the information used by the READ statement to read *all* the 50 elements of the array marks. The first DO loop picks the highest element of marks and stores it in first. In the second DO loop all the elements of marks equal to first are skipped and second highest component picked from among the rest. Instead of using two DO loops as shown in this solution it is possible to write a program with a single DO loop. It is also possible to solve this problem without using an array. The reader should try to solve this problem both ways and he would then appreciate the flexibility and power afforded by subscripts.

The general form of an array variable is:

v(i)

where v is a variable name which may be of type integer or real and i is a subscript. The subscript may be any valid integer constant, integer variable name or integer expression. Subscripts may be negative, zero or positive. Negative subscripts are allowed provided it leads to a meaningful value within the bounds of the array.

Example

i, j, code i * 4 – k, 2 * i/p are valid subscripts provided i, j, code, k, p are integer variable names. The following are invalid:

a(2i), c(2.6), x(i = p/4), p[i]

The following are valid:

a(2 * i) , b(i + 1) , q(9/2) , d(k – 1)

A declaration of a variable name as representing an array provides information to the Fortran 90 compiler to enable it to:

i. identify the variable name as an array name
ii. reserve locations in memory to store all the elements of an array.

Observe that Fortran 90 assumes that the subscripts evaluated during computation will never exceed the size declared in a declaration statement. If it does exceed, wrong answers may be printed. Thus it is a programmer's responsibility to see that array bounds are not violated. The declaration INTEGER :: a(5) reserves five locations for array a and by default assumes that the subscript starts with 1. The locations are labelled a(1), a(2), a(3), a(4), a(5). If we want the array subscript to have a different range of values then we can use the declaration

INTEGER :: a (–1 : 3)

The above declaration reserves 5 locations in memory for a and the locations are identified by a(– 1), a(0), a(1), a(2), a(3). In the declarations:

```
INTEGER, DIMENSION (0:3) :: b
INTEGER, DIMENSION (–3: –1) :: d
```

The array b has 4 elements b(0), b(1), b(2), b(3) and d has 3 elements d(–3), d(–2) and d(–1). The following are illegal:

```
INTEGER :: a (– 4 : – 6)     (Second value smaller than first)
INTEGER :: b (2 : 2 + 6)     (Expression not allowed)
INTEGER :: d (0; 4)          (; not allowed)
```

Example 10.2

We will now write a program which interchanges the odd and even components of an array. The program is given as Example Program 10.3.

Example Program 10.3 Interchanging odd and even components of a vector

```
!PROGRAM 10.3
!THIS PROGRAM INTERCHANGES THE COMPONENTS OF A VECTOR
PROGRAM interchange
   IMPLICIT NONE
   INTEGER :: a(10),i,temp
   PRINT *, " Type 10 components of vector "
   READ *,a
   DO i=1,9,2
      temp = a(i)
      a(i) = a(i+1)
      a(i+1) = temp
   END DO
   PRINT *,"interchanged array =", a
END PROGRAM interchange
```

Example 10.3

We will now write a program to evaluate a polynomial

$$p(x) = a_n x^n + a_{n-1} x^{n-1} + a_{n-2} x^{n-2} + \dots + a_1 x + a_0$$

Evaluating this polynomial by writing an arithmetic statement is simple but inefficient. It will require n (n + 1)/2 multiplication operations and n addition operations. We will use an alternative method of writing the polynomial and write a program to evaluate the polynomial. This method requires only n multiplications and n additions.

$$\begin{aligned} p(x) &= a_0 + a_1 x + a_2 x^2 + \dots + a_{n-1} x^{n-1} + a_n x^n \\ &= a_0 + x(a_1 + x(a_2 + x(a_3 + \dots + x(a_{n-1} + x a_n)))\dots) \end{aligned}$$

We start evaluating the expression in the innermost parentheses and successively multiply by x in a DO loop. The coefficients a_0, a_1, a_2 ..., a_n are stored in an array a(n). The program is written as Example Program 10.4.

Example Program 10.4 Evaluating a polynomial

```
!PROGRAM 10.4
!THIS PROGRAM EVALUATES POLYNOMIALS UPTO ORDER 20
PROGRAM poly
   IMPLICIT NONE
   INTEGER :: i, n
   REAL ::x, polynomial
   REAL, DIMENSION(0:20)::a
   PRINT *, "Type order of polynomial n and x"
   READ *, n, x
!n IS THE ORDER OF THE POLYNOMIAL TO BE EVALUATED
!AND IS READ AS INPUT. n SHOULD BE LESS THAN OR EQUAL TO 20
   PRINT *,  " Type components of a"
   READ *, (a(i), i=0, n)
!a(0), a(1), a(2)...a(n) TYPED IN ONE OR MORE LINES
   polynomial = a(n)
   DO i=n, 1, -1
   polynomial = a(i-1)+x*polynomial
  END DO
  PRINT *, "x=", x, "Polynomial value =", polynomial
END PROGRAM poly
```

In Example Program 10.4 we assume that the maximum number of polynomial coefficients is 20. Thus the size of the array a storing the coefficients is declared with DIMENSION (0 : 20). If the order of polynomial is less than 20 then this program will work. We now explain the program. The first DO loop reads all values of the coefficients of the polynomial into the array a. The second DO loop is traced in Table 10.1.

Table 10.1 Tracing DO Loop in Example Program 10.4

Index i	*Polynomial*
Initialization	a(n)
n	a(n – 1) + x * a(n)
n – 1	a(n – 2) + x(a(n – 1) + x * a(n))
n – 2	a(n – 3) + x(a(n – 2) + x(a(n – 1) + x * a(n)))
.	
.	
.	
1	a(0) + x * (a(1) + x * (a(2) + x * (a(3) + ...)))

Observe that the index starts with n and is decremented at the end of each execution of the statement:

```
polynomial = a (i – 1) + x * polynomial
```

which is the only statement in the DO loop.

As it is desirable to write a general program to evaluate polynomials it would have been nice to declare the array with DIMENSION (0 : n) with n being a variable. We will see later how this can be done in Fortran 90.

10.2 USE OF MULTIPLE SUBSCRIPTS

In the last section we explained the use of a single dimensional array. Two dimensional arrays called matrices also occur often in practice. Thus the two dimensional array shown below:

$$a = \begin{bmatrix} 2.6 & 3.2 & 0.0 & 3.9 \\ 1.4 & 5.6 & -8.1 & 4.5 \\ 9.5 & -4.2 & 3.8 & -8.3 \end{bmatrix}$$

may be given a single name, say a, and an element of the matrix identified by using two subscripts. Thus the element in the second row and third column may be identified by attaching the subscripts (2, 3) to the array name. In this matrix a(2, 3) = – 8.1. A general element may be signified by using the notation a(i, j) where i is the row subscript and j the column subscript. We will now consider an example of use of an array variable with two subscripts.

Assume that a store stocks several brands of electric bulbs and that each brand is coded using a unique integer. For example: GEC – 1, Philips – 2, Crompton – 3, Bengal – 4, Mysore – 5, Bajaj – 6. Further assume that each wattage is also coded using an integer. For example: 15 watts – 1, 25 watts – 2, 40 watts – 3, 60 watts – 4, 100 watts – 5. The number of bulbs of each category in the store may be represented by the array variable bulbs (brand, watts) as shown in Table 10.2 (the variables brand and watts are declared integers).

Table 10.2 Table showing Stock Position of Bulbs

		WATTS				
		15	25	40	60	100
		1	2	3	4	5
	GEC 1	10	12	0	4	9
B	Philips 2	0	10	5	2	8
R	Crompton 3	10	0	25	4	8
A	Bengal 4	9	8	0	10	12
N	Mysore 5	10	5	6	6	8
D	Bajaj 6	20	12	0	9	12

Matrix bulbs

Thus bulbs (4, 5) indicates the number of Bengal 100 watts bulbs and from the table it is seen to be 12. As new bulbs of a particular brand and wattage are received in the store Example Program 10.5 would add the number to the appropriate component of bulbs (brand, watts). The data gives the serial number, brand code, the wattage code and the number of bulbs.

Example Program 10.5 Illustrates use of 2 subscripts

```
!PROGRAM 10.5
!THE FOLLOWING PROGRAM ILLUSTRATES HOW THE NUMBERS OF BULBS
!IN STOCK IS UPDATED WHEN NEW STOCK IS RECEIVED
PROGRAM update
   IMPLICIT NONE
   INTEGER, DIMENSION(6, 5)::bulbs
   INTEGER ::serial, brand_code, watt_code, number
!serial = 0 INDICATES END OF DATA
   DO
      READ*, serial, brand_code, watt_code, number
      IF(serial == 0)EXIT
      bulbs(brand_code, watt_code) =bulbs(brand_code, watt_code)+ number
   END DO
   PRINT *, " Bulbs = ", bulbs
END PROGRAM update
```

If the data read is 1, 4, 5, 10 then the statement:

```
bulbs (brand_code, watt_code) = bulbs (brand_code, watt_code) + number
```

would give:

```
bulbs (4, 5) = bulbs (4, 5) + 10 = 12 + 10 = 22
```

Observe the statement

```
INTEGER, DIMENSION (6, 5) :: bulbs
```

This statement gives information to the compiler that bulbs is an integer variable name, has two subscripts and that the maximum values of the subscripts are 6 and 5 respectively. One may also write:

```
INTEGER :: bulbs (6, 5)
```

If the dimensions of the array are declared in the TYPE declaration no separate DIMENSION statement should be given for that variable.

One may have situations where more than 2 subscripts may be required. In the above example if each wattage bulb also comes in three varieties, say, transparent, translucent and gas filled then a third subscript which indicates the type of the bulb may be used. Thus if transparent is coded 1, translucent as 2 and gas filled as 3 then bulbs (4, 2, 2) would mean the number of Bengal brand, 25 watts, translucent bulbs.

Fortran 90 allows up to seven subscripts. In practice, however, more than three subscripts are rarely used.

10.3 DO TYPE NOTATION FOR INPUT/OUTPUT STATEMENTS

At the beginning of this chapter the following statement was introduced to read data into an array:

```
READ *, (marks (i), i = 1, 50)
```

The above statement will read 50 values and assign them respectively to marks (1), marks (2), ... marks (50). In other words the first value will be stored in marks (1), the second in marks (2) etc. Data will be read till values are assigned to all the 50 components of marks.

Such a statement is said to incorporate an implied DO. The full generality of DO statements is available for such READ statements. For example, if the values of the odd components of an array are to be read, the following statement may be used

```
READ *, (a (i), i = 1, 10, 2)
```

This statement will assign succeeding numbers to a(1), a(3), a(5), a(7) and a(9). More than one array may be specified in a read statement. For example, the statement

```
READ*, ((a (i), b (i)), i = 1, 10)
```

reads numbers and assigns the first number to a(1), the second number to b(1), the third number to a(2), fourth to b(2) and so on till the last number which is assigned to b(10).

Two dimensional arrays may also be read by a similar READ statement. For example, the statement:

```
READ *, ((a (i, j), i = 1, 10), j = 1, 5)
```

will read in successive numbers and assign them respectively to:

```
a(1, 1), a(2, 1), a(3, 1), .... a(10, 1),
a(1, 2), a(2, 2), a(3, 2), .... a(10, 2),
   .        .        .
   .        .        .
   .        .        .
a(1, 5), a(2, 5), a(3, 5), .... a(10, 5),
```

Observe that the inner parentheses with the index i corresponds to an inner DO loop and the outer parentheses to an outer DO loop. This statement and the nested DO loops shown below (Fig. 10.1) assign the same values to the components of the matrix.

```
!A program segment illustrating storing
!numbers in a matrix
!- - - - - - - - - - - - - - - - - - - - -
   IMPLICIT NONE
   REAL DIMENSION (10, 5) :: a
   INTEGER :: i, j
   DO j = 1, 5
      DO i = 1, 10
         READ *, a (i, j)
      END DO
   END DO
```

Fig. 10.1 Nested DO loops to read two dimensional array.

The statement of Fig. 10.1 read data in the order of a(1, 1), a(2, 1), a(3, 1), ... a(10, 1), a(1, 2), a(2, 2), ... a(10, 2), ... a(1, 5), ... a(10, 5). However, 50 READ operations are executed. Observe that the elements of the matrix are read columnwise by both the above statements.

The statement:

```
READ *, ((a (i, j), j = 1, 5), i = 1, 10)
```

will read in successive numbers from the input unit and assign them respectively to a(1, 1), a(1, 2), a(1, 3) ... a(1, 5), a(2, 1). a(2, 2) ... a(2, 5) .... a(10, 1), a(10, 2) ... a(10, 5).

We will illustrate reading and printing a matrix with Example Program 10.6. This program reads a 2×3 matrix:

$$\begin{bmatrix} 1 & 3 & 5 \\ 2 & 4 & 6 \end{bmatrix}$$

The values are input columnwise. The matrix stored in the memory is then printed rowwise. Example Program 10.6 gives the program, the input and the output.

Example Program 10.6 Reading and printing a matrix

```
!PROGRAM 10.6
!ILLUSTRATES READING A MATRIX

PROGRAM mat_read
   IMPLICIT NONE
   INTEGER, DIMENSION(2, 3) :: matrix
   INTEGER :: i, j
   PRINT *, "Type elements of matrix columnwise"
   READ*, ((matrix(i, j), i=1, 2), j=1, 3)
   PRINT*, (matrix(1, j), j=1, 3)
   PRINT*, (matrix(2, j), j=1, 3)
END PROGRAM
```

```
   Type elements of matrix columnwise
1 2 3 4 5 6
   Output of the program
1 3 5
2 4 6
```

The implied DO read statement may also be used to read more than one array. For example the statement:

```
READ *,  ((a(i, j), b(i, j), i = 1, 10), j = 1, 2)
```

will assign successive data items to:

```
a(1, 1), b(1, 1), a(2, 1), b(2, 1), .... a(10, 1), b(10, 1)
a(1, 2), b(1, 2), a(2, 2), b(2, 2), .... a(10, 2), b(10, 2)
```

The full generality of indexing available in a DO statement is also available for the implied DO. Thus the indices used in the implied DO read statement may themselves be integer variables provided they are defined before they are used. For example, the statement:

```
READ *, (a (i), i = k, j, m)
```

is valid provided k, j and m are defined earlier.

The implied DO may also be used for reading 3 dimensional (or higher dimensional) arrays. For example,

```
READ *, (((a(i, j, k), i = 1, 5), j = 1, 2), k = 1, 3)
```

will read data into the components of a in the order:

```
a(1, 1, 1), a(2, 1, 1), a(3, 1, 1), ......  a(5, 1, 1),
a(1, 2, 1), a(2, 2, 1), a(3, 2, 1), ......  a(5, 2, 1),
a(1, 1, 2), a(2, 1, 2), a(3, 1, 2) .......  a(5, 1, 2)
    .           .           .               .
    .           .           .               .
    .           .           .               .
a(1, 2, 3), a(2, 2, 3), ....................  a(5, 2, 3)
```

It is similar to the nested DO (Fig. 10.2) as regards the order in which data are assigned to the components of the arrray.

```
!Program segment illustrating storing
!numbers in a three dimensional array a
!- - - - - - - - - - - - - - - - - - - - - -
REAL, DIMENSION (5, 2, 3) :: a
  INTEGER :: i, j, k
  DO k = 1, 3
    DO j = 1, 2
      DO i = 1, 5
        READ *, a (i, j, k)
    END DO
  END DO
END DO
!- - - - - - - - - - - - - - - - - - - - - -
```

Fig 10.2 Nested DO loops to read a three dimensional array.

Fortran 90 also allows one to read the entire matrix columnwise without explicitly using subscripts. Thus in Example Program 10.6 the READ statement may be replaced by

```
READ *, matrix
```

This method of reading subscripted variables may be used for arrays of higher dimensions also. For example we may write:

```
REAL, DIMENSION (4, 3, 2) :: z
READ *, z
```

The data in this case is to be presented in the order

z(1, 1, 1), z(2, 1, 1), z(3, 1, 1), z(4, 1, 1),
z(1, 2, 1), z(2, 2, 1), z(3, 2, 1), z(4, 2, 1),
z(1, 3, 1), z(2, 3, 1), z(3, 3, 1), z(4, 3, 1),
z(1, 1, 2), z(2, 1, 2), z(3, 1, 2), z(4, 1, 2),
z(1, 2, 2), z(2, 2, 2), z(3, 2, 2), z(4, 2, 2),
z(1, 3, 2), z(2, 3, 2), z(3, 3, 2), z(4, 3, 2),

Observe that the first subscript is varied first, the second subscript next and finally the last subscript is varied. The READ statement may be replaced by the explicit statement:

```
READ*, (((z (i, j, k), i = 1, 4), j = 1, 3), k = 1, 2)
```

The implicit READ statement which does not require the use of explicit subscripts should be used with care because a beginner often forgets the order in which data is expected by the statement. It is thus advisable to print a row of the matrix immediately after it is read and check it for validity.

The rules given for writing a READ statement with implied DO apply without any change to PRINT statements also. Thus

```
PRINT*, ((a(i , j), i = 1, 10), j = 1, 5)
```

will print the components of a in the order:

a(1, 1), a(2, 1), a(3, 1), ... a(10, 1)
....
a(1, 5), a(2, 5), a(3, 5), ... a(10, 5)

In writing all the above READ and PRINT statements a common mistake committed by beginners is in omitting a comma. All the commas are essential and should be used as indicated. Other common errors are forgetting the order in which data are assigned to components, and forgetting to pair parentheses.

Some invalid READ and PRINT statements using implied DO are given below:

```
PRINT*, ((a(i, j) i = 1, 5) j = 1, 5)        (commas missing)
READ*, (a(i, j), i = 1, 5), j = 1, 5)        (Parentheses missing)
READ*, (a(i), i = 15)                        (incomplete)
```

The most important point to remember while reading entire matrices using a READ statement of the type

```
READ *, matrix
```

is that the Fortran 90 compiler expects the data to be presented in what is known as column major order as Fortran 90 stores data columnwise. In other words, the input data has to be presented with values of the first column, followed by second column and so on. If the matrix to be stored is

$$\begin{bmatrix} 1 & 2 & 3 \\ 4 & 5 & 6 \\ 7 & 8 & 9 \end{bmatrix}$$

the input data must be presented as:

1, 4, 7, 2, 5, 8, 3, 6, 9

For inputing arrays with more than 2 subscripts the values should be given in the order with first subscript changing most rapidly then second subscript and finally the third subscript as in the statement:

```
READ *, (((z(i, j, k), i = 1, 4), j = 1, 3), k = 1, 2)
```

10.4 INITIALIZING ARRAYS

An array b is declared below:

```
INTEGER, DIMENSION (0 : 4) :: b
```

It may be initialized using an array constructor as follows:

```
b = (/ 4, 5, 8, 7, 6 /)
```

The values to be assigned to the elements of the array b are enclosed by slashes /. The first value 4 is assigned to b(0), 5 to b(1), 8 to b(2), 7 to b(3) and 6 to b(4).

This method is said to use an array constructor. It is simple to use provided the array size is small. If the array is long and values to be assigned to the elements follow a regular pattern then a method analogous to DO loop can be used. For example if d is a 50 element vector and its element values are to be set to 1, 2, 3, 4 ... 50 then one may use the array constructor

```
d = (/ (i, i = 1, 50) /)
```

The constructor

```
d = (/ 5, 8, (2 * i, i = 1, 47), 9/)
```

will set d(1) = 5, d(2) = 8, d(3) = 2, d(4) = 4, d(5) = 6, ... d(49) = 94 and d(50) = 9.

More than one implied loops can be used in an array constructor. For example,

The constructor

```
b = (/ (i, i = 1, 10), (3 * i, i = 1, 10) /)
```

will assign b(1) = 1, b(2) = 2 ... b(10) = 10, b(11) = 3, b(12) = 6 ... b(20) = 30.

If all elements of an array are to be set to zero we may use the statement:

```
INTEGER, DIMENSION (20) :: a = 0
```

which will initialize all elements of a to 0.

Initializing multidimensional arrays is more complicated. Before we discuss it, it is necessary to remember that the Fortran 90 compiler stores multidimensional arrays in a computer's memory columnwise.

Thus if we want to initialize the values of the matrix bulbs given in Table 10.1 we must use the array constructor statement:

```
INTEGER, DIMENSION (6, 5) :: bulbs = &
RESHAPE ((/ 10, 0, 10, 9, 10, 20, 12, 10, 0, 8, 5, 12, 0, 5, 25, 0, 6, 0, &
            4, 2, 4, 10, 6, 9, 9, 8, 8, 12, 8, 12 /), (/ 6, 5 /))
```

Observe that we have given the values columnwise following RESHAPE. The values are followed by a comma and the number of rows and columns in the array enclosed in parentheses with slashes as shown.

Consider another example of initial values to be assigned to the matrix:

```
REAL, DIMENSION (3, 4) :: x
```

The values are given below:

$$\text{Matrix x} = \begin{bmatrix} 2.0 & 3.0 & 4.0 & 5.0 \\ 6.0 & 7.0 & 8.0 & 9.0 \\ 10.0 & 11.0 & 12.0 & 13.0 \end{bmatrix}$$

The initializing statement is

```
REAL, DIMENSION (3, 4) :: x = &
RESHAPE ((/ 2.0, 6.0, 10.0, 3.0, 7.0, 11.0, 4.0, 8.0, 12.0, 5.0, 9.0, 13.0 /), (/ 3, 4 /))
```

The declaration

```
INTEGER, DIMENSION (3, 2, 2) :: y = RESHAPE (/ (2 * i, i =1, 12) /), (/ (3, 2, 2) /)
```

will assign the values

```
y(1, 1, 1) = 2, y(2, 1, 1) = 4, y(3, 1, 1) = 6
y(1, 2, 1) = 8, y(2, 2, 1) = 10, y(3, 2, 1) = 12
y(1, 1, 2) = 14, y(2, 1, 2) = 16, y(3, 1, 2) = 18
y(1, 2, 2) = 20, y(2, 2, 2) = 22, y(3, 2, 2) = 24
```

to the three dimensional array y.

10.5 TERMINOLOGY USED FOR MULTIDIMENSIONAL ARRAYS

We have so far used single dimensional and two dimensional arrays. Fortran 90 allows arrays with upto seven dimensions. Fortran 90 uses a number of technical terms to specify arrays. We will describe them now.

The declaration:

```
REAL, DIMENSION (– 1 : 5, 0:10) :: b
```

states that b is an array with two subscripts. The first subscript has a *lower bound* = – 1 and *upper bound* = 5. The number of elements in the first dimension is 5 – (–1) + 1 = 7. It is calculated using the formula

$$\text{No. of elements} = \textit{upper bound} - \textit{lower bound} + 1.$$

The number of elements in this dimension, namely, dimension 1 is called the *extent* of the array in dimension 1. The extent of array b in the second dimension is 10 – 0 + 1 = 11.

The number of subscripts in an array is called its *rank.* Thus the rank of array b is 2.

The *size* of the array is the total number of elements in it. In one dimensional array the size is equal to its extent. In a two dimensional array it is the product of the extent of the array in dimension 1 and the extent in dimension 2. The size of the array b is thus 7 × 11 = 77.

The *shape* of an array b is a vector. The number of elements in the shape vector of b equals the rank of b. The value of each element of the shape vector equals the extent of b in each of its dimensions. Thus the shape vector of b has 2 elements. The first element is 7 and the second is 11. Shape of b is (7, 11). The shape of the array d declared below is:

INTEGER, DIMENSION (–2 : 6, 4 : 10, 15) :: d
Shape of d = (9, 7, 15)
The *rank* of d is 3, $extent_1$ = 9, $extent_2$ = 7, $extent_3$ = 15,
The size of d is 9 × 7 × 15 = 945

In general:

- The *rank* is the number of subscripts
- The number of elements along each dimension is the *extent* in that dimension
- The *size* is the product of the extents
- The *shape* is a one dimensional array with number of elements equal to the rank and each element is equal to the extent in that dimension.

We will conclude by taking another example.
The array g declared below:

REAL, DIMENSION (–1: 5, 0 : 8, 15, 5) :: g

has

rank = 4
$extent_1$ = 7, $extent_2$ = 9, $extent_3$ = 15, $extent_4$ = 5
size = 7 * 9 * 15 * 5 = 4725
shape = (7, 9, 15, 5)

10.6 USE OF ARRAYS IN DO LOOPS

In this section we will illustrate the use of subscripts within DO loops. Such use of subscripts is very useful in practice.

Example 10.4

The program for fitting a straight line through a given set of points which was given as Example Program 7.8 is rewritten as Example Program 10.7 using arrays.

Example Program 10.7 Fitting a straight line

```
!PROGRAM 10.7
!FITTING A STRAIGHT LINE
!USE OF SUBSCRIPTED VARIABLES
PROGRAM fit_line
   IMPLICIT NONE
   REAL :: m, c, realn, numerator, denominator
   REAL :: sumx=0, sumy=0, sumxy=0, sumxsq=0
   REAL, DIMENSION(50):: x, y
   INTEGER :: n, i
   PRINT *, " Type no. of points n"
   READ *, n
   PRINT *, "Type", n, "pairs of x, y values"
   READ *, (x(i), y(i), i=1, n)
   DO i=1, n
      sumx=sumx + x(i)
      sumy=sumy + y(i)
      sumxy=sumxy + x(i)*y(i)
      sumxsq=sumxsq + x(i)*x(i)
   END DO
   realn = n
   numerator = realn*sumxy - sumx*sumy
   denominator = realn * sumxsq - sumx * sumx
   m = numerator/denominator
   c = (sumy - m * sumx)/realn
   PRINT *, "Equation of straight line "
   PRINT *, "y =", m, "*x + ", c
END PROGRAM fit_line
```

Observe that in Example Program 10.7 all the x and y coordinates are read and stored in memory by the single READ statement:

```
READ *, (x (i), y (i), i = 1, n)
```

This should be contrasted with Example Program 7.8 in which each pair of x and y values are read in a DO loop. In Example Program 10.4 only 2 READ instructions are executed whereas in Example Program 7.8 the number of READ instruction executed equals the number of pairs of x and y values + 1 (for READ *, n). As reading is time consuming Example Program 10.7 will take less time to execute compared to Example Program 7.8 but it will need more storage. Observe that x and y are declared as having DIMENSION (50) assuming that the number of points will be less than 50. It would be preferable to use a variable DIMENSION appropriate to the number of actual points in a given problem. Fortran 77 did not have a provision for variable DIMENSION whereas Fortran 90 has the provision to allocate a space as required for an array. We will accordingly modify Example Program 10.7. The declaration of the array is changed to

```
REAL, ALLOCATABLE, DIMENSION (:) :: x, y
```

Observe that instead of giving 50 as the DIMENSION, a colon : is used to indicate that the value is to be allocated. The actual allocation is done by the statement:

```
READ*, n
ALLOCATE (x (n), y (n))
```

This will allocate space for x and y to store n components of x and n components of y. The statement READ *, n reads the value of n. For example, if n = 20 then 20 locations will be reserved for x and 20 for y.

Example Program 10.8 Fitting a straight line—Version 2

```
!PROGRAM 10.8
!FITTING A STRAIGHT LINE
!MODIFICATION OF PROGRAM 10.7 WITH ALLOCATABLE ARRAYS
PROGRAM fit_line_v2
  IMPLICIT NONE
  REAL :: sumx=0, sumy=0, sumxy=0, sumxsq=0, m, c, realn, numerator, denominator
  INTEGER :: i, n, ok
  REAL, ALLOCATABLE, DIMENSION(:)::x, y
  PRINT *,  " Type no. of points n "
  READ *, n
  ALLOCATE(x(n), y(n), STAT = ok)
  IF(ok /=0) THEN
!ALLOCATION NOT SUCCESSFUL .STOP.
    PRINT *, "Space not allocated to x, y"
    STOP
  ENDIF
  READ *, (x(i), y(i), i=1, n)
  DO i=1, n
    sumx = sumx + x(i)
    sumy = sumy + y(i)
    sumxy = sumxy + x(i)*y(i)
    sumxsq = sumxsq + x(i)*x(i)
  END DO
  realn = n
  numerator = realn*sumxy - sumx*sumy
  denominator = realn*sumxsq - sumx*sumx
  m = numerator/denominator
  c = (sumy - m*sumx)/realn
  PRINT *, "equation of straight line"
  PRINT *, "y =", m, "*x + ", c
  END PROGRAM fit_line_v2
```

If for some reason the compiler is not able to allocate the required storage it has a provision to inform the programmer about it. In order to use this facility the ALLOCATE statement should be changed to

```
ALLOCATE (x(n), y(n), STAT = ok)
```

In the above statement STAT is known as the allocation status indicator. If allocation is successful then the variable name following STAT = will be set to 0. If unsuccessful the variable name will be a non zero integer. Thus in the above example, the variable name ok will be 0 if allocation is successful. If allocation is not successful then program should be stopped. This is done by the statements:

```
ALLOCATE (x(n), y(n), STAT = ok)
IF (ok /= 0) THEN
!Allocation unsuccessful. Stop
      PRINT *, "Space not allocated to x(n), y(n)"
      STOP
END IF
!If allocation successful control reaches this point
```

It is a good programming practice to check the status variable as shown above so that if there is a problem a clear message is given by the program.

In large programs where there is not enough memory available it is convenient if the space occupied by an array is released after use. Such a facility is available in Fortran 90.

After arrays x and y are used the space may be released by the statement

```
DEALLOCATE (x(n), y(n))
```

In this case also STAT can be optionally used to check whether deallocation is sucessful

```
DEALLOCATE (x(n), y(n), STAT = done)
IF (done /= 0) THEN
   PRINT *, "Arrays not released"
   STOP
ENDIF
```

In Example Program 10.4 we arbitrarily set the polynomial size as 20. We can modify the program with allocatable array as shown

```
REAL, ALLOCATABLE, DIMENSION (:) :: a
READ *, n, x
ALLOCATE (a(0 : n), STAT = done)
IF (done /= 0) THEN
   PRINT *, 'Allocation unsuccessful'
   STOP
ENDIF
READ *, (a(i), i = 0, n)
!Continue with rest of the program
```

The reader is advised to rewrite Example Program 10.4 with allocatable array size to test it.

Example 10.5

Consider the example of array variable bulbs with two subscripts explained in Section 10.3. The array variable bulbs is used to indicate the number of bulbs of a given brand and wattage. Assume that the cost of a bulb of a specified brand and wattage is given in another array named cost shown on the right in Table 10.3 (These are not real costs but fictitious numbers used for illustration). A program is to be written which will do the following:

i. Print out the brand, and wattage codes for items out of stock, and
ii. calculate and print the total cost of bulbs in the inventory.

Table 10.3 Bulbs and Cost Arrays

Brand	Wattage 15	25	40	60	100						
	1	2	3	4	5	Codes	1	2	3	4	5
GEC 1	10	12	0	4	9	1	4.95	5.00	5.05	5.10	5.25
Philips 2	0	10	5	2	8	2	7.00	7.00	7.10	7.15	7.30
Crompton 3	10	0	25	4	8	3	5.9	5.5	5.5	5.5	5.5
Bengal 4	9	8	0	10	12	4	3.95	3.95	3.95	4.2	4.5
Mysore 5	10	5	6	6	8	5	5.95	6.05	6.10	6.15	6.25
Bajaj 6	20	12	0	9	12	6	7.00	7.00	7.10	7.20	7.30
	bulbs						cost				

A program to do these is given as Example Program 10.9.

Example Program 10.9 Cost calculation with 2 dimensional array

```
!PROGRAM 10.9
!STOCK ... AND COST DETERMINATION

PROGRAM stock_cost
   IMPLICIT NONE
   INTEGER :: brand,watts
   INTEGER, DIMENSION(6, 5)::bulbs
   REAL, DIMENSION(6, 5)::cost
   REAL::tcost=0, abulbs
   PRINT *, " Type stock of bulbs "
   READ *, bulbs
   PRINT *, " Type cost of bulbs "
   READ *, cost
   DO brand=1, 6
      DO watts=1, 5
         IF(bulbs(brand, watts)==0) THEN
            PRINT*, "Out of stock"
            PRINT*, "Brand code =", brand, " Watt code =", watts
         ELSE
            abulbs = bulbs(brand, watts)
            tcost = tcost + cost(brand, watts)*abulbs
         ENDIF
      END DO
   END DO
   PRINT *, "Total value of bulbs =", tcost
END PROGRAM stock_cost
```

The Example Program illustrates a number of points. Observe that the arrays are read by the simple READ statements. These are equivalent to the statements:

```
READ*, ((bulbs (brand, watts), brand = 1, 6), watts = 1, 5)
READ*, ((cost (brand, watts), brand = 1, 6), watts = 1, 5)
```

The simple read statements given in the program are particularly relevant if the entire array is to be read in as in this case. The input data should be presented columnwise, that is, bulbs (1, 1), bulbs (2, 1), bulbs (3, 1) is the order in which the data should be presented. The variable abulbs is used to convert each component of the array bulbs to real mode to be used in the arithmetic statement for cost calculation. The cost array is real.

Example 10.6

At the beginning of this chapter we considered a program to pick the first and the second highest marks in a class of nstud students. In this example we will extend it to arrange the marks in a descending order, that is, in an order starting from the highest to the lowest marks. We will consider first a technique which is simple but inefficient. We will consider later a more efficient method.

The procedure we will follow is to read the marks into an array named marks. We will then compare marks (1) with marks (2) and interchange them if marks (1) is less than marks (2). Now marks (1) will contain the larger value. We will next compare marks (3) with marks (1) and interchange them if marks (1) < marks (3). This procedure will be repeated till marks(nstud) is compared with marks (1). At the end of this pass marks (1) will have the highest marks. This procedure may be implemented with a DO loop as shown in Program Segment 10.10.1.

Example Program 10.10.1 Placing highest marks in marks (1)

```
!PROGRAM 10.10.1 DEVELOPMENT
!PLACING LARGEST MARK IN marks(1)

PROGRAM sort_v1
   IMPLICIT NONE
   INTEGER, ALLOCATABLE, DIMENSION(:):: marks
   INTEGER :: i, nstud, ok
   READ *, nstud
!nstud IS THE NUMBER OF STUDENTS IN THE CLASS
   ALLOCATE(marks(nstud), STAT = ok)
   IF(ok /=0) THEN
      PRINT *, "space for marks not allocated"
      STOP
   ENDIF
   READ *, marks
   DO i=1, (nstud - 1)
      IF(marks(1) >= marks(i+1)) CYCLE
      CALL exchange(marks(1), marks(i+1))
   END DO
   PRINT *, "Marks array =", marks
   CONTAINS
      SUBROUTINE exchange(a, b)
      INTEGER, INTENT(INOUT) :: a, b
      INTEGER :: temp
      temp = a
      a = b
      b = temp
   END SUBROUTINE exchange
   END PROGRAM sort_v1
```

Observe that the last value of the index i of the DO loop should be (nstud –1) as we are comparing marks (1) with marks (i + 1). In this example observe that we have used a SUBROUTINE EXCHANGE to interchange values marks (1) and marks (i + 1). This makes the program readable.

Having placed the highest marks in marks (1) we now repeat the procedure starting from marks(2). At the end of this step marks (2) will have the second highest marks. This can be done by modifying the previous program segment as shown in Example Program 10.10.2.

Example Program 10.10.2 Placing highest and next highest in marks (1) and marks (2)

```
!PROGRAM 10.10.2
!PLACING FIRST AND SECOND MARKS IN marks(1) and marks(2)

PROGRAM sort_v2
   IMPLICIT NONE
   INTEGER, ALLOCATABLE, DIMENSION(:) :: marks
   INTEGER :: i, k, nstud, ok
   READ *, nstud
!nstud IS THE NUMBER OF STUDENTS IN THE CLASS
   ALLOCATE(marks(nstud), STAT = ok)
   IF(ok /= 0) THEN
      PRINT *, "Space for marks not allocated"
      STOP
   ENDIF
   READ *, marks
   DO k=1, 2
      DO i=k, (nstud - 1)
         IF(marks(k) >= marks(i+1)) CYCLE
         CALL exchange(marks(k), marks(i+1))
      END DO
   END DO
   PRINT *, "marks array =", marks
   CONTAINS
      SUBROUTINE exchange(a, b)
      INTEGER, INTENT(INOUT) :: a, b
      INTEGER :: temp
      temp = a
      a = b
      b = temp
   END SUBROUTINE exchange
END PROGRAM sort_v2
```

Program Segment 10.10.1 may be generalised to arrange the marks in descending order. The complete program is given as Example Program 10.10.3.

Example Program 10.10.3 Sorting an array of marks

```
!PROGRAM 10.10.3 FINAL VERSION
!SIMPLE SORTING OF MARKS
PROGRAM sort_v3
   IMPLICIT NONE
   INTEGER, ALLOCATABLE, DIMENSION(:) :: marks
   INTEGER :: i, k, nstud, ok
   READ *, nstud
!nstud IS THE NUMBER OF STUDENTS IN THE CLASS
   ALLOCATE(marks(nstud), STAT = ok)
   IF(ok /= 0) THEN
      PRINT *, "Space for marks not allocated"
      STOP
   ENDIF
   READ *, marks
   DO k=1, (nstud - 1)
      DO i=k, (nstud - 1)
         IF(marks(k) >= marks(i+1)) CYCLE
         CALL exchange(marks(k), marks(i+1))
      END DO
   END DO
   PRINT *, "marks array =", marks
   CONTAINS
      SUBROUTINE exchange(a, b)
      INTEGER, INTENT(INOUT) :: a, b
      INTEGER :: temp
      temp = a
      a = b
      b = temp
      END SUBROUTINE exchange
   END PROGRAM sort_v3
```

Example Program 10.10.3 may be used to sort the marks of any class of students as we have declared marks with ALLOCATABLE DIMENSION. The actual number of students in a given class is read as data. The required storage is thus allocated.

We will now develop a method of arranging the marks in descending order which is more efficient than the method presented in Example Program 10.10.3 particularly when the marks are already partially sorted. The basic strategy may be developed by first roughly sketching it as shown in the following Steps 1–4:

Step 1 Let the number of students be nstud. Read the marks array into memory.

Step 2 For all i from i = 1 to (nstud –1) compare marks (i) with marks (i + 1) and interchange if marks (i) < marks (i + 1). Observe that the last array index compared is (i + 1) = (nstud – 1 + 1) = nstud. Note the last array index which needed interchange. Call it last switch index. (This means that all marks in indices greater than last switch index are already in descending order).

Step 3 Repeat step 2 for i = 1 to (lastswitch –1)

Step 4 When lastswitch = 1 the entire array is in descending order.

We may now refine the above rough sketch of the procedure as the algorithm given below:

Step 1 Read marks (i) for i = 1 to nstud
Step 2 Initialize limit ← (nstud –1) and lastswitch ← (nstud)
Step 3 Repeat Step 4 to 6 while (lastswitch > 1)
Step 4 Initialise lastswitch ← 1
Step 5 For i = 1 to limit. Compare marks (i) with marks (i + 1) and interchange if marks (i) < marks (i + 1). Store in lastswitch the last value of i when an interchange took place
Step 6 limit ← (lastswitch – 1).

In the above algorithm in Step 2 lastswitch is initialized to (nstud) which could be its "worst" value. This is required in Step 3 (the Repeat While statement) where lastswitch is tested. Step 4 re-initializes lastswitch to 1 because if the array is in right order no interchange would take place in Step 5 and lastswitch will retain its initialized value.

The above algorithm is converted to Example Program 10.11.

Example Program 10.11 An efficient sorting program

```
!PROGRAM 10.11
!SORTING A SET OF STUDENT MARKS
!AN EFFICIENT VERSION
PROGRAM sort_v3
   IMPLICIT NONE
   INTEGER, ALLOCATABLE, DIMENSION(:) :: marks
   INTEGER :: i, nstud, ok, lastsw, k, limit
   READ *, nstud
!nstud IS THE NUMBER OF STUDENTS IN THE CLASS
   ALLOCATE(marks(nstud), STAT = ok)
   IF(ok /= 0) THEN
      PRINT *, "Space for marks not allocated"
      STOP
   ENDIF
   READ *, marks
   lastsw = nstud
   limit = nstud - 1
   DO k=1, nstud
      IF(lastsw == 1) EXIT
      lastsw = 1
      DO i=1, limit
         IF(marks(i) >= marks(i+1)) CYCLE
         CALL exchange(marks(i), marks(i+1))
         lastsw = i
      END DO
   limit = lastsw - 1
   END DO
   PRINT *, "Sorted marks array"
   PRINT *, marks
   CONTAINS
      SUBROUTINE exchange(a, b)
      INTEGER, INTENT(INOUT) :: a, b
      INTEGER :: temp
      temp = a ; a = b ;b = temp
      END SUBROUTINE exchange
  END PROGRAM sort_v3
```

Example 10.7

A Fibonacci number is defined as follows:

Fibonacci(0) = 0
Fibonacci(1) = 1
Given the above two
Fibonacci(2) = Fibonacci(1) + Fibonacci(0)

and in general

Fibonacci(i) = Fibonacci(i − 1) + Fibonacci(i − 2)

Example Program 10.12 generates the first 12 Fibonacci numbers and prints them.

Example Program 10.12 Generating a Fibonacci sequence

```
!PROGRAM 10.12
!GENERATING FIBBONACCI NUMBERS

PROGRAM fib
   IMPLICIT NONE
   INTEGER, DIMENSION(0:11) :: fibonacci
   INTEGER :: i
   fibonacci(0) = 0
   fibonacci(1) = 1
   DO i=2, 11
      fibonacci(i) = fibonacci(i - 1) + fibonacci(i - 2)
   END DO
   PRINT *, "Fibonacci numbers"
   PRINT *, fibonacci
END PROGRAM fib
```

Example 10.8

Two matrices are given:

$$[a_{ij}] = \begin{bmatrix} a_{11} & a_{12} & a_{13} \\ a_{21} & a_{22} & a_{23} \end{bmatrix}$$

$$[b_{ij}] = \begin{bmatrix} b_{11} & b_{12} \\ b_{21} & b_{22} \\ b_{31} & b_{32} \end{bmatrix}$$

It is required to multiply these matrices and get the product matrix c_{ij} which is defined as

$$[c_{ij}] = \begin{bmatrix} a_{11}b_{11} + a_{12}b_{21} + a_{13}b_{31} & a_{11}b_{12} + a_{12}b_{22} + a_{13}b_{32} \\ a_{21}b_{11} + a_{22}b_{21} + a_{23}b_{31} & a_{21}b_{12} + a_{22}b_{22} + a_{23}b_{32} \end{bmatrix}$$

In general, given a matrix [a] with i rows and j columns and a matrix [b] with j rows and k columns the product matrix has i rows and k columns. The two matrices [a] and [b] cannot be multiplied if the number of columns in the first matrix [a] does not equal the number of rows of the matrix [b].

Example Program 10.13 A program to multiply matrices

```
!PROGRAM 10.13
!MATRIX MULTIPLICATION WITH INTRINSIC FUNCTION
!MATRIX SIZE ALLOCATABLE

PROGRAM mat_mult
   IMPLICIT NONE
   INTEGER, ALLOCATABLE, DIMENSION(:, :):: a, b, c
   INTEGER :: i, j, k, a_rows, a_cols, b_rows, b_cols, c_rows, c_cols, ok
   PRINT *,  "Type no. of rows and columns in a and b "
   PRINT *, "Type in the order a_row, a_column, b_row, b_column"
   READ *, a_rows, a_cols, b_rows, b_cols
   ALLOCATE(a(a_rows, a_cols), STAT =ok)
   IF(ok /= 0) THEN
      PRINT *, "allocation failure for a"
      STOP
   ENDIF
   ALLOCATE(b(b_rows, b_cols), STAT = ok)
   IF(ok /= 0) THEN
      PRINT *, "Allocation failure for b"
      STOP
   ENDIF
   PRINT *, "Type elements of a columnwise "
   READ*, a !READ COLUMNWISE
   PRINT *,  "Type elements of b columnwise "
   READ*, b !READ COLUMNWISE
   c_rows = a_rows
   c_cols = b_cols
   ALLOCATE(c(c_rows, c_cols), STAT = ok)
   IF(ok /= 0) THEN
      PRINT *, "Allocation failure for c"
      STOP
      ENDIF
!INITIALISE MATRIX c TO 0
DO i = 1,  c_rows
   DO j =1, c_cols
      c(i, j) = 0
   END DO
END DO

!MATRIX MULTIPLICATION PERFORMED IN THE FOLLOWING THREE LOOPS
   DO k = 1,  c_rows
      DO i = 1, b_cols
         DO j = 1, a_cols
            c(k, i) = c(k, i) + a(k, j) * b(j, i)
         END DO
      END DO
   END DO
!MATRIX c PRINTED COLUMNWISE
   PRINT *, "Matrix c columnwise"
   PRINT *, c
END PROGRAM mat_mult
```

Example Program 10.13 multiplies two matrices and prints the product matrix. In this program we have declared the matrices a, b and c to have allocatable DIMENSIONs. The matrix c has been initialized with zeros stored in its components. The first READ statement reads values for the number of rows and columns of matrices a and b. After that matrices a and b are read columnwise. Number of rows and columns of c are now initialized from the known values of the rows and columns of a and b respectively.

The next set of three DO loops perform the matrix multiplication. In Table 10.4 we trace these DO loops to illustrate how the multiplication is performed. We use the matrices defined at the beginning of this example. Table 10.4 tabulates the values of i, j, k and c(k, i) when the three nested loops are executed.

Table 10.4 Illustrating how Example Program 10.13 does Matrix Multiplication
(max) k = c_rows = a_rows = 2; (max) i = b_cols = 2, (max) j = a_cols = 3

k	i	j	c (k, i)		
1	1	1	c_{11}	=	$c_{11} + a_{11}\ b_{11}$
1	1	2	c_{11}	=	$a_{11}\ b_{11} + a_{12}\ b_{21}$
1	1	3	c_{11}	=	$a_{11}\ b_{11} + a_{12}\ b_{21} + a_{13}\ b_{31}$
1	2	1	c_{12}	=	$c_{12} + a_{11}\ b_{12}$
1	2	2	c_{12}	=	$a_{11}\ b_{12} + a_{12}\ b_{22}$
1	2	3	c_{12}	=	$a_{11}\ b_{12} + a_{12}\ b_{22} + a_{13}\ b_{31}$
2	1	1	c_{21}	=	$c_{21} + a_{21}\ b_{11}$
2	1	2	c_{21}	=	$a_{21}\ b_{11} + a_{22}\ b_{21}$
2	1	3	c_{21}	=	$a_{21}\ b_{11} + a_{22}\ b_{21} + a_{23}\ b_{31}$
2	2	1	c_{22}	=	$c_{22} + a_{21}\ b_{12}$
2	2	2	c_{22}	=	$a_{21}\ b_{12} + a_{22}\ b_{22}$
2	2	3	c_{22}	=	$a_{21}\ b_{12} + a_{22}\ b_{22} + a_{23}\ b_{32}$

We wrote Example Program 10.13 to multiply two matrices. Fortran 90 provides very powerful built-in (or intrinsic) functions to perform many common mathematical operations on arrays. For example, the entire procedure for multiplication of matrices which used three nested DO loops can be replaced by the single statement:

```
c = MATMUL (a, b)
```

In Example Program 10.14 we have illustrated use of this function.

Example Program 10.14 Matrix multiplication using intrinsic function

```
!PROGRAM 10.14
!MATRIX MULTIPLICATION WITH INTRINSIC FUNCTION
!MATRIX SIZE ALLOCATABLE

PROGRAM mat_mult_v2
   IMPLICIT NONE
   INTEGER, ALLOCATABLE, DIMENSION(:, :):: a, b, c
   INTEGER :: i, j, k, a_rows, a_cols, b_rows, b_cols, c_rows, c_cols, ok
   PRINT *, " Type no. of rows and columns in a and b"
   READ *, a_rows, a_cols, b_rows, b_cols
   ALLOCATE(a(a_rows, a_cols), STAT =ok)
   IF(ok /= 0) THEN
```

```
      PRINT *, "allocation failure for a"
      STOP
    ENDIF
    ALLOCATE(b(b_rows, b_cols), STAT = ok)
    IF(ok /= 0) THEN
      PRINT *, "Allocation failure for b"
      STOP
    ENDIF
    PRINT *, " Type elements of a columnwise "
    READ*, a !READ COLUMNWISE
    PRINT *,  " Type elements of b columnwise "
    READ*, b !READ COLUMNWISE
    c_rows = a_rows
    c_cols = b_cols
    ALLOCATE(c(c_rows, c_cols), STAT = ok)
    IF(ok /= 0) THEN
      PRINT *, "Allocation failure for c"
      STOP
    ENDIF
  !INITIALISE MATRIX c TO 0
    c = 0 !THIS SETS ALL ELEMENTS OF C TO 0
  !MATRIX MULTIPLICATION USING INTRINSIC FUNCTION
    c = MATMUL(a, b)
  !MATRIX c PRINTED COLUMNWISE
    PRINT *, "Matrix c columnwise"
    PRINT *, c
  END PROGRAM mat_mult_v2
```

Another intrinsic function of importance is:

```
matrix_a = TRANSPOSE (matrix_b)
```

Besides these there are a number of useful intrinsic functions for arrays which are given in Table 10.5.

Table 10.5 Intrinsic Functions for Vectors and Matrices

Name	*Arguments*	*Result*
MATMUL (a, b)	Conformable matrices a and b or a matrix and b vector	Matrix product
DOT_PRODUCT (a, b)	a, b vectors	Scalar product = $a_1b_1 + a_2b_2 \ldots a_nb_n$
TRANSPOSE (a)	a matrix	Transpose of a
MAXVAL (a)	a an array or a(N, i) where N is a constant	Maximum value among all elements of an array
MINVAL (a)	Same as above	Minimum value among all elements of an array
PRODUCT (a)	Same as above	$a_1 * a_2 * a_3 * \ldots * a_n$
SUM (a)	Same as above	$a_1 + a_2 + a_3 + \ldots + a_n$

10.7 WHOLE ARRAY OPERATIONS

Two arrays are said to be *conformable* if they have the same shape. In other words the arrays have the same number of subscripts and their extents along each subscript dimension are equal. Various operations defined for scalars are extendable to conformable arrays. Let us consider an example of adding two arrays x and y using DO loops as shown below:

```
REAL, DIMENSION (10) :: x, y, z
DO i = 1, 10
   z(i) = x(i) + y(i)
END DO
```

The above DO loop can be replaced by

```
z = x + y
```

as x and y are conformable arrays. The + symbol here indicates element by element addition of array elements of x and y.

Let us consider another example:

```
INTEGER, DIMENSION (10, 10) :: z
INTEGER, DIMENSION (–5 : 4, 0 : 9) :: x
INTEGER, DIMENSION (2:11, –2:7) :: y
DO i = 1, 10
   DO j = 1, 10
      z (i, j) = x (i –6, j –1) * y (i + 1, j –3)
   END DO
END DO
```

The DO loops above may be replaced by the statement

```
z = x * y
```

Observe that arrays x, y, z are conformable.

The examples above show the ease with which operations on whole arrays can be carried out in Fortran 90. Besides simplicity this method is less prone to error. Further, if the program is executed on a parallel computer the appropriate compiler detects array operations easily if they are on whole arrays and effectively utilizes the parallel hardware of the computer.

We stated in the last para that two arrays are conformable if they have the same shape. A scalar, including a constant, is conformable with any array. Thus if we write:

```
INTEGER :: p
INTEGER, DIMENSION (10, 10) :: a, b
a = b + p
```

then p is added to each element of b and stored in a.

If we write

```
a = 0
```

Each element a is set to 0. The above statement is very useful to initialize arrays. In fact we used this in Example Program 10.14. Besides arithmetic operations, logical operations are also allowed between conformable arrays. If arrays a and b are conformable, we write:

```
IF (a <= b) THEN
block of statements
ENDIF
```

the block of statements will be executed if every element of a is <= every element of b.

Many of the intrinsic functions defined in Fortran 90 may be used with arrays as arguments. In the following example:

```
REAL, DIMENSION (10, 10) :: a, b
b = SIN(a)
```

b will be a (10×10) matrix with each $b_{ij} = \text{Sin}(a_{ij})$ for i, j = 1, 10.

There are also special intrinsic functions such as sum, product etc. For example if we write:

```
INTEGER, DIMENSION (10, 5) :: a
INTEGER : p
p = SUM(a)
```

then $$p = \sum_{i=1}^{10} \sum_{j=1}^{5} a_{ij}$$

In Example Program 10.9 we found the total inventory cost of bulbs. The part calculating the total cost can be written in one statement without a DO loop as:

```
tcost = SUM(cost * REAL(bulbs))
```

The matrices cost and bulb are multiplied element by element and a new matrix is created. All the elements of this matrix are added and stored in tcost. Observe the function REAL (bulbs). It converts the integer matrix bulbs to real. It is not necessary, as Fortran 90 allows multiplication of reals by integers giving a real answer. We have used it to illustrate the use of whole array functions. Such functions are also known as *elemental functions* as they operate element by element.

There are other useful operations on arrays. One is masking which allows operating on selected parts of an array based on results of testing a condition. The other is a feature which allows creating subarrays from arrays. We will discuss these features when need arises to use them in some examples. In Appendix A we have listed array intrinsic functions.

SUMMARY

1. An array is a set of quantities arranged in some order. The entire set is referred to by a single name.
2. Each item in the array is called an array element.
3. An individual element in an array is identified by the array name followed by a subscript expression enclosed in parentheses. Only integers are allowed as subscript expressions.
4. A variable name is declared as an array by a DIMENSION statement.
5. Upto seven subscripts are allowed for an array. Each subscript refers to one dimension of an array. In the DIMENSION statement the lower bound and the upper bound of each subscript is specified. These bounds define the range of allowable subscript values for that dimension.
6. Values may be assigned to array elements by READ statement using an implied DO loop.

7. Entire arrays may be read by a single READ statement. In this case the values of the elements are input with the first subscript varying most rapidly, the second subscript next and so on. This is called column major order. The order for a two dimensional array is a_{11}, a_{21}, a_{31}, a_{12}, a_{22}, a_{32}, a_{13}, a_{23}, a_{33} for an array declared as REAL, DIMENSION (3, 3) :: a with a READ statement

```
READ *, a
```

8. Arrays may be printed with an implied DO loop in a PRINT statement. They may also be printed with a statement such as

```
PRINT *, a
```

in which case the array elements are printed in column major order.

9. Arrays may be initialized using an array constructor.
10. The terminology used to describe multidimensional arrays are:
    i. The number of elements in each dimension is called the *extent* in that dimension.
    ii. The number of dimensions of an array is called its *rank*.
    iii. The *size* of an array is the total number of elements in it.
    iv. The *shape* of an array is a vector whose elements are the extent of the array in each of its dimensions.
11. The extents of an array need not be explicitly specified in Fortran 90. If an array is declared ALLOCATABLE the actual extents can be allocated at execution time by an ALLOCATE statement.
12. Two arrays are said to be conformable if they have the same shape. A scalar is conformable with any array.
13. All operators such as +, *, –, >, == (known as intrinsic operators) may be used to operate on conformable arrays. Operations are then carried out element by element. For example if a, b, c are conformable arrays then if we write c = a + b, then each element of c is obtained by adding the corresponding elements of a and b.
14. A number of intrinsic functions such as MATMUL, TRANSPOSE etc., are defined with arrays as operands. Table 10.5 enumerates some of these.

EXERCISES

10.1 Write a program to transpose the following matrix:

$$A = \begin{bmatrix} -9 & 8 & 7 & 16 & 0 \\ 4 & 13 & 2 & -1 & 5 \\ -9 & 4 & 3 & 1 & -8 \end{bmatrix}$$

10.2 Write a program to rearrange the elements of each row of the above matrix such that the elements of each row are arranged in a descending order as shown below:

$$\begin{bmatrix} 16 & 8 & 7 & 0 & -9 \\ 13 & 5 & 4 & 2 & -1 \\ 4 & 3 & 1 & -8 & -9 \end{bmatrix}$$

10.3 Write a program to find the sum of squares of elements on the diagonal of a square matrix.

10.4 Write a program to find if a square matrix is symmetric.

10.5 A factory has 3 divisions and stocks 4 categories of products. An inventory table is updated for each division and for each product as they are received. There are three independent suppliers of products to the factory:

Design a data format to represent each transaction
Write a program to take a transaction and update the inventory
If the cost per item is also given write a program to calculate the total inventory value.

10.6 The data obtained from life tests of 50 electric bulbs is tabulated below. Write a program to obtain a frequency distribution table conforming to the following specifications:

992	1007	1001	1010	1001
1009	990	1003	1008	999
1014	992	991	1006	998
986	996	1010	1008	1008
998	1004	999	1000	1002
994	1002	1005	1008	1025
1003	981	1014	982	997
1009	1001	988	1018	991
1028	1000	1011	1012	1012
1010	1017	1010	996	996

i. Put all bulbs with life less than 985 hours in group 1.
ii. Put all bulbs with life greater than 1024 hours in the last group.
iii. Divide the region between 985 and 1024 hours into eight intervals such that each interval encompasses a life-time of 5 hours (e.g. 985 to 989 is one interval).

Write a general program so that you can accommodate upto 200 data and 20 class intervals. Read the following as the first data.

n = No of data = 50 in this specific case.
lowlimit = Lowerlimit. All data less than lowlimit will be put in class 1.
hilimit = Highlimit. All data greater than hilimit will be put in the last class.
interval = interval width, it is 5 in this example.

Do all calculations in integer mode.

10.7 Write a program to solve the following simultaneous equation by Gauss method and by Gauss-Jordan method. Evaluate the determinant of the matrix of coefficients:

$$x_1 + 2x_2 + 3x_3 = 6$$
$$x_1 + 10x_2 + 4x_3 = .29$$
$$-2x_1 - 4x_2 + x_3 = 9$$

10.8 Economic order quantity may be calculated from the equation

$$Q = (2RS/I)^{0.5}$$

where R is the yearly requirement, S the setup cost and I the carrying cost per item. The values of R, S and I for 15 items in a factory are given. Write a program using DO loop and arrays to calculate the economic order quantity for each of these items.

10.9 Write a program to read two one-dimensional arrays of integers and print a third array which is the union of the two arrays (e.g. union of (1, 3, 6, 8) (4, 7, 6) is (1, 3, 4, 7, 6, 8) and the intersection of the arrays (the intersection of the two arrays above is (6)).

10.10 The dot product of two vectors (a_1, a_2, a_3) and (b_1, b_2, b_3) is defined as $a_1b_1 + a_2b_2 + a_3b_3$. The cross product of a and b is defined as the vector $a_2b_3 - a_3b_2$, $a_3b_1 - a_1b_3$, $a_1b_2 - a_2b_1$. Write programs to find the dot product and cross product of two conformable vectors of arbitrary extent.

11. *Elementary Format Specifications*

Learning Objectives

In this chapter we will learn:

1. How to write FORMAT statements to read data and print outputs in a more flexible form
2. The various edit descriptors to describe editing of data
3. How to print strings of characters
4. How to read and write logical quantities
5. How to read/write data from input/output units other than terminals

---

So far we considered "free style" input and output statements. The list directed (format-free) statement simplifies programming for the beginner at the expense of flexibility in presenting output data and in reading input data. By including a Format specification a programmer gains a great deal of freedom in the way he wants to input data into the machine and the way he wants the results of computations to be printed out. The FORMAT statement is a non-executable statement. It merely supplies information to the compiler on how data will be found and how results are to be presented.

The following terms will be used in discussing FORMAT statements:

i. **A list:** This is the group of variables specified in a READ or PRINT or WRITE statement. The variables are separated by commas.

ii. **A Record:** This is the contents of one 80 column line on a terminal to be read in or the group of values to be printed on one line of 132 character width. If the output is to be typed on a terminal then a record is one 80 column line.

iii. **A Field:** A record consists of a number of fields. A field is an individual element of a record describable as a unit. A field is normally the set of columns reserved for the value of one variable. The number of columns in a field is called the width of the field. For example, the number 95.42 has a width of five. The decimal point is to be counted as a character.

A Format statement is given as a part of a READ or a PRINT statement and describes, in the case of the READ statement, how the data is laid out and in the case of the PRINT statement in what form it is to be printed out.

An example of a READ statement with FORMAT specified is:

```
  READ 5, a, b, n
5 FORMAT (F5.2, E12.4, I5)
```

In this example the number 5 in the READ statement refers to the statement number of the corresponding FORMAT specification. The statement number is an integer > 0. The list is a, b, n. The record is one data line with the values of a, b and n. The quantities inside the parentheses in the FORMAT statement, namely, F5.2, E12.4, I5 describe the fields of the individual quantities a, b and n and are called *edit descriptors*. The string F5.2, E12.4, I5 is called a *format string*. The general form of a READ or PRINT statement with a FORMAT specification is shown below:

$$\text{READ } n, \textit{List}$$
$$n \text{ FORMAT } (S_1, S_2, \ldots\ldots, S_m)$$

Here *n* is the statement number of the FORMAT statement referred to, and $S_1, S_2, \ldots, S_m$ are edit descriptors which will be discussed in detail in what follows. The same FORMAT statement may be used by many input-output statements.

11.1 FORMAT DESCRIPTION FOR NUMERICAL DATA; READ STATEMENT

Numerical quantities may be specified in three forms: (i) integer, (ii) real in fractional form, and (iii) real in exponent notation.

11.1.1 Specification of Integers

If a data field is in integer mode it is specified by using the code I*w*. The letter I indicates that it is an integer and *w*, the number of columns occupied by the data. Thus, if a number 1942 is to be read in, the specification given is FORMAT (I4).

The data to be input on a line of a terminal is as shown below:

Col. →	1	2	3	4
Data →	1	9	4	2

More columns may be reserved for a data field than are required to accommodate the number in that field. The extra columns should be on the *left* of the number. Thus if the number is typed as □□□□1942, the FORMAT description should be I8. Blanks* on the right of the number or blanks embedded within a number are taken to be zeros. Thus if the number is typed as □□□1942□ with specification I8 it will be taken to mean 19420.

11.1.2 Specification for Reals in Fractional Form

A real number typed in fractional form is specified using the code F*w.d* where the letter F indicates that the number is in the fractional form, *w* specifies the number of columns occupied by the number, and *d* the number of digits appearing after the decimal point. The record with the four fields as shown below is specified by the statement:

FORMAT (F4.2, F5.2, F4.0, F6.2)

Column number →	1 2 3 4	5 6 7 8 9	10 11 12 13	14 15 16 17 18 19
Data →	1 • 2 5	8 • 4 2	4 2	1 • 5
	←Field 1→	← Field 2 →	← Field 3 →	← Field 4 →

* Blanks are represented by □ in this book.

Observe that by a proper field specification in the FORMAT statement blank columns may be left on either side of the number.

11.1.3 Specification for Reals in Exponent Form

The FORMAT specification for a real number, in exponent notation, is E*w.d*. The letter E indicates that the number uses exponent notation, *w* is the number of columns occupied by the number and *d* is the number of digits appearing to the right of the decimal point in the mantissa part of the number. The two numbers in the exponent notation typed as shown below are specified by the format statement:

```
FORMAT (E8.2, E6.0)
```

Column number →	1 2 3 4 5 6 7 8	9 10 11 12 13 14
Data →	– • 1 2 E – 0 2	1 • E + 0 5
	← Field 1 →	← Field 2 →

A single Format statement may, of course, describe both integers and reals in input. Thus the statement:

```
   INTEGER :: i
   REAL :: g, h
   READ 40, g, h, i
40 FORMAT (F6.2, E8.2, I6)
```

may be used to input the data:

Column number →	1 2 3 4 5 6	7 8 9 1 1 1 1 1 0 1 2 3 4	1 1 1 1 1 2 5 6 7 8 9 0
Data →	– 6 1 • 5 4	2 • 4 5 E – 2 8	2 4 8 7 6 2
	← 6 columns →	← 8 columns →	← 6 columns →

```
   INTEGER :: j
   REAL :: p, q
   READ 50, p, q, j
50 FORMAT (E8.2, E5.0, I4)
```

may be used to read the data:

Column number →	1 2 3 4 5 6 7 8	9 1 1 1 1 0 1 2 3	1 1 1 1 4 5 6 7
Data →	– 6 1 • 5 4	2 • E 1 5	2 4 6 8
	← 8 columns →	← 5 columns →	← 4 columns →

All the READ statements given in this section have been collected together and given as Example Program 11.1. The printed output obtained using the list directed PRINT statement corresponding to each READ command is also given in Fig. 11.1.

Example Program 11.1 Illustrating format statements

```
!PROGRAM 11.1
!CONSOLIDATED READ AND FORMAT EXAMPLES
PROGRAM form_1
  IMPLICIT NONE
  INTEGER :: int,i,j
  REAL :: a,b,c,d,e,f,g,h,p,q
  READ 10,int
  10 FORMAT(I4)
  READ 20,a,b,c,d
  20 FORMAT(F4.2,F5.2,F4.0,F6.2)
  READ 30,e,f
  30 FORMAT(E8.2,E6.0)
  READ 40,g,h,i
  40 FORMAT(F6.2,E8.2,I6)
  READ 50,p,q,j
  50 FORMAT(F8.2,E5.0,I4)
  PRINT *,"———OUTPUT RESULTS———"
  PRINT *,int
  PRINT *,a,b,c,d
  PRINT *,e,f
  PRINT *,g,h,i
  PRINT *,p,q,j
  PRINT *,"————————————————"
END PROGRAM form_1
```

```
INPUT DATA for PROGRAM 11.1
1942
1.258.42 42 1.51
-.12E-021.E+05
-61.542.45E-282468762
-61.542.E152468
———OUTPUT RESULTS———
1942
1.250000000 8.420000076 42.00000000 1.509999990
-0.1200000057E-02 100000.0000
-61.54000092 0.2450000038E-27 246876
-61.54000092 0.1999999974E+16 2468
————————————————
```

Fig. 11.1 Input/Output of Example Program 11.1.

11.2 FORMAT DESCRIPTION FOR PRINT STATEMENT

FORMAT statements for printing are similar to those presented for READ except for the following:

i. The record length, that is the number of characters which could be printed is for one line of VDU.

ii. The first element in the list of the FORMAT statement of a PRINT statement is the carriage control information and is an essential piece of information. This character is not printed. The carriage control characters are given in Table 11.1. (There would be some variations for different processors and the programmer should check this for the particular computer being used.)

Table 11.1 Carriage Control Characters

FORMAT code in PRINT	Effect
blank or 1X	Single space before printing
0	Double space before printing
1	Skip to next page before printing
+	Over print on the same line

The main point one must remember while writing formats for print statements is that the contents of memory are printed by such statements and very often the value which will be printed is not known ahead of time. Thus one should provide enough columns in the Format specification to accommodate the largest possible number, sign, decimal points, the letter E for E format etc. Further, enough blank space should be provided between printed values for easy readability. Appropriate captions must also be printed to help the user understand the output.

While planning input formats the main concern is to reduce manual effort in typing and hence unnecessary blank columns should not be there. This requirement is quite opposite to that which is desirable for output, namely, using plenty of blank columns to aid readability.

The format specifications I*w*, F*w.d* and E*w.d* are again used with PRINT statements where *w* is the width of the field. Thus the statement

```
      INTEGER :: mj
      REAL :: a, b
      PRINT 25, mj, a, b
   25 FORMAT (1X, I8, F10.6, E15.8)
```

would allocate 8 columns for the value of mj, 10 columns for a and 15 columns for b. The programmer should allow enough columns to accommodate the size of the number, decimal point, sign and extra space for easy readability.

We will now discuss a few examples of output formats.

Example 11.1

The program shown below:

```
      INTEGER :: i, j, k
      i = –12589
      j = 455
      k = – 48989
      PRINT 35, i, j, k
   35 FORMAT (1X, I6, I4, I5)
```

will print one line in the form:

– 12589□455 *****

The asterisks indicate that enough number of columns were not provided by the FORMAT for the last integer. Further, the output is obviously not very readable as no blank spaces between the values of i, j, k have been provided for in the FORMAT specification. A better FORMAT for this example would be:

```
45 FORMAT (1X, I8, I6, I8)
```

which would cause the following output:

□□−12589 □□□455□□− 48989

Blank columns may be left between data fields in the output using the specification *w*X where *w* is the number of columns to be left blank. Using this facility the FORMAT for printing may be written as:

```
    INTEGER :: i, j, k
    PRINT 55, i, j, k
55 FORMAT(1X, 2X, I6, 3X, I3, 2X, I6)
```

which will give the same output as:

```
65 FORMAT (1X, I8, I6, I8)
```

To output real numbers the fractional form specification is useful only when a fairly good idea of the magnitude of the number in storage is known. If the magnitude is not known it would be preferable to use the exponent form specification for output.

Example 11.2

The following statements illustrate printed outputs in F-Format:

```
    REAL:: a, b, c
    a = – 193.4589
    b = .4589
    c = – .008946
    PRINT 75, a, b, c
75 FORMAT (1X, F7. 4, F6. 4, F8.6)
```

The output would be:

******* □ .4589 – .008946

As enough columns have not been provided for a in the format, asterisks appear instead of the value of a. (Some processors would print a truncated number without giving any indication to the user!) Further the output is not properly spaced. A better FORMAT specification is:

```
75 FORMAT (1X, F11.4, F8.4, F11.6)
```

which would print the output as:

Column number →	1 2 3 4 5 6 7 8 9 1 1 0 1	1 1 1 1 1 1 1 1 2 3 4 5 6 7 8 9	2 2 2 2 2 2 2 2 2 2 3 0 1 2 3 4 5 6 7 8 9 0
Data →	−1 9 3 . 4 5 8 9	0 . 4 5 8 9	−0 . 0 0 8 9 4 6

← 11 columns →← 8 columns →← 11 columns →

The same numbers may be printed in exponent notation by the FORMAT statement:

```
75 FORMAT (1X, E15.8, E11.4, E12.4)
```

which would print the output as:

```
– 0.19345890E+03□0.4589E+00□– 0.8946E–02
```

While writing E type FORMAT specification for output one must satisfy the inequality $w \geq d + 7$. That is, the total width of the field must exceed the number of digits required on the right of the decimal point by at least seven. These seven columns are required for (i) two digits of the exponent part, (ii) one position for exponent symbol E, (iii) one position for the sign of the exponent (if the exponent is positive some processors leave a blank column in the output), (iv) one position for the decimal point of the mantissa, (v) one position for the sign of the mantissa, and (vi) one position for a zero which is printed by most processors between the sign and the decimal point of the mantissa. If all the digits stored in a real variable name are to be printed, the Format used should be E15.8 (assuming the computer stores 8 significant digits for a mantissa).

The output for Example 11.2 will be much more readable with the format:

```
100 FORMAT (1X, E17.8, E17.8, E17.8)
```

Example 11.3

Two real numbers a and b are to be printed in the exponent notation (with eight significant digits) and an integer n of 3 digit length is also to be printed. FORMAT specification is:

```
    INTEGER :: n; REAL :: a,b
    PRINT 105, a, b, n
105 FORMAT (1X, E15.8, 5X, E15.8, 5X, I5)
```

The output will then appear as shown below:

± 0.XXXXXXXXE ± XX	□□□□□	0.XXXXXXXXE ± XX	□□□□□	□ ± XXX
← 15 Cols →	← 5 Cols →	← 15 Cols →	← 5 Cols →	← 5 Cols →

Example 11.4

Three real numbers a1, b1 and c1 which are known to be less than one are to be printed with 6 decimal digits accuracy. An integer n of 4 digits lengths is also to be printed. The output statement in this case may be written as:

```
    INTEGER :: n; REAL :: a1,b1,c1
    PRINT 115, a1, b1, c1, n
115 FORMAT (1X , 3X, F8.6, 3X, F8.6, 3X, F8.6, 3X, I5)
```

The FORMAT specification may also be written as:

```
116 FORMAT (1X, F11.6, F11.6, F11.6, I8)
117 FORMAT (1X, 3F11.6, I8)
```

Thus, if n successive fields within one record are to be printed in the same fashion, then it may be specified by writing n before the E, F or I specification.

Thus the Format of Example 11.3 may also be written as:

```
110 FORMAT (1X, 2(E15.8, 5X), I5)
```

Example 11.5

Three real numbers x, y, z whose values are not known are to be printed out. In this case E Format should be used. An appropriate Format could be:

```
READ:: x, y, z
PRINT 125, x, y, z
125 FORMAT (1X, 3E17.8)
```

In this Format enough space is reserved for each variable and 2 blanks between variables would be available. If x, y, z are respectively

$$1.25*10^{-2}, \; -4.8549423*10^{10}, \; 4859448.5$$

the output will appear as shown below:

□□□0.12500000E−01□□−0.48549423E+11□□□0.48594485E+07

All the PRINT statements along with Formats given in this section have been consolidated as Example Program 11.2. The requisite input data is read using list directed input statements. Comments have been included in lower case along with the output for ease of understanding.

Example Program 11.2 Consolidated format examples of Sec. 11.2

```
!PROGRAM 11.2
!CONSOLIDATES ALL EXAMPLES IN SECTION 11.2

PROGRAM form_2
   IMPLICIT NONE
   INTEGER :: i,j,k,n,mj
   REAL :: a,b,c,a1,b1,c1,x,y,z
   READ *,mj,a,b
   PRINT 25,mj,a,b
   25 FORMAT(1X,I8,F10.6,E15.8)
   READ*,i,j,k
   PRINT 35,i,j,k
   35 FORMAT(1X,I6,I4,I5)
   PRINT 45,i,j,k
   45 FORMAT(1X,I8,I6,I8)
   PRINT 55,i,j,k
   55 FORMAT(1X,2X,I6,3X,I3,2X,I6)
   PRINT 65,i,j,k
   65 FORMAT(1X,I8,I6,I8)
   READ *,a,b,c
   PRINT 75,a,b,c
```

```
75 FORMAT(1X,F7.4,F6.4,F8.6)
PRINT 85,a,b,c
85 FORMAT(1X,F11.4,F8.4,F11.6)
PRINT 95,a,b,c
95 FORMAT(1X,E15.8,E11.4,E12.4)
PRINT 100,a,b,c
100 FORMAT(1X,E17.8,E17.8,E17.8)
READ *, a, b, n
PRINT 105,a,b,n
105 FORMAT(1X,E15.8,5X,E15.8,5X,I5)
PRINT 110,a,b,n
110 FORMAT(1X,2(E15.8,5X),I5)
READ *,a1,b1,c1,n
PRINT 115,a1,b1,c1,n
115 FORMAT(1X,3X,F8.6,3X,F8.6,3X,I5)
PRINT 116,a1,b1,c1,n
116 FORMAT(1X,F11.6,F11.6,F11.6,I8)
PRINT 117,a1,b1,c1,n
117 FORMAT(1X,3F11.6,I8)
READ *,x,y,z
PRINT 125,x,y,z
125 FORMAT(1X,3E17.8)
END PROGRAM form_2
```

```
OUTPUT of PROGRAM 11.2
   1245 66.822998 0.25600000E–14
   –12589 455*****
   –12589 455 –48989
   –12589 455 –48989
   –12589 455 –48989
   *******0.4589–.008946
   –193.4589 0.4589 –0.008946
   –0.19345889E+03 0.4589E+00 –0.8946E–02
   –0.19345889E+03 0.45890000E+00 –0.89459997E–02
   –0.26798501E+04 0.10654320E+02 468
   –0.26798501E+04 0.10654320E+02 468
   ******** ******** *****
   0.000000
   4686.432129–256.324005 42.650002 348
   4686.432129–256.324005 42.650002 348
   0.12500000E–01 0.48549421E+11 0.48594485E+07
```

Fig. 11.2 Output of Example Program 11.2.

11.3 MULTI-RECORD FORMATS

If input is to be read from more than one input record or output is to be printed on more than one line then a multi-record format is to be specified. In order to understand this specification it is helpful to know how the compiler interprets FORMAT statements.

When the object program encounters an input/output statement it scans the corresponding FORMAT specification from left to right and simultaneously scans the variables in the list. Each element in the list is printed or read according to the given format. When the computer encounters the *final* parenthesis in the format code it checks if all the elements in the list are exhausted. If the list is not exhausted and the Format statement has only one pair of parentheses then the same Format is used repeatedly till all the elements in the list are read or printed. For example,

```
   INTEGER :: n, k, m
   READ 66, n, k, m
66 FORMAT (I3)
```

will read the values of n, k, m from three successive records all with FORMAT (I3). The statement:

```
   INTEGER, DIMENSION (6) :: x
   READ 88, (x(i), i = 1, 6)
88 FORMAT (3F8.3)
```

will read 3 items each from 2 successive records.

If a Format statement has more than one pair of parentheses and the first scan of the Format is not sufficient to account for all the elements in the list of variables then the same Format statement is used for the rest of the list elements using the following *Format rescan rule.*

When the rightmost parenthesis of the Format specification is reached and variables in the corresponding input/output list are not exhausted then a rescan of the Format is initiated backwards from right to left. The rescan is started at the last right parenthesis and is stopped at the next *left* parenthesis. The rest of the list elements use the Format specification between this parenthesis and the rightmost parenthesis.

The statement

```
   INTEGER :: k, m; REAL :: a, b, c, d
   PRINT 77, k, m, a, b, c, d
77 FORMAT (1X, 2I3, (1X, F10.4))
```

will print k, m and a on the first line and b, c, d on the next three lines using FORMAT (1X, F10.4).

The following statement

```
   REAL :: a, b, g (1:5); INTEGER :: knt (1:5)
   PRINT 35, a,b, (g(i), knt (i), i = 1, 5)
35 FORMAT (3X, 2E15.8, (10X, F10.6, 5X, I6))
```

will print a, b, g(1), knt(1) with FORMAT(3X, E15.8, E15.8, 10X, F10.6, 5X, I6) on the first line and print g(2), knt (2) on the second line with FORMAT (10X, F10.6, 5X, I6), g(3), knt (3) on the third line with the same FORMAT and continue printing the succeeding components of g and knt on successive lines. In other words the above statements are equivalent to the following:

```
   PRINT 36, a, b, g (1), knt (1)
36 FORMAT (3X, 2E15.8, 10X, F10.6, 5X, I6)
   PRINT 37, (g (i),knt (i), i = 2, 5)
37 FORMAT(10X, F10.6, 5X, I6)
```

Two more examples below illustrate how the Format rescan point is determined:

```
FORMAT (1X, (3I2, F10.8), F7.5, (1X, I8, F8.6, F5.2), I4)
                                ↑                      ↑
                          rescan point          end of rescan

FORMAT (1X, 2(3(1X, F8.4, I3), F5.2), I8)
             ↑                       ↑
        rescan point          end of rescan
```

Record spacing

A slash (/) may be used in FORMAT codes to deal with lists which are to be printed on more than one line or read from more than one record. It may also be employed to provide blank lines in a printed output. The occurrence of a slash is a command to go to the next record. For example the statements

```
   REAL :: p (1:7)
   PRINT 38, (p(i), i = 1, 7)
38 FORMAT (1X, 3F10.2 / / / 1X, 4F10.4)
```

will print the values of p(1), p(2), p(3) on the first line, nothing on the next two lines and p(4), p(5), p(6) and p(7) on the next line. Observe the carriage control character 1X which is needed for each new line to be printed.

The following statements:

```
   INTEGER :: k., k1, m, n; REAL :: a, b, c
   PRINT 40, a, b, c, k,k1, m, n
40 FORMAT (1X, 3F10.2 / 1X, 4I8)
```

will print a, b, c on the first line and k, k1, m, n on the next line. The specification

```
45 FORMAT (1X/ 3F10.2 / (1X, 4I8))
```

will leave a blank line, print 3 fields on the second line and will print four integer fields on all succeeding lines. Observe that a slash in the middle of a FORMAT specification indicates the end of a record and a command to go to the next record.

```
80 FORMAT (1X / 1X, 3F10.2 / (1X, 4I8 / ))
```

will leave one blank line after printing each line with 4 integer fields. The statement:

```
    REAL :: a, b, c; INTEGER :: m, nt (1: 28)
    PRINT 10, a, b, c, (nt (m), m = 1, 28)
120 FORMAT (1X, 3F10.2 / (1X, 4I8/1X, 3I6))
```

will print three real fields on the first line, 4 integers on the second line and 3 integers on the third line, and alternately 4 and 3 integers on all succeeding lines.

As a slash is a command to go to the next record, n slashes in the middle of a Format specification leave $(n - 1)$ blank records. However, n slashes at the beginning of a Format specification will leave n blank records.

All the examples in this section have been consolidated as Example Program 11.3. The input and output are also given with appropriate comments for ease of understanding in Fig. 11.3.

Example Program 11.3 Consolidation of Sec. 11.3 examples

```
!PROGRAM 11.3
!CONSOLIDATES ALL EXAMPLES IN SECTION 11.3

PROGRAM form_3
   IMPLICIT NONE
   INTEGER :: knt(1:5),nt(1:28),n,k,m,k1,i
   REAL :: g(1:5),p(1:7),x(1:6),a,b,c,d
   READ 66,n,k,m
   66 FORMAT(I3)
   PRINT *, "Printing n, k, m"
   PRINT *,n,k,m
   READ 88,(x(i),i=1,6)
   88 FORMAT(3F8.3)
   PRINT *, "Printing (x(i),i=1,6)"
   PRINT 89,(x(i),i=1,6)
   89 FORMAT(1X,3F8.3)
   READ *,k,m,a,b,c,d
   PRINT *, "Printing k,m,a,b,c,d"
   PRINT 77,k,m,a,b,c,d
   77 FORMAT(1X,2I3,(1X,F10.4))
   READ *,a,b,(g(i),knt(i),i=1,5)
   PRINT *, "Printing a,b,(g(i),knt(i),i=1,5) "
   PRINT 35,a,b,(g(i),knt(i),i=1,5)
   35 FORMAT(3X,2E15.8,(1X,10X,F10.6,5X,I6))
   PRINT *, "Printing a,b,g(1),knt(1) "
   PRINT 36,a,b,g(1),knt(1)
   36 FORMAT(1X,3X,2E15.8,10X,F10.6,5X,I6)
   PRINT *, "Printing (g(i),knt(i),i=1,5) "
   PRINT 37,(g(i),knt(i),i=1,5)
   37 FORMAT(1X,10X,F10.6,5X,I6)
   READ *,(p(i),i=1,7)
   PRINT *, " Printing (p(i),i=1,7) "
   PRINT 38,(p(i),i=1,7)
   38 FORMAT (1X,3F10.2///1X,4F10.4)
   READ*,a,b,c,k,k1,m,n
   PRINT *, "Printing a,b,c,k,k1,m,n "
   PRINT 40,a,b,c,k,k1,m,n
   40 FORMAT(1X,3F10.2/1X,4I5)
   PRINT *, "Printing a,b,c,k,k1,m,n "
   PRINT 45,a,b,c,k,k1,m,n
   45 FORMAT(1X/1X,3F10.2/(1X,4I8))
   READ *,a,b,c,(nt(m),m=1,28)
   PRINT *, "Printing a,b,c,(nt(m),m=1,28) "
   PRINT 60,a,b,c,(nt(m),m=1,28)
   60 FORMAT(1X/1X,3F10.2/(1X,4I8)/)
   PRINT *, "Printing a,b,c,(nt(m),m=1,28) "
   PRINT 80,a,b,c,(nt(m),m=1,28)
   80 FORMAT(1X,//1X,3F10.2/(1X,4I8)/)
   PRINT *, "Printing a,b,c,(nt(m),m=1,28) "
   PRINT 120,a,b,c,(nt(m),m=1,28)
   120 FORMAT(1X,3F10.2/(1X,4I8/1X,3I6))
END PROGRAM form_3
```

```
INPUT of PROGRAM 11.3
42
53
63
24.65,256.4,-46.2
25.68,34.26,84.95
56,-4,265.43,-36.85,42.65,48.45
22.65,42.85,4.6,3,4.8,8,9.3,4,4.8,9,8.9,28
22.85,33.65,-42.65,95.92,72.72,95.56,25.5
2.62,3.45,4.85,-92,45,36,72
4.85,3.82,-9.65,1,2,3,4,5,6,7,8,9,10,11,12,13,14,15,16,17,18,
19,20,21,22,23,24,25,26,27,28
```

```
OUTPUT of PROGRAM 11.3
Printing n, k, m
42 53 63

Printing (x(i),i=1,6)
   24.650 256.400 -46.200
   25.680 34.260 84.950

Printing k,m,a,b,c,d
56 -4 265.4300
    -36.8500
    42.6500
    48.4500

Printing a,b,(g(i),knt(i),i=1,5)
  0.22650000E+02 0.42849998E+02      4.600000        3
      4.800000          8
      9.300000          4
      4.800000          9
      8.900000         28

Printing a,b,g(1),knt(1)
  0.22650000E+02 0.42849998E+02      4.600000        3

Printing (g(i),knt(i),i=1,5)
      4.600000          3
      4.800000          8
      9.300000          4
      4.800000          9
      8.900000         28

Printing (p(i),i=1,7)
   22.85     33.65      -42.65
   95.9200  72.7200  95.5600  25.5000

Printing a,b,c,k,k1,m,n
   2.62   3.45   4.85
   -92   45   36   72

Printing a,b,c,k,k1,m,n
   2.62   3.45   4.85
   -92   45   36   72
```

Fig. 11.3 (*Contd.*)

```
Printing a,b,c,(nt(m),m=1,28)
   4.85     3.82     -9.65
     1    2     3      4
     5    6     7      8
     9   10    11     12
    13   14    15     16
    17   18    19     20
    21   22    23     24
    25   26    27     28
Printing a,b,c,(nt(m),m=1,28)
   4.85     3.82     -9.65
     1    2     3      4
     5    6     7      8
     9   10    11     12
    13   14    15     16
    17   18    19     20
    21   22    23     24
    25   26    27     28
Printing a,b,c,(nt(m),m=1,28)
   4.85     3.82     -9.65
     1    2     3      4
   5    6    7
     8    9    10     11
  12    13   14
    15   16    17     18
  19    20   21
    22   23    24     25
  26    27   28
```

Fig. 11.3 Input/Output of Example Program 11.3.

Tabulation

When data is to be skipped or re-read from an input device or is to be printed in certain specified columns then a *Tab edit descriptor* is used. The three forms of this are:

T*n*: which causes data to be read from n^{th} column or printed from n^{th} column
TR*n*: which causes data to be read or printed *n* columns to the *right of the present position*
TL*n*: which causes data to be read or printed *n* columns to the *left of the present position*

Observe that Tn is an absolute tab, that is, it does not depend on the current column which is being read or printed. TR and TL on the other hand are relative to column being currently printed. In the following statement:

```
INTEGER :: a, b, c
READ 15, a, b, c
15 FORMAT (T6, I2, T9, I3, T2, I4)
```

The value of a will be read from the 6th column, the value of b from 9th column and the value of c from 2nd column. The values of a, b, c should be placed in the input unit as shown below:

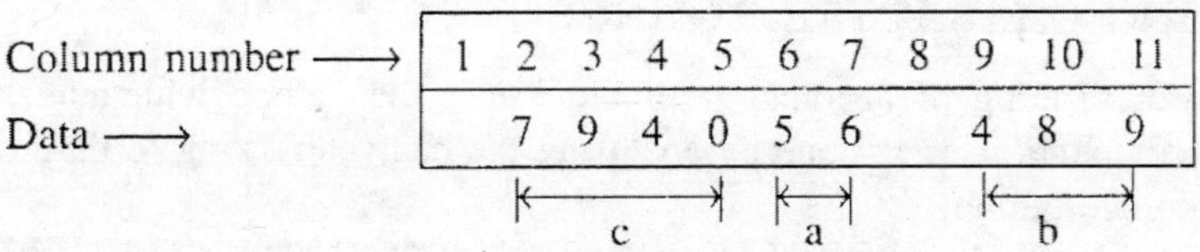

The same effect may be obtained by the statement:

```
      READ 25, a, b, c
   25 FORMAT (T6, I2, TR1, I3, TL10, I4)
```

Thus Tab edit descriptor can be used to skip data fields. It can also be used to re-read parts of data.

The Tab edit descriptor is particularly useful in printing headings of tables. For example if the heading in a table shown below are to be printed, the print statement is:

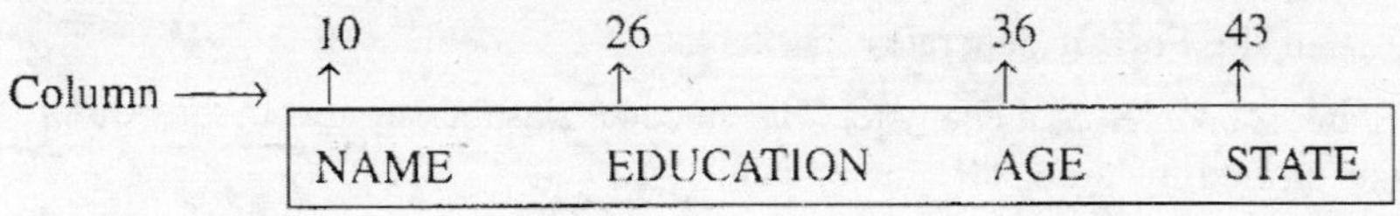


```
      PRINT 25
   25 FORMAT (T10, "NAME", T26, "EDUCATION", T36, "AGE", T43, "STATE")
```

Example Program 11.4 consolidates the examples in this section. The output of this program is given in Fig. 11.4.

Example Program 11.4 Use of tab format

```
!PROGRAM 11.4
!ILLUSTRATES TAB CHARACTERS

PROGRAM form_4
   IMPLICIT NONE
   INTEGER :: a,b,c
   READ 15,a,b,c
   ! 794056 489 INPUT
   15 FORMAT (T6,I2,T9,I3,T2,I4)
   PRINT 16,a,b,c
   16 FORMAT (1X,"a = ",I6, " b = ", I6, " c = ", I6)
   READ 25, a,b,c
   25 FORMAT (T6,I2,TR1,I3,TL10,I4)
   ! 794056 489 INPUT
   PRINT 16, a,b,c
   PRINT 35
   35 FORMAT(T10,"NAME",T26,"EDUCATION",T39,"AGE",T45,"STATE")
END PROGRAM form_4
```

```
OUTPUT of PROGRAM 11.4
a = 56 b = 489 c = 7940
a = 56 b = 489 c = 7940
   NAME          EDUCATION AGE STATE
```

Fig. 11.4 Output of Example Program 11.4.

11.4 PRINTING CHARACTER STRINGS

One often requires printing of headings, variable names etc., along with numerical results calculated by a computer. This is done by enclosing the character string to be printed within apostrophes or double quotes.

Suppose the title ABC EXPORT CORPORATION PVT. (LTD.) is to be printed on a 80 column printer. This title should be properly centred on the 80 column line. Counting characters in the title we have 34 characters including blanks. Thus (80 – 34) / 2 = 23 blanks must be left before the title. This title may be obtained using the following statement:

```
    PRINT 100
100 FORMAT (1X, 23X, "ABC EXPORT CORPORATION PVT.(LTD)")
```

Observe the following points:

1. 1X at the beginning is a carriage control character.
2. 23X in the Format generates 23 blanks.
3. Blank is counted as a character. The characters as they appear in the FORMAT declaration are printed by the PRINT statement.
4. Observe that the PRINT statement has no variable list. This is allowed as only a title is to be printed in this case.

Values of variables could also be printed out along with their names. Example Program 11.5 prints out the data centered on a line below the company's name ABC EXPORT CORPORATION PVT. (LTD.).

Example Program 11.5 illustrates how values of variables may be printed with appropriate captions.

Example Program 11.5 Printing strings of character

```
!PROGRAM 11.5
!ILLUSTRATES PRINTING STRINGS USING FORMAT

PROGRAM form_5
  IMPLICIT NONE
  INTEGER :: day=25
  PRINT 100
  100 FORMAT(1X,23X,"ABC EXPORT CORPORATION PVT.(LTD.)")
  PRINT 110,day
  110 FORMAT(1X,32X,"JANUARY",I3," 1996")
END PROGRAM form_5
```

11.5 READING AND WRITING LOGICAL QUANTITIES

Fortran 90 uses an edit descriptor L*w* to READ logical quantities. Logical quantities have a value *true* or *false*. On input *true* is represented by .T. or T or TRUE and *false* by .F., F or FALSE. The descriptor L*w* assumes that the next *w* characters are to be taken to represent a logical quality. The presence of t, T, .t or .T as the first letter(s) is taken as true and stored as logical *true*. Similarly f, F, .f or .F is taken as false. Once a T or F is read as first letter other letters are ignored as shown in Table 11.2.

Table 11.2 Explaining L*w* Descriptor

Data interpreted as true	*Data interpreted as false*
.t	.f
T	F
.T	.F
true	false
TRUE	FALSE
.TRUE.	.FALSE.
tool	foot
.true	.false

On output if a logical quality is true it is printed as ␣␣␣ T with edit descriptor L4 or as T with descriptor L1. In general if the edit descriptor is L*w* then ($w - 1$) blanks are left followed by T or F depending on whether the logical variable is True or False.

11.6 GENERALIZED INPUT/OUTPUT STATEMENTS

The READ and PRINT statements considered so far give the programmer access to the VDU and the printer. Most computers have besides these other input-output media like terminals, magnetic tapes and discs. Fortran 90 provides generalized input-output statements which allow the programmer to specify the particular input-output unit he wants to use. In this section we will consider some of these statements.

The general input statement available in Fortran 90 is:

READ (*unit, format*) *list*

where *unit* is an integer variable name or an integer constant which refers to a code assigned to the input unit to be accessed and *format* is the statement number of the Format declaration for the list.

The code for an input unit is assigned by the computer installation. A programmer should check the installation codes for the computer he intends to use. Assume that unit 5 is default input unit (VDU) and unit 6 is the default output unit (Printer).

Thus the statements:

```
   READ (5,25) a, b, c
25 FORMAT (3F10.6)
```

commands the computer to read values a, b, c from the VDU using Format 3F10.6.

The general output statement is:

WRITE (*unit, format*) *list*

where *unit, format* and *list* have the same meaning as in the READ statement. For printing the results one may thus use the statement:

```
   WRITE (3, 35) x, y, z
35 FORMAT (1X, 3E15.8)
```

If a programmer wants to generalize his program and make it independent of the specific codes for I/O units in an installation he may use the following artifice:

```
! ILLUSTRATING USE OF UNITS
  INTEGER::PRNTR, DISK, READER, TERMNL
  READ*,PRNTR, DISK, READER, TERMNL
  ____________________________
  READ (READER, 25) a, b, c
  ____________________________
  WRITE (PRNTR, 40) x, y, z
  ____________________________
  WRITE (TERMNL, 50) w,r, s
  ____________________________

  ____________________________
```

The data read should contain the integer codes for printer, disk file, reader and terminal appropriate for the computer being used.

The statement

WRITE (PRNTR, 40) x, y, z

is equivalent to the statement: PRINT 40, x, y, z

The statement

READ (READER, 25) a, b, c

is equivalent to the statement: READ 25, a, b, c.

All the discussions on Formats given so far are applicable to the generalized I/O statements given in this section. The only point to be remembered if a video terminal is to be used as an input/output device is that they normally accommodate 80 characters per line and 24 lines per page frame. Video terminals display results on a television screen. A printed copy may be obtained either by a hard copy attachment to a video terminal or a teletype terminal.

Fortran 90 allows the use of the character * to indicate a device by default. The device assumed for input when the device code is not specified is the keyboard of VDU. Thus one may write

READ (*, 25) a, b, c

If the input format is also not specified and a list directed input is desired one may write:

READ(*,*) a, b, c

The default device for output is the video display and one may thus write as per Fortran 90 standard

WRITE (*, 20) x, y, z

for output to be displayed. A list directed output statement may be written as:

WRITE (*,*) x, y, z

We have used a brief version of READ and WRITE statements. In general the form of the statement is

READ (c_*list*) input_list
or WRITE (c_*list*) output_list

where *c_list* is called the *control information list*. An expanded version of *c_list* is

READ (UNIT = 5, FMT = 125, IOSTAT = ioerror) input_list.

In the above form UNIT is the unit number of the unit from which data is to be read. FMT is the statement number of FORMAT specification and IOSTAT is an internal variable whose value is set to 0 if no error has occurred and a positive number if an error has occurred. Other values are set for end of file and end of record conditions which do not concern us now. We will discuss this later. IOSTAT is optional in *c_list*. Also writing UNIT = , FMT = is optional as we have seen. But if these key words are used their order of occurrence is not important in *c_list*. We can thus write:

```
READ (FMT = 25, UNIT = 5) a, b, c
```

If key words are not used, the unit number must come first and then the format number.

Fortran 90 also allows FORMAT string to be specified without a separate FORMAT statement. We can thus write:

```
INTEGER :: a; REAL :: b, c
READ, "(I2, F6.2, F8.3)", a, b, c
```

if a default input unit is to be used.

We may also write:

```
READ (UNIT = 5, FMT = "(I2, F6.2, F8.3)") a, b, c
or
READ ( 5, "(I2, F6.2, F8.3)") a,b, c
```

if UNIT 5 is to be used.

Some writers prefer writing FORMAT in the READ or WRITE statement as it does not require writing a separate FORMAT statement with a statement number. The only disadvantage of writing the FORMAT string as part of READ or PRINT statement is it sometimes becomes too long and unreadable. A separate FORMAT statement can be used by more than one READ or PRINT statement. It also makes the FORMAT readable and easy to change.

11.7 SOME COMMENTS ON FORMATS

In Section 11.1 the rules for writing Format statements for input data were presented. They were kept intentionally "strict" to reduce possible confusion to beginners. The rules are in fact less rigid so that the manual labour in data input is reduced. The following points illustrate how input formats may be simplified.

1. The presence of a decimal point in the field of input data specified using F or E format overrides the "d" specification in formats Ew.d and Fw.d. Thus if the data is typed as shown below:

   123.45□□11.45E10

   and specified by the format:

   ```
   FORMAT (F6.0, 2X, E8.1)
   ```

   The data would be correctly read, even though the stricter format would be:

   ```
   FORMAT (F6.2, 2X, E8.2)
   ```

2. In the E and F specifications a decimal point need not be explicitly typed. If it is not typed the number of digits after the decimal point as given in the Format statement is taken. Thus if the number 10524 is typed with the corresponding Format given as FORMAT (F5.2) then the number will be taken as 105.24. If it is typed as 10524E–02 with FORMAT (E9.2) the number will be taken as 105.24E–02.

3. Data typed in E format need not have an E explicitly typed. Thus a number typed as 145.1+2 with FORMAT (E7.1) will be read in as 145.1E2. Observe that the + sign instead of E for the exponent is essential. A number typed as 14.25–4 with FORMAT (E7.2) will be taken as 14.25E–4.

4. The specification wX in an input format ignores the contents of the specified w columns in the input record. For example, the following statements:

```
   REAL :: h, p
   READ 25, h, p
25 FORMAT (F6.2, 5X, F6.2)
```

Data

```
145.32 VALUE 125.45
```

would read in 145.32 into h and 125.45 into p and ignore the characters VALUE as though they were blanks.

The points on input data preparation given in this section are consolidated as Example Program 11.6. Both the input and output are given along with the program.

Example Program 11.6 Consolidated examples of Sec. 11.7

```
!PROGRAM 11.6
!CONSOLIDATES EXAMPLES IN SECTION 11.7
!TESTING INPUT DATA TYPED IN SHORT FORM

PROGRAM form_6
  IMPLICIT NONE
  REAL :: a,b,c,d,e,e2,f,f1,g,g1,h,p
  READ "(F6.0,2X,E8.1)",a,b
  READ "(F6.2,2X,E8.2)",c,d
  READ 30,e
  30 FORMAT(F5.2)
  READ 35,e2
  35 FORMAT(E9.2)
  READ 40,f
  40 FORMAT(F5.2)
  READ 50,g
  50 FORMAT(E7.2)
  READ 55,f1,g1
  55 FORMAT(E7.1,E7.2)
  READ 60,h,P
  60 FORMAT(F6.2,5X,F6.2)
  PRINT *,"PRINTED RESULTS"
  PRINT 80,a,b
  80 FORMAT(" a = ",F6.2,2X, " b = ", E12.4)
  PRINT 90, c,d
  90 FORMAT(" c = ", F6.2,2X," d = ", E12.4)
  PRINT 95, e
  95 FORMAT(" e = ",F8.2)
```

```
    PRINT 98, e2
    98 FORMAT(" e2 = ",E12.5)
    PRINT 100, f
    100 FORMAT(" f = ", F8.2)
    PRINT 102,g
    102 FORMAT(" g = ", E12.5)
    PRINT 105, f1, g1
    105 FORMAT("f1 = ", E12.5," g1 = ", E12.5)
    PRINT 110, h, p
    110 FORMAT(" h = ", F10.2,2X," p = ", F10.2)
END PROGRAM form_6
```

```
123.45 11.45E10
123.45 11.45E10
10524
10524
10524
1052E-2
145.1+214.25-4
145.32VALUE125.45
```

Fig. 11.5 Input to Example Program 11.6.

```
PRINTED RESULTS
a = 123.45 b = 0.1145E+12
c = 123.45 d = 0.1145E+12
e = 105.24
e2 = 0.10524E+03
f = 105.24
g = 0.10520E+00
f1 = 0.14510E+05 g1 = 0.14250E-02
h = 145.32 p = 125.45
```

Fig. 11.6 Output of Example Program 11.6.

To conclude we will present a list of points to be checked while writing Format statements. These points are as follows:

1. The order in which data are typed should correspond to the order in which the variables in the input list are specified.
2. Input data (in I, E and F formats) should be right adjusted within their respective fields. The type of variable name and the corresponding Format declaration should tally. Thus reals should use E or F Formats and integers I Format.
3. The list elements in READ should be variable names and not expressions.
4. In output statements one extra column should be left for the sign of the number.
5. If the approximate range of values of a real number to be printed is not known E Format should be used. A safe E Format is E15.8 (in such cases) for computers which have 8 significant digit mantissa. A safe format for integers is I12.

6. In PRINT statements the first edit descriptor in FORMAT is a carriage control character and the appropriate character should be used.
7. The number of characters to be printed per line should not exceed the capacity of the printer.

SUMMARY

1. If data is available in a specified form and if output is to be printed in a specified form then it is necessary to use a FORMAT specification in READ and PRINT statements.
2. The general form of READ and PRINT statements with FORMAT specification are

   READ n, *list*
   n FORMAT (*list of edit descriptors*)
   or
   READ "(*list of edit descriptors*)", *list*
   or
   READ (UNIT = integer, FMT = n) *list*
   n FORMAT (*list of edit descriptors*)
   or
   READ (UNIT = *integer*, FMT = "(*list of edit descriptors*)") *list*
   or READ (*integer, integer*) *list*

   For example

   ```
      READ 25, a, b, c
   25 FORMAT (F6.2, F7.3, F9.4)
   or READ "(F6.2, F7.3, F9.4)", a, b, c
   or READ (UNIT = 5, FMT = 25) a, b, c
   25 FORMAT (F6.2, F7.3, F9.4)
   ```

   are all equivalent.

   The UNIT specifies the number given to units such as VDU, magnetic disk file etc., by an installation. They have to be found out in a given installation.

3. The general form of a PRINT statement is
   PRINT *n, list*
   n FORMAT (*list of edit descriptors*)
   or PRINT " (*edit descriptors*)", *list*
   PRINT is normally used for default output device (usually a VDU)
   For other output devices the form is:
   WRITE (UNIT = *n*, FMT = *m*) list
   m FORMAT *(edit descriptors)*
   or WRITE (*n*, m) *list*
   m FORMAT (*edit descriptors*)
   or WRITE (n, "(*edit descriptors*)") *list*
   or WRITE (*, *m*) *list*
   m FORMAT (*edit descriptors*)
   (* means default device)

4. Table 11.2 gives a list of edit descriptors and their meaning for input data.

Table 11.2 Edit Descriptors for Input

Descriptor	*Meaning*
I*w*	Read next *w* characters as an integer
F*w.d*	Read next *w* characters as a REAL with *d* digits after decimal point
E*w.d*	Read next *w* characters as REAL in exponent form. Assume *d* digits after decimal point in mantissa
*n*X	Ignore next *n* characters
L*w*	Read next *w* characters as representation of a logical value. First character T or t for *true* and F or f for *false*
T*n*	Read next character from position n
TL*n*	Read next character *n* characters to the left of the current position
TR*n*	Read next character *n* characters to the right of the current position

5. Table 11.3 gives a list of edit decriptors and their meanings for output.

Table 11.3 Edit Descriptors for Output

Descriptor	*Meaning*
I*w*	Output an integer in the next *w* columns
F*w.d*	Output a REAL in the next *w* columns with d digits following the decimal point
E*w.d*	Output a REAL in the next *w* columns using Exponent form. *d* digits are to be printed after the decimal point in the mantissa. Four characters must be reserved to print the exponent symbol E, sign and exponent digits.
*n*X	Leave *n* blank columns
L*w*	Output (*w* – 1) blank columns followed by T for true or F for false
T*n*	Output next item starting in position *n*
TL*n*	Output next item starting from *n* positions to left of the current position
TR*n*	Output next item starting from *n* positions to right of current position
"C_1 , C_2.....C_n" or 'C_1, C_2.....C_n'	Output string C1, C2 ....Cn starting at the next column.

6. A slash (/) is used as an edit descriptor to advance to next line in input or output.

7. If the number of edit descriptors in a FORMAT specification are not sufficient to satisfy the list of variables to be read/output then the FORMAT string is rescanned. The place from which rescanning starts is defined in the rescan rule described in Section 11.3.

EXERCISES

11.1 Present the output of Problem 10.6 in the following form:

Class Intervals	No. in each interval	Percent of Total
1	XX	XX
2	XX	XX
3	XX	XX
.	.	.
.	.	.
.	.	.
.	.	.

Total data points = XXX

11.2 It is intended to mechanise the payroll calculations in a company. The company has about 1000 employees. The payroll list has the following information:

i. Gross pay
ii. If gross pay is more than Rs. 2,000/- but less than Rs. 3000/- per month income tax is deducted at 5 percent of gross pay. On incomes between Rs. 3000/- per month and Rs. 8000/- per month the tax is at 10 percent. On salaries above Rs. 8000/- per month 20% tax is deducted at source. No tax is due for gross pay less than Rs. 2000/- per month.
iii. 8.33 percent provident fund is deducted from each employee.
iv. House rent at the rate of 10% of gross pay is deducted.
v. Any deduction authorized by an employee subject to a maximum of Rs. 1000 is made from the pay

(a) Prepare a format for input data
(b) Write a program to print employee identification number, gross pay, deduction and net pay to nearest paisa as shown below:

Employee id	*Gross pay*	*Tax*	*Other deductions*	*Net Pay*
4562	6000	600	1500	3900

(c) Check your program with appropriate sample data.

11.3 Write FORMAT statements to present the results of solving quadratic equations of Example 6.4 in the following form:

	a	b	c	xr_1	xr_2	xi_1	xi_2	Remarks
Case 1								
Case 2								
.								
.								
Case 5								

with neat placement of columns.

11.4 Write a FORMAT statement for Exercise 6.10 in the following form:

Customer A/c No.	Deposit	Years	Interest	Amount Due
48945	10000	3	5609	15609
.	.	.	.	.
.	.	.	.	.
.	.	.	.	.

11.5 A power series representation of Sin x is Sin x = $x - x^3/3! + x^5/5! - x^7/7! + x^9/9!$ .... Write a program to evaluate Sin x to 4 significant digits for the values of x = 0.5, – 2.5, 22.2 radians. Print the result in a nice format indicated below:

x	Sin x from series	No. of terms used	Sin x from library	% Error

11.6 Present the results of Exercise 7.10 using a nice format.

11.7 Present the results of Exercise 7.11 using a nice format.

11.8 Present the results of Exercise 7.12 using a nice format.

11.9 Present the results of Exercise 7.5 for the following values of a, b, c, d in a nice format.

x	a	b	c	d	f(x)
0.5	2.5	3.5	4.5	1.5	
1.5	2.5	3.5	4.5	1.5	
1.0	2.5	3.5	4.5	1.5	
2.5	2.5	3.5	4.5	1.5	

11.10 Present the results of Exercise 7.8 in a tabular form with appropriate headings.

12. *Processing Strings of Characters*

Learning Objectives

In this chapter we will learn:

1. How to declare, read and write strings of characters
2. How to manipulate strings of characters using intrinsic functions provided by Fortran 90
3. How to develop functions to process strings

So far we have considered only the simplest types of data available in Fortran 90, namely, integers and reals. These data types are sufficient for most numerical applications. Fortran 90 provides many new features to solve non-numeric problems among which is the facility to declare and manipulate variables in which strings of characters are stored. In this chapter we will learn how to declare variable names in which strings of characters are stored and how to manipulate strings.

12.1 THE CHARACTER DATA TYPE

We have seen that a real or an integer is stored in a memory box which is 32 bits long (In some recent computers this is being increased to 64 bits). A character, on the other hand, is coded as an 8 bit byte. Thus more than one character can be stored in a memory box. In Fortran 90 a variable name can be declared to store an arbitrary number of characters. If we want to store the string of characters raja in a variable name first-name we may write:

```
CHARACTER (LEN = 4 ) :: first_name
first-name = "raja"
```

Observe that a string is enclosed in double quotes. There are other equivalent forms of declaring variable names which store strings. They are:

```
CHARACTER ( 4 ) :: first_name
```

or

```
CHARACTER :: first_name * 4
```

or

```
CHARACTER * 4 :: first_name
```

If a number of variable names are to be declared each storing strings of different lengths we need a different declaration. For example, if first-name is to store "Pankaj" middle-name "Ram" and last name "Gupta". We may use the following declarations:

```
CHARACTER (LEN = 6 ) :: first_name
CHARACTER (LEN = 3 ) :: middle_name
CHARACTER (LEN = 5) :: last_name
```

or

```
CHARACTER :: first_name * 6, middle_name *3, last_name *5
```

The first form is lengthy but perhaps clearer. The second form is shorter and reasonably easy to understand. We will use either of these as appropriate. Fortran 90 allows integer expression (using constants only) for length specification. For example, we can write:

```
CHARACTER (LEN = 8-2) :: first_name
```

or

```
CHARACTER :: first_name * ( 8 -2 )
```

In the second form, the integer constant expression should be enclosed within parentheses.

Character strings may be read into character variable name by using list directed input statement as follows:

```
CHARACTER :: first_name *6, last_name *5
READ *, first_name, last_name
```

Data →"Pankaj", "Gupta"

A READ statement with FORMAT specification can also be used as shown below:

```
   CHARACTER :: first_name *6, last_name *5
   READ 20, first_name, last_name
20 FORMAT (A6, A5)
```

(Data) : PankajGupta

Observe that the edit descriptor in FORMAT for reading characters is Aw where w is the width of the character field to be read. Thus first 6 characters from the input data line will be stored in first_name and the next 5 characters in last_name. If A format is used the data string need not be enclosed by quote marks.

If the character length declaration is smaller than the number of characters in input data then the input data is truncated and the number of characters specified in the declaration is stored. For example if we write:

```
CHARACTER :: first_name *6
READ *, first_name
```

Data → "Pankajam"

Pankaj is stored in first_name. The letters a and m in the input string are ignored. The same happens when FORMAT declaration is used as shown below:

```
   CHARACTER :: first_name *6
   READ 20, first_name
20 FORMAT (A6)
```

Data → Pankajam

Pankaj is again stored in first_name. The letters a and m are truncated.

If the data string is shorter than that declared in CHARACTER then blanks are added to the right of the string to make up the length. For example, if we write:

```
CHARACTER :: first_name *6
READ *, first_name
```

Data → "Pank"

then Pank▯▯ (where ▯ is a blank space) will be stored in first_name.

Besides reading strings into variable names declared as CHARACTER, we may also assign strings using assignment statement as shown below:

```
CHARACTER :: first_name *6, last_name *5
first_name = "Pankaj"
last_name = "Gupta"
```

If a string longer than the declared length of the character variable is assigned to it then the excess characters at the right end of the string are truncated. For example, if we write

```
first_name = "Pankajam"
```

then Pankaj will be assigned to first_name. On the other hand, if a shorter string is assigned, blanks are appended on its right and the string of current length is stored. For example, if we write

```
first_name = "Pank"
```

then Pank□□ is stored in first_name.

12.2 MANIPULATING STRINGS

Fortran 90 provides one operator for operating on strings. This is the *concatenation operator.* A concatenation operator symbol is // (two slashes). It is used to join two strings.

Example Program 12.1 Use of concatenation operator

```
!PROGRAM 12.1
!ILLUSTRATING CONCATENATION OPERATOR //

PROGRAM concatenate_1
  IMPLICIT NONE
  CHARACTER :: first_name*20,last_name*20,full_name*40
  PRINT *, "Type first name and last name"
  READ *,first_name,last_name
  full_name = first_name//last_name
  PRINT *, full_name
END PROGRAM concatenate_1
```

Example Program 12.1 reads the first_name and last_name of a person separately and prints a single string full_name. The main problem with this program is that we do not know ahead of time the exact length of first_name and last_name. We have arbitrarily allocated 20 characters for each of these. If they are short as shown below:

```
first_name = "Ramnath"
last_name = "Yadav"
```

then full_name will be printed as:

```
full_name = Ramnath             Yadav
               |← 13 blanks →|
```

The blanks after Yadav are not objectionable. However, those separating first_name and last_name give a bad appearance. They should be removed. There is an intrinsic function in

Fortran 90 TRIM which removes the trailing blanks. If we write TRIM (first_name) then only Ramnath with no trailing blanks will be obtained. This is done in Example Program 12.2. Observe that the function TRIM removes all trailing blanks. We have thus concatenated a blank space between first_name and last_name to get the full_name.

Example Program 12.2 Use of TRIM function

```
!PROGRAM 12.2
!ILLUSTRATES CONCATENATION WITH TRIM

PROGRAM concatenate_2
   IMPLICIT NONE
   CHARACTER :: first_name*20,last_name*20,full_name*40
   PRINT *," Type first name and last name"
   READ *,first_name,last_name
   full_name = TRIM(first_name)//" "//last_name
   PRINT *,full_name
END PROGRAM
```

Another useful intrinsic function provided by Fortran 90 is LEN. If we write LEN (*string*) the number of characters in *string* is returned by the function.

For example, if first_name = "Ramaswamy" then LEN (first_name) = 9.

Another useful feature of Fortran 90 is a method of picking substrings of strings. This is done by following the character constant or character variable name by two integers or integer expressions separated by a colon and enclosing these in parentheses. For example, if we write "Ramaswamy" (3:5) it will return a substring "mas", that is, the substring starting with the 3rd character of "Ramaswamy" upto and including the fifth character. If we write "Ramaswamy" (:3) it will return the first three characters, namely, "Ram". On the other hand, if we write "Ramaswamy" (5:) then substring starting with the 5th character upto end of string will be returned. In this case it is the substring "swamy". Instead of a string constant we may use string variable name. For example if

person_name = "Sivaramakrishnan".

Then person_name (5:8) = "rama",

person_name (:4) = "Siva"

and person_name (9:) = "krishnan"

If i = 5, then person_name (i : i + 8) = "ramakrish"
person_name (i : i) = "r"
person_name (i : i – 1) = null (i.e., no character)

The last intrinsic function we will consider in this section is ADJUSTL. This removes all leading blanks from a string. Thus:

ADJUSTL ("□□□ Ramanath") = "Ramanath"

The argument of ADJUSTL can also be a character variable name in which case the leading blanks in the string stored are removed. For example if:

```
person_name = "□□□ krishnan"
```

then

```
person_name = ADJUSTL (person_name)
```

will store "krishnan" in person_name.

We will now use these facilities to write some string manipulation programs.

Example 12.1

Given a set of names a program is needed which will count the number of a's in each name and print it along with the name. We will assume that the input is presented in the form

Ramanathan
Arunkumar
Sivaramakrishnan
Rajaraman
End_of_names

We have written Example Program 12.3 to solve this problem. Observe that we have assumed that no name exceeds 40 characters as per the FORMAT edit specification A40. After reading a name, the trailing blanks are removed by the TRIM function. We now check if the end of list of names is reached. Observe the use of the relational operator == to compare two strings. This is allowed in Fortran 90. (There are some intrinsic functions also to compare strings. We will discuss why they are needed later in this chapter.) The program exits if the End_of_names is reached. If the End_of_names is not reached, the program finds out the number of characters in a name. Observe that LEN_TRIM function finds the length of the trimmed name. This function rather than LEN should be used as LEN will also count the trailing blanks in name. The next DO loop counts the number of 'a's or 'A's in the name. Observe how a single character is picked and compared with "a" or "A". If there is a match, count is incremented. After all characters in a name are compared the name and count of 'A's are printed.

Example Program 12.3 Counting a or A in names

```
!PROGRAM 12.3
!ILLUSTRATES MANIPULATION OF STRINGS

PROGRAM count_a
   IMPLICIT NONE
   CHARACTER(LEN=40)::name,temp_name
   INTEGER :: count,name_length,i
outer : DO
      READ 40,temp_name
      40 FORMAT(A40)
      name = TRIM(temp_name)
      IF(name == "End_of_names") EXIT
      name_length = LEN_TRIM(name); count = 0
   inner : DO i=1,name_length
         IF(name(i:i) == "a" .OR. name(i:i) == "A") count=count+1
         END DO inner
      PRINT 50,temp_name,count
      50 FORMAT(1X,A40,2X,"Count of a's =",2X,I2)
   END DO outer
END PROGRAM count_a
```

Example 12.2

We will now write a program to rearrange a set of names. We assume that the names are given in one of the following forms:

First name ▯ or .middle name ▯ or .Last name
First name ▯ or .Last name
First name
First name ▯ or .middle initial ▯ or .Last name
First initial ▯ or .middle name ▯ or .Last name

For example

Ram Kumar Gupta
S. Raju
Arvind
Ram K. Vepa
V. Ram Kumar
A.V. Ganesh
V.K.R.V. Rao

The names are to be rearranged with last name first

Gupta Ram Kumar
Raju S.
Arvind
Vepa Ram K.
Kumar V. Ram
Ganesh A.V.
Rao V.K.R.V.

The strategy of the algorithm is given as Algorithm 12.1.

Algorithm 12.1 Algorithm to rearrange names

DO until End_of_names reached
  Read full name
  Trim trailing and leading blanks
  Find length of full name
  Scan full name from right to left till the first occurrence of a blank or. Note this position and call it p
  Copy substring from position (p + 1) to end of substring into last name
  Concatenate to the right of last name, first name, initials, etc.
  Print the rearranged names

Example Program 12.4 Rearranging names

```
!PROGRAM 12.4
!PROGRAM TO REARRANGE NAMES

PROGRAM rearrange_names
  IMPLICIT NONE
  INTEGER :: length_name,i,p
  CHARACTER(LEN=40) :: last_name,first_name
  CHARACTER(LEN=80) :: full_name
  CHARACTER(LEN=40) :: temp_name
  DO
    p=0
    READ 40,full_name
    40 FORMAT(A80)
    temp_name = TRIM(full_name)
    length_name = LEN_TRIM(temp_name)
    temp_name = ADJUSTL(temp_name)
    IF(temp_name == "End_of_names") EXIT
    DO i=length_name,1,-1
    IF(temp_name(i:i) == " ".OR.temp_name(i:i) ==".") THEN
      p=i
      EXIT
      ENDIF
    END DO
    IF(p/=0) THEN
      last_name = temp_name(p+1:length_name)
      first_name = temp_name(1:p)
      full_name = TRIM(last_name)//" "//first_name
    ENDIF
    PRINT 50,full_name
    50 FORMAT(1X,A80)
  END DO
END PROGRAM rearrange_names
```

Algorithm 12.1 is implemented as Example Program 12.4. The program is a straightforward implementation of the algorithm. Observe the usefulness of the simple method of extracting substrings from strings.

Example 12.3 Insertion of a string in a given string

The following information is given:

given_string, string_to_insert, position from which it is to be inserted p.

For example given a string: "Sivasubramanian"

string_to_insert = "rama"

position at which to insert: from 5th character.

Resulting string: "Siva*rama*subramanian"

↓

Inserted string

This is fairly straightforward. A program to do this is given as Example Program 12.5.

Example Program 12.5 Inserting a string in a given string

```
!PROGRAM 12.5
!PROGRAM TO INSERT A STRING

PROGRAM insert
   IMPLICIT NONE
   INTEGER :: p,i
   CHARACTER(LEN=40) :: given_string,string_to_insert,temp
   CHARACTER(LEN=80) :: new_string
   PRINT *, "Type an integer p which is position to insert string"
   PRINT *, "Type given string and the string to be inserted "
   READ *,p,given_string,string_to_insert
   new_string=given_string(1:p-1)//TRIM(string_to_insert)//given_string(p:)
   PRINT *," The new string is ", new_string
END PROGRAM insert
```

12.3 COMPARING CHARACTER STRINGS

Fortran 90 standard defines a Fortran Character set which consists of

26 upper case letters A, B, C, D ...... Z
10 decimal digits 0, 1, ... 9
Underscore character _
21 special characters

Lower and upper case letters are considered identical in identifiers. This set is shown in Table 12.1.

Table 12.1 Fortran Characters

A B C D E F G H I J K L M N O P Q R S T U V W X Y Z
0 1 2 3 4 5 6 7 8 9
_ (underscore)
□ = + − * / ( ) , . ' : ! " % & ; < > ? $

Fortran characters are different from the actual set of characters available on computers. Most computers use the character set called ASCII set (American Standard Code for Information Interchange) now standardized by International Standards Organization. This set is allowed in character strings used in Fortran 90 programs. Characters are coded as sequence of binary digits and stored in computer's memory. Each code has a decimal equivalent. These decimal numbers can be ordered in ascending sequence called a *collating sequence*. The ASCII collating sequence is given in Table 12.2.

Table 12.2 ASCII Codes for Characters

Left Digits ↓ / Right Digit →	0	1	2	3	4	5	6	7	8	9
3			▯	!	"	#	$	%	&	.
4	(	)	*	+	,	–	.	/	0	1
5	2	3	4	5	6	7	8	9	:	;
6	<	=	>	?	@	A	B	C	D	E
7	F	G	H	I	J	K	L	M	N	O
8	P	Q	R	S	T	U	V	W	X	Y
9	Z	[	\	]	^	_	'	a	b	c
10	d	e	f	g	h	i	j	k	l	m
11	n	o	p	q	r	s	t	u	v	w
12	x	y	z	{	|	}	~			

Observe that in the ASCII code the codes for upper and lower case characters are different. We have used the symbol ▯ to represent a blank or space.

Codes 00 to 31 and code 127 represent special control characters which cannot be printed. Code 00 represents null and code 32 represents a blank character. The code for Z, for example, is 90 (in decimal) and its binary representation in the computer would be 1011010.

Strings of characters can be compared in Fortran 90. It is safe to use intrinsic functions to compare strings as these functions use ASCII character ordering. These functions are given in Table 12.3.

Table 12.3 Intrinsic Functions to Compare Character Strings

LGT (s1, s2) is equivalent to s1 > s2
LGE (s1, s2) is equivalent to s1 > = s2
LLE (s1, s2) is equivalent to s1 < = s2
LLT (s1, s2) is equivalent to s1 < s2

The intrinsic function LGT ("Aswin", "Ela") gives a result *false* as A has a smaller value in the collating sequence compared to E.

LGT ("Adam", "Adamant") is *false* as blank is smaller than all characters in the collating sequence of ASCII code. The relational operator = = can be used to compare character strings.

Fortran 90 also has intrinsic functions to find ASCII code of a character and the character corresponding to ASCII digits. These are ACHAR (Integer) which returns ASCII character corresponding to Integer. Integer should lie within the range of the ASCII codes (126 ≥ Integer ≥ 32).

A companion function which returns a character corresponding to its integer code is IACHAR (ch) which returns the position of the character ch in the ASCII collating sequence. For example, IACHAR (+) = 43.

We will now take examples in string manipulation which uses this function.

Example 12.4

An identifier in a language is defined as a string of 8 or less characters with the first character being an uppercase letter. The other characters are uppercase letters or digits or underscores. No other characters are allowed. A function has to be developed which will return *true* if it is a legal identifier and *false* otherwise. An appropriate message is to be printed.

Example Program 12.6 Checking legal identifiers

```
!PROGRAM 12.6
!FUNCTION TO CHECK IF IDENTIFIER IS LEGAL

LOGICAL FUNCTION check_id(identifier)
   IMPLICIT NONE
   CHARACTER(LEN=8),INTENT(IN):: identifier
   INTEGER :: i
   IF(LGE(identifier(1:1),"A") .AND.LLE(identifier(1:1),"Z")) THEN
      check_id = .TRUE.
   ELSE
      check_id = .FALSE.
      PRINT *,"First character not upper case"
   ENDIF
   DO i=2,8
      IF(identifier(i:i) == " ") EXIT
      IF((LGE(identifier(i:i),"A") .AND.LLE(identifier(i:i),"Z")) .OR. &
         (LGE(identifier(i:i),"0") .AND.LLE(identifier(i:i),"9")) .OR. &
         (identifier(i:i) == "_")) THEN
            check_id = check_id .AND. .TRUE.
      ELSE
         check_id = .FALSE.
         PRINT *,"Character ",i," illegal"
      ENDIF
   END DO
END FUNCTION check_id

!MAIN PROGRAM
PROGRAM legal_identifier
   IMPLICIT NONE
   LOGICAL :: check_id
   CHARACTER(LEN=8) :: var_name
   DO
   READ 50,var_name
   50 FORMAT(A8)
   IF(var_name == "****") EXIT
   IF(check_id(var_name)) THEN
      PRINT *,"Identifier name legal"
   ELSE
      PRINT *,"Identifier illegal"
   ENDIF
   ENDDO
END PROGRAM legal_identifier
```

Example Program 12.6 implements these rules. Observe that we have used the function LGE, LLT. In this case, as collating sequence of upper case letters and digits are clearly known ("A" < "Z" and "0" < "9"). We could use the statement:

```
IF ((identifier (i : i) > = "A") .AND.(identifier (i : i) < = "Z" )) .OR. &
   ((identifier (i : i) > = "0") .AND.(identifier (i : i) < = "9")) .OR. &
   (identifier (i : i) = = "_")) THEN
   check_id = check_id .AND. .TRUE.
ELSE
   check_id = .FALSE.
   PRINT *, "character", i, "illegal"
ENDIF
```

in Example Program 12.6.

Example 12.5

In this example we will write a FUNCTION which will return .TRUE. if a string is a Palindrome and .FALSE. if it is not. A string is said to be a Palindrome if it reads the same when read from left to right or right to left. For example, ABBA is a Palindrome. ADA is a Palindrome. A famous Palindrome is ABLE WAS I ERE I SAW ELBA. The algorithm to find if a string is a Palindrome is simple. We compare the first and last character. If they match we compare the 2nd character with the 2nd character from the end. If at any time there is no match we leave the function after setting Palindrome as FALSE. If all matches succeed we return from the FUNCTION with Palindrome = .TRUE.

This algorithm is translated into a Fortran 90 program (Example Program 12.7).

Example Program 12.7 Finding if a string is a palindrome

```
!PROGRAM 12.7
!FINDING IF A STRING IS A PALINDROME

PROGRAM pal
   IMPLICIT NONE
   CHARACTER(LEN=80) :: string
   LOGICAL :: palindrome
   DO
   READ "(A)",string
   string = TRIM(string)
   IF( string == "*") EXIT
   IF(palindrome(string)) THEN
      PRINT *,string
      PRINT *,"String is a palindrome"
   ELSE
      PRINT *,string
      PRINT *,"String is not a palindrome"
   ENDIF
   ENDDO
END PROGRAM pal
```

```
LOGICAL FUNCTION palindrome(char_str)
  IMPLICIT NONE
  CHARACTER(LEN=*),INTENT(IN)::char_str
  INTEGER :: i,j,length
  LOGICAL :: temp = .TRUE.
  length = LEN_TRIM(char_str)
  DO i=1,(length/2)
     j = length -i + 1
     IF(char_str(i:i) == char_str(j:j) ) THEN
        temp = .TRUE.
     ELSE
        temp = .FALSE.
           EXIT
     ENDIF
  END DO
  palindrome = temp
END FUNCTION palindrome
```

Observe the declaration:

CHARACTER (LEN = *), INTENT (in) :: string

in the LOGICAL FUNCTION Palindrome (char_string). The length declaration LEN = * specifies the length as arbitrary as we do not know the length the character string to be passed by the main program. Observe that in the DO loop (in the FUNCTION) pairs of characters taken from the two ends of the string are compared. If any of them does not match temp is set to .FALSE. and control leaves the loop. If all pairs match then Palindrome is .TRUE. The variable name temp is initialized to .TRUE. Thus in the degenerate case if the string has only one character temp is set .TRUE. A null character string is also declared a Palindrome by this program.

Observe in the calling program the statement READ "(A)", string. This format allows character srings of arbitrary length to be read.

Example 12.6

A program will be developed which gives the decimal equivalent of a number written using a Roman numeral system. For example, the decimal equivalent of XVIII is 18, that of CLXVI is 166. Table 12.4 gives the symbols used in Roman numeral system and their decimal equivalents.

Table 12.4 Roman Numeral and Decimal Equivalents

Roman	M	D	C	L	X	V	I
Decimal	1000	500	100	50	10	5	1

Algorithm 12.2 gives the method of converting a Roman numeral string $r_1\ r_2\ r_3\ ....r_n$ to decimal.

Algorithm 12.2 Roman to decimal conversion

decimal equivalent = 0
Read a character r_1 from the input roman string
    v_1 = value of r_1 (As given in Table 12.4)
    DO i = 2 to length of roman string
    v_2 = value of roman string (i)
        if $v_1 \geq v_2$ *then*
            add v_1 to decimal equivalent
        else
            subtract v_1 from decimal equivalent
        endif
            $v_1 \leftarrow v_2$
    END DO
add v_1 to decimal equivalent
Print decimal equivalent

Example Program 12.8 Decimal equivalent of roman numeral

```
!PROGRAM 12.8
!PROGRAM TO FIND DECIMAL EQUIVALENT OF ROMAN NUMERAL

PROGRAM roman_no
   IMPLICIT NONE
   CHARACTER(LEN=20)::roman
   INTEGER :: dec_eqv=0,length,dec_1,dec_2,value,i
   CHARACTER :: rom_1,rom_2
   PRINT *, "Type a roman numeral "
   READ "(A)",roman
   length = LEN_TRIM(roman)
   rom_1 = roman(1:1)
   dec_1 = value(rom_1)
   DO i=2,length
      rom_2 = roman(i:i)
      dec_2 = value(rom_2)
      IF(dec_1 >= dec_2) THEN
      dec_eqv = dec_eqv + dec_1
      ELSE
      dec_eqv = dec_eqv - dec_1
      ENDIF
      dec_1 = dec_2
   END DO
   dec_eqv = dec_eqv + dec_1
   PRINT 25,roman,dec_eqv
   25 FORMAT("Decimal equivalent of ",A20," is ",I10)
END PROGRAM roman_no
```

```
INTEGER FUNCTION value(rom)
  IMPLICIT NONE
  CHARACTER :: rom
  SELECT CASE(rom)
    CASE("M")
    value = 1000
    CASE("D")
    value = 500
    CASE("C")
    value = 100
    CASE("L")
    value = 50
    CASE("X")
    value = 10
    CASE("V")
    value = 5
    CASE("I")
    value = 1
    CASE DEFAULT
    PRINT *,"Error in roman numeral"
    PRINT *,rom
    END SELECT
END FUNCTION value
```

Example Program 12.8 has been developed using Algorithm 12.2. Observe the use of separate FUNCTION to find the decimal values of roman numerals. The program is a straightforward translation of Algorithm 12.2 into Fortran 90. To check the correctness of the program we have traced it with an input string CMXXIV. The trace is given in Table 12.5.

Table 12.5 Trace of Example Program 12.8

Input string CMXXIV
len = 6, rom_1 = C, dec_1 = 100, dec_equiv = 0

rom_1	dec_1 (initial)	i	rom_2	dec_2	dec_equiv	dec_1 (final)
C	100	2	M	1000	−100	1000
	1000	3	X	10	900	10
	10	4	X	10	910	10
	10	5	I	1	920	1
	1	6	V	5	919	5
	out of loop				924	

We have used many intrinsic functions for characters in this chapter. There are many more functions available in Fortran 90. These are consolidated and placed in Appendix A.

SUMMARY

1. Fortran 90 has a data type called CHARACTER data type to store characters. A variable name is declared CHARACTER with a specification of the length of strings which can be stored in it. If first_name is a string of 8 characters it may be declared in one of many equivalent forms:

   ```
   CHARACTER (LEN = 8) :: first_name
   CHARACTER * 8 :: first_name
   CHARACTER :: first_name * 8
   CHARACTER ( 8 ) :: first_name
   ```

   If a variable name s stores a single character it is declared as:

   ```
   CHARACTER :: s
   ```

   More than one character string may be declared in a single declaration. For example,

   ```
   CHARACTER :: x * 8, y * 4, z * 3
   ```

   declares x as a string of length 8, y as a string of length 4 and z as a string of length 3
2. A character string constant is a string of characters enclosed in double quotes as shown below:

   "This is a string"

   If double quote itself is part of a string, single quotes may be used to enclose the string. For example, 'Rama said "I am happy"'
3. Character strings may be read by a list directed read statement. In this case the input data string is enclosed in double quotes. They may also be read using FORMAT statement. A is the edit descriptor for reading characters. A descriptor A*w* reads *w* characters. In this case strings need not be enclosed in double quotes.
4. Character strings may be printed using list directed output or output with FORMAT. A*w* is the edit descriptor to print *w* characters.
5. Fortran 90 provides an operator // to concatenate (join together) two strings.
6. A substring of a string str may be picked by writing str (p : k) which is a substring starting with p^{th} character of str ending with k^{th} character, str (p:p) picks a single character, namely, the pth character of str.
7. There are many intrinsic functions in Fortran 90 for character variables. Among the ones used often are LEN (str) which gives the number of characters in str, TRIM (str) which removes the trailing blanks in str, LEN_TRIM(str) which gives the number of characters in str after removing trailing blanks, ADJUSTL (str) which removes the leading blanks in str and a set of functions to compare strings. A list of intrinsic functions is given in Appendix A.

EXERCISES

12.1 Write a program to delete all vowels from a sentence. Assume that the sentence is not more than 80 characters long.

12.2 Write a program to count the number of words in a sentence.

12.3 Write a program which will read a line and squeeze out all blanks from it and output the line with no blanks.

12.4 Write a program which will read a line and delete from it all occurrences of the word 'the'.

12.5 Write a program to encript a sentence using the strategy of replacing a letter by the next letter in its collating sequence. Thus every A will be replaced by B, every B by C and so on and finally Z will be replaced by A. Blanks are left undisturbed.

12.6 Write a program which takes a set of names of individuals and abbreviates the first, middle and other names except the last name by their first letter. For example RAMA RAO would become R.RAO and SURESH KUMAR SHARMA would become S.K.SHARMA.

12.7 Write a program to read a sentence and substitute every occurrence of the word 'POST" by the word 'DAK'. Use the following sentence to test your program.

Input line: "The postman came from the post office bringing post"

Output line: "The dakman came from the dak office bringing dak"

12.8 Write a program to convert decimal numbers to hexadecimal. For example the hexadecimal equivalent of

$$\begin{aligned} AC8D &= A * 16^3 + C * 16^2 + 8 * 16^1 + D * 16^0 \\ &= 10 * 16^3 + 12 * 16^2 + 8 * 16 + 13 \\ &= 44173 \end{aligned}$$

12.9 Write a program to convert decimal numbers to hexadecimal. For example the hexadecimal equivalent of 43919 is AB8F.

12.10 Write a program to count the number of occurrences of any two vowels in succession in a line of text. For example, in the following sentence:

"Please allow a studious girl to read behavioural science"

such occurrences are:

ea, io, ou, ea, io, ou, ie.

Observe that in a word such as studious we have counted "io" and "ou" as two separate occurrences of two consecutive vowels.

12.11 Write a program to arrange a set of names in alphabetic order. The sorting is to be on the first two characters of the last name. For example, given the list:

Ramaswamy. R.
Arumugam. B
Agarwal. K.
Sarma. A.B.
Bagchi. D.R.

the sorted list should be

Agarwal. K.
Arumugam. B.
Bagchi. D.R.
Ramaswamy. R.
Sarma. A.B.

13. *Program Examples*

Learning Objectives

In this chapter we will learn:

1. How to simulate a small computer
2. How to develop a complete program from a given problem statement
3. How to write complex FORMAT statements

Many important instruction types in Fortran 90 have now been discussed and it will be worthwhile to write complete programs to solve some interesting problems. We will consider three examples in this chapter.

13.1 DESCRIPTION OF A SMALL COMPUTER

In this section we will write a program to simulate the detailed working of a small hypothetical computer. The program is called a simulator program for SMAC (SMALL Computer). This technique of simulating the function of a computer on an already existing computer is widely used for developing software for new computers. Further, this example will illustrate the internal structure and functioning of a typical digital computer.

SMAC has the following specifications:

- 1000 memory locations
- Each memory location can accommodate 5 digits and a sign. We will call a sequence of 5 digits of the form ± XXXXX which can be stored in one location in memory a *word.*
- Each word stored in the memory can be an instruction or a data.
- An instruction for this machine consists of two parts. One part gives the code for the operation to be performed and the other part gives the location in memory where the operand will be found. The sign is assumed to be positive in an instruction and not explicitly shown. Figure 13.1 illustrates this. As the memory has a total of 1000 locations, three digits (000 to 999) are needed to address all the locations.

The remaining 2 digits in the word may be used to code the various operations to be performed by the computer. Theoretically 100 operations may be coded with two digits. We will, however, have a much smaller number of operation codes.

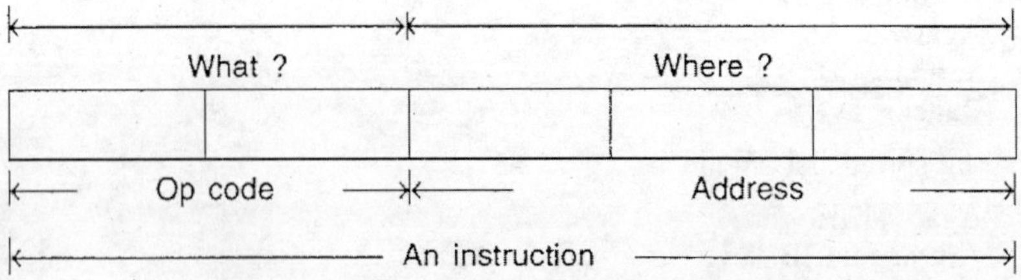

Fig. 13.1 Instruction format of SMAC.

- SMAC has an arithmetic logic unit (abbreviated ALU) where all arithmetic operations are performed. The ALU has a one word length (5 digits) register called an accumulator register where the results of arithmetic operations are temporarily stored. The accumulator register is also used as an implied operand in arithmetic operations.
- The ALU also decodes instructions and supervises execution of programs. It has an instruction register where the operation code and the address part of an instruction are stored and an instruction counter which stores the address of the next instruction to be executed. The first two digits of the instruction register contain the OP code and the last 3 digits the address of the operand to be accessed.
- It has an input unit which reads information from a terminal and an output unit which displays the results on a VDU.

A block diagram of the computer with all the registers used in it is shown in Fig. 13.2. A program for SMAC consists of a set of machine instructions followed by data. Each data (or operand) can have at most 5 digits and a sign.

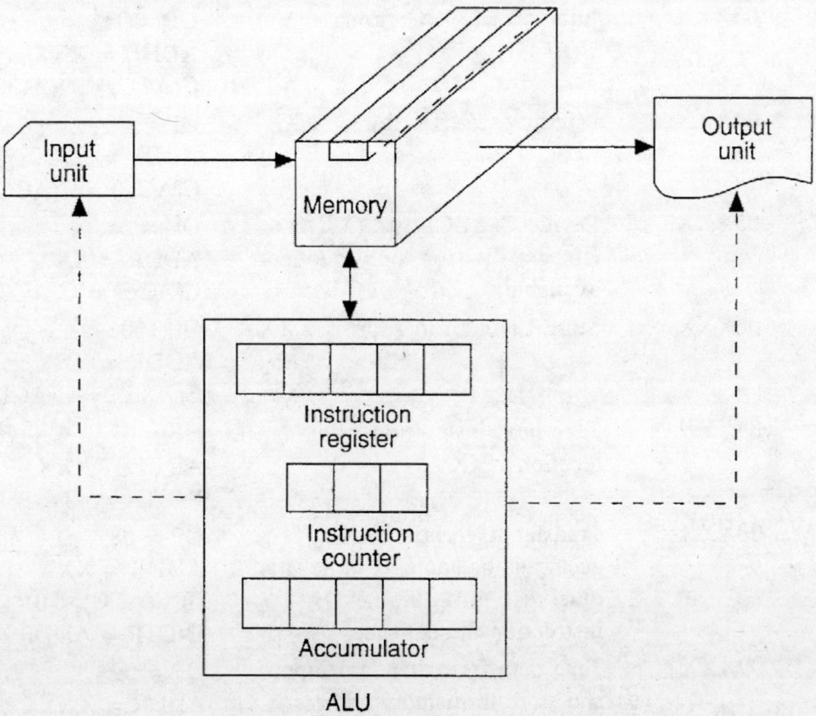

Fig. 13.2 Block diagram of SMAC.

The computer operates in two phases. In the first phase the list of instructions is read and stored in the memory starting from address 000. The end of the list of instructions is signalled by a specially coded line. Data follow this line and are not read during this phase.

In the second phase the instruction counter in the control unit is set to 000 and the instruction stored in memory location 000 is sent to the instruction register. The instruction counter is incremented by one to point to the next instruction to be executed.

The operation code (abbreviated OP code) is retrieved from the instruction register and decoded. The ALU activates the appropriate part of the computer for executing the instruction.

For example, data will be brought in and stored in memory if the instruction is an input instruction. If the instruction is a branch instruction the content of the instruction counter is determined by the executed instruction. If it is not a branch instruction the order given by the current OP code is executed. The instruction counter gives the address of the next instruction in sequence. The list of OP codes and their purpose is given in Table 13.1. The following

Table 13.1 The Meaning of Operation Codes of SMAC

OP code	*Instruction format*	*Meaning*	*Status of registers*
01	01XXX	Clear accumulator and transfer C(XXX) to accumulator	OP = 01 ADDR = XXX C(ACC) = C(XXX)
02	02XXX	Add C(XXX) to accumulator	OP = 02 ADDR = XXX C(ACC) = C(ACC) + C(XXX)
03	03XXX	Subtract C(XXX) from C(ACC)	OP = 03 ADDR = XXX C(ACC) = C(ACC) – C(XXX)
04	04XXX	Multiply C(XXX) by C(ACC)	OP = 4 ADDR = XXX C(ACC) = C(ACC) * C(XXX)
05	05XXX	Divide C(ACC) by C(XXX) (Integer division, only quotient available)	OP = 05 ADDR = XXX C(ACC) = C(ACC)/C(XXX)
06	06XXX	Store C(ACC) in address XXX	OP = 06 ADDR = XXX C(XXX) = C(ACC)
07	07XXX	Take next instruction from location XXX	OP = 07 ADDR = XXX INCTR = ADDR
08	08XXX	Transfer to location XXX if accumulator contents is negative, otherwise go to the next instruction in sequence	OP = 08 ADDR = XXX IF(C(ACC) < 0) THEN INCTR = ADDR
09	09XXX	Take data from standard input and store in memory address XXX	OP = 09 ADDR = XXX
10	10XXX	Print the contents of location XXX	OP = 10 ADDR = XXX
11	11XXX	Stop executing program Address part not used	OP = 11

abbreviations are used:

ACC:	Accumulator
INCTR:	Instruction counter
ADDR:	Address part of an instruction

OP: Operation part of an instruction
OP Code 01: Instruction Form: 01XXX where XXX is the address part of the instruction
Meaning: Clear the accumulator register and enter the contents of memory location XXX in it.

In working with machine instructions it is very important to distinguish between the address of a word in memory and the actual contents of the word. We will use the notation C(XXX) to denote the contents of address XXX. An equal to symbol (=) will be used to denote "replaces".

13.2 A MACHINE LANGUAGE PROGRAM

We will now write a small program in the machine language of this machine to compare the magnitudes of two numbers and output the larger of the two. The program is given as Table 13.2. In the program of Table 13.2 columns 2 and 3 contain the machine instruction executed by the machine. Column 1 tells where this instruction is stored in memory. This information is required to write the program. For instance in the program of Table 13.2 the instruction 08 007 commands that if the contents of the accumulator is negative the next instruction to be executed should be taken from location 007. A programmer should thus know the instruction stored in location 007.

Table 13.2 A Machine Language Program to Find the Larger of Two Numbers

Memory location where machine code is stored	*Machine code*		*Explanation of machine instruction*
	OP code	*Address*	
000	09	100	Read from input a number and store it in 100, C(100) = I
001	09	110	Read from input unit a number and store in 110, C(110) = J
002	01	100	ACC = C(100) = I
003	03	110	ACC = ACC – C (110) = I – J
004	08	007	If ACC < 0 take next instruction from 007
005	10	100	Print C(100) (if I > J Print I)
006	11	000	Stop
007	10	110	Print C(110) (If J > I Print J)
008	11	000	Stop
– 10	00	000	End of machine language program

The last column in Table 13.2 contains comments to enable a reader to understand the program.

The machine language program is typed with the location of the instruction in the first three columns followed by a blank column, the operation code in the next two columns, a blank column and the operand address in the last three columns.

The machine stores the program in memory starting from location 000. The programmer has to remember this in writing a program and start the first instruction from location 000. He has to know, besides, exactly where each one of the machine instructions is stored in memory. The end of the machine language program is indicated by a data line with a negative number. Storing of the program is stopped when this data line is encountered.

13.3 AN ALGORITHM TO SIMULATE THE SMALL COMPUTER

An algorithm to simulate the operation of the small computer is given as Algorithm 13.1. The algorithm is divided into two phases, namely, storing instructions in Phase I and interpreting and executing instructions in Phase II.

Algorithm 13.1 Algorithm to simulate SMAC

Phase I: Storing machine language instructions in memory
Instruction counter = 0
Read a machine instruction
While end of machine language is not reached
{Store machine instruction in memory address given by instruction counter;
Add 1 to instruction counter;
Read a machine instruction};

Control will reach this point as soon as all machine language instructions are stored.

Phase II: Interpreting and executing machine language instructions
Instruction counter = 0 !First instruction is in location 0

Repeat the following steps until the stop instruction of a machine language program is reached.

Step 2.1: Retrieve machine instruction from location given by instruction counter.
Step 2.2: Add 1 to instruction counter
Step 2.3: Branch to actions depending on operation code
OP Code 1: C(ACC) = C(ADDR)
OP Code 2: C(ACC) = C(ACC) + C(ADDR)
OP Code 3: C(ACC) = C(ACC) − C(ADDR)
OP Code 4: C(ACC) = C(ACC) * C(ADDR)
OP Code 5: C(ACC) = C(ACC) / C(ADDR)
OP Code 6: C(ADDR) = C(ACC)
OP Code 7: Instruction counter = ADDR
OP Code 8: *if* C(ACC) < 0 *then* Instruction counter = ADDR
OP Code 9: Read data and store in specified ADDR
OP Code 10: Print contents of specified ADDR
OP Code 11: Stop execution
end of algorithm

13.4 A SIMULATION PROGRAM FOR THE SMALL COMPUTER

A simulation program will now be written to simulate SMAC. The composition of the complete program is shown in Fig. 13.3. The program itself is given as Example Program 13.1. This program is essentially Algorithm 13.1 rewritten in Fortran 90.

Example Program 13.1 implements the two phases specified in the simulation algorithm (Algorithm 13.1). In phase I the machine language program is read and stored in memory starting from location 0. In phase II machine language instructions are retrieved from memory starting from location 0, the operation code is decoded and the specified operation performed. A loop is used to read and store the machine language in the simulated memory. The end of

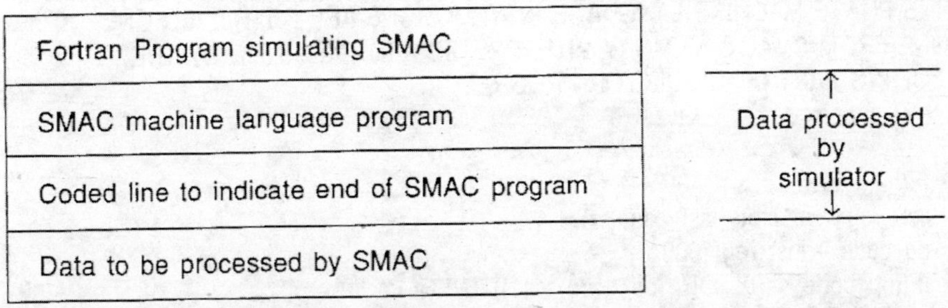

Fig. 13.3 Composition of program and data to use SMAC simulator.

machine language program is indicated by a dummy instruction with a negative number in its location field. Observe that as a data with a negative number in its location field is not a machine instruction it should not be stored in the simulated memory. Thus when we read such a data we should exit from the loop. Another loop simulates the execution of machine instructions.

It is a good programming practice to introduce in the program statements to check whether values assigned to variables go outside the specified range. When such an error is detected informative messages should be printed along with the status of the important registers in the simulated computer. This has been done in the simulation program. If the address part of the instruction or the OP code or the instruction counter assume values outside the specified range then an appropriate message is printed and the program unconditionally jumps to the end of the program stopping further execution. A CASE statement is ideally suited to decode an operation code and perform different actions depending on this code. This is done in the program. When the operation code for stopping execution of SMAC is encountered the variable halt is set equal to .TRUE. and this terminates the machine language program.

Example Program 13.1 Simulator of a small computer

```
!PROGRAM 13.1
!SIMULATOR FOR A SMALL COMPUTER SMAC

PROGRAM smac
   IMPLICIT NONE
   INTEGER :: inst_counter=0,address,op_code,instrn, &
      acc=0, inst_reg,location
   INTEGER,DIMENSION(0:999) :: memory
   LOGICAL :: halt = .FALSE.
!THE FOLLOWING LOOP READS SMAC MACHINE LANGUAGE PROGRAM
!GIVEN AS DATA TO SIMULATOR AND STORES IT IN SMAC'S MEMORY
   DO
   READ 40,location,op_code,address
   40 FORMAT(I3,2X,I2,2X,I3)
      IF(location < 0) EXIT
      instrn = op_code*1000 + address
      memory(inst_counter) = instrn
      inst_counter = inst_counter + 1
      IF(inst_counter > 999) THEN
         PRINT *,"Program overflows memory"
         STOP
      ENDIF
   END DO
!STORING OF PROGRAM OVER
```

```
!IN THIS PHASE MACHINE LANGUAGE INSTRUCTIONS ARE RETRIEVED ONE
!BY ONE FROM SMAC'S MEMORY INTERPRETED AND EXECUTED BY THE
!FOLLOWING PART OF SIMULATOR PROGRAM
   inst_counter = 0
   DO
      IF(halt) EXIT
      inst_reg = memory(inst_counter)
      op_code = inst_reg/1000
      IF((op_code <= 0) .OR. (op_code > 11)) THEN
         PRINT *,"Illegal op-code"
         PRINT *,"inst-counter =",inst_counter," op-code =",op_code
         STOP
      ENDIF
      address = MOD(inst_reg,1000)
      !PRINT *,inst_counter,op_code,address,acc
      inst_counter = inst_counter + 1
      SELECT CASE(op_code)
         CASE(1) !LOAD ACCUMULATOR
         acc = memory(address)
      CASE(2) !ADD TO ACCUMULATOR
         acc = acc + memory(address)
      CASE(3) !SUBTRACT FROM THE ACCUMULATOR
         acc = acc - memory(address)
      CASE(4) !MULTIPLY ACCUMULATOR
         acc = acc * memory(address)
      CASE(5) !DIVIDE ACCUMULATOR
         IF(memory(address) == 0) THEN
            PRINT *,"Attempt to divide by zero"
            PRINT *,inst_counter-1,op_code,address
            STOP
         ENDIF
         acc = acc/memory(address)
      CASE(6) !STORE ACCUMULATOR IN MEMORY
         memory(address) = acc
      CASE(7) !UNCONDITIONAL JUMP
         inst_counter = address
      CASE(8) !CONDITIONAL JUMP
         IF(acc < 0) inst_counter = address
      CASE(9) !READ DATA INTO SMAC'S MEMORY
         READ *,memory(address)
      CASE(10) !PRINT CONTENTS OF SPECIFIED ADDRESS
         PRINT *,memory(address)
      CASE(11) !STOP EXECUTION
         halt = .TRUE.
      END SELECT
   END DO
   PRINT *,"Program terminates normally"
   PRINT *, "Instruction counter = ", inst_counter - 1
END PROGRAM smac
```

The status of all the important registers of SMAC in each execution cycle may be printed by inserting the statement:

```
PRINT *, inst-counter, op-code, address, acc
```

before the statement, inst_counter = inst_counter + 1 in the DO loop. This would give what is known as the execution trace of the machine language program. This is very useful in debugging the machine language program. This is shown as a comment in Example Program 13.1.

13.5 A STATISTICAL DATA PROCESSING PROGRAM

We will consider in this section a typical statistical data processing problem. In this problem a table of the marks obtained by each student in a class along with his/her average marks and division is required. Besides this, the average performance of the class in each subject and some statistical measures relating the performance of the class in different subjects are required. A program for obtaining these will be developed in this section.

The problem specifications are given below:

i. The class has 100 or less students.

ii. Each student takes 6 subjects, namely, Physics, Chemistry, Mathematics, Engineering Science, Technical Arts and Humanities.

iii. The maximum marks in each subject is 100.

iv. A student passes in the first division if he or she gets more than 60 marks on the average, in the second division if he or she gets an average between 50 and 59, in the third division if he or she gets between 40 and 49 and fails if his or her average marks is below 40.

v. The program should compute the average marks and the division of each student.

vi. It is required to find the performance of the class as a whole in each subject. This is indicated by the class average and the standard deviation of the marks in each subject.

vii. It is also required to correlate the performance of the class in different subjects. One wants to draw conclusions such as "if a class does well in mathematics it also does well in Physics", "the performance of a class in Humanities is uncorrelated with its performance in Mathematics". To draw such conclusions a statistical measure called the correlation coefficient is used. The program should compute the matrix of correlation coefficients relating the performance of students in various subjects. The class average, standard deviation, covariance and correlation coefficient are given by the following equations:

The class average in a subject is given by:

$$\overline{m}_i = \frac{1}{N}(\Sigma\, m_{ik}) \qquad k \text{ varying from 1 to N} \qquad (13.1)$$

where m_{ik} is the marks obtained by the kth student in the ith subject and N is the total number of students in the class.

The standard deviation of the marks obtained by students in subject i is given by:

$$s_i = \frac{1}{N}(\Sigma\, (m_{ik} - \overline{m}_i)^2)^{0.5} \qquad k \text{ varying from 1 to N} \qquad (13.2)$$

The covariance between the marks obtained by students in subject i and subject j is defined by the equation

$$c_{ij} = \frac{1}{N} \Sigma (m_{ik} - \overline{m}_i)(m_{jk} - \overline{m}_j) \quad \text{k varying from 1 to } N$$

$$= \frac{1}{N} \Sigma (m_{ik}\, m_{jk} - \overline{m}_i\, \overline{m}_j) \qquad (13.3)$$

From Eq. 13.3 above it is seen that

$$c_{ii} = \frac{1}{N} \Sigma ((m_{ik})^2 - (\overline{m}_i)^2) \quad \text{k varying from 1 to N} \qquad (13.4)$$

The quantity c_{ii} is called the variance of the marks in subject i and is the square of the standard deviation. In the computer c_{ij} will be computed and c_{ii} obtained as a by-product by setting j = i.

The gross structure of the procedure may be stated as:

Algorithm 13.2 Procedure to compute class statistics

while student records are not yet over do
  {Read a student record
  Accumulate count of students
  Find total marks of the student
  Find average marks of the student
  Find the division of the student based on the average marks
  Accumulate marks of students in each subject
  Accumulate products of marks in pairs of subject
  Print name, marks in each subject, total marks,
  average marks and division of the student}

Calculate class average marks for each subject based on accumulated totals and student count.
Calculate standard deviation and correlation coefficients.
Print all the calculated values.
end of algorithm

Example Program 13.2 Class statistics calculation

```
!PROGRAM 13.2
!PROCESSING OF STUDENTS RESULTS

PROGRAM student_grades
  IMPLICIT NONE
  INTEGER :: total_stud = 0,marks_total,i,j,avg_marks
  INTEGER,DIMENSION(6) :: marks,subj_avg,total_subj,std_dev
  REAL,DIMENSION(6,6) :: cross_product,correl
  INTEGER,DIMENSION(6,6) :: covnce
  CHARACTER (LEN = 20) :: name
  CHARACTER (LEN = 15) :: division
  total_subj = 0
  cross_product = 0
```

```
outer_loop:DO
      READ 50,name,marks
    50 FORMAT(A20,6(2X,I3))
  !NAME OCCUPIES FIRST 20 COLUMNS
    !EACH SUBJECT MARKS OCCUPIES 5 COLUMNS RIGHT JUSTIFIED
    IF(TRIM(name) == "end_of_data") EXIT
    total_stud = total_stud + 1
      marks_total = SUM (marks)
    avg_marks = REAL(marks_total)/6.0 + 0.5
    IF(avg_marks >= 60) THEN
      division = "PASSED DIV I"
    ELSE IF(avg_marks >= 50) THEN
      division = "PASSED DIV II"
    ELSE IF(avg_marks >= 40) THEN
      division = "PASSED DIV III"
    ELSE
      division = "FAILED"
    ENDIF
    PRINT 60,name,marks,avg_marks,division
    60 FORMAT (1X,A20,7(3X,I3),2X,A15)
!ACCUMULATE TOTAL IN EACH SUBJECT TO FIND CLASS AVERAGE
    DO i=1,6
    total_subj(i) = total_subj(i) + marks(i)
    DO j=1,6
      cross_product(i,j) = cross_product(i,j) + &
      marks(i)*marks(j)
    END DO
    END DO
  END DO outer_loop
    PRINT 70
    70 FORMAT(33X,"CLASS AVERAGES")
    DO i=1,6
      subj_avg(i) = total_subj(i)/total_stud
    END DO
    PRINT 80 !THIS PRINTS COLUMN HEADING OF TABLES
    80 FORMAT(19X,"PHYS",4X,"CHEM",4X,"MATH",4X,"T.A.",4X,&
    "E.SC",4X,"HSS")
    PRINT 90,subj_avg
    90 FORMAT(1X,"AVERAGES",10X,6(I4,4X))
    DO i=1,6
      DO j=1,6
        covnce(i,j) = cross_product(i,j)/total_stud&
        - subj_avg(i)*subj_avg(j)
      END DO
    END DO
    DO i=1,6
      std_dev(i) = SQRT(REAL(covnce(i,i)))
    END DO
    PRINT 100,std_dev
    100 FORMAT(1X,"STD.DEVIATIONS",4X,6(I4,4X))
    PRINT 110
```

```
    110 FORMAT(25X,"THE VARIANCE COVARIANCE MATRIX")
          PRINT 80 !THIS PRINTS COLUMN HEADINGS OF TABLE
          PRINT 120,((covnce(i,j),j=1,6),i=1,6)
       !THIS PRINTS ROW HEADINGS OF TABLE
    120 FORMAT(1X,"PHYS",14X,6(I4,4X)/1X,"CHEM",14X,&
          6(I4,4X)/1X,"MATH",14X,6(I4,4X)/1X,"T.A.",&
          14X,6(I4,4X)/1X,"E.SC",14X,6(I4,4X)/1X,&
          "HSS.",14X,6(I4,4X))
       DO i=1,6
            DO j=1,6
               correl(i,j) = REAL(covnce(i,j))/&
               (SQRT(REAL(covnce(i,i)*covnce(j,j))))
            END DO
       END DO
            PRINT 130
    130 FORMAT(24X,"THE CORRELATION COEFFICIENT MATRIX")
       PRINT 80 !PRINTING COLUMN HEADINGS OF TABLE
       PRINT 140,((correl(i,j),j=1,6),i=1,6)
    140 FORMAT(1X,"PHYS",14X,6(F4.2,4X)/&
            1X,"CHEM",14X,6(F4.2,4X)/&
            1X,"MATH",14X,6(F4.2,4X)/&
            1X,"T.A.",14X,6(F4.2,4X)/&
            1X,"E.SC",14X,6(F4.2,4X)/&
            1X,"HSS.",14X,6(F4.2,4X))
END PROGRAM student_grades
```

A program written in Fortran 90 to accomplish this is given as Example Program 13.2. We will now examine this program and comment on some of its important features. The array marks (i) stores the marks of each student in the six subjects. Observe that i ranges over 1 to 6. The arrays total-subj (i) and cross-product (i, j) accumulate the subject total and cross product total respectively. These are initialized at the beginning of the program. Observe how whole arrays can be initialized in Fortran 90 using DO loops. The statement following the initialization statements reads the student name in A format and marks in the six subjects. The IF statement following the FORMAT statement (statement 50) needs some comments. As the number of students in a batch is arbitrary the program should be independent of the actual number of students in a batch. This independence is gained by placing a record with the data end_of_data in the name field as the last record of the data. As each record is read in, the IF statement checks to see if it is the last record. If it is the last record the first phase of the program is skipped and control is transferred to the second phase where the class averages are computed. Observe the use of whole array addition function SUM(marks).

Observe the FORMAT statements 60, 70, 80, 90, 100, 110, 120, 130 and 140 which together are planned to give a good looking output with the proper titles. The FORMAT specifications are very important in data processing problems and the reader is urged to spend some time studying the specifications in this example.

A sample input data and the corresponding output are shown in Fig. 13.4. This is mainly intended for the reader to understand the FORMAT and the corresponding printed outputs.

```
INPUT DATA for PROGRAM 13.2
S.Agarwal         30   40   50   60   70   80
A.S.Bhatia        40   30   40   30   40   34
A.B.Chamanlal     70   60   60   50   60   65
S.Duraiswamy      50   35   45   35   40   40
P.R.Ganapathy     40   60   50   70   60   80
V.B.Narayanan     30   30   60   50   35   45
end_of_data       00   00   00   00   00   00

S.Agarwal          30   40   50   60   70   80   55    PASSED DIV II
A.S.Bhatia         40   30   40   30   40   34   36    FAILED
A.B.Chamanlal      70   60   60   50   60   65   61    PASSED DIV I
S.Duraiswamy       50   35   45   35   40   40   41    PASSED DIV III
P.R.Ganapathy      40   60   50   70   60   80   60    PASSED DIV I
V.B.Narayanan      30   30   60   50   35   45   42    PASSED DIV III

                              CLASS AVERAGES
                    PHYS    CHEM    MATH    T.A.    E.SC    HSS
AVERAGES              43      42      50      49      50     57
STD.DEVIATIONS        14      14      11      14      15     19

                      THE VARIANCE COVARIANCE MATRIX
                    PHYS    CHEM    MATH    T.A.    E.SC    HSS
PHYS                 217     135      75     -15      75     25
CHEM                 135     206      95     146     175    217
MATH                  75      95     137      95     100    110
T.A.                 -15     146      95     203     175    260
E.SC                  75     175     100     175     254    289
HSS.                  25     217     110     260     289    385

                      THE CORRELATION COEFFICIENT MATRIX
                    PHYS    CHEM    MATH    T.A.    E.SC    HSS
PHYS                1.00    0.64    0.43   - .07    0.32   0.09
CHEM                0.64    1.00    0.57    0.71    0.77   0.77
MATH                0.43    0.57    1.00    0.57    0.54   0.48
T.A.               - .07    0.71    0.57    1.00    0.77   0.93
E.SC                0.32    0.77    0.54    0.77    1.00   0.92
HSS.                0.09    0.77    0.48    0.93    0.92   1.00
```

Fig. 13.4 Input and output of Example Program 13.2.

13.6 PROCESSING SURVEY DATA WITH COMPUTERS

A frequent use of digital computers is in the tabulation of the results of surveys. The general principles involved in planning the collection of survey data which are to be ultimately processed by digital computers and the programming aspects may be illustrated by considering an example. The example chosen is the processing of questionnaires (distributed to the participants of a short course on computers) shown as Table 13.3.

The objectives of the survey are to obtain the following tables:

i. The distribution of participants by sex.
ii. The average age of the participants.
iii. The distribution of the participants by institutional affiliation.

Table 13.3 A Sample Questionnaire

Please record the answers to the following questions by entering the code number corresponding to your choice in the box on the right of each question.

	Serial Number *For Office use only*		*Column Number*
			1 2 3
1.	What is your sex? Male = 1 Female = 2		4
2.	Age: What was your age at the last birthday? IF it is, say, 25 enter it as:	2 5	5 6
3.	What is your institutional affiliation?		7
	Private Sector	1	
	Educational Institution	2	
	Government Office	3	
	Public Sector Firm	4	
	Research Laboratory	5	
	Unemployed	6	
4.	What is your primary interest?		8
	Science	1	
	Engineering	2	
	Mathematics	3	
	Social Sciences	4	
	Business Data Processing	5	
5.	What is the highest degree obtained by you?		9
	High School	1	
	Intermediate	2	
	Bachelor's	3	
	Master's	4	
	Ph.D.	5	

iv. The distribution of the participants as a function of their primary interest.
v. The distribution of the participants as a function of their educational background.
vi. A table giving the number of participants with specified interests from different types of institutions.

After deciding on the number of groups of each type into which the participants are to be divided it is necessary to uniquely code each group. The division into groups is obvious if sex is the distinguishing characteristic. In this case there are two groups and each one is given a code number. A code 0 is assigned to males and 1 to females. As our aim is to count the number of males and females respectively among the participants it is conveniently done by taking the participants' sex as an array with two components. The first component corresponds to males and the second to females. If the participants are to be grouped using another characteristic, say their educational background, then this information may be coded into a set of integers. These codes may be thought of as subscripts which group the participants into distinct classes.

Example Program 13.3 Questionnaire analysis program principles

```
!PROGRAM 13.3
!SER_NO IS SERIAL NUMBER
!SEX_CODE IS THE CODE FOR SEX
!bad_data IS USED TO COUNT RECORDS WITH ERRORS
!no_quest IS THE NUMBER OF VALID QUESTIONNAIRES

PROGRAM simple_quest
  IMPLICIT NONE
  INTEGER :: ser_no,sex_code,bad_data=0,no_quest=0
  INTEGER,DIMENSION(2):: sex = 0
  DO
    READ 15,ser_no,sex_code
    15 FORMAT(I3,I1)
    IF(ser_no == 0) EXIT
    IF((sex_code == 0) .OR. (sex_code > 2)) THEN
      PRINT 20,ser_no,sex_code
      20 FORMAT(1X,"Error in sex code "," ser no =",I3,&
      "sex code =",I1)
      bad_data = bad_data + 1
    ELSE
      sex(sex_code) = sex(sex_code) + 1
      no_quest = no_quest + 1
    ENDIF
  END DO
  PRINT 30,no_quest,bad_data
  30 FORMAT(1X,"No.of valid questionnaires tabulated =",I3/&
  1X,"No.of bad records= ",I3)
  PRINT 40,sex(1),sex(2)
  40 FORMAT(1X,"No.of Males =",I3,/1X,"No.of Females =",I3)
END PROGRAM simple_quest
```

The main idea used in processing survey questionnaires may be illustrated by considering the following example in which the participants are grouped into two groups, males and females. Assume that one data is typed per participant and that it has a serial number in columns 1 to 3 and the sex code (1 or 2) in column 5. The program to divide the participants into two groups (namely, males and females) is given as Example Program 13.3. In this program the "bin" sex (1) is set up to count data lines which have sex_code = 1 and "bin" sex (2) to count those with sex_code = 1. After clearing sex(1) and sex (2) to zeros a data is read. If the code is less than 1 or greater than 2 then it is illegal. In other words, the data has been wrongly typed. This is indicated in the program and the number of such bad cards are counted. For correct data if sex_code = 1, sex (1) is incremented by 1 and if sex_code = 2 then sex (2) is incremented by 1. Thus the value of the sex_code "sorts" the data into appropriate "bins"

Extension of this technique to the case when the number of groups is greater than 2 is obvious. A program to process the questionnaire given at the beginning of this section is given as Example Program 13.4. The student is urged to study this carefully. It will be observed that the programming job by itself is very simple. Most of the work is in obtaining proper formats for spacing, headings, etc.

Example Program 13.4 Analysis of questionnaire data

```
!PROGRAM 13.4
!QUESTIONNAIRE ANALYSIS PROGRAM
!COMPLETE VERSION WITH FULL FORMATTING

PROGRAM questionnaire
   IMPLICIT NONE
   INTEGER :: sex_code,inst_code,intrt_code,degree_code, &
      age,sum_age=0,avg_age,serial_no,bad_data=0, &
      no_quest=0,i,j,inp_error
   INTEGER :: sex(1:2),degree(1:5),interest(1:5),institution(1:9)
   INTEGER,DIMENSION(6,5) :: inst_vs_intrt
!THE FOLLOWING STATEMENTS CLEAR ALL TABLES
   sex(1) = 0
   sex(2) = 0
   DO i=1,5
      degree(i) = 0
      interest(i) = 0
   END DO
   DO i=1,6
      institution(i) = 0
   END DO
   DO i=1,6
      DO j=1,5
         inst_vs_intrt(i,j) = 0
      END DO
   END DO
   PRINT *,"Output tables"
main_loop : DO
      READ 40,serial_no,sex_code,age,inst_code,intrt_code, degree_code
   40 FORMAT(I3,I1,I2,3I1)
      IF(serial_no == 0) EXIT
      inp_error = 0
      IF((sex_code < 1) .OR. (sex_code > 2)) THEN
            inp_error = 1
            PRINT *,"Error in sex code. Serial no =",serial_no
      ENDIF
      IF((age < 0).OR.(age > 75)) THEN
         inp_error = 1
      PRINT *,"Error in age.Serial no =",serial_no
      ENDIF
      IF((inst_code < 1).OR.(inst_code > 6)) THEN
         inp_error = 1
         PRINT *,"Error in institution code.Serial no =", serial_no
      ENDIF
```

```
      IF((intrt_code < 0).OR.(intrt_code > 5)) THEN
         inp_error = 1
         PRINT *,"Error in interest code.Serial no =",serial_no
      ENDIF
      IF((degree_code < 0).OR.(degree_code > 5)) THEN
         inp_error = 1
         PRINT *,"Error in degree code.Serial no=",serial_no
      ENDIF
      IF(inp_error == 1) THEN
         bad_data = bad_data + 1
      ELSE
         sex(sex_code) = sex(sex_code) + 1
         institution(inst_code) = institution(inst_code)+1
         interest(intrt_code) = interest(intrt_code)+1
         degree(degree_code) = degree(degree_code)+1
         sum_age = sum_age + age
         no_quest = no_quest + 1
         inst_vs_intrt(inst_code,intrt_code) = &
         inst_vs_intrt(inst_code,intrt_code) + 1
      ENDIF
   END DO main_loop
      avg_age = sum_age/no_quest
      PRINT 50,no_quest,bad_data
      50 FORMAT(1X,"NO.of valid questionnaires tabulated=",I3/&
      1X,"No.of bad data records=",I3)
      PRINT 60,avg_age
      60 FORMAT(1X,"The average age of the group=",I3)
      PRINT 70,sex
      70 FORMAT(1X,/1X,"Distribution of participants by sex"/&
      1X,"Males =",i3,"Females=",I3)
      PRINT 80,institution
      80 FORMAT(1X,/"Distribution of participants by ",&
      "institution",//1X,"PVT=",I3,"EDN ="I3,"GOVT=",I3,&
      "P.SEC=",I3,"RES=",I3,"UNEM=",I3)
      PRINT 90,interest
      90 FORMAT(1X,/"Distribution of participants by",&
      "interest",//1X,"SCIENCE=",I3,"ENGG=",I3,"MATH=",I3,&
      "SOC.SC =",I3,"BUSINESS=",I3)
      PRINT 100,degree
      100 FORMAT(1X,/"Distribution of participants by",&
      "qualification"//1X,"HSC=",I3,"INTER=",I3,"BA/BSc",I3,&
      "M.A./MSc=",I3,"Phd=",I3)
      PRINT 110
      110 FORMAT(1X,"Institutional affiliation related to interest")
      PRINT 120
      120 FORMAT(11X,"PVT.",2X,"EDN",2X,"GOVT",2X,"PUB.",2X,&
      "RES",2X,"UNEMP")
      PRINT 130,((inst_vs_intrt(i,j),j=1,6),i=1,5)
      130 FORMAT(1X/1X,"SCIENCE",3X,6(I3,3X)/&
            1X,"ENGG.",5X,6(I3,3X)/&
            1X,"MATHS.",4X,6(I3,3X)/&
            1X,"SOC.SC.",3X,6(I3,3X)/&
            1X,"BUSINESS",2X,6(I3,3X))
END PROGRAM questionnaire
```

The input and output Example Program 13.4 (Questionnaire analysis program) are given in Fig. 13.5.

```
INPUT DATA of PROGRAM 13.4
124025343
128135463
129145212
130038321
131128110
132030000
133145123
134145654
140135454
141065544
142099334
000000000
   Output tables
   Error in sex code. Serial no = 124
   Error in interest code.Serial no = 128
   Error in sex code. Serial no = 130
   Error in degree code.Serial no = 131
   Error in sex code. Serial no = 132
   Error in institution code.Serial no = 132
   Error in interest code.Serial no = 132
   Error in degree code.Serial no = 132
   Error in sex code. Serial no = 141
   Error in sex code. Serial no = 142
   Error in age.Serial no = 142
   No. of valid questionnaires = 4
   No. of bad data records = 7
   The average age of the group = 42

Distribution of participants by sex

   Males = 4 Females = 0

Distribution of participants by institution

   PVT = 1 EDN = 1 GOVT = 0 P.SEC = 1 RES = 0 UNEM = 1

Distribution of participants by interest

   SCIENCE = 1 ENGG = 1 MATH = 0 SOC.SC = 0 BUSINESS = 2

Distribution of participants by qualification

   HSC = 0 INTER = 1 BA/BSc = 1 M.A./MSc = 2 Phd = 0

Institutional affiliation related to interest
                PVT.    EDN   GOVT  P.SEC.     RES  UNEMP
SCIENCE          0       1     0     0          0     0
ENGG.            1       0     0     0          0     0
MATHS.           0       0     0     0          0     0
SOC.SC.          0       0     0     0          0     0
BUSINESS         0       0     0     1          0     1
```

Fig. 13.5 Input and output of questionnaire analysis program.

EXERCISES

13.1 Write a machine language program for SMAC which will pick the largest of 10 numbers. Test this program with the simulator.

13.2 Write a machine language program for SMAC which will add two 10 component vectors.

13.3 It is desired to add more instructions to SMAC. Some of the machine instructions and their meanings are given below. Rewrite SMAC with these additions and test it.

OP code: 21 Instruction form: 21XXX
Meaning: C(ACC) = C(ACC) + XXX
OP code: 22 Instruction form: 22XXX
Meaning: C(ACC) = C(ACC) – XXX
OP code: 31 Instruction form: 31XXX
Meaning: Shift C(ACC) right by XXX positions.

13.4 Income-tax rules define three categories of persons for tax computation:

i. Residents
ii. Resident but not ordinarily resident
iii. Non-resident

Definition of resident:
If a person satisfies any one of the following rules he is considered a resident during a specified year.

i. He lived in India for at least 182 days during the year.
ii. He maintained a home in India for at least 182 days and lived for atleast 30 days in India during the year.
iii. He lived in India in the four preceding years for at least 365 days and lived in India for 60 days during the given year.

Definition of resident but not ordinarily resident:
A person is considered ordinarily resident in India during a year if he satisfies both the conditions given below in addition to being a resident during the year:

i. If during preceding 10 years he is a resident of India for at least 9 years.
ii. If during preceding seven years he lived in India for a total of 760 days or more.

If he does not satisfy any one of the conditions above he is considered a resident but not ordinarily resident.

Non-resident
A person who is not resident in India is called non-resident.

i. Obtain a decision table to decide into which category a person falls given the required data.
ii. How many previous years' data are required to decide about the status of a person in a given year?
iii. Write a computer program which prints out the category to which a person belongs given the required data.

13.5 A sociologist conducts a survey among college students and collects the following data:

1. Age
2. Sex
3. Marital status
4. No. of years in college
5. Percentage marks obtained in the last 3 examinations
6. Time spent in studies/week
7. Time spent in extra-curricular activities/week
8. Financial support (Parents/guardian/government/charitable organization/other (Here the student may get support from more than one source).
9. No. of cinemas seen per month
10. Opinion about usefulness of education (very useful/doubtful/useless):

    i. Prepare a code to convert the information to one which would be suitable for processing on a computer.

    ii. Write a program to tabulate the results.

13.6 A hospital keeps a file of blood donors in which each record has the format:

Name:	20 columns
Address:	40 columns
Age:	2 columns
Blood type:	2 columns (Type A, B, O or AB)

Write a program to print out all blood donors whose age is below 25 and blood is type B.

13.7 Develop a program to process grades of students with the following specifications: Students take 5 courses and are given grades A, B, C, D or F. A grade equals 10 points, B grade 8 points, C grade 6 points, D grade 4 points and F grade 0 points. The program should read a student record in the format:

Roll No.	Name	Grade in 5 subjects
← 5 cols. →	← 20 cols. →	← 5 cols →

and print the output in the form:

42565 A.B.C. RAO ABCBA 8.4

Performance index is calculated by adding point equivalent in 5 subjects and dividing by 5. The performance index for the above example is (10 + 8 + 6 + 8 + 10)/5 = 8.4.

The program should also find the average performance of students in each course by computing the class average points.

14. *Procedures with Array Arguments*

Learning Objectives

In this chapter we will show:

1. How arrays can be used as dummy arguments of procedures.

2. The use of MODULES and explicit INTERFACE to facilitate communication between calling and called programs.

3. The need to ensure that the DIMENSIONS of arrays used as dummy arguments in procedures match with the corresponding arrays used in calling program.

4. How to declare and use temporary arrays in procedures.

5. How to use function names (both external and intrinsic) as arguments of procedures.

14.1 INTRODUCTION

In Chapter 10 we wrote a program to evaluate a polynomial (Example Program 10.4). We have rewritten it as a function in Example Program 14.1.

Example Program 14.1 Polynomial evaluation

```
!PROGRAM 14.1
!A FUNCTION TO EVALUATE A POLYNOMIAL OF DEGREE 10
FUNCTION polynomial(x,a)
   IMPLICIT NONE
   REAL,INTENT(IN) :: x
   REAL,DIMENSION(0:10),INTENT(IN) :: a
   INTEGER :: i !LOCAL VARIABLE
   REAL :: polynomial
   polynomial = a(10)
   DO i=10,1,-1
      polynomial = a(i-1) + x*polynomial
   END DO
END FUNCTION polynomial
!LISTING OF CALLING PROGRAM
PROGRAM poly_1
   IMPLICIT NONE
   INTEGER ::i
   REAL,DIMENSION(0:10)::p
   REAL :: z,poly_value,polynomial
   !p(0)+p(1)*z+p(2)*z**2+p(3)*(z**3)+...+p(10)*(z**10) IS THE
   !POLYNOMIAL TO BE EVALUATED
   READ *,z,p
   poly_value = polynomial(z,p)
   PRINT *,"z =",z
   PRINT *,"polynomial coefficients =",p
   PRINT *,"polynomial value =",poly_value
END PROGRAM poly_1
```

Observe that the dummy arguments used in the FUNCTION polynomial are:

x (a scalar), and a which is an array of polynomial coefficients a(0), a(1) ....a(10). The degree of the polynomial which can be evaluated is 10 as the DIMENSION of a is declared as (0:10) in the DIMENSION declaration. The DO loop also uses a(0) to a(10). The calling program can thus only evaluate polynomial of degree 10 as there is no dummy argument to specify the degree of the polynomial to be evaluated. Writing a FUNCTION of this type is rigid and does not serve any purpose as the primary reason for writing a FUNCTION is to evaluate the value of a polynomial of arbitrary degrees. We have thus rewritten the FUNCTION as Example Program 14.2. In this program we have introduced a third dummy argument n which specifies the degree of the polynomial to be evaluated. The calling program (PROGRAM poly) calls the FUNCTION with an actual argument m which will be used as the value of n during the FUNCTION evaluation. Observe that the maximum degree of the polynomial in the calling program is max_degree which is specified as a PARAMETER and equals 30. Observe that the declaration for a specifies its DIMENSION as (0:n). The value of the actual parameter passed by the calling program will be substituted for n. This method of writing a function allows it to be used much more flexibly.

Example Program 14.2 Polynomial evaluation—generalized

```
!PROGRAM 14.2
!A FUNCTION TO EVALUATE A POLYNOMIAL

FUNCTION polynomial(x,a,n)
      IMPLICIT NONE
      REAL,INTENT(IN) :: x
      INTEGER,INTENT(IN) :: n
      REAL,DIMENSION(0:n),INTENT(IN) :: a
      INTEGER :: i !LOCAL VARIABLE
      REAL :: polynomial
      polynomial = a(n)
      DO i=n,1,-1
      polynomial = a(i-1) + x*polynomial
   END DO
END FUNCTION polynomial
!THE ABOVE FUNCTION IS CALLED AS SHOWN BELOW

PROGRAM poly_2
   IMPLICIT NONE
   INTEGER ::m,i
   INTEGER,PARAMETER :: max_degree=30
   REAL,DIMENSION(0:max_degree)::p
   REAL :: z,poly_value,polynomial
   !p(0)+p(1)*z+p(2)*(z**2)+p(3)*(z**3)+...+p(10)*(z**10) IS THE
   !POLYNOMIAL TO BE EVALUATED
   READ *,z,m
   READ *,(p(i),i=0,m)
   poly_value = polynomial(z,p,m)
   PRINT *,"z =",z,"m =",m
   PRINT *,"polynomial coefficients"
   PRINT *,(p(i),i=0,m)
   PRINT *,"polynomial value =",poly_value
END PROGRAM poly_2
```

There is yet another method of writing the function which is quite flexible. This is shown as Example Program 14.3. In this case the DIMENSION declaration of a is:

REAL, DIMENSION (0:), INTENT (IN) :: a

Observe that the upper value of DIMENSION is not specified. This method of declaration is allowed in FUNCTION and SUBROUTINE. It is called an *assumed shape array* declaration. If the DIMENSION is given as DIMENSION (:) then it is assumed that the lower bound of the array is 1. We have explicitly given the lower bound as 0 as the polynomial coefficients are assumed to be a(0), a(1), ...a(max_degree). The extent of the array can be found by the intrinsic function SIZE (a). Thus the actual dimension of the array passed by the calling program is found in the FUNCTION and used in the DO loop. Fortran has traditionally allowed separate compilation of procedures and appropriate information for this is needed. Fortran 90 requires that when an assumed shape array is used by a procedure (FUNCTION or SUBROUTINE) a program which calls it must have an *explicit* INTERFACE which gives all the declarations used by the procedure. Thus in Example Program 14.3 the calling program has an INTERFACE block shown. Observe that the INTERFACE block starts with INTERFACE and ends with END INTERFACE. The FUNCTION statement and all the declarations used by the FUNCTION are contained in the INTERFACE block. Observe that the declarations of local variables are not needed in the INTERFACE block. The actual procedure used by the FUNCTION *is not included* in the INTERFACE block. After duplication of the declarations relevant to the dummy arguments, the END FUNCTION statement is written. If an INTERFACE is used the FUNCTION name (in this case polynomial) should not be declared in the main PROGRAM.

Example Program 14.3 Illustrating use of explicit INTERFACE

```
!PROGRAM 14.3
!EVALUATING POLYNOMIAL WITH AN ASSUMED ARRAY SHAPE

FUNCTION polynomial(x,a)
  IMPLICIT NONE
  REAL,INTENT(IN) :: x
  REAL,DIMENSION(0:),INTENT(IN) :: a
  INTEGER :: i,n !LOCAL VARIABLES
  REAL :: polynomial
  n = SIZE(a)
  polynomial = a(n)
  DO i=n,1,-1
    polynomial = a(i-1) + x*polynomial
  END DO
END FUNCTION polynomial
!THE PROGRAM IS CALLED AS SHOWN BELOW

PROGRAM poly_3
  IMPLICIT NONE
  INTEGER ::i,m
  INTEGER,PARAMETER :: max_degree=30
  REAL,DIMENSION(0:max_degree)::p
  REAL :: z,poly_value,polynomial
  !INTERFACE BLOCK STARTS HERE
  INTERFACE
    FUNCTION polynomial(x,a)
```

```
      IMPLICIT NONE
         REAL,INTENT(IN) :: x
         REAL,DIMENSION(0:),INTENT(IN) :: a
         REAL :: polynomial
      END FUNCTION polynomial
   END INTERFACE
   READ *,z,m
   READ *,(p(i),i=0,m)
   poly_value = polynomial(z,p)
   PRINT *,"z =",z
   PRINT *,"polynomial coefficients =",p
   PRINT *,"polynomial value =",poly_value
END PROGRAM poly_3
```

Instead of using an INTERFACE specification we can also define a MODULE in which the data used by a set of procedures are declared. This MODULE is made available to all the procedures that need the data. We define a data MODULE for the polynomial evaluation problem in Fig. 14.1.

```
MODULE poly_data
   IMPLICIT NONE
   SAVE
   INTEGER, PARAMETER :: max_degree = 30
   REAL, DIMENSION (0 : max_degree) :: a
END MODULE poly_data
```

Fig. 14.1 Defining a data MODULE.

Let us first examine the MODULE defined in Fig. 14.1. The MODULE starts with the key word MODULE followed by an identifier which is the name of the MODULE. The MODULE body follows. The MODULE ends with the statement END MODULE *module name*. In the body of the MODULE we begin with the statement IMPLICIT NONE which will enforce the declaration of all variables in the MODULE. The statement SAVE following it is to ensure that data stored in the variables in the MODULE are not lost between invocations of the MODULE. (We will explain this point in greater detail in 16.9) This is followed by the declaration of the array of coefficients of the polynomial. Observe that we have allowed upto 30th degree polynomial.

Example Program 14.4 Illustrates use of data MODULE

```
!PROGRAM 14.4
!ILLUSTRATING USE OF DATA MODULE
!EVALUATING A POLYNOMIAL

MODULE poly_data
   IMPLICIT NONE
   SAVE
   INTEGER,PARAMETER :: max_degree = 5
   REAL,DIMENSION(0:max_degree) :: a
END MODULE poly_data
```

```
FUNCTION polynomial(x,n)
   USE poly_data
   IMPLICIT NONE
   REAL,INTENT(IN) :: x
   INTEGER,INTENT(IN) :: n
   INTEGER :: i !LOCAL VARIABLE
   REAL :: polynomial
   polynomial = a(n)
   DO i=n,1,-1
      polynomial = a(i-1) + x*polynomial
   END DO
END FUNCTION polynomial
!LISTING OF CALLING PROGRAM

PROGRAM poly_4
   USE poly_data
   IMPLICIT NONE
   INTEGER ::m
   !m IS THE DEGREE OF THE POLYNOMIAL TO BE EVALUATED
   REAL :: z,poly_value,polynomial
   z=1.2 ;m = 5 ; a = (/1,2,3,4,5,6/)
   poly_value = polynomial(z,a)
   PRINT *,"z =",z,"m =",m
   PRINT *,"polynomial coefficients =",a
   PRINT *,"polynomial value =",poly_value
END PROGRAM poly_4
```

In Example Program 14.4 in the FUNCTION subprogram we have the statement USE poly_data as the first statement. This is equivalent to "inserting" the declarations in the data MODULE poly_data as part of the data declarations in the FUNCTION polynomial. Observe that the data MODULE poly_data declares only the coefficients of the polynomial. Thus the dummy arguments of FUNCTION polynomial are the polynomial variable x and the degree of the polynomial n. There is no change in the computational statements used in the FUNCTION. In the calling program also we insert USE poly_data before IMPLICIT NONE. Thus storage is allocated for the coefficients of the polynomial. The main purpose of the DATA MODULE (in this example) is to provide a storage area in which data can be stored and made accessible to a set of procedures. The same data area is shared by PROGRAM poly_4 and FUNCTION polynomial. Thus there is no need for specifying the polynomial coefficients as dummy argument in FUNCTION polynomial. The degree of the polynomial to be evaluated is, however, required as a dummy argument. The degree should be less than or equal to max_degree specified in MODULE poly_data.

In this section we have examined 4 different methods of calling a FUNCTION which has an array as a dummy argument. We compare these 4 methods in Table 14.1.

14.2 PROCEDURES WITH MULTI-DIMENSIONAL ARRAYS

In this section we will examine how multi-dimensional arrays are passed as arguments to

Table 14.1 Comparison of Calling Methods

Example Program	*Dummy argument*	*Dummy array DIMENSION declaration*	*Remarks*
14.1	x, a	Fixed = 10. Both Calling and Called program have identical array size.	Inflexible. Meant only for degree 10 polynomial. Poor design.
14.2	x, a, n	Variable. Value of array size passed by calling program.	Flexible. Can go upto polynomial degree max_size.
14.3	x, a	Assumed shape array. Explicit INTERFACE needed in calling program to convey SIZE of actual array.	Flexible. More general than 14.2 as SIZE of a is not a dummy argument.
14.4	x, n	Array defined in DATA MODULE and made available to both calling and called programs. Array need not be explicity passed.	Flexible. As DATA MODULE is shared global storage can be altered by any of the programs sharing it.

procedures. The most important point to remember is that the main memory of computers consists of a sequence of addresses and is a one dimensional array as shown in Fig. 14.2.

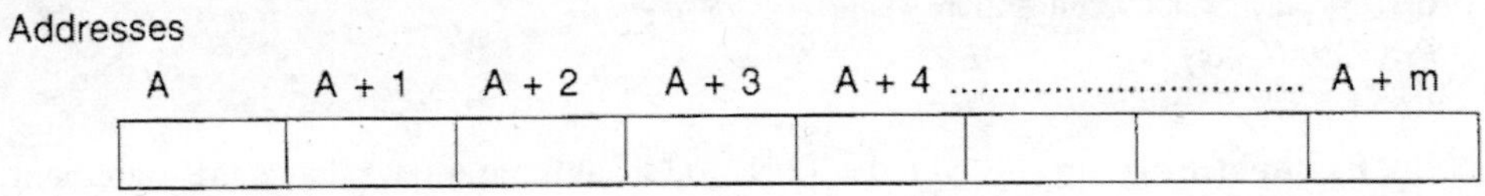

Fig. 14.2 Main memory.

To store a multi-dimensional array, the elements have to be "linearly ordered" and fitted into a one-dimensional memory. Thus an array t of DIMENSION (2, 3) shown in Fig. 14.3

$$\begin{bmatrix} t(1, 1) & t(1, 2) & t(1, 3) \\ t(2, 1) & t(2, 2) & t(2, 3) \end{bmatrix}$$

Fig. 14.3 Array of DIMENSION (2, 3).

has to be appropriately ordered. In Fortran 90 the convention is to *store arrays columnwise* as we saw in Chapter 10. Thus t will be stored as shown in Fig. 14.4. This has an important

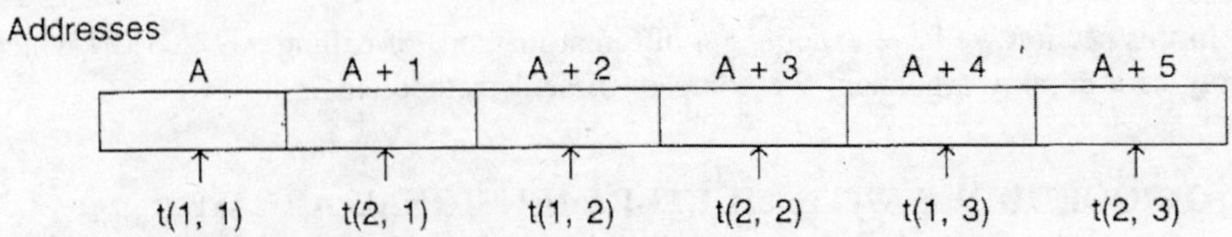

Fig. 14.4 Linearly storing a two-dimensional array.

bearing while associating dummy arrays with actual arrays in called programs. Thus if an array d in a calling program is declared as:

```
REAL, DIMENSION (2, 3) :: d
```

and that in the subroutine is declared as:

```
REAL, DIMENSION (2, 3) :: b
```

then the first element of d is associated with the first element of b and the rest columnwise as shown in Fig. 14.5.

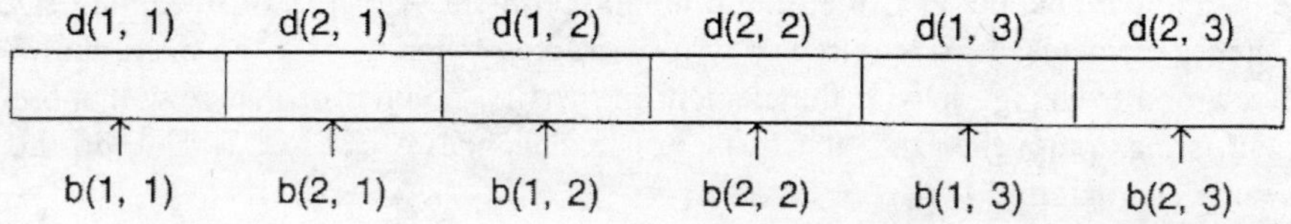

Fig. 14.5 Association of arrays in calling and called programs.

Arrays of different DIMENSIONs can also be associated in a similar way. For example, if an array f in the calling program is:

```
REAL, DIMENSION (3, 2) :: f
```

and that in the subroutine is:

```
REAL, DIMENSION (2, 3) :: b
```

the association of elements will be as shown in Fig. 14.6.

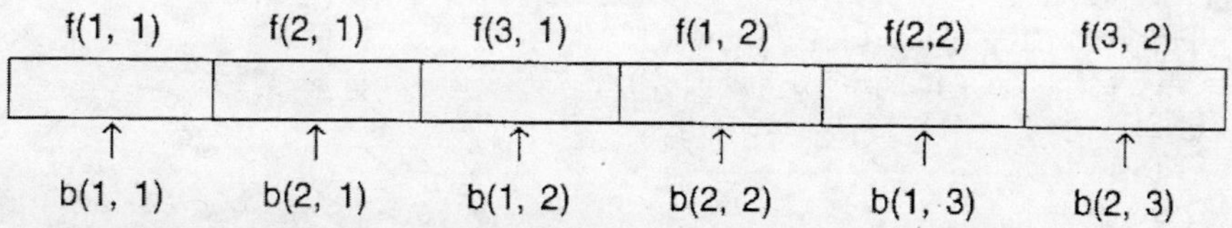

Fig. 14.6 Association of arrays of two different DIMENSIONs.

Even a one dimensional array in a calling program can associate with a 2 dimensional array in a called program. If the array b in the calling program is:

```
REAL, DIMENSION (2, 3) :: b
```

and that in the called program is

```
REAL, DIMENSION (6) :: g
```

the association of elements will be as shown in Fig. 14.7.

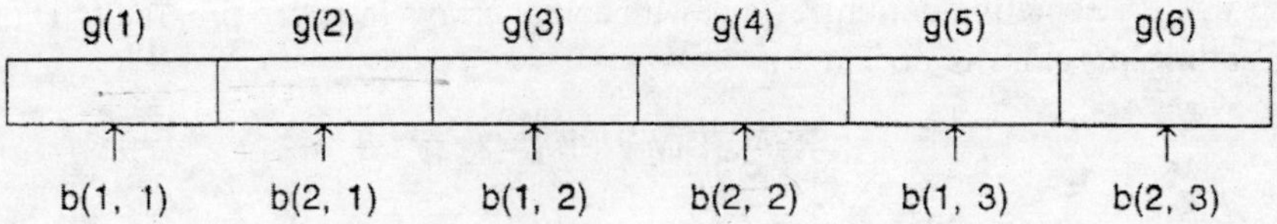

Fig. 14.7 Association of a one-dimensional array in calling program with a 2 dimensional array in the subroutine.

Example 14.1

We will consider in this example how multi-dimensional arrays are defined in a SUBROUTINE and how they are called. Consider the following problem. A matrix of maximum size 10 × 10 has integer elements. It is required to write a SUBROUTINE to pick the maximum element in each row and exchange it with the element in the first column of that row. If more than one element is maximum then the first of them is exchanged. A SUBROUTINE to do this is given as Example Program 14.5.

Example Program 14.5 Putting maximum value of each row of a matrix as first element—Version 1

```
!PROGRAM 14.5
!EXAMPLE OF A SUBROUTINE WITH A TWO DIMENSIONAL ARRAY AS
!DUMMY ARGUMENT

SUBROUTINE max_row(g_matrix,rows,cols)
   IMPLICIT NONE
   INTEGER,DIMENSION(10,10) :: g_matrix
   INTEGER,INTENT(IN) :: rows,cols
   INTEGER :: i,j !LOCAL VARIABLES
   DO i=1,rows
   DO j=1,cols
      IF(g_matrix(i,j) > g_matrix(i,1)) THEN
      CALL exchange(g_matrix(i,j),g_matrix(i,1))
      ENDIF
      END DO
   END DO
END SUBROUTINE max_row

PROGRAM sample_1
   IMPLICIT NONE
   INTEGER,DIMENSION(10,10) :: h
   INTEGER :: m_rows,n_cols,i,j
   READ *,m_rows,n_cols
   !READ MATRIX ROW-WISE
   DO i=1,m_rows
      READ *,(h(i,j),j=1,n_cols)
   END DO
   !PRINT MATRIX ROW WISE
   CALL mat_print(h,m_rows,n_cols)
   !CALL SUBROUTINE TO TRANSFORM THE MATRIX
   CALL max_row(h,m_rows,n_cols)
```

```
!PRINT TRANSFORMED MATRIX ROW-WISE
   CALL mat_print(h,m_rows,n_cols)
END PROGRAM sample_1
SUBROUTINE exchange(x,y)
   IMPLICIT NONE
   INTEGER :: x,y,temp
   temp = x
   x = y
   y = temp
END SUBROUTINE exchange

SUBROUTINE mat_print(g,row,col)
   INTEGER :: row,col,i,j
   INTEGER,DIMENSION(10,10) :: g
   DO i=1,row
      PRINT *,(g(i,j),j=1,col)
   END DO
END SUBROUTINE mat_print
```

Observe that the DIMENSION of the dummy matrix g_matrix in the SUBROUTINE is declared 10×10 (fixed) corresponding to the maximum size of matrix specified. The actual matrix and its size are the dummy arguments of the SUBROUTINE. SUBROUTINE max_rows uses another SUBROUTINE exchange. The calling program also specifies the DIMENSION of the matrix to be transformed, namely, h, as 10×10. The actual size of h is read as variables m_rows and n_cols. The following points are again emphasized:

i. SUBROUTINE max_row transforms the matrix h sent to it by the called program as per the rules specified and leaves it in storage. Control is returned to the calling program to the statement immediately following the CALL statement.
ii. A SUBROUTINE should be made as general as possible.
iii. A SUBROUTINE can call other SUBROUTINES to accomplish its job. In this example SUBROUTINE exchange is CALLED by the SUBROUTINE max_row.
iv. Observe that the DIMENSION of the matrix in the called and calling program are identical. We will have to examine whether this can be relaxed.
v. As SUBROUTINEs are separately compiled the same variable names may occur in many SUBROUTINEs or main program without any ambiguity as long as they are local variables. If a value stored in a variable name is to be transmitted to a SUBROUTINE it can be done only through the argument list or by using MODULEs.
vi. The arguments of the calling program agree in number, order, dimension and mode with those of the dummies in the SUBROUTINE.

In this example we have assumed that the DIMENSION of dummy array in the SUBROUTINE and the calling program are equal and constant. A question which arises is whether the DIMENSION of array declared in the SUBROUTINE can be kept as a variable and the actual dimension passed using a dummy argument. We have done this in the case of a one-dimensional array in the example in the last section. The question is whether it can be done for multi-dimensional arrays also. The answer is yes. It is, however, essential to ensure that the dimensions of the dummy array match those declared for the corresponding actual array in the calling program. We will illustrate the problems which would arise if this is not done using the SUBROUTINE mat_print written as part of Example Program 14.5. Suppose the matrix h, which is to be printed, has m_rows = 3 and n_cols = 4 and its elements are as shown below.

$$h = \begin{bmatrix} 9 & 6 & 3 & 4 \\ 7 & 3 & 7 & 4 \\ 8 & 7 & 4 & 2 \end{bmatrix}$$

Suppose we declare the DIMENSION of g in the SUBROUTINE mat_print as:

```
INTEGER, DIMENSION (row, col) :: g
```

and not as:

```
INTEGER, DIMENSION (10, 10) :: g
```

which is the DIMENSIONs declared for h in the calling program.

The dummy array g is taken as 3 × 4 as row = m_rows = 3 and col = n_cols = 4. As the actual array h is stored columnwise as per its DIMENSION (10 × 10) declared in the calling PROGRAM sample_1 it is stored as shown in Fig. 14.8. The correspondence between the elements

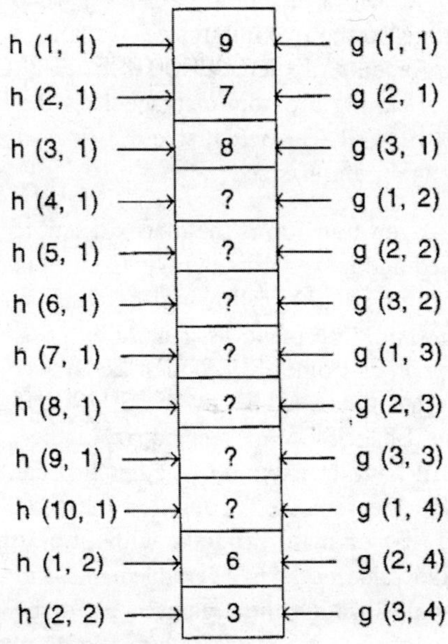

Fig. 14.8 Establishing correspondence between the elements of h and g.

of h and g is established as shown in Fig. 14.8 by the compiler. The SUBROUTINE will thus print the 3 × 4 array as shown below.

$$\begin{bmatrix} 9 & ? & ? & ? \\ 7 & ? & ? & 6 \\ 8 & ? & ? & 3 \end{bmatrix}$$

where ? indicates undefined values. The correct method of dealing with adjustable dimensions is to pass the DIMENSION declared in the calling program to the SUBROUTINE (called program) as an actual argument in the CALL. This is shown in Example Program 14.6.

Example Program 14.6 Printing a matrix—need to match dimensions of calling and called programs

```
!PROGRAM 14.6
!PROGRAM ILLUSTRATES THE CORRECT DIMENSION DECLARATION FOR
!MULTI DIMENSIONAL ARRAYS

PROGRAM print_matrix
  IMPLICIT NONE
  INTEGER,PARAMETER::max_rows=10,max_cols=10
  INTEGER,DIMENSION(max_rows,max_cols) :: h
  INTEGER :: n_rows,n_cols,i,j
  READ *,n_rows,n_cols
  READ *,((h(i,j),i=1,n_rows),j=1,n_cols)
  !MATRIX h READ ROW-WISE BY READ
  CALL mat_print(h,max_rows,max_cols,n_rows,n_cols)
  !SUBROUTINE mat_print PRINTS THE MATRIX
END PROGRAM print_matrix
!SUBROUTINE TO PRINT MATRIX
SUBROUTINE mat_print(g,maxr,maxc,row,col)
  IMPLICIT NONE
  INTEGER :: maxr,maxc
  INTEGER,DIMENSION(maxr,maxc) :: g
  INTEGER,INTENT(IN) :: row,col
  INTEGER :: i,j !LOCAL VARIABLES
  DO i=1,row
    PRINT *,(g(i,j),j=1,col)
  END DO
END SUBROUTINE mat_print
```

An important point to observe is that the declared DIMENSION of multi-dimensional arrays in a calling program *should exactly match* with that of the called program. If this is not done the results will be wrong. Unfortunately such an error will not be detected by the compiler. This is probably the single most common cause of bugs in Fortran 90. The reader must thus take special note of this point.

Can we avoid sending the DIMENSIONs declared in the calling program to the SUBROUTINE through explicit arguments? The answer is yes.

Use of a data MODULE is an appropriate method in this problem. Example Program 14.5 is modified and written as Example Program 14.7 using data MODULE. Observe that we have declared the matrix h in a data MODULE and made the MODULE available to the SUBROUTINEs that need them. By doing this it is not necessary to explicitly pass matrices via dummy arguments to SUBROUTINEs. Only one copy of h is maintained. Observe that the original matrix h is overwritten by the transformed matrix.

Example Program 14.7 Putting maximum value of each row of a matrix as first element—Version 2

```
!PROGRAM 14.7
!USE OF DATA MODULE WITH TWO DIMENSIONAL ARRAY

MODULE matrix_data
   IMPLICIT NONE
   SAVE
   INTEGER,PARAMETER :: max_rows=20,max_cols=20
   INTEGER,DIMENSION(max_rows,max_cols) :: h
END MODULE matrix_data
PROGRAM sample_2
   USE matrix_data
   IMPLICIT NONE
   INTEGER :: m_rows,m_cols,i,j
   READ *,m_rows,m_cols
   !READ MATRIX ROW-WISE
   DO i=1,m_rows
      READ *,(h(i,j),j=1,m_cols)
   END DO
   !PRINT INPUT MATRIX ROW-WISE
   CALL mat_print(m_rows,m_cols)
   !TRANSFORM MATRIX
   CALL max_row(m_rows,m_cols)
   !PRINT TRANSFORMED MATRIX ROW-WISE
   CALL mat_print(m_rows,m_cols)
END PROGRAM sample_2

SUBROUTINE max_row(rows,cols)
   USE matrix_data
   IMPLICIT NONE
   INTEGER,INTENT(IN) :: rows,cols
   INTEGER :: i,j !LOCAL VARIABLES
   DO i=1,rows
      DO j=1,cols
      IF(h(i,j) > h(i,1)) THEN
         CALL exchange(h(i,j),h(i,1))
         ENDIF
      END DO
   END DO
END SUBROUTINE max_row

SUBROUTINE mat_print(row,col)
   USE matrix_data
   IMPLICIT NONE
   INTEGER,INTENT(IN) :: row,col
   INTEGER :: i,j !LOCAL VARIABLE
   DO i=1,row
      PRINT *,(h(i,j),j=1,col)
   END DO
END SUBROUTINE mat_print
```

```
SUBROUTINE exchange(x,y)
   IMPLICIT NONE
   INTEGER,INTENT(INOUT) :: x,y
   INTEGER :: temp !LOCAL VARIABLE
   temp = x
   x = y
   y = temp
END SUBROUTINE exchange
```

Example 14.2

A program which determines the number of data points in each one of a set of assigned intervals will now be developed. Such a grouping of data into intervals is known as a frequency table and is used extensively in statistics.

The strategy we will adopt to develop the program is as follows:

i. Given the data array to be grouped in a frequency table find the maximum and minimum values of the data in the array.
ii. Given the maximum and minimum values of the data and the interval size, the number of intervals is found by dividing (maximum data – minimum data) by the size of the interval and rounding it to the next higher integer value.
iii. Having found the number of intervals, a datum is taken and the interval in which it is to be placed is determined by a DO loop. The loop also counts the number of data items.

A number of points worth noting are:

i. MODULE data_arrays is used by the main program, SUBROUTINE freq_table and FUNCTIONs maximum and minimum. Thus arrays are not passed explicitly as dummy arguments.
ii. We did not use the intrinsic function MAXVAL (data_in) to find the maximum value of the elements in the input data array as the actual array read in may have fewer elements compared to the size of data_in as defined in the MODULE data_arrays.

Example Program 14.8 Frequency table generation

```
!PROGRAM 14.8
!PROGRAM TO OBTAIN FREQUENCY TABLE
!THE FOLLOWING MODULE DEFINES THE DATA

MODULE data_arrays
   IMPLICIT NONE
   SAVE
   INTEGER,PARAMETER :: max_data=200,max_inter=50
   INTEGER,DIMENSION(max_data) :: data_in
   INTEGER,DIMENSION(max_inter) :: freq
END MODULE data_arrays
!THE FOLLOWING PROGRAM CALLS SUBROUTINE freq_table TO PRINT THE
!FREQUENCY ARRAY FOR A GIVEN DATA ARRAY data_in WHICH HAS n_data
!ELEMENTS.THE INTERVAL FOR FREQUENCY TABLE IS NAMED intervals
```

```
PROGRAM main
   USE data_arrays
   IMPLICIT NONE
   INTEGER :: n_data,intervals,min,max,i,j,m
   READ *,n_data,intervals
   READ *,(data_in(i),i=1,n_data)
   CALL freq_table(intervals,n_data,min,max)
   j = (max-min)/intervals + 1
   PRINT 50,max,min,j
50 FORMAT(1X,"Max data =",I4,"Min data =",I4,"No.of intervals=",I3)
   PRINT 60,(freq(m),m=1,j)
60 FORMAT(15X,"FREQUENCY TABLE"/(1X,10I6))
END PROGRAM main
!THE FOLLOWING SUBROUTINE GATHERS DATA ARRAY INTO A FREQUENCY TABLE.
!INPUT DATA ARE DATA READ,INTERVALS.THE OUTPUTS ARE MAXIMUM DATA VALUE
!MINIMUM DATA VALUE AND THE FREQUENCY TABLE WHICH IS STORED IN THE
!ARRAY.freq DEFINED IN THE DATA MODULE

SUBROUTINE freq_table(intl,no_data,min,max)
   USE data_arrays
   IMPLICIT NONE
   INTEGER,INTENT(IN) :: no_data,intl
   INTEGER,INTENT(OUT) :: min,max
   INTEGER :: no_intervals,i,low_lim,k,minimum,maximum
   max = maximum(no_data)
   min = minimum(no_data)
   no_intervals = (max - min)/intl + 1
   DO i=1,no_intervals
      freq(i) = 0
   END DO
   DO i=1,no_data
      low_lim = min + intl
      DO k=1,no_intervals
      IF(data_in(i) < low_lim) THEN
         freq(k) = freq(k) + 1
         EXIT
         ENDIF
      low_lim = low_lim + intl
      END DO
   END DO
END SUBROUTINE freq_table
!THE FOLLOWING FUNCTION FINDS THE MAXIMUM VALUE IN AN ARRAY.
!AS THE ARRAY SIZE IS VARIABLE WE HAVE NOT USED THE INTRINSIC WHOLE
!ARRAY FUNCTION MAXVAL
integer FUNCTION maximum(n_data)
   USE data_arrays
   IMPLICIT NONE
   INTEGER,INTENT(IN) :: n_data
   !n_data IS NUMBER OF DATA IN ARRAY data_in
   !INTEGER,INTENT(OUT) :: maximum
   INTEGER :: i
   maximum = data_in(1)
```

```
   DO i=2,n_data
      IF(data_in(i) > maximum) THEN
      maximum = data_in(i)
      ENDIF
   END DO
END FUNCTION maximum
!FUNCTION TO FIND MINIMUM DATA
!PROCEDURE SIMILAR TO MAXIMUM
FUNCTION minimum(n_data)
   USE data_arrays
   INTEGER,INTENT(IN) :: n_data
   INTEGER,INTENT(OUT) :: minimum
   INTEGER :: i !LOCAL VARIABLE
   minimum = data_in(1)
   DO i=2,n_data
      IF(data_in(i) < minimum) THEN
      minimum = data_in(i)
      END IF
   END DO
END FUNCTION minimum
```

14.3 TEMPORARY ARRAYS IN PROCEDURES

There are many situations where arrays (one- or multi-dimensional) may be required to store temporary data in a procedure (SUBROUTINE or FUNCTION). In such cases these arrays are not dummy arguments but are local variables within a procedure. If these arrays are of fixed size they may be declared with appropriate DIMENSION within the procedure. As these are within procedures, space for these arrays is allocated when the procedure is invoked. These arrays, however, have only a transient existence as long as the procedure is active. When control leaves the procedure the space is deallocated. Such arrays are known as *automatic arrays.*

The temporary arrays within a procedure may also have variable DIMENSIONs. The size may depend upon a dummy argument passed to the procedure. A program segment is given in Fig. 14.9 to illustrate this.

```
SUBROUTINE sample_1 (x, y, n)
IMPLICIT NONE
REAL, DIMENSION (10, 10) :: x
REAL, DIMENSION (n, n) :: y
! local temporary arrays
REAL, DIMENSION (20, 20) :: a
INTEGER, DIMENSION (n * n, 0 : n + 2) :: b
.
.
.
```

Fig. 14.9 Illustrating use of temporary arrays.

Observe that the DIMENSION of x is fixed and that of y variable. It should be ensured that the DIMENSION of the array in the calling program corresponding to x and y match those declared in the SUBROUTINE sample_1 for x and y. Thus if the calling program is cal_samp_1 then it must have declaration as shown in Fig. 14.10.

```
PROGRAM cal_samp_1
   IMPLICIT NONE
   REAL, DIMENSION (10, 10) :: x1
   INTEGER, DIMENSION (20, 20) :: y1
   m = 20
   .
   .
   .

   CALL sampl_1 (x1, y1, m)
   .
   .
   .
```

Fig. 14.10 Segment of program calling sample_ 1.

We saw in Chapter 10 that Fortran 90 allows arrays to be declared ALLOCATABLE and the DIMENSION of such an array can be variable determined at execution time. Allocatable arrays are allowed as temporary arrays in procedures. Allocatable arrays, however, cannot be used as dummy arguments in procedures. Use of ALLOCATABLE arrays in procedures for temporary arrays is better than using automatic arrays as a programmer has greater control of allocatable arrays.

14.4 FUNCTIONS AS DUMMY ARGUMENTS

Fortran 90 permits the use of a procedure (FUNCTION or SUBROUTINE) name as dummy argument(s) in a SUBROUTINE or FUNCTION. The fact that the argument is a procedure has to be specified by declaring it with an attribute EXTERNAL.

We will illustrate the use of a procedure as a function argument with an example. Suppose a function f(x) is to be integrated from x_0 to x_n. A simple method is to use trapezoidal rule to evaluate the integral as integral of $f = h * [\frac{1}{2} f(x_0) + f(x_1) + f(x_2) + ... + f(x_{n-1}) + \frac{1}{2} f(x_n)]$

where

$$h = (x_n - x_0)/n$$

We have written a SUBROUTINE to compute the integral as Example Program 14.9. Observe that in the SUBROUTINE we have used f as a dummy argument. The compiler should be told that the argument f is not a variable name but is a function name. This is done in the declaration:

```
REAL, EXTERNAL :: f
```

The SUBROUTINE is a straightforward implementation of the trapezoidal rule.

Example Program 14.9 Subroutine to integrate function f(x)

```
!PROGRAM 14.9
!SUBROUTINE TO INTEGRATE FUNCTION f(x)
 SUBROUTINE integral(f,n,int_of_f,x0,xn)
!n IS THE NUMBER OF INTERVALS,x0 IS THE FIRST ORDINATE AND xn IS THE
!LAST ORDINATE
!INTEGRAL IS RETURNED AS VALUE OF VARIABLE int_of_f.TRAPEZOIDAL RULE
!IS USED
   IMPLICIT NONE
!DECLARATION EXTERNAL SPECIFIES THAT f IS A FUNCTION AND NOT A VARIABLE
!NAME
   REAL,EXTERNAL :: f
   INTEGER,INTENT(IN):: n
   REAL,INTENT(IN) :: x0,xn
   REAL,INTENT(OUT) :: int_of_f
   INTEGER :: i !LOCAL VARIABLE
   REAL :: h,sum !LOCAL VARIABLE
   h = (xn - x0)/n
   sum = (f(x0) + f(xn))/2.0
   DO i=1,n-1
      sum = sum + f(x0 + i*h)
   END DO
   int_of_f = sum * h
END SUBROUTINE integral
!THE FOLLOWING PROGRAM CALLS THE SUBROUTINE TO COMPUTE THE INTEGRAL OF
!SIN(x) FOR x=0 TO pi/2
PROGRAM find_integral_1
   IMPLICIT NONE
   REAL,PARAMETER :: pi_by_two = 1.5707963
   REAL,INTRINSIC :: SIN
!AS SINE IS BEING USED AS THE FUNCTION AND IT IS AN INTRINSIC FUNCTION
!THIS DECLARATION IS REQUIRED.THE INTEGRAL USES 30 POINTS FROM
!0 to pi/2
   REAL :: int_sine
   CALL integral(SIN,30,int_sine,0.0,pi_by_two)
   PRINT *,"Integral =",int_sine
END PROGRAM find_integral_1
```

The program which calls this SUBROUTINE is find_integral_1. This program requests the integration of SIN(x). The program thus passes SIN as a calling argument. The fact that SIN is an intrinsic function being passed as an argument should be told to the compiler. This is done by the declaration

```
REAL, INTRINSIC :: SIN
```

In PROGRAM find_integral_2 (Example Program 14.10) we have integrated a function f (x) = x Sin(x) using the SUBROUTINE integral. The fact that f is a function name in the calling argument list while calling integral is informed to the compiler by the declaration

```
REAL, EXTERNAL :: f
```

in the calling program.

Example Program 14.10 Finding integral of x Sin(x)

```
!PROGRAM 14.10
!SUBROUTINE TO INTEGRATE FUNCTION f(x)
SUBROUTINE integral(f,n,int_of_f,x0,xn)
!n IS THE NUMBER OF INTERVALS,x0 IS THE FIRST ORDINATE AND xn IS THE
!LAST ORDINATE
!INTEGRAL IS RETURNED AS VALUE OF VARIABLE int_of_f.TRAPEZOIDAL RULE
!IS USED
   IMPLICIT NONE
!DECLARATION EXTERNAL SPECIFIES THAT f IS A FUNCTION AND NOT A VARIABLE
!NAME
   REAL,EXTERNAL :: f
   INTEGER,INTENT(IN):: n
   REAL,INTENT(IN) :: x0,xn
   REAL,INTENT(OUT) :: int_of_f
   INTEGER :: i !LOCAL VARIABLE
   REAL :: h,sum !LOCAL VARIABLE
   h = (xn - x0)/n
   sum = (f(x0) + f(xn))/2.0
   DO i=1,n-1
   sum = sum + f(x0 + i*h)
   END DO
   int_of_f = sum * h
END SUBROUTINE integral
!THE FOLLOWING PROGRAM CALLS THE SUBROUTINE TO COMPUTE THE INTEGRAL OF
!f(x) = xSIN(x) FROM x=0.5 to 2.5.TWENTY POINTS ARE USED
PROGRAM find_integral_2
   IMPLICIT NONE
   REAL,EXTERNAL :: f !f IS AN EXTERNAL FUNCTION
   REAL :: int_s !INTEGRAL RETURNED IN THIS VARIABLE
   CALL integral(f,20,int_s,0.5,2.5)
   PRINT *,"Integral =",int_s
END PROGRAM find_integral_2
!FUNCTION xSIN(x)
FUNCTION f(x)
   IMPLICIT NONE
   REAL,INTENT(IN) :: x
   REAL :: f
   f = x*SIN(x)
END FUNCTION f
```

In Example Program 14.11 we have given an alternate way of informing the compiler that f in the calling argument list of the SUBROUTINE is a function name by using an INTERFACE declaration in the calling PROGRAM find_integral_3. This is an alternate method allowed in Fortran 90.

Example Program 14.11 Finding integral—Use of INTERFACE

```
!PROGRAM 14.11
   SUBROUTINE integral(f,n,int_of_f,x0,xn)
!SUBROUTINE TO INTEGRATE FUNCTION f(x)
!n IS THE NUMBER OF INTERVALS,x0 IS THE FIRST ORDINATE AND xn IS THE
!LAST ORDINATE
!INTEGRAL IS RETURNED AS VALUE OF VARIABLE int_of_f.TRAPEZOIDAL RULE
!IS USED
   IMPLICIT NONE
!DECLARATION EXTERNAL SPECIFIES THAT f IS A FUNCTION AND NOT A VARIABLE
!NAME
   REAL,EXTERNAL :: f
   INTEGER,INTENT(IN):: n
   REAL,INTENT(IN) :: x0,xn
   REAL,INTENT(OUT) :: int_of_f
   INTEGER :: i !LOCAL VARIABLE
   REAL :: h,sum !LOCAL VARIABLE
   h = (xn - x0)/n
   sum = (f(x0) + f(xn))/2.0
   DO i=1,n-1
      sum = sum + f(x0 + i*h)
   END DO
   int_of_f = sum * h
END SUBROUTINE integral

!ALTERNATE DECLARATION WHEN A PROGRAM USES A FUNCTION AS
!AN ARGUMENT IN CALLING SUBROUTINE
PROGRAM find_integral_3
   IMPLICIT NONE
   INTERFACE
      FUNCTION f(X)
      REAL,INTENT(IN) :: x
      REAL :: f
      END FUNCTION f
   END INTERFACE
   REAL :: int_s
   CALL integral(f,20,int_s,0.5,2.5)
   PRINT *,"Integral =",int_s
END PROGRAM find_integral_3
```

SUMMARY

1. Arrays may be passed as dummy arguments to procedures.
2. The DIMENSION of the dummy array should equal the DIMENSION of the corresponding array in the calling program.
3. The DIMENSION of the dummy array(s) in a procedure need not be explicitly specified. It may be passed via another dummy argument by a calling program provided the point mentioned in 2 above is satisfied.

4. A MODULE is a program unit in which data and/or procedures may be included. The structure of a MODULE is:

   MODULE *name*
   {MODULE body (data and (or) procedures)}
   END MODULE *name*

5. A MODULE may be used to store arrays which can be made accessible to a group of programs by inserting a statement:

   USE *module name*

   in each program in the group. USE *module name* must be the first statement in all procedures.

6. An explicit INTERFACE may be used in a calling program in which all the declarations of a called procedure are placed. This facilitates correct communication between the calling program and the called procedures.

7. Multi-dimensional arrays are stored in column major order in memory. This is an important point which one should remember. Multi-dimensional arrays may be used as dummy arguments of procedures and the calling array may have a different shape. The correspondence between elements of the arrays in calling and called programs must be examined carefully by a user remembering arrays are stored in column major order.

8. Temporary arrays in procedures can, however, not be used as dummy arguments of procedures.

9. FUNCTIONS or SUBROUTINES may be used as dummy arguments of procedures. They should however be declared as EXTERNAL in the FUNCTION/SUBROUTINE. The argument corresponding to the dummy function argument in a calling program may be an intrinsic function. In such a case it should be declared as INTRINSIC in the calling program.

EXERCISES

14.1 The intrinsic trigonometric functions for SIN, COS, TAN, ASIN etc., have arguments in radians. Write a trigonometric function which will accept arguments given in degrees, minutes and seconds. The function should be of the type:

REAL FUNCTION trig_degree (trig_fun, degrees, minutes, seconds)

trig_degree (SIN, degrees minutes, seconds) should give the value of SIN(angle) where angle is in degrees, minutes and seconds.

14.2 Write a SUBROUTINE to multiply a $(n \times n)$ square matrix by a $(n \times 1)$ vector. The CALL statement will give the size of the matrix and the names of the matrix and the array.

14.3 Use the SUBROUTINE of Exercise 14.2 to generate a (8×8) matrix whose elements are given by $a_{ij} = 2^{-(i-j)}$.

14.4 Write a SUBROUTINE to find the trace of a matrix. The trace is defined as the sum of the diagonal elements of the matrix. How will the matrix be called?

14.5 Write a FUNCTION to find the norm of a (n × n) matrix. The norm is defined as the square root of the sum of squares of all the elements in the matrix.

14.6 Write a SUBROUTINE to accept a (n × n) matrix and output a matrix whose diagonal elements contains the maximum value of elements in each row. For example, given a matrix

$$a = \begin{bmatrix} 1 & 4 & 9 \\ 19 & 3 & 6 \\ 4 & 20 & 8 \end{bmatrix} \qquad \text{the transformed matrix is: } \begin{bmatrix} 9 & 4 & 1 \\ 3 & 19 & 6 \\ 4 & 8 & 20 \end{bmatrix}$$

14.7 Write a procedure to validate the elements of a (n × n) matrix. The validation rules are:
All diagonal entries should be > 0.
The matrix should be symmetric.
All the non-diagonal elements must be < 0 or = 0.

14.8 Write a FUNCTION to find the integral of a function using Simpson's rule (see a book on Numerical techniques to get Simpson's rule). Use this to integrate $x^2 e^{-x}$ from x = 0 to 2.

14.9 Write a SUBROUTINE to solve a (n × n) simultaneous linear algebraic equations using Gauss elimination method.

14.10 Write a SUBROUTINE to multiply a (n × m) matrix by a (m × n) matrix.

15. Derived Types

Learning Objectives

In this chapter we will learn:

1. How to declare our own data types known as derived types
2. How to use derived types (namely user defined data type) in applications
3. How derived types are used as dummy arguments to procedures
4. How arrays of derived type data can be used

So far we have used the built-in or intrinsic data types available in Fortran 90. Besides the intrinsic type, Fortran 90 allows a user to define his/her own data type. This enhances the readability of programs and also allows writing more powerful programs. In what follows we will describe how a user can define his/her own data type known as derived type in Fortran 90.

15.1 DEFINING DERIVED TYPES

There are many applications where it is convenient to treat related data items as one entity. Individual components of such an entity would usually be of different data types. Such an entity is called a *structure* and the related data items used in it are called its components. For example, consider items in a store. Each item in the store may be described by its code, current stock and its price. Such a structure is called a *derived type* in Fortran 90. A definition for item_in_store using Fortran 90 syntax is given below:

```
TYPE item_in_store
   INTEGER :: item_code
   INTEGER :: qty_in_stock
   REAL :: price
END TYPE item_in_store
```

The following declaration declares soap and hair_oil to be of TYPE item_in_store:

```
TYPE (item_in_store) :: soap, hair_oil
```

Some more derived type definitions are given below:

```
TYPE date
   INTEGER :: day, month, year
END TYPE date
```

Observe that in the above definition all three components are integers. This is allowed. We can now declare

```
TYPE (date) :: birth_day, marriage_day
```

Some more examples are:

```
TYPE person
   CHARACTER LEN (30) :: name
   CHARACTER LEN (50) :: address
   INTEGER :: phone_no
END TYPE person

TYPE student
   INTEGER : roll_no
   CHARACTER LEN(30) :: name
   INTEGER : year_joined
END TYPE student
```

15.2 USING DERIVED TYPES

Let us consider the variable name soap which is declared to be of TYPE (item_in_store). If we want to find the price of soap we use the notation:

soap% price

Similarly the item_code and qty_in_stock of soap may be found by using the notation:

soap%item_code, soap% qty_in_stock

The storage assignment for storing information about soap is shown in Table 15.1.

Table 15.1 Storage of TYPE (item_in_store)

soap	soap% item_code	2678
	soap% qty	95
	soap% price	6.50

Example Program 15.1 is written to find the total inventory value of various brands of soap stored in a shop. Each brand of soap will have different item code. The program also finds the number of different brands of soap in the store. An item code of 0 indicates end of items in store.

Example Program 15.1 Use of derived type—inventory value calculation

```
!PROGRAM 15.1
!ILLUSTRATES THE USE OF DERIVED TYPE AND ITS USE

PROGRAM inv_value
   IMPLICIT NONE
   TYPE item_in_store
      INTEGER :: item_code,qty_in_stock
      REAL :: price
   END TYPE item_in_store
   TYPE(item_in_store) :: soap
   INTEGER :: no_of_brands = 0
   REAL :: total_value=0
   DO
      READ *,soap
      IF(soap%item_code == 0) EXIT
      total_value = total_value + soap%qty_in_stock *soap%price
      no_of_brands = no_of_brands + 1
   END DO
   PRINT *,"No.of brands of soap =",no_of_brands
   PRINT *,"Total value of inventory =",total_value
END PROGRAM inv_value
```

We can read a derived type variable using a READ statement by simply using the variable name. The data supplied should have one to one correspondence with the individual components of the derived type and presented in the order in which the components occur in the TYPE definition.

For example we can write

```
READ*, soap
```

and if the data presented is

```
2678, 95, 6.50
```

then these values will be stored as shown in Table 15.1. Similarly if we write:

```
PRINT*, soap
```

then the values printed will be in the order soap% item_code, soap% qty and soap% price. If we want to assign a value to soap using an assignment statement then we should write:

```
soap = item_in_store (2678, 95, 6.5)
```

This method of assigning a constant value for a derived type variable is called a *structure constructor*.

As another example we will reconsider the example given in Chapter 8 (Example Program 8.4). The problem is: given today's date and the date an employee joined a job to find if he or she has completed one year service. We will use a derived type to solve the problem.

Example Program 15.2 Finding completion of one year service

```
!PROGRAM 15.2
!PROGRAM CHECKS COMPLETION OF ONE YEAR SERVICE
!ILLUSTRATES USE OF DERIVED TYPE

PROGRAM service_dt
   IMPLICIT NONE
   TYPE date
      INTEGER :: day,month,year
   END TYPE date
   INTEGER :: emp_no
!emp_no = 0 INDICATES END IF DATA
   TYPE(date) :: todate,joining_date,diff_date
   READ *,todate
   PRINT 25,todate
   25 FORMAT(1X,"Todays date =",I3,"/",I3,"/",I4)
   DO
      READ *,emp_no,joining_date
      PRINT 30,joining_date
      30 FORMAT(1X,"Joining date=",I3,"/",I3,"/",I4)
      IF(emp_no == 0) EXIT
      diff_date%day=todate%day - joining_date%day
      diff_date%month = todate%month – joining_date%month
      diff_date%year = todate%year – joining_date%year
      IF((diff_date%year > 1).OR.&
         ((diff_date%year == 1).AND.(diff_date%month > 0)).OR.&
         (((diff_date%year == 1).AND.(diff_date%month == 0)).AND.&
         (diff_date%day >= 0))) THEN
         PRINT *,"emp no=",emp_no," is eligible"
      ELSE
         PRINT *,"emp no =",emp_no," is not eligible"
      ENDIF
   END DO
END PROGRAM service_dt
```

The derived type used is date which is defined in Example Program 15.2. The main advantage of using a derived type in this case is a uniform data type definition of the two dates of relevance in this problem. The rest of the program 15.2 is self-explanatory.

15.3 USING DERIVED TYPES IN PROCEDURES

A question which naturally arises is whether derived types can be used as dummy arguments of procedures. If the procedure is a FUNCTION, can a derived type be returned as a value of the FUNCTION? If a derived type is defined in a calling program it will not be known to a called program and vice-versa (Remember that in Fortran 90 procedures are separately compiled). Thus a derived type must be globally defined and made available to all procedures which use that type as arguments. We have seen that global accessibility is provided by MODULEs. Thus derived type definition should be placed in a MODULE and the MODULE used by procedures which need that data type. We illustrate this in Example Program 15.3. In this program we implement functions to perform the operations of addition, multiplication and division of complex numbers. The definition of these operations are given in the next page.

Example Program 15.3 Use of MODULE for derived type

```
!PROGRAM 15.3
!USE OF DERIVED DATA TYPES IN FUNCTIONS
!DEFINITION OF MODULE COMPLEX
   MODULE complex
   IMPLICIT NONE
   SAVE
   TYPE complex_number
      REAL :: real,imag
   END TYPE complex_number
END MODULE complex

PROGRAM comp_arithmetic
   USE complex
   IMPLICIT NONE
!DEFINE EXTERNAL FUNCTIONS
   TYPE(complex_number) :: sum,product,quot
!DEFINE COMPLEX VARIABLES
   TYPE(complex_number) :: x,y
!READ COMPLEX NUMBERS
   PRINT *,"Please supply x_real,x_imaginary and y_real"&
      ,"y_imaginary as a sequence of 4 numbers separated by commas"
   READ *,x,y
   !CALCULATE sum,product and quotient using functions
   PRINT *,"Sum of x and y is =",sum(x,y)
   PRINT *,"Product of x and y is=",product(x,y)
 PRINT *,"Quotient of x and y is=",quot(x,y)
END PROGRAM comp_arithmetic

FUNCTION sum(a,b)
   USE complex
   IMPLICIT NONE
   TYPE(complex_number) :: sum
   TYPE(complex_number),INTENT(IN) :: a,b
   sum%real = a%real + b%real
   sum%imag = a%imag + b%imag
END FUNCTION sum
```

```
FUNCTION product(a,b)
   USE complex
   IMPLICIT NONE
   TYPE(complex_number) :: product
   TYPE(complex_number),INTENT(IN) :: a,b
   product%real = a%real * b%real - a%imag * b%imag
   product%imag = a%real * b%imag + a%imag * b%real
END FUNCTION product
FUNCTION quot(a,b)
   USE complex
   IMPLICIT NONE
   TYPE(complex_number) :: quot
   TYPE(complex_number),INTENT(IN) :: a,b
   REAL :: denom
   denom = b%real ** 2+b%imag ** 2
   quot%real = (a%real*b%real + a%imag*b%imag)/denom
   quot%imag = (a%imag*b%real - a%real*b%imag)/denom
END FUNCTION quot
```

Given two complex numbers (a1 + ia2) and (b1 + ib2) we define:

sum: (a1 + ia2) + (b1 + ib2) = (a1 + b1) + i (a2 + b2)

product: (a1 + ia2) * (b1 + ib2) = (a1b1 _ a2b2) + i (a1b2 + a2b1)

quotient: (a1 + ia2) / (b1 + ib2) = {(a1b1 + a2b2) + i (a2b1 _ a1b2)} / ($b1^2 + b2^2$)

In Example Program 15.3 we first define MODULE complex in which we define the derived type complex_number. This MODULE is available for use by any program. FUNCTIONs sum, product and quot return values which are of TYPE (complex_number) and their dummy arguments are also of TYPE (complex_number). At the beginning of each of these FUNCTIONs we have written USE complex which will access MODULE complex. This module facilitates defining TYPE (complex_number). In the calling PROGRAM comp_arithmetic also we write USE complex at the beginning to access the MODULE complex. It is essential to declare sum and product as EXTERNAL procedures. Otherwise the compiler will get confused as there are intrinsic functions sum and product. Observe that in the PRINT statements we have called FUNCTIONS sum, product and quot. The pair of values of sum (x,y) will be printed by the first print statement. The following PRINT statements will print product and quot. Even though Fortran 90 has an intrinsic type COMPLEX we have defined a derived type primarily for illustration.

15.4 USING DERIVED TYPES IN ARRAYS

So far we have considered arrays in which the individual elements were scalars. Consider a derived type declaration

```
TYPE item
   INTEGER :: item_code
   CHARACTER (LEN = 20) :: item_name
   INTEGER :: qty_in_stock
   REAL :: price
END TYPE item
TYPE (item), DIMENSION (100) :: inventory
```

This defines inventory to be an array of TYPE (item) having 100 components. We could also write this declaration as:

TYPE (item) :: inventory (100)

Each element of the array will have storage allocated as shown in Table 15.2.

Table 15.2 Illustrating an Array whose Elements are of Derived Type

	item_code INTEGER	*item_name* CHARACTER (LEN=20)	*qty_in_stock* INTEGER	*price* REAL
inventory (1)	2678	RICE BASMATI	200	32.5
inventory (2)	7742	MARGO SOAP	350	8.5
.				
.				
.				
inventory (100)				

An individual item is referred to as

inventory (1) % price

In this case the value of this is 32.5 as shown in Table 15.2. We illustrate the use of this array in Example Program 15.4 which lists items out of stock in the store and computes the total value of inventory kept in the store.

Example Program 15.4 Use of derived type in an array

```
!PROGRAM 15.4
!ILLUSTRATES USE OF DERIVED DATA TYPE IN ARRAY

PROGRAM structure_array
   IMPLICIT NONE
   TYPE item
      INTEGER :: item_code
      CHARACTER(LEN=20) :: item_name
      INTEGER :: qty_in_stock
      REAL :: price
   END TYPE item
   TYPE(item),DIMENSION(100) :: inventory
   INTEGER :: no_of_items,i
   REAL :: inv_value=0
   PRINT *,"Please type the number of items in store"
   READ *,no_of_items
   DO i=1,no_of_items
      READ *,inventory(i)
      IF(inventory(i)%qty_in_stock == 0) THEN
      PRINT *,"Item code=",inventory(i)%item_code," out of stock"
      ELSE
         inv_value = inv_value + inventory(i)%qty_in_stock* inventory(i)%price
      ENDIF
   END DO
   PRINT 25,inv_value
   25 FORMAT(1X,"Inventory value= Rs.",F8.2)
END PROGRAM structure_array
```

It is also possible to define derived types within derived types. Suppose it is required to describe suppliers who supply items to a store. This may be declared by the structure:

```
TYPE address
   CHARACTER (LEN = 20) :: street
   CHARACTER (LEN = 15) :: city
   INTEGER :: pin_code
END TYPE address

   TYPE supplier
      INTEGER :: supp_code
      CHARACTER (LEN = 20) :: supp_name
      TYPE (address) :: supp_address
   END TYPE supplier
TYPE (supplier), DIMENSION (50) :: supp_group
```

Observe that the address of the supplier is declared as a TYPE(address) within the TYPE (supplier). The program segment shown in Fig.15.1 illustrates how such derived type can be used. This program is to find the address of all suppliers whose pin code is 500042.

```
DO i = 1, 50
   IF(supp_group (i)%supp_address%pin_code = = 500042) THEN
      PRINT*, "Supplier address is",supp_group(i)%supp_address
   ENDIF
END DO
```

Fig. 15.1 Use of derived type within a derived type.

Suppose it is required to find out the address of all suppliers who supply a particular item to a store. In the current structure describing an item in store there is no reference to who supplies the item. Similarly there is no information in supplier record about what items the supplier is capable of supplying. Thus it is not possible to find out who could supply an item which is out of stock in a store. We will alter the derived type item to include supp_code of all suppliers who supply this item. The altered TYPE is shown below:

```
TYPE item
   INTEGER :: item_code
   CHARACTER (LEN = 20) :: item_name
   INTEGER :: qty_in_stock
   REAL :: price
   INTEGER :: supp_code (3)
END TYPE item
```

In TYPE (item) we have assumed upto three suppliers for each item is stored. These three suppliers' codes are stored in the array supp_code.

Example Program 15.5 Use of arrays in derived data types

```
!PROGRAM 15.5
!ILLUSTRATES USE OF ARRAYS IN DERIVED DATA TYPES
```

```
PROGRAM supplier_select
   IMPLICIT NONE
   TYPE item
      INTEGER :: item_code
      CHARACTER(LEN=20) :: item_name
      INTEGER :: qty_in_stock
      REAL :: price
      INTEGER :: supp_code(3)
   END TYPE item
   TYPE(item),DIMENSION(100) :: inventory
   INTEGER :: no_of_items,i,j
   PRINT *,"Please type the number of items in store"
   READ *,no_of_items
   DO i=1,no_of_items
      READ *,inventory(i)
      IF(inventory(i)%qty_in_stock == 0) THEN
      PRINT *,"Item code=",inventory(i)%item_code, "is out of stock"
!FIND OUT SUPPLIERS OF THIS ITEM
         PRINT *,"Suppliers of this item are:"
      DO j=1,3
         PRINT *,inventory(i)%supp_code(j)
      END DO
      ENDIF
   END DO
END PROGRAM supplier_select
```

In Example Program 15.5 we have written a program to print the supplier codes of suppliers who can supply items which are out of stock in the store.

If we want to print the name and address of the supplier given the supplier code we need to have access to the supplier information. In Example Program 15.6 the main PROGRAM supplier_data_base creates the data base of suppliers. SUBROUTINE print_address prints the address of a supplier whose supplier code is given. Observe the use of MODULE supplier_struct which defines the derived data type used in this program.

Example Program 15.6 Printing supplier details from supplier codes

```
!PROGRAM 15.6
!ILLUSTRATES PRINTING SUPPLIER DETAILS GIVEN SUPPLIER CODE
MODULE supplier_struct
   SAVE
   IMPLICIT NONE
   TYPE address
      CHARACTER(LEN=20) :: street
      CHARACTER(LEN=15) :: city
      INTEGER :: pin_code
   END TYPE address
   TYPE supplier
      INTEGER :: supp_code
      CHARACTER(LEN=20) :: supp_name
      TYPE(address) :: supp_address
   END TYPE supplier
END MODULE supplier_struct
```

```
SUBROUTINE print_address(supp_group,in_code,n_supp)
   USE supplier_struct
   IMPLICIT NONE
   INTEGER,INTENT(IN) :: in_code,n supp
   TYPE(supplier),DIMENSION(n_supp),INTENT(IN)::supp_group
   INTEGER :: i !LOCAL VARIABLE
   DO i=1,n_supp
      IF(in_code == supp_group(i)%supp_code) THEN
         PRINT 25,supp_group(i)%supp_name,supp_group(i)%supp_address%street,&
         supp_group(i)%supp_address%city,supp_group(i)%supp_address%pin_code
         25 FORMAT(1X,A20/A20/A15/"PIN ",I7)
      ENDIF
   END DO
END SUBROUTINE print_address
PROGRAM supp_data_base
   USE supplier_struct
   IMPLICIT NONE
   TYPE(supplier),DIMENSION(50) :: supp_group
   INTEGER :: code,i,no_supp
   PRINT *,"Please type the number of suppliers"
   READ *,no_supp
   DO i=1,no_supp
      PRINT *,"Type supplier code"
      READ *,supp_group(i)%supp_code
      PRINT *,"Type supplier name < 20 characters"
      READ *,supp_group(i)%supp_name
      PRINT *,"Type supplier street"
      READ *,supp_group(i)%supp_address%street
      PRINT *,"Type supplier city"
      READ *,supp_group(i)%supp_address%city
      PRINT *,"Type pin code"
      READ *,supp_group(i)%supp_address%pin_code
      PRINT *,"Next supplier"
   END DO
   PRINT *,no_supp,"data input"
 !PRINT ADDRESS OF SUPPLIERS OF OUT STOCK ITEMS
   DO i=1,3
      PRINT *,"Type code of supplier of out of stock item"
      READ *,code
      PRINT *,"Address of supplier with code=",code
      CALL print_address(supp_group,code,no_supp)
   END DO
 END PROGRAM supp_data_base
```

We can integrate Programs 15.5 and 15.6 into one program to create inventory data base, supplier data base and print the addresses of suppliers of out of stock item. This is left as an exercise to the student (Exercise 15.7).

SUMMARY

1. There are many applications where it is preferable to treat related data items usually of different data types as one entity. Such an entity is called a derived data type in Fortran 90.
2. A derived data type to describe data on students is shown below:

```
TYPE student
INTEGER :: roll-no
CHARACTER (LEN = 30) :: name
INTEGER :: age, sex
END TYPE student
```

3. A declaration of a variable or an array can be of a specified TYPE may be written as:

```
TYPE (STUDENT), DIMENSION(50) :: b_student
```

4. An individual data element in a derived type b_student is referred to by the notation:

```
b_student (i)%name
```

5. In order to use a derived type as a dummy argument in procedures, it should be placed in a MODULE and the MODULE used in relevant procedures.
6. Arrays may be used as components of a derived type. A derived type may include another derived type as its component.

EXERCISES

15.1 Define a derived type point and use it to define type triangle. Use this type to find the perimeter and area of the triangle. Write a procedure to find if the given triangle is

  i. right angled triangle,
  ii. isosceles triangle.

15.2 Define a derived type circle. Use this to find the area of a circle.

15.3 Create a derived type to specify data on students given below:

Roll number, Name, Department, Course, Year of joining. A typical students data will be:

1456 S.Sunder, E.E. M.E. 1994

Assume that there are less than 500 students:

  i. Create a sample data base of 20 students.
  ii. Write a procedure to print the names of all students who joined in a specified year.
  iii. Write a procedure to print the data on a student given his/her roll number.

15.4 Create a derived data to specify data on customers in a bank. The data to be stored is:

Acct.No., Name, Balance in Account. Assume max. of 500 customers in the bank:

i. Create a sample data base of 20 accounts.
ii. Write a procedure to print the account number and names of customers with balance below Rs. 500.
iii. A customer gives a request for withdrawal of deposit in the form:

Account Number, amount, Code D for deposit, Code W for withdrawal

If the balance in the account is insufficient for withdrawal write a procedure to print a message "The balance insufficient".

15.5 Create a derived data type for items in an inventory with the following specifications:

Part No., Part name, qty. in hand, re-order level, re-order quantity, supplier(s) codes

Assume 200 items in the inventory:

i. Create a sample data base with 15 items.
ii. Write a procedure to print details of items whose stock is below the re-order level.
iii. Write a procedure to re-order items whose stock is below the re-order level.

15.6 Create a derived data type to store employees' data with the following specifications:

Employee No., Employee name, Employee's pay, date of joining

i. Create a sample data base of 20 employees.
ii. Write a procedure to implement the following decision on revision of salaries:

Pay ≤ Rs.5000	increase by 15%
Pay ≤ 25000	increase by 10%
Pay > 25000	no increase

iii. Write a procedure to print details of employees who have completed 20 years service on a specified date.

15.7 Integrate the programs given in the text for inventory creation and printing addresses of all suppliers of items out of stock.

16. *Additional Features in Procedures*

Learning Objectives

In this chapter we will learn:

1. How recursive procedures are defined and used
2. How to define and use generic procedures
3. How it is possible for a user to define his/her operators for operations appropriate in an application. In this context we will also see how intrinsic operators of Fortran can be overloaded. In other words, how they can be used to perform different operations depending on the type of operands
4. How to create array valued functions
5. How optional and keyword arguments may be used in procedures
6. Scoping rules in procedures

16.1 A REVIEW OF PROCEDURES

We will first quickly review and consolidate various aspects of procedures we have discussed in previous chapters. A Fortran 90 program normally consists of a main program which has the form shown in Fig. 16.1.

```
                  PROGRAM p_name
                  USE module_names (if any)
  ------->           < declaration of variables_1 >
Main Program         < declaration of TYPE block(s) if any >
                     < declaration of INTERFACE block(s) if any >
                     < executable statements >
                     CALL to external or internal subprograms
                  CONTAINS
                      SUBROUTINE s_name (< dummy arguments >)
                         < declaration of variables_2 >
Internal  ------->       < executable statements >
Subprograms           END SUBROUTINE s_name
                      FUNCTION f_name (< dummy arguments >)
                         < declaration of variables_3 >
                         < executable statements >
                      END FUNCTION f_name

                  END PROGRAM p_name
```

Fig. 16.1 Structure of a Fortran 90 main PROGRAM.

A PROGRAM consists of USE *module_name* if it uses a module. This is followed by declaration of variables needed by it, derived type definition, INTERFACE block in case external programs being called have special type of dummy variables, followed by executable statements and calls (if any) to external or internal subprograms. After this it may have the statement CONTAINS followed by one or more complete subprograms. These are internal subprograms used by PROGRAM. Internal subprograms are not allowed to CONTAIN other subprogram(s).

A procedure or subprogram is of two types: a function subprogram in which a single value is returned via the name of the function and a subroutine subprogram in which value or values may be returned via dummy arguments or no value may be returned. In a function subprogram the values of the dummy variables are not altered. Functions and Subroutines are known as *external subprograms* or procedures. External procedures may contain within them other functions or subroutines. The structure of an external subprogram is shown in Fig. 16.2.

```
SUBROUTINE name (dummy arguments)
USE module_names (if any)
        < declaration of variables >                External subprogram
        < executable statements >              <-------------------
        CALL to external or internal subprograms

    CONTAINS                              <------- Internal subprograms
        < internal subprograms >
        < internal subprograms >

END SUBROUTINE name
```

Fig. 16.2 Structure of an external subprogram.

A third type of program unit is called a MODULE. The structure of a MODULE is shown in Fig. 16.3. We have used MODULEs so far which had only specification statements.

```
MODULE module name
        < variable declarations >
        < Type blocks (if any) >
    CONTAINS
        < internal subprogram_1 >
        < internal subprogram_2 >
END MODULE module name
```

Fig. 16.3 Structure of MODULE.

In this chapter we will see how MODULE containing internal subprograms are used. A MODULE is invoked by the statement:

USE < *module name* >

We have so far stated that a procedure can call other procedures but not itself. This was true in Fortran 77. In Fortran 90, however, procedures can call themselves either directly or indirectly. This is called *recursion.* We will discuss recursion in the next section.

16.2 RECURSIVE FUNCTIONS

Recursion is the name given to the technique of defining a function or a procedure in terms of itself. The best known example of a recursively defined function is the factorial function defined as follows:

Factorial function

0! = 1
n! = n (n – 1)!

Here n! is defined in terms of (n – 1)! which is in turn defined in terms of (n – 2)! and so on till we reach 0! which is explicitly defined to have a value of 1. Any recursive definition must have an explicit definition for some value or values of the argument(s); otherwise the definition would be circular. Some more recursively defined functions are:

Fibonacci Numbers

i. Fib (0) = 0; Fib (1) = 1
ii. Fib (n + 1) = Fib (n) + Fib (n – 1)

Arithmetic Expression

i. < arith.expn. > : = < variable name >
ii. < arith.expn. > : = < arith.expn. > < operator > < arith.expn. >
where < operator > is +, –, * or /

If a function *f* contains an explicit reference to itself, then it is said to be *directly recursive.* If *f* contains a reference to another function *g* which contains a reference to *f*, then *f* is said to be *indirectly recursive.*

The following algorithm gives a recursive definition of n!

Algorithm 16.1

```
integer factorial (integer n)
    {integer result;
        if (n = = 0)
            result = 1
        else
            result = n * factorial (n – 1)}
    return result to factorial
end factorial
```

Algorithm 16.1 is written as Example Program 16.1. The definition of a recursive function starts with the statement:

RECURSIVE FUNCTION factorial(n) RESULT(fact_n).

Example Program 16.1 Calculating factorial (n)

```
!PROGRAM 16.1
!ILLUSTRATION OF A RECURSIVE FUNCTION

PROGRAM fact_1
   IMPLICIT NONE
   INTEGER :: m,factorial
   READ *,m
   PRINT *,m
   IF(m < 0) THEN
      PRINT *,"m < 0 not allowed"
      STOP
   END IF
   PRINT *,"m= ",m,"factorial(m) =",factorial(m)
END PROGRAM fact_1
RECURSIVE FUNCTION factorial(n) RESULT (fact_n)
   IMPLICIT NONE
   INTEGER :: n,fact_n
   IF(n == 0) THEN
      fact_n = 1
   ELSE
      fact_n = n*factorial(n-1)
   ENDIF
END FUNCTION factorial
```

Observe that we have to add the word RECURSIVE before FUNCTION. Also see that we have to use a variable name to store the result and this is specified as RESULT (fact_n). The TYPE of the result variable namely, fact_n is declared within the FUNCTION body. As the name of function is used within the FUNCTION for recursive function call, to avoid ambiguity, a separate result variable is needed to give the final result of the function. In fact a RESULT variable could be used in *all function definitions* and some authors recommend it. When RESULT variable is used there is no need to declare the type of function name as the RESULT variable is declared and its TYPE is the type of the function. The program FUNCTION factorial (n) closely follows Algorithm 16.1. Observe the declaration of fact_n in the FUNCTION. The function factorial calls itself. A recursive function is called by the main program in our example by the appearance of the function name as usual.

Observe that in the main program we have used the statement STOP. This will unconditionally stop execution of the program. It is used only in abnormal conditions to prevent execution from proceeding any further. In our example factorial (n) is undefined for negative n. If by mistake a negative value is input the calling program gives a message and halts execution. Similar to use of STOP in a main program a statement RETURN is used in a subprogram.

Example Program 16.2 A subroutine to compute factorial(n)

```
!PROGRAM 16.2
!ILLUSTRATING A RECURSIVE SUBROUTINE

PROGRAM fact_2
   IMPLICIT NONE
   INTEGER :: m,fact_m
   LOGICAL :: error
   READ *,m
   CALL factorial(m,fact_m,error)
   IF(error) THEN
      PRINT *,"Input value m=",m,"is illegal"
   ELSE
      PRINT *,"factorial of ",m," is ",fact_m
   ENDIF
END PROGRAM fact_2
!DEFINITION OF RECURSIVE SUBROUTINE
RECURSIVE SUBROUTINE factorial (n,fact_n,error_flag)
   IMPLICIT NONE
   INTEGER,INTENT(IN) :: n
   INTEGER,INTENT(OUT) :: fact_n
   LOGICAL,INTENT(OUT) :: error_flag
   error_flag = .false.
   IF(n < 0) THEN
      error_flag = .true.
      RETURN
   ENDIF
   IF(n == 0) THEN
      fact_n = 1
   ELSE
      CALL factorial(n-1,fact_n,error_flag)
      !THIS WILL RETURN factorial(n-1)
      fact_n=n*fact_n
   ENDIF
END SUBROUTINE factorial
```

In Example Program 16.2 we have written a SUBROUTINE to calculate factorial(n). Notice that the check for n < 0 is done in the subprogram. If n < 0, an error-flag is set .TRUE. and control returns to the calling program by use of the statement RETURN. Observe that we have written a SUBROUTINE to calculate factorial(n) as we are returning more than one output value to the calling program.

We will now write one more recursive function. The function is to calculate Fibonacci numbers. Fibonacci numbers are recursively defined as follows:

$$\text{fib}(0) = 0;\ \text{fib}(1) = 1$$
$$\text{fib}(n + 1) = \text{fib}(n) + \text{fib}(n - 1)$$

Example Program 16.3 computes Fibonacci numbers.

Example Program 16.3 Calculation of Fibonacci numbers

```
!PROGRAM 16.3
!CALCULATION OF FIBONACCI NUMBERS

PROGRAM fib_1
   IMPLICIT NONE
   INTEGER :: m,fibonacci
   READ *,m
   PRINT *,"m =",m
   IF(m < 0) THEN
      PRINT *, m ," is illegal"
      STOP
   ENDIF
   PRINT 25,m,fibonacci(m)
   25 FORMAT(1X,"fibonacci(",I4,")=",I6)
END PROGRAM fib_1
RECURSIVE FUNCTION fibonacci(n) RESULT(fib_n)
   IMPLICIT NONE
   INTEGER,INTENT(IN) :: n
   INTEGER,INTENT(OUT) :: fib_n
   IF(n == 0) THEN
      fib_n = 0
   ELSE IF(n== 1) THEN
      fib_n = 1
   ELSE
      fib_n = fibonacci(n-1) + fibonacci(n-2)
   ENDIF
END FUNCTION fibonacci
```

If n = 5 the RECURSIVE FUNCTION fibonacci will activate itself 15 times as shown in Fig. 16.4. The value of fibonacci(5) is calculated working backwards starting from the leaf nodes of the tree of Fig. 16.4 and ending in the root node. It is clear that the total number of calls to fibonacci and consequently computing it will grow exponentially with n. Each call requires reservation of storage for values and links. Such a recursive program to solve the problem needs extra resources. These resources are, however, "released" after the computation of the function.

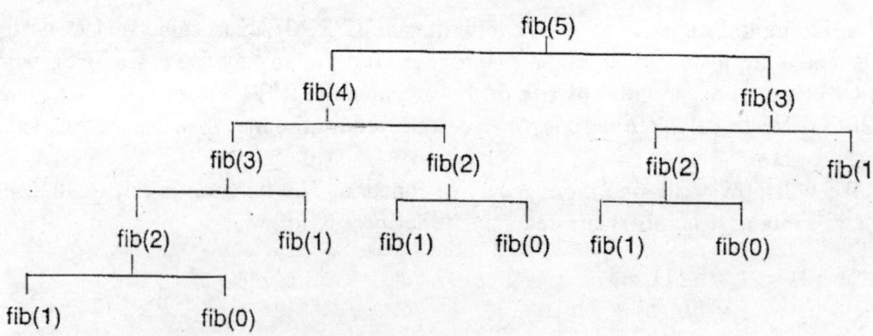

Fig. 16.4 The calls made to Fibonacci when n = 5.

Example Program 16.4 An iterative method to calculate fibonacci numbers

```
!PROGRAM 16.4
!CALCULATING FIBONACCI NUMBERS BY ITERATION

FUNCTION fibonacci(n) RESULT(fib_n)
   IMPLICIT NONE
   INTEGER,INTENT(IN) :: n
   INTEGER :: fib_n
!LOCAL VARIABLES
   INTEGER :: i,prev,current,next
   IF(n == 0) THEN
      fib_n = 0;
   ELSE IF(n == 1) THEN
      fib_n = 1;
   ELSE
      prev = 0
      current = 1
      DO i = 2,n
         next = prev + current
         prev = current
         current = next
      END DO
         fib_n = current
   ENDIF
END FUNCTION fibonacci
```

Fibonacci numbers may be generated iteratively as illustrated in Example Program 16.4. In this iterative algorithm the number of computations performed increases linearly with n. It is thus much more efficient compared to the recursive program. Observe, however, that it is not as "elegant" as the recursive program. The recursive program closely follows the problem specification which is itself recursive. Inspite of the elegance of recursive programs sometimes it is worthwhile to explore alternative method based on iteration due to considerations of efficiency. A thumb rule is to use a recursive program if there is no *obvious* iterative program to solve the problem.

16.3 GENERIC PROCEDURES

We have seen some intrinsic generic functions in Fortran 90. For example, the intrinsic function ABS can have an argument which can be either real, integer or complex. A function whose dummy argument(s) can be one of many types is called a *generic function*. Fortran 90 allows users to define generic functions. Generic functions are convenient to use for different argument types as we do not have to invent different names. In this section we will see how generic procedures can be defined.

Consider the problem of rotating the values of 3 variables. Given three variables a, b, c the value of a is shifted to b, b to c and c to a, as shown in Fig. 16.5.

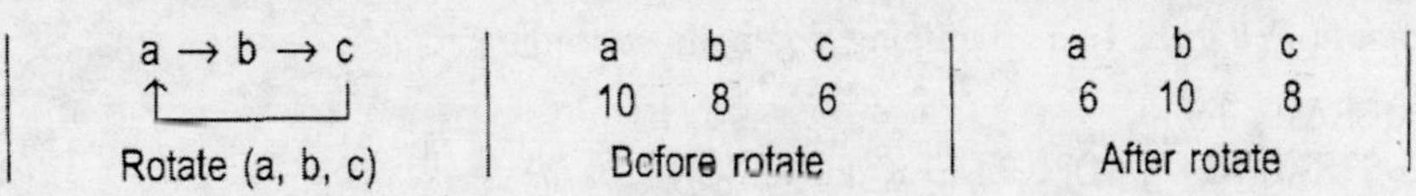

Fig. 16.5 Defining a procedure rotate.

Suppose in one case a, b, c are integers and in another instance a, b, c are characters. We have written two procedures for rotate in Figs. 16.6 and 16.7 respectively.

```
SUBROUTINE rotate_int (a, b, c)
    IMPLICIT NONE
    INTEGER :: a, b, c, temp
        temp = c
        c = b
        b = a
        a = temp
END SUBROUTINE rotate_int
```

Fig. 16.6 Procedure to rotate integers.

```
SUBROUTINE rotate_char (a, b, c)
    IMPLICIT NONE
    CHARACTER :: a, b, c, temp
        temp = c
        c = b
        b = a
        a = temp
END SUBROUTINE rotate_char
```

Fig. 16.7 Procedure to rotate characters.

If we want to give a single name rotate to both these functions, we may do it by writing an INTERFACE block shown in Fig. 16.8.

```
INTERFACE rotate
    SUBROUTINE rotate_int (a, b, c)
        IMPLICIT NONE
        INTEGER :: a, b, c, temp
    END SUBROUTINE rotate_int
    SUBROUTINE rotate_char (a, b, c)
        IMPLICIT NONE
        CHARACTER :: a, b, c, temp
    END SUBROUTINE rotate_char
END INTERFACE rotate
```

Fig. 16.8 Interface block defining generic procedure name rotate.

In Example Program 16.5 we see how a calling program can use the generic procedure. The generic procedures are external subroutines in Example Program 16.5.

Example Program 16.5 Defining a generic procedure rotate

```
!PROGRAM 16.5
!ILLUSTRATING USE OF GENERIC FUNCTION
!MAIN PROGRAM CALLS THE GENERIC PROCEDURE
```

```
PROGRAM generic_1
   IMPLICIT NONE
   INTEGER :: x,y,z
   CHARACTER :: p,q,r
   INTERFACE rotate
      SUBROUTINE rotate_int(a,b,c)
         INTEGER :: a,b,c,temp
      END SUBROUTINE rotate_int
      SUBROUTINE rotate_char(a,b,c)
         CHARACTER :: a,b,c,temp
      END SUBROUTINE rotate_char
   END INTERFACE
   READ *,x,y,z
   PRINT *,"x =",x,"y =",y,"z =",z
   CALL rotate(x,y,z)
   PRINT *,"x =",x,"y =",y,"z =",z
   READ *,p,q,r
   PRINT *,"p =",p,"q =",q,"r =",r
   CALL rotate(p,q,r)
   PRINT *,"p =",p,"q =",q,"r =",r
END PROGRAM generic_1

SUBROUTINE rotate_int(a,b,c)
   IMPLICIT NONE
   INTEGER :: a,b,c,temp
   temp = c;c = b;b = a;a = temp
END SUBROUTINE rotate_int
SUBROUTINE rotate_char(a,b,c)
   IMPLICIT NONE
   CHARACTER :: a,b,c,temp
   temp = c;c = b;b = a;a = temp
END SUBROUTINE rotate_char
```

If the procedures are encapsulated in a MODULE then an INTERFACE block in the calling program does not have to repeat the SUBROUTINE and variable declarations as they are available through USE < module name > statement in the calling program. The INTERFACE block takes the form:

```
INTERFACE rotate
   MODULE PROCEDURE rotate_int
   MODULE PROCEDURE rotate_char
END INTERFACE
```

Fig. 16.9 Interface block to define generic procedure included in a MODULE.

Example Program 16.6 illustrates how the INTERFACE block is used.

Example Program 16.6 Defining a generic procedure with a MODULE

```
!PROGRAM 16.6
!ILLUSTRATING USE OF GENERIC FUNCTION

MODULE shift_circ
   CONTAINS
   SUBROUTINE rotate_int(a,b,c)
      IMPLICIT NONE
      INTEGER :: a,b,c,temp
      temp = c;c = b;b = a;a = temp
   END SUBROUTINE rotate_int
   SUBROUTINE rotate_char(a,b,c)
      IMPLICIT NONE
      CHARACTER :: a,b,c,temp
      temp = c;c = b;b = a;a = temp
   END SUBROUTINE rotate_char
END MODULE shift_circ

!MAIN PROGRAM WHICH USES MODULE
PROGRAM generic_2
   USE shift_circ
   IMPLICIT NONE
   INTERFACE rotate
      MODULE PROCEDURE rotate_int
      MODULE PROCEDURE rotate_char
   END INTERFACE
   INTEGER :: x,y,z
   CHARACTER :: p,q,r
   READ *,x,y,z
   PRINT *,"x =",x,"y =",y,"z =",z
   rotate(x,y,z)
   PRINT *,"x =",x,"y =",y,"z =",z
   PRINT *," Character Rotation"
   READ *,p,q,r
   PRINT *,"p =",p,"q =",q,"r =",r
   rotate(p,q,r)
   PRINT *,"p =",p,"q =",q,"r =",r
END PROGRAM generic_2
```

It is also possible to define a generic procedure in a MODULE by including the INTERFACE block specification of Fig. 16.9 in its body. In such a case a calling program which uses the MODULE does not require an INTERFACE block.

The main point while defining generic procedures is that the TYPE of at least one dummy argument of the constituent procedures must be different.

16.4 USER DEFINED OPERATORS

Fortran 90 allows a user to define his/her own operator for operations on derived type variables. It is also possible to "overload" intrinsic operators + , −, *, /, ** etc. In other words, the same operator may have a different meaning depending on the TYPE of the operands. The new meaning may be defined by a user. We will illustrate this with a simple example of a program which computes the sum and product modulo 8 of two vectors whose elements are octal digits (digits to base 8). The sum/product is the sum/product of the corresponding elements of the vector modulo 8 as we want the elements of the sum vector also to be single octal digits. We give two examples below:

a = [7 3 2 0 6]
b = [6 4 3 1 5]
a + b (modulo 8) = [5 7 5 1 3]
a * b (modulo 8) = [2 4 6 0 6]

The operators + and * are "overloaded". They do not stand for the normal addition and multiplication but octal modulo 8 addition and multiplication. The + and * are *not* vector operators.

Example Program 16.7 Octal addition and multiplication

```
!PROGRAM 16.7
!PROGRAM TO ADD & MULTIPLY OCTAL VECTORS
!ILLUSTRATES DEFINING OF "OVERLOADED" OPERATORS

MODULE oct_add_mult
   INTEGER :: x,y,z
   SAVE
   IMPLICIT NONE
   TYPE octal
      INTEGER :: val
   END TYPE octal
   INTERFACE OPERATOR(+)
      MODULE PROCEDURE octal_add
   END INTERFACE
   INTERFACE OPERATOR (*)
      MODULE PROCEDURE octal_mult
   END INTERFACE
   CONTAINS
      FUNCTION octal_add(x,y) RESULT(z)
      TYPE(octal),INTENT(IN) :: x,y
      TYPE(octal) :: z
      IF((ABS(x%val) > 7).OR.(ABS(y%val) > 7)) THEN
            PRINT *,"Error in input vectors"
         RETURN
      ENDIF
      z%val = MOD((x%val+y%val),8)
   END FUNCTION octal_add
   FUNCTION octal_mult(x,y) RESULT(z)
   TYPE(octal),INTENT(IN) :: x,y
   TYPE(octal) :: z
      IF((ABS(x%val) >7).OR.(ABS(y%val) > 7)) THEN
      PRINT *,"Error in input vectors"
      RETURN
      ENDIF
      z%val = MOD((x%val*y%val),8)
   END FUNCTION octal_mult
END MODULE oct_add_mult
```

```
PROGRAM vec_sum_prod_octal
   USE oct_add_mult
   IMPLICIT NONE
   TYPE(octal),DIMENSION(5) :: a,b,c,d
   INTEGER :: i
   a%val = (/ 7, 3, 2, 0, 6 /)
   b%val = (/ 6, 4, 3, 1, 5 /)
   DO i=1,5
      c(i) = a(i)+b(i) !OBSERVE USE OF "USER" DEFINED + FOR ADDITION
      d(i) = a(i)*b(i)
   END DO
      PRINT *,"Vector a:"
      PRINT *, a%val
      PRINT *,"Vector b:"
      PRINT *, b%val
      PRINT *,"Sum of vectors a,b"
      PRINT *,c%val
      PRINT *,"Product of vectors a, b"
      PRINT *, d%val
END PROGRAM vec_sum_prod_octal
```

We have developed Example Program 16.7 to solve this problem. Observe in the program we have created a MODULE in which we first define a derived type octal. Following this we have written two FUNCTIONs octal_add (x,y) and octal_mult (x,y). Consider FUNCTION octal_add (x,y). We first declare x,y,z as of TYPE (octal). We next check that x%val, y%val are between 0 and 7. If any one of them is not in this range we give an error message and return control to the calling program. We then calculate x%val = MOD ((x%val + y%val), 8) which is the octal sum of x%val and y%val. FUNCTION octal_mult (x,y) similarly gives an output which is the product of x and y modulo 8. Following the MODULE we have the main PROGRAM. In the program we have a statement USE oct_add_mult (x,y) which makes the MODULE oct_add_mult available to the main PROGRAM. After declaring the necessary variables we have written:

```
INTERFACE OPERATOR (+)
MODULE PROCEDURE octal_add
END INTERFACE
```

This defines the operator +. FUNCTION octal_add (x,y) in the MODULE defines the addition operation for variables declared TYPE (octal). The symbol + which is normally used for decimal addition is now said to be "overloaded" as it will add operands which are octal numbers. The precedence of this operator is identical to that of the intrinsic operator + of Fortran 90. We have used this operator to add the components of an array whose elements are of TYPE (octal). We have also overloaded the operator for multiplying variables of TYPE (octal) by writing:

```
INTERFACE OPERATOR (*)
   MODULE PROCEDURE octal_mult
END INTERFACE
```

The precedence of * for octals is the same as that of the intrinsic operator *.

Observe that the + and * operators are overloaded only to octal add, multiply respectively of scalar quantities. They do not apply for vector quantities. We have used an explicit DO loop for this reason in Example Program 16.7.

We could have defined different operator(s) instead of overloading + and *. If we write

```
INTERFACE OPERATOR (.ADDO.)
   MODULE PROCEDURE octal_add
END INTERFACE
```

then .ADDO. is a new operator. If we write

```
z_sum = x .ADDO. y
```

then x and y are added using octal addition. The operator can be any identifier enclosed by dots (.). In this case the precedence of ADDO is lowest.

We have defined binary operators, that is, operators which operate on two operands. While writing a program we should make sure that the procedure defining the operation has two dummy arguments of the appropriate TYPE.

We can also define a unary operator which operates on a single operand. As an example we will define an operator which will rotate clockwise an array by one position. For example if an array a is

```
         a = [ 1 6 7 9 4 3 ]
.ROTATE. a = [ 3 1 6 7 9 4 ]
```

Example Program 16.8 implements this unary operation .ROTATE. Observe that FUNCTION rot in the MODULE rotate_vec implements rotation of input array. Only a function can be used to define an operator (user defined or overloaded) and it should not have any side effects. In other words it should operate on input and not alter any other variables. Observe that in FUNCTION rot(a) we have used RESULT(rot_array) to return the result. This is necessary. When an operator is overloaded the meaning of the operator can be extended but not changed. In other words the operator + can be used to add new type of quantities but not used to, for example, multiply. The INTERFACE definition of .ROTATE. is

```
INTERFACE OPERATOR (.ROTATE.)
   MODULE PROCEDURE rot
END INTERFACE
```

and it is placed in the MODULE itself. The entire MODULE including the INTERFACE definition is available to the calling program by writing USE rotate_vec. The FUNCTION rot is called by the appearance of .ROTATE. in the calling program. The rest of the program is self-explanatory.

Example Program 16.8 Use of unary operator—.ROTATE.—Version 1

```
!PROGRAM 16.8
!PROGRAM TO ROTATE AN ARRAY CLOCKWISE BY ONE POSITION

MODULE rotate_vec
   INTERFACE OPERATOR (.ROTATE.)
      MODULE PROCEDURE rot
   END INTERFACE
      CONTAINS
   FUNCTION rot(a) RESULT(rot_array)
      IMPLICIT NONE
      INTEGER,DIMENSION(:),INTENT(IN) :: a
      INTEGER,DIMENSION(SIZE(a)) :: rot_array
      INTEGER :: i,n
      n=SIZE(a)
      rot_array(1) = a(n)
      DO i=1,n-1
         rot_array(i+1) = a(i)
      END DO
   END FUNCTION rot
END MODULE rotate_vec

PROGRAM vec_rotate
   USE rotate_vec
   IMPLICIT NONE
   INTEGER :: i,m
   INTEGER,DIMENSION(:), ALLOCATABLE :: b,b_out
   PRINT *,"Type no. of components in array"
   READ *,m
   PRINT *,"Please type",m,"elements of array"
   ALLOCATE(b (m))
   ALLOCATE(b_out (m))
   READ *,(b(i),i=1,m)
   b_out = .ROTATE. b
   PRINT *,"rotated array =",(b_out(i),i=1,m)
END PROGRAM vec_rotate
```

Instead of using a MODULE we can also write Example Program 16.8 in a different form with only a FUNCTION as shown in Example Program 16.9. In this program using .ROTATE. is equivalent to calling the FUNCTION rot by the main program.

Example Program 16.9 Use of unary operator .ROTATE.—Version 2

```
!PROGRAM 16.9
!VERSION 2 OF PROGRAM 16.8

FUNCTION rot(a) RESULT(rot_array)
   IMPLICIT NONE
   INTEGER,DIMENSION(:),INTENT(IN) :: a
   INTEGER,DIMENSION(SIZE(a)) :: rot_array
   INTEGER :: i,n
   n = SIZE(a)
   rot_array(1) = a(n)
   DO i=1,n-1
      rot_array(i+1) = a(i)
   END DO
END FUNCTION rot
PROGRAM vec_rotate_2
   INTERFACE OPERATOR (.ROTATE.)
      FUNCTION rot(a) RESULT(rot_array)
         INTEGER,DIMENSION(:),INTENT(IN) :: a
         INTEGER,DIMENSION(SIZE(a)) :: rot_array
      END FUNCTION rot
   END INTERFACE
   IMPLICIT NONE
   INTEGER :: i,m
   INTEGER,DIMENSION(:), ALLOCATABLE :: b,b_out
   PRINT *,"Type no. of components in array"
   READ *,m
   ALLOCATE(b (m))
   ALLOCATE(b_out (m))
   PRINT *,"Please type",m,"elements of array"
   READ *,(b(i),i=1,m)
   b_out = .ROTATE.b
   PRINT *,"Rotated array =",(b_out(i),i=1,m)
END PROGRAM vec_rotate_2
```

16.5 OVERLOADING ASSIGNMENT

In the last section we saw how intrinsic operators may be used to operate on user defined data types besides their normal operation. We called this overloading an operator. It is also possible to extend the meaning of assignment to enable assignment of the value of an expression of one data type to a variable name of another type. In fact, as we have already seen, Fortran 90 allows assigning a real expression to an integer variable name and vice versa. We can go beyond this by overloading = using an INTERFACE block. For example we can assign the value of a logical expression to an integer variable by setting an integer variable to 1 when a logical quantity becomes .TRUE. and to 0 when it becomes .FALSE.

In order to overload an assignment we write a SUBROUTINE which does the assignment using two dummy arguments. It is a good practice to have as the first dummy argument of the SUBROUTINE a variable whose type is the same as the variable on the left of the assignment symbol (=). Thus the first dummy will be declared with INTENT (OUT) and the second dummy with INTENT(IN). A SUBROUTINE to set an integer to a logical value is given in Example Program 16.10. In the calling program we have an INTERFACE block to associate the

Example Program 16.10 Use of = to assign a logical value to integer

```
!PROGRAM 16.10
!ILLUSTRATES OVERLOADING AN ASSIGNMENT
SUBROUTINE logical_to_int(in_t,boolean)
   IMPLICIT NONE
   LOGICAL,INTENT(IN) :: boolean
   INTEGER,INTENT(OUT) :: in_t
   IF(boolean) THEN
      in_t = 1
   ELSE
      in_t = 0
   ENDIF
END SUBROUTINE logical_to_int
PROGRAM test
   IMPLICIT NONE
   INTEGER :: i
   LOGICAL :: a,b,c
   INTERFACE ASSIGNMENT(=)
      SUBROUTINE logical_to_int(in_t,boolean)
      LOGICAL,INTENT(IN) :: boolean
      INTEGER,INTENT(OUT) :: in_t
      END SUBROUTINE logical_to_int
   END INTERFACE
   PRINT *,"Please type three logical values as T or F",&
      "blank space must separate values"
   READ 25,a,b,c
25 FORMAT(L1,1X,L1,1X,L1)
   PRINT 30,a,b,c
30 FORMAT(1X,L1,1X,L1,1X,L1)
   i = a .AND. b .OR. c
   PRINT *,"i =",i
END PROGRAM test
```

assignment (=) with the appropriate SUBROUTINE which specifies this assignment. Observe that in the calling program we have assigned a logical quantity to an integer.

16.6 ARRAY VALUED FUNCTIONS

Fortran 90 allows arrays to be returned as values of functions. Array results can be obtained using SUBROUTINEs as we saw. Sometimes use of FUNCTION is more convenient, particularly, as operations are allowed on whole arrays in Fortran 90. We illustrate this by writing a simple FUNCTION which uses two arrays as dummy arguments and returns an array as result. The FUNCTION adds modulo 10 corresponding elements of two conformable arrays (that is arrays of equal size) and return the sum array.

We have named the FUNCTION:

```
FUNCTION mod_sum_arr (arr_x, arr_y)
```

This FUNCTION adds modulo 10 arrays input via dummy arguments arr_x, arr_y and returns the sum in mod_sum_array. The FUNCTION is developed in Example Program 16.11. We have declared the dummy arguments arr_x and arr_y as assumed shape arrays in the FUNCTION.

The two arrays must have equal extents. The result array mod_sum_arr (which is returned in the name of the FUNCTION) is declared to be of SIZE (arr_x) which is the extent of one of the input arrays. The arrays are added modulo 10 by a DO loop. We could have used array addition allowed in Fortran 90 but used a DO loop instead for illustration.

Example Program 16.11 An array valued function

```
!PROGRAM 16.11
!WE DEFINE ARRAY VALUED FUNCTION BELOW

FUNCTION mod_sum_arr(arr_x,arr_y)
  IMPLICIT NONE
  INTEGER,DIMENSION(:) :: arr_x,arr_y
  INTEGER,DIMENSION(SIZE(arr_x)) :: mod_sum_arr
!WE HAVE DEFINED INPUT ARRAYS arr_x, arr_y TO THE FUNCTION
!AS ASSUMED SHAPE ARRAY.THEY ARE ASSUMED TO BE OF EQUAL
!SIZE.THE RESULT ARRAY RETURNED VIA mod_sum_arr
  INTEGER :: i !LOCAL VARIABLE
  DO i=1,SIZE(arr_x)
    mod_sum_arr(i) = MOD((arr_x(i) + arr_y(i)),10)
  END DO
!WE HAVE USED DO LOOP TO ADD COMPONENTS OF ARRAY
!WE COULD HAVE USED ARRAY ADDITION
!mod_sum_arr=MOD((arr_x+arr_y),10)

END FUNCTION mod_sum_arr

!PROGRAM ILLUSTRATES USE OF ARRAY VALUED FUNCTION
PROGRAM mod_10_sum
  IMPLICIT NONE
!MAXIMUM SIZE OF INPUT ARRAYS IS 20
!INPUT ARRAYS ARE arr_p,arr_q.ASSUME ELEMENTS < 10.
!arr_r IS THE MODULO 10 SUM OF ARRAYS arr_p and arr_q
  INTEGER,DIMENSION(10) :: arr_p,arr_q,arr_r
!AN EXPLICIT INTERFACE IS NEEDED TO CALL
!AN ARRAY VALUED FUNCTION
  INTERFACE array_sum
    FUNCTION mod_sum_arr(arr_x,arr_y)
      IMPLICIT NONE
      INTEGER,DIMENSION(:) :: arr_x,arr_y
      INTEGER,DIMENSION(SIZE(arr_x)) :: mod_sum_arr
      END FUNCTION
  END INTERFACE array_sum
  PRINT *,"Input elements of arr_p . Each element < 10"
  READ *,arr_p
  PRINT *,"Input elements of arr_q . Each element < 10"
  READ *,arr_q
  IF(SIZE(arr_p) /= SIZE(arr_q)) THEN
    PRINT *,"Input arrays are of different size, they cannot be added"
  ELSE
    arr_r = mod_sum_arr(arr_p,arr_q)
    PRINT 25,arr_p,arr_q,arr_r
  25 FORMAT(1X,"arr_p=",10I3/"arr_q=",10I3/"arr_r=",10I3)
    ENDIF
END PROGRAM mod_10_sum
```

The FUNCTION is called by PROGRAM mod_10_sum in which we have declared arrays arr_p, arr_q, arr_r of maximum DIMENSION 20. We have assumed that the elements are < 10. This assumption is not necessary. In fact the program will work with integers of any size. Observe the use of an explicit INTERFACE in the calling PROGRAM. This is essential when an array valued FUNCTION is called. An explicit INTERFACE is required when assumed shape arrays are used as dummy arguments of procedures. The rest of the program is self-explanatory.

16.7 USE OF OPTIONAL AND KEYWORD ARGUMENTS IN PROCEDURES

There are many situations in practice when all arguments in a procedure are not required. Consider the following simple example of summing a series:

$$\text{sum} = \sum_{i=p}^{q} ax_i + b * i$$

Assume the following cases. If p is not specified it is assumed to be 1 and if q is not specified it is assumed to be 20. If we write a function it could be:

FUNCTION s_sum (arr_x, a, b, p, q)

The dummy variables p and q are optional. If p is not present it is assumed to be 1; if q is not present it is assumed to be 20. If both p and q are not present they are taken as 1 and 20 respectively. We can call the FUNCTION as:

```
      s_sum (x_in, a_in, b_in, l_bound, u_bound)
or    s_sum (x_in, a_in, b_in, l_bound)
or    s_sum (x_in, a_in, b_in)
```

Fortran 90 allows one to specify OPTIONAL dummy variables in procedures. There is an intrinsic function

PRESENT (*dummy variable name*)

to enquire whether a dummy variable name is present in the calling program FUNCTION invocation. If it is PRESENT the function PRESENT returns TRUE, else it returns FALSE.

We have written FUNCTION s_sum (arr_x, a, b, p, q) in Example Program 16.12. Observe that in the declaration the dummy arguments p and q have the qualifier OPTIONAL. This informs the compiler that these dummies may or may not be present. In the sequence of IF statements we check which optional dummy arguments are present and based on this assign appropriate values to p and q. When p, q or both are not present they are undefined. Thus we have declared variables temp_p and temp_q which are given appropriate values when p or q or both are not present. Observe that in the case when lower bound is not present if we call the FUNCTION as s_sum(x_in, a_in, b_in, u_bound) the compiler has no way of knowing that u_bound is to be associated with q and not p. Thus Fortran 90 allows dummy argument of a FUNCTION to be used as a keyword: We have thus written the CALL in this case as s_sum (x_in, a_in, b_in, q = u_bound). The rest of the FUNCTION is self-explanatory.

Example Program 16.12 Use of optional arguments in functions

```
!PROGRAM 16.12
!ILLUSTRATES USE OF OPTIONAL ARGUMENTS IN FUNCTIONS

FUNCTION s_sum(arr_x,a,b,p,q)
   IMPLICIT NONE
   REAL,INTENT(IN),DIMENSION(:) :: arr_x
   INTEGER,INTENT(IN),OPTIONAL :: p,q
   REAL,INTENT(IN) :: a,b ; REAL :: s_sum
   INTEGER :: i,temp_p,temp_q !LOCAL VARIABLE
   s_sum = 0
   print *,present(p),present(q)
   IF(.NOT.PRESENT(p))temp_p = 1
   IF(.NOT.PRESENT(q))temp_q = 20
   print *,temp_p,temp_q,a,b
   DO i=temp_p,temp_q
      s_sum = s_sum + arr_x(i)*a + b*i
   END DO
END FUNCTION s_sum
!CALLING PROGRAM
PROGRAM add_series
   IMPLICIT NONE
   REAL,DIMENSION(20) :: x_in
   REAL :: a_in,b_in,sum_series
   INTEGER :: u_bound,l_bound,i
   INTERFACE
      FUNCTION s_sum(arr_x,a,b,p,q)
      REAL,INTENT(IN),DIMENSION(:) :: arr_x
      INTEGER,OPTIONAL :: p,q
      REAL,INTENT(IN) :: a,b
      REAL :: s_sum
      END FUNCTION
   END INTERFACE
   PRINT *,"Type 20 components of array"
   READ *,x_in
   PRINT *,"Type a_in, b_in"
   READ *,a_in,b_in
   sum_series = s_sum(x_in,a_in,b_in)
   PRINT *,"Series sum : Case 1 =",sum_series
   PRINT *,"Type u_bound and l_bound"
   READ *,u_bound,l_bound
   PRINT *,"Type elements of the array"
   READ *,(x_in(i),i=l_bound,u_bound)
   sum_series = s_sum(x_in,a_in,b_in,l_bound,u_bound)
   PRINT *,"Series sum :Case 2 =",sum_series
   PRINT *,"Type u_bound"
   READ *,u_bound
   READ *,(x_in(i),i=1,u_bound)
   sum_series = s_sum(x_in,a_in,b_in,q=u_bound)
   PRINT *,"Series sum :Case 3 =",sum_series
END PROGRAM add_series
```

The calling program add_series has an explicit INTERFACE in which the FUNCTION s_sum and all its declarations are included. An explicit INTERFACE is required whenever a called procedure has optional arguments. The rest of the calling program is self-explanatory.

We saw in Example Program 16.12 the need for Fortran 90 to allow dummy arguments of a procedure to be used as keywords when a procedure is called. This also enhances readability of the program, particularly when there is a long list of dummy arguments. For instance we could have written in Example Program 16.12

```
      s_sum (arr_x = x_in, a = a_in, b = b_in, p = l_bound, q = u_bound)
or    s_sum (a = a_in, b = b_in, arr_x = x_in, q = u_bound, p = l_bound)
or    s_sum (a = 5.0, b = 10.5, arr_x = x_in, p = 10, q = 20)
or    s_sum (x_in, a_in, b_in, p = l_bound)
or    s_sum (x_in, a_in, b_in, p = l_bound, q = u_bound)
```

In the second example we have changed the order of the arguments in the call. This is allowed. In the last example we have mixed positional arguments and keyword arguments. This is allowed provided after the first use of a keyword argument, the remaining arguments are also keyword arguments. When keyword arguments are used, an explicit INTERFACE is required in the calling program.

16.8 SCOPE OF NAMES IN FORTRAN 90

We saw in Section 16.1 that there are three types of program units in Fortran 90. Let us first consider main program unit whose first line is PROGRAM program_name and last line END PROGRAM program_name. In Fig. 16.1 we have given the structure of this unit. The major question which arises is the scope of the variable names used in the PROGRAM. By scope we mean the set of lines in a program where a variable name can be used and its value is applicable. Identifiers used to refer to subprogram names, TYPE names etc., must also have a unique interpretation within their scope.

The scope of variables declared in a PROGRAM block begins from the first line and is upto END PROGRAM line. In other words if a variable name is declared in the PROGRAM it is available to all statements in the PROGRAM. All internal subprograms contained in the PROGRAM can use them.

Variables declared in the internal subprogram are private to it (i.e., they have no meaning outside the internal subprogram). We will explain these points using the Example Program 16.13.

Example Program 16.13 Program illustrates scope rules—Version 1

```
!PROGRAM 16.13
!ILLUSTRATES SCOPE RULES

PROGRAM scope_rules
   IMPLICIT NONE
   INTEGER :: x,y,z,a,b,p
   x = 16;y = 9;a = 2;b = 4;
   z = fun_1(x,y) * b
   CALL sub_1(x,y,p)
   PRINT *,"Values printed in main program"
   PRINT *,"x =",x,"y=",y,"a =",a,"b =",b
```

```
PRINT *,"z =",z,"p =",p
CONTAINS
  FUNCTION fun_1(p,q)
  INTEGER,INTENT(IN) :: p,q
  INTEGER :: fun_1
  INTEGER :: b=16 !LOCAL VARIABLE
  b = p * q
  fun_1 = a*SQRT(real(p)) + b*SQRT(real(q))
  PRINT *,"Values printed in fun_1"
  PRINT *,"p =",p,"q =",q,"b =",b,"a =",a
  PRINT *,"fun_1 =",fun_1,"x =",x,"y =",y
END FUNCTION fun_1
SUBROUTINE sub_1(p,q,r)
  INTEGER,INTENT(IN) :: p,q
  INTEGER,INTENT(OUT) :: r
  r = b*SQRT(real(p)) + q*q
  PRINT *,"Values printed in sub_1"
  PRINT *,"p =",p,"q =",q,"r =",r,"b =",b
END SUBROUTINE sub_1
END PROGRAM scope_rules
```

In PROGRAM scope_rules, the variables x, y, z, a, b, p are declared INTEGER and their scope is the entire program. Values are assigned to x, y, a, b and are 16, 9, 2 and 4 respectively. The values stored are shown in the first line of Table 16.1. In the statement,

z = fun_1 (x, y) * b

the function fun_1 is called with x, y. Referring to the statement FUNCTION fun_1(x,y), variables x, y correspond to the dummies p, q in fun_1. The values of p, q in fun_1 are shown in the second

Table 16.1 Values of Variables in Example Program 16.13

	MAIN						fun_1				sub_1		
	x	y	z	a	b	p	p	q	fun_1	b	p	q	r
INPUT	16	9	–	2	4	–	–	–	–	16			
	16	9	1760	2	4	97	16	9	440	144	16	9	97

line of Table 16.1. In FUNCTION fun_1, b is declared as a local variable. This is *private* to fun_1. Even though b is declared in the main program and has a value 4 it is not applicable in fun_1, as it is declared again in fun_1 and assigned a value 16. The value of b remains 4 in the calling PROGRAM. The function fun_1 is calculated as:

fun_1 = 2 * 4 + 144 * 3 = 440

Observe that the value of a from the main PROGRAM is used in fun_1 as a is not redeclared in fun_1.

When control returns to the calling program z is calculated as:

z = 440 * 4 = 1760

PROGRAM scope-rules after computing z, calls sub_1. The dummy variables p, q in the SUBROUTINE are assigned values 16 and 9 respectively by the main program. In SUBROUTINE the variable b is not declared. Thus the value assigned in the main PROGRAM which CONTAINS the SUBROUTINE is applicable. Thus r is calculated in the SUBROUTINE as:

$$r = 4 * 4 + 9 * 9 = 97$$

This value is returned in p declared in the calling program. Observe that the dummy variable p declared in SUBROUTINE and the variable p used in the calling program are different. Each one is entirely local in its own scope. The value of p printed in SUBROUTINE sub_1 in PROGRAM scope-rules will be different as seen from Table 16.1. The Example Program given is a contrived one to illustrate points. Normally when subprograms are contained in another program dummy arguments are hardly used.

Example Program 16.14 Illustrates scope rules—Version 2

```
!PROGRAM 16.14
!ILLUSTRATES SCOPE RULES
PROGRAM scope_2
   IMPLICIT NONE
   INTEGER :: x,y,z,a,b,p
   x = 16;y = 9;a = 2;b = 4
   z = fun_1() * b
   CALL sub_1(p)
   PRINT *,"Values printed in the main program"
   PRINT *,"x =",x,"y =",y,"a =",a,"b =",b
   PRINT *,"z =",z,"p =",p
   STOP
   CONTAINS
   INTEGER FUNCTION fun_1()
   !x,y NEED NOT BE DECLARED AS THEY ARE DECLARED IN THE
   !CONTAINING PROGRAM
      INTEGER :: b=16 !LOCAL VARIABLE
      b = x*y
      fun_1 = a*SQRT(REAL(x)) + b*SQRT(REAL(y))
      PRINT *,"Values printed in fun_1"
      PRINT *,"fun_1 =",fun_1,"a =",a,"b =",b
   END FUNCTION fun_1
   SUBROUTINE sub_1(r)
      INTEGER,INTENT(OUT) :: r
      r = b*SQRT(REAL(x)) + y*y
      PRINT *,"Values printed in sub_1"
      PRINT *,"b =",b,"r =",r
   END SUBROUTINE sub_1
END PROGRAM scope_2
```

We have illustrated the fact that the scope of variables declared in PROGRAM includes the internal subprograms contained in it in Example Program 16.14.

The second program unit we considered are external subprograms (see Fig. 16.2). External programs are compiled independently. Thus all local variables declared in them are private to them. The only communication with other programs is through dummy arguments. The names of external subprograms should, of course, be known to all calling programs. If external subprograms contain within them internal subprograms then the rules we already discussed apply.

Apart from variable names, statement labels, statement numbers, names of internal programs, names of TYPE declarations are all private to external subprograms. Similarly local names used in the main program are private to them and not available to external subprograms.

Lastly we come to MODULES (see Fig. 16.3). A module contains declaration of names of variables, parameters, types etc., between the MODULE statement and the CONTAIN statement. This is followed by the full source code of subprograms internal to it ending with END MODULE *name* statement. When a module is included in a program (or another module) with a USE statement, it is as if all declarations made in the module were made at the place where the USE statement appears (We will see later that some variables, types etc., can be declared PRIVATE in a module and these are not available even when USE statement appears in a program). Thus if a MODULE containing only variables and TYPE declarations are placed in a number of external subprograms then these variables are accessible to all of them and they can each store and change values independently in them. They are thus common to all programs which use them (In Fortran 77 there was a statement called COMMON which defined a COMMON area in memory shared by many subprograms. MODULE serves a similar purpose in a much neater way).

When MODULEs contain subprograms then these subprograms are accessible and can be called by any program in which the MODULE is included by a USE statement. This is to be contrasted with internal subprograms which are available only to programs in which they are included and are not callable by other subprograms.

16.9 SAVING VALUES OF VARIABLES IN SUBPROGRAMS

Normally when control leaves a subprogram all the local variables are freed and any data stored in them is lost. If we want them to be saved it can be done in two ways. One of them is to initialize their values when they are declared. Example Program 16.15 illustrates this. The values stored in good_data and sum_age are to be accumulated in the SUBROUTINE and not lost when control leaves it. We have initialized good_data and sum_age when they are declared in the SUBROUTINE. They are thus saved.

Example Program 16.15 Illustrates use of SAVE attribute

```
!PROGRAM 16.15
!EXAMPLE TO SHOW THE USE OF SAVE ATTRIBUTE

PROGRAM save_attr
   IMPLICIT NONE
   INTEGER :: serial_no,age
   PRINT *,"Type serial no,age"
   PRINT *,"End of data indicated by serial no=0"
   DO
      READ *,serial_no,age
      CALL sum_good_age(age)
      IF(serial_no == 0) EXIT
   END DO
END PROGRAM save_attr
```

```
SUBROUTINE sum_good_age(age)
  IMPLICIT NONE
  INTEGER :: avg_age
  INTEGER,INTENT(IN) :: age
  INTEGER :: good_data =0, sum_age=0
  IF((age < 25).AND.(age > 3)) THEN
    good_data = good_data + 1
    sum_age = sum_age + age
  ENDIF
  IF (age == 0) THEN
    avg_age = sum_age/good_data
    PRINT *,"No. of good data =",good_data
    PRINT *,"Average age =",avg_age
  ENDIF
END SUBROUTINE sum_good_age
```

The other method is to use a SAVE attribute in the declaration of the variables whose values are to be saved. Thus if the values of variables good_data and sum_age are to be saved we write:

```
INTEGER, SAVE :: good_data, sum_age
```

As a good programming practice, in order to remember which local variables are SAVED in successive invocation of the SUBROUTINE it is better to write:

```
INTEGER, SAVE :: good_data = 0, sum_age = 0
```

The dummy variables of SUBROUTINE should not have a SAVE attribute. The SAVE attribute is relevant only to the *local variables* in procedures.

The values of all variables declared in the main program are automatically saved. No SAVE attribute is needed in the main PROGRAM.

If a MODULE is used in the main program, the values of all local variables in the MODULE are automatically saved. If a MODULE is used only in a subprogram and if values of the variables declared in the MODULE are to be saved then we write SAVE after the MODULE statement. In fact we have done it in earlier occasions just to prevent loss of data inadvertently.

SUMMARY

1. A FUNCTION or a SUBROUTINE can call itself. In such a case it is called a recursive subprogram. The fact that a subprogram is recursive is indicated by using the word RECURSIVE as a prefix of FUNCTION or SUBROUTINE statement.
2. A procedure whose dummy argument(s) can be one of many types is called a generic procedure. For example, the procedure rotate (a, b, c) when a, b, c can be either integers or characters is called a generic procedure. A procedure can be defined as generic in Fortran 90 by writing multiple versions of the procedure one for each type of dummy argument(s). The declarations of all of these procedures are included in an INTERFACE block in which a common generic name is given to the procedure. The declaration of INTERFACE block:

```
INTERFACE rotate
   SUBROUTINE rotate_int (a, b, c)
      INTEGER :: a, b, c, temp
   END SUBROUTINE rotate_int
   SUBROUTINE rotate_char (a, b, c)
      CHARACTER :: a, b, c, temp
   END SUBROUTINE rotate_char
END INTERFACE rotate
```

gives a single name rotate for rotation of either integer variables or characters.

3. In Fortran 90 a user can define his own operations or overload intrinsic operators to do one of a set of operations. The operator can be either unary or binary. For example if octal addition of elements of two arrays are needed we can "overload" the operator + which is used for decimal addition to also do octal addition. This is done by defining an INTERFACE block to define +. The block is

```
INTERFACE OPERATOR (+)
   MODULE PROCEDURE octal_add
END INTERFACE
```

   in which a procedure octal_add defined in a MODULE gives the algorithm to add two octal numbers. Now + can be used to perform octal addition of variables declared to be of TYPE octal in a program. An overloaded operator can only extend the meaning of an operator but not redefine it. The MODULE PROCEDURE can only be a function and not a subroutine. A unary operator can be similarly defined. Instead of overloading an intrinsic operator a new operator can be defined by using an identifier enclosed by dots (.). For example .ADDO. can be used as octal addition operator.

4. The assignment operator can also be overloaded to assign the value of an expression formed by variables of one type to a variable of another type.

5. An array can be returned as value of a FUNCTION. An explicit INTERFACE giving the name of the FUNCTION and all the declarations of variables in it is required in the calling program.

6. Fortran 90 allows some of the dummy variables in a SUBROUTINE or FUNCTION to be optional. An explicit INTERFACE containing the declarations of the FUNCTION is required in the calling program.

7. By scope of a variable in a procedure we mean the set of lines in the procedure where the variable name can be used unambiguously. The scope of a variable name in a main PROGRAM is the whole program from PROGRAM *name* to END PROGRAM statement including the subprograms contained in it. The scope of variable declared in a subprogram, is the entire subprogram. Variables appearing as local variables in a subprogram are private to it. They can not be used by other subprograms or main program. When a MODULE is placed in a program with a USE statement, the variables and procedures defined in the MODULE become available to the subprogram in which it is placed. MODULEs are a convenient way of sharing variables/procedures among many programs.

8. When control leaves an external subprogram, the values stored in all local variables declared in it are not saved. They can be saved either by initializing the local variables with values when they are declared or by including an attribute SAVE in their declarations. The values of variables in MODULE placed in a main PROGRAM are automatically saved. If a MODULE is placed only in an external subprogram, variable values can be saved by writing SAVE after the MODULE statement.

EXERCISES

16.1 Write a recursive function to compute a**n where a is real and n is an integer. Compare it with an iterative function.

16.2 The Ackerman's function is defined as follows:

$A(0, n) = n + 1$
$A(m, 0) = A(m - 1, 1) \quad (m > 0)$
$A(m, n) = A(m - 1, A(m, n - 1)) \quad (m, n > 0)$

Using the above definition show that A(2, 2) = 7.

Write a recursive function to compute A (m, n).

16.3 Let committee (n, k) be the number of committees of k persons which can be formed from among n persons. For example, committee (4, 3) = 4. Show that Committee (n, k) = Committee $(n - 1, k)$ + Committee $(n - 1, k - 1)$; $(n, k > 0)$

Committee (1, 1) = 1, Committee (2, 1) = 2.

Write a recursive program to compute Committee (n, k) for $n, k \geq 1$.

16.4 Write a recursive program to print out all possible character strings of length n by picking characters out of a set of k characters. For example, if the given set of characters is 'A', 'B', 'C', then 9 possible strings exist of length n = 2 and they are AA, BB, CC, AB, BA, AC, CA, BC, CB.

16.5 Write a generic procedure to

```
interchange (a, b)
```

to interchange values of a and b. a, b can be of type REAL, INTEGER or CHARACTER.

16.6 Use the procedure of Exercise 16.5 to interchange neighbouring elements of an array x_arr with n elements (n odd or even) x_arr can have REAL, INTEGER or CHARACTER elements.

16.7 Write a generic procedure to find the sum of diagonal elements of a square matrix of size (n × n). The elements can be REAL, INTEGER or COMPLEX.

16.8 Overload the operator + to concatenate two strings of characters.

16.9 Overload the operator – to subtract Modulo 16 two hexadecimal digits. Apply it to two arrays whose elements are hexadecimal digits.

16.10 Define a unary operator .SUCC. which will return the ASCII character following the specified character. For example

```
.SUCC. "A" = "B"
```

Extend it to integers.

16.11 Overload the assignment operator to assign a logical value to an integer expression. A logical value .FALSE. is assigned when an integer expression is 0 and .TRUE. if it is > 0. It is undefined for expressions < 0.

16.12 Overload the assignment operator to assign to a character string variable an integer.

For example if

CHARACTER, LEN (5) :: p and if a is declared INTEGER :: a= 726578 then if we write p = a then

p = <u>72</u> <u>65</u> <u>78</u>

using ASCII coding "HAN" will be stored in p. Pairs of digits taken from the right end are used to get equivalent character code. Digit pairs < 32 are taken as null.

16.13 Given two 8 element arrays of base 4 digits, write an array valued function to return an array whose elements are sum modulo 4 of these arrays. Overload + operator for base 4 addition.

16.14 Write a subroutine to find the mean and the standard deviation of a set of data. SUBROUTINE should have two optimal arguments which specify data to be rejected if it is above a specified value or below a specified value. Rewrite the SUBROUTINE with keyword arguments.

16.15 Write a SUBROUTINE to fit a straight line through a set of points. Use an optional argument to refit the straight line after rejecting points which are too far away from the fitted straight line.

17. *Processing Files in Fortran*

Learning Objectives

In this chapter we will learn how to:

1. Create a sequential file of records on a magnetic medium
2. Read the file and update it with new data
3. Search a sequential file for a specified record
4. Merge two sequential files
5. Create a random file of records, update the file and search the file

In Chapter 11 we defined a field and a record. For example, a line of printed output is a record. A collection of related records is called a *file*. For example, each employee of a company may have a pay record which will consist of his number, name, gross pay and deductions. A collection of all the pay records of individual employees would constitute a payroll file. The individual records in a file can be arranged in two ways. One method of arranging the records is as a *sequential file*. Records are stored on a magnetic tape sequentially. For example, if we consider an audio tape recorder (which is somewhat similar to the tape unit in a computer) songs are recorded in it one after the other sequentially. If one wants to retrieve and play a particular song which happens to be in the middle of the tape one cannot do it without passing (may be at a high speed) through the earlier parts of the tape.

The second method of arranging records as a file is called *direct access file*. In this arrangement a specified record can be directly retrieved without reading or passing through other records in the file. Records may be stored on magnetic disk as a direct access file. We may take a Compact Disk (CD) audio record as an analogy to the magnetic disk. If a particular song is to be retrieved the CD player places the head directly on the required track (which may be the innermost band) without hearing the songs recorded on the outer tracks.

As records in a sequential file can be retrieved only in a rigid order it is necessary to arrange them systematically using one of the unique fields in the records as a key. Usually the records in the file are arranged in ascending or descending order of this *key field*. For example, in a student file the roll number is usually used as the key field as it is unique to each student.

The records in a direct access file (also known as a random access file) need not be arranged in a rigid ascending or descending order by key. Given the key of a record to be retrieved it is transformed to a disk address by the processor and the record is directly retrieved.

Compared to direct access files, sequential files require less computer storage and take less time to process. If only a few records are to be read or altered, however, direct access files are faster. Programs to manipulate direct access files are easier to write compared to those for manipulating sequential files.

Whereas only sequential files may be stored on tapes, both sequential and direct access files may be stored on magnetic disks. As sequential files are more economical in using computer resources most files on disks are also stored as sequential files.

So far in this book we dealt only with small collections of data records assumed to be typed on a keyboard. For small computations it is sufficient to work with such small collection of data records. When a program requires a large collection of data to be processed it is advisable to create a file using the editor of the operating system being used and store the data in it. This will facilitate easy correction of data if data is to be changed and append new data as necessary. Such a method is much better than typing data from the terminal every time a program is run. We will examine how such files can be input to Fortran Programs and processed. Fortran also has statements to create sequential or random access files using data typed on terminals. In the next section we will see how sequential files can be created.

17.1 CREATING A SEQUENTIAL FILE

In this section we will introduce the Fortran statements necessary to create a sequential file on a magentic device. The records of the file are typed on a terminal, one record per line, containing the following data:

Fields ⟶	Roll number	Name	Marks 1	Marks 2	Marks 3
	4 digits	Maximum 25 chars.	Maximum 3 digits	Maximum 3 digits	Maximum 3 digits

A typical record would be typed as:

```
3468, A.B. RAMCHANDANI, 85, 48, 92
```

and will be read by a format free READ statement. We will also assume that the records are input in ascending order of roll number. The roll number is unique and will be used as the key field for each record. A record containing 0 in the roll number field will be used to indicate end of records and will be typed as the last record on the terminal. We will assume that the records are arranged in ascending order of roll number while being typed on the terminal. We will write a program (Example Program 17.1) in Fortran 90 to read these records and store them in a file in a magnetic medium in the computer. The magnetic medium is normally a disk. The file we create will be a sequential file as the records will be arranged in ascending order of roll number which is the key field.

(The records typed on the terminal could be stored in a file using an editor available in the operating system of the computer. Such a file, which is normally stored on a disk and given a name by a programmer, can also be read by a Fortran 90 program. Example Program 17.1 is primarily intended to show how a file can be created and stored using the commands available in Fortran 90).

Referring to Example Program 17.1 after the declarations the following statement is written:

```
OPEN (unit = disk, FILE = "stud_file", STATUS = "NEW", IOSTAT = ios)
```

This statement is required to specify a logical unit number and connect a file with a given name to it. The logical unit number varies from one computer to another. We will thus use either a parameter to specify a unit number or read the unit number into an integer variable name and use the integer variable name as UNIT number. It is compulsory to specify a unit number in the OPEN statement. The other compulsory specification in OPEN statement is:

FILE = *file_name*

Example Program 17.1 Creating a file in Fortran 90

```
!PROGRAM 17.1
!ILLUSTRATES CREATION OF SEQUENTIAL FILE ON DISK

PROGRAM create_file
   IMPLICIT NONE
   INTEGER :: roll_no,marks(3),ios
   CHARACTER(LEN=25) :: name
   INTEGER,PARAMETER :: dsk=20
   OPEN(UNIT = dsk,FILE = "stud_file",STATUS = "NEW",IOSTAT = ios)
   IF(ios /= 0) THEN
      PRINT *,"File dsk cannot be opened"
      STOP
   ENDIF
   REWIND dsk
   DO
      READ *,roll_no,name,marks
      IF(roll_no == 0) EXIT
      WRITE(UNIT = dsk,FMT = 50)roll_no,name,marks
      50 FORMAT(I4,A25,3I3)
   END DO
   END FILE dsk
   REWIND dsk
   CLOSE(dsk)
END PROGRAM create_file
```

The file name can be any logical Fortran identifier. It is the name of a file where the data will be stored. This file will be connected to the specified UNIT. Valid file names are:

stud_file, master_file, xyz, trans_file_2

In the open statement the file name given, namely, stud_file, master_file etc., are enclosed in double quotes. A file can be connected to only one unit at a given time.

Some of the other details about a file given in an OPEN statement are:

- STATUS = file_status

  where file_status is one of the following:

  - "OLD" if the file is an existing file.
  - "NEW" if it is a new file to be opened. If the file name already exists an error condition will be signalled.
  - "SCRATCH" if the file is to be used temporarily. A "SCRATCH" file will be deleted when program comes to an end.
  - "REPLACE" if the named file is to replace an existing named file which would be deleted.
- FORM = "FORMATTED" or "UNFORMATTED". The default mode is FORMATTED if this specification is omitted. A file to be printed should be FORMATTED.
- IOSTAT = integer variable name (e.g. ios). IOSTAT gives the status of the file commands. The status is an integer which can be assigned to an integer variable name. If opening the file is successful then ios = 0. If attempt to open fails ios is non-zero. A programmer can use this fact to print an appropriate message and exit. Failure may be due to a file not being connected to a unit.

There are some more specifications which we will not be using in our examples. In Table 17.1 we have summarized all the specifics which may be used in an OPEN statement.

Table 17.1 Options Available in Open Statement

Specifier	*Quantity on right of =*	*Remarks*
UNIT =	Integer constant, variable, or expression.	Specifies unit number of external file. Cannot be omitted.
FORM =	FORMATTED or UNFORMATTED.	Optional. Default is FORMATTED.
FILE =	File name allowed in the computer being used. Usually a character string.	Optional but preferable to specify.
STATUS =	OLD, NEW, REPLACE, SCRATCH or UNKNOWN.	Default value is UNKNOWN. System dependent
IOSTAT =	integer variable name, for example ios.	= 0 if currently opened. Optional.
ACCESS =	SEQUENTIAL or DIRECT.	Default SEQUENTIAL.
RECL =	An integer constant or expression > 0. Specifies max.length of record in direct access files.	Compulsory for direct access files.
ACTION =	READ, WRITE or READWRITE. If READ specified cannot WRITE and vice versa.	Optional. Default is READ/WRITE.
ERR =	Statement number to which control jumps if error found.	Optional.

If we write OPEN (20, "stud_file") the first integer is taken as specifying a unit number and "stud_file" taken as FILE = stud_file

Reverting to Example Program 17.1

```
OPEN (UNIT = dsk, FILE = "stud_file", STATUS = "NEW", IOSTAT = ios)
```

will connect file name stud_file to the logical unit dsk. It states that stud_file is a NEW file. If a file with the same name exists then OPEN will fail. The failure or success of OPEN is indicated in IOSTAT. If it is not 0 then OPEN has failed. Thus in the program we have checked if ios = 0. If it is not 0 then we print a message stating that the specified file cannot be opened and halt. If OPEN is successful then we REWIND dsk which rewinds the file connected to unit disk (namely stud_file) and keeps it ready for processing.

A DO loop is used to read records from the terminal and store them in the specified file. The format free READ statement:

```
READ *, roll_no, name, marks
```

reads data typed on the first line and it is stored in stud_file connected to UNIT = dsk by the statement

```
WRITE (UNIT = dsk, FMT = 50) roll_no, name, marks
50 FORMAT (I4, 1X, A25, 3I3)
```

Observe that marks is declared as a three component array. Thus three fields are read and stored in marks (1), marks (2) and marks (3) respectively. READ and WRITE are repeated in DO loop until an input data line with roll_no = 0 is read which indicates end of input records. When this record is read control leaves the DO loop indicating writing is complete. When this happens we execute the statements

```
END FILE dsk
```

which places a special record known as end of file record at the end of the file connected to UNIT dsk, namely, stud_file. We will see later that an end of file record can be sensed by IOSTAT in a READ statement. After placing the end of file record (or marker) we rewind the file using the statement

```
REWIND dsk
```

Finally the statement

```
CLOSE (dsk)
```

terminates I/O operations on the specified file, releases the device and other computer resources allocated to process the file. The specified file cannot be used again unless it is opened by an OPEN statement.

Figure 17.1 illustrates how records are arranged on a sequential file. Observe that after each record a small gap is left. This would allow positioning a file to a required record by counting the number of "gaps". Also observe the special indicators used to mark the beginning and the end of the sequential file.

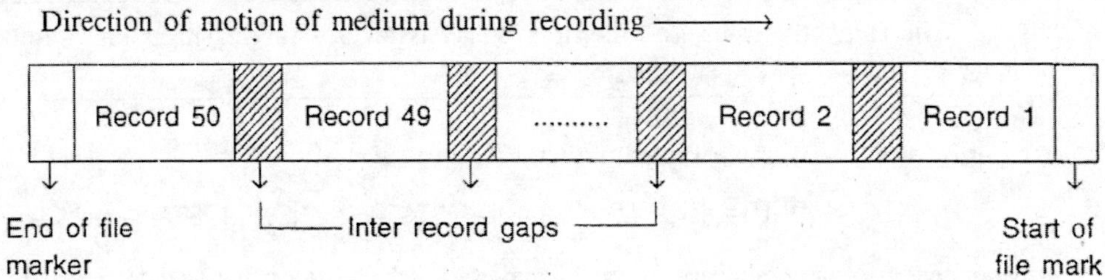

Fig. 17.1 Illustrating arrangement of records in a sequential file.

In writing Example Program 17.1 we have assumed that the input data is sorted and in strict sequential order by roll_no. If, by chance, records get interchanged then the file created will not be in the right sequence and would lead to difficulties during further processing. It is thus a good practice to check if the records are in the right sequence before recording the information in a magnetic file. Any records not in the right sequence must not be stored and information about them should be printed out. It is also necessary to check if the data being stored is correct. For example, if marks is greater than 100 or less than 0 it is an obvious error and such data should not be stored. Similarly data with roll_no > 9999 or < 1 should be rejected.

Example Program 17.2 reads the file stud_file stored in Example Program 17.1 detects any error in the file and writes out an edited file. The program is self-explanatory.

Example Program 17.2 Editing a file stored in a disk

```
!PROGRAM 17.2
!ILLUSTRATES EDITING A SEQUENTIAL FILE

PROGRAM edit_file
   IMPLICIT NONE
   INTEGER :: roll_no,marks(3),ios,prev_no = 0,i
   CHARACTER(LEN=25) :: name
   INTEGER,PARAMETER :: dsk = 20; LOGICAL :: good_data
   OPEN(UNIT = dsk,FILE = "stud_file",STATUS = "old",IOSTAT = ios)
   IF(ios /= 0) THEN
   PRINT *,"stud_file cannot be opened"
   STOP
   ENDIF
   REWIND dsk
   DO
      READ(UNIT = dsk,FMT = 50,IOSTAT = ios)roll_no,name,marks
      IF(ios < 0) EXIT !ios < 0 INDICATES END OF FILE
      IF((roll_no > 999) .OR. (roll_no < 1)) THEN
         PRINT *,"Incorrect roll_no",roll_no,name,marks
         CYCLE
      ENDIF
   good_data = .TRUE.
   DO i=1,3
      IF((marks(i) <= 100).AND.(marks(i) >= 0)) THEN
         good_data = good_data .AND. .TRUE.
      ENDIF
   END DO
      IF(.NOT.(good_data)) THEN
         PRINT *,"Marks out of range",roll_no,name,marks
         CYCLE
      ENDIF
      IF(roll_no <= prev_no) THEN
         PRINT *,"Roll_no not in sequence",roll_no,name,marks
         CYCLE
      ELSE
         prev_no = roll_no
      ENDIF
      WRITE(dsk,FMT=50)roll_no,name,marks
      50 FORMAT(I4,A25,3I3)
   END DO
   END FILE dsk
   REWIND dsk
   CLOSE(dsk)
END PROGRAM edit_file
```

17.2 SEARCHING A SEQUENTIAL FILE

In this section we will develop a Fortran program to retrieve a record with a specified key from a sequential file. We will assume that the sequential file is arranged in ascending order of the key field. A program to do this is given as Example Program 17.3. At the beginning of the

Example Program 17.3 Searching a sequential file

```
!PROGRAM 17.3
!ILLUSTRATES SEARCHING A SEQUENTIAL FILE

PROGRAM search_file
  IMPLICIT NONE
  INTEGER :: roll_no,marks(3),search_no,dsk,ios
  CHARACTER(LEN=25) :: name
  READ *,dsk,search_no
  OPEN(UNIT = dsk,FILE = "stud_file",STATUS = "old", IOSTAT = ios)
  IF(ios /= 0) THEN
    PRINT *,"File on unit",dsk,"cannot be opened"
    STOP
  ENDIF
  REWIND dsk
  DO
    READ (UNIT = dsk,FMT = 50,IOSTAT=ios)roll_no,name,marks
    50 FORMAT(I4,A25,3I3)
    IF(ios < 0) EXIT !ios < 0 INDICATES END OF FILE
    IF(roll_no == search_no) THEN
      PRINT *,"Record being searched found in file"
      PRINT *,"Details of required record follows"
      PRINT 60,roll_no,name,marks
      60 FORMAT(1X,I6,A30,3I6)
      EXIT
    ELSE IF(roll_no > search_no) THEN
      PRINT *,"Roll_no =",search_no,"not in file"
      EXIT
    ENDIF
  END DO
  REWIND dsk
  CLOSE(dsk)
END PROGRAM search_file
```

program the key of the record to be retrieved is read into search_no. The number of the logical unit to which the sequential file is connected is also read into dsk. This makes the program somewhat machine independent as the specific unit number may be different in different installations and an appropriate number may be read into dsk. In the DO loop a record is read from the file ed_stud_file connected to dsk. The key of this record is compared with the key search_no of the record to be retrieved. If they match no further search is needed (as the key is assumed unique). Thus control passes out of the DO loop, and details of the retrieved record are printed before leaving the loop. The file is rewound and closed and the program halts. If the key field read from the sequential file becomes greater than the search key without the two becoming equal at any point during search it means that the key being searched is not in the file. We can come to this conclusion because the file is arranged in ascending order of keys. The key of a record read from the file can become larger than the search key without the two keys matching only if the key being searched is not in the file. When such a condition is detected further search is abandoned and an appropriate message is printed. If the search_no is greater than all the roll numbers in the file then end of file will be reached without either of the two conditions in the loop being satisfied. In this case also a message that the record is not in the file is to be printed. This is done in the Example Program 17.3.

It should now be evident why sequential files are arranged strictly in ascending or descending order of the key.

17.3 UPDATING A SEQUENTIAL FILE

In Example Program 17.1 each student's record had marks in 3 subjects. Suppose the marks in a fourth subject become available. A program is required to do the following:

- Include the marks in the fourth subject in each student's record stored in the file
- Compute the total marks in the four subjects and include it in each student's record on the file
- Print out the student's record.

We will assume that the marks in the fourth subject are entered as shown below and arranged in ascending order of Roll Numbers.

Roll No.	*Marks (4)*
Columns 1 to 4	Columns 5 to 7

The program to be written is known in computer jargon as updating the records in a master file with records in a transaction file and creating a new master file. The updating program is given as Example Program 17.4.

Example Program 17.4 Updating a sequential file

```
!PROGRAM 17.4
!ILLUSTRATING UPDATING SEQUENTIAL FILE

PROGRAM update_file
   IMPLICIT NONE
   INTEGER :: roll_no,marks(4),dsk,dsk_new,dsk_tr,i,ios,roll_no_tr,total_marks
   CHARACTER(LEN=25) :: name
   CHARACTER(LEN=10) :: trans_file
   READ *,dsk,dsk_new,dsk_tr !read unit numbers of the three files
   OPEN(UNIT = dsk,FILE ="stud_file",STATUS ="old",IOSTAT=ios)
   IF(ios /= 0) THEN
      PRINT *,"stud_file cannot be opened"
      STOP
   ENDIF
   OPEN(UNIT=dsk_new,FILE="new_file",STATUS="new",IOSTAT=ios)
   IF(ios /= 0) THEN
      PRINT *,"New file cannot be opened"
      STOP
   ENDIF
   PRINT *,"Give name of file in which marks(4) is entered"
   READ 25,trans_file
   25 FORMAT(A) !THIS WILL READ CHAR FIELD OF ARBITRARY LENGTH
   OPEN(UNIT=dsk_tr,FILE=trans_file,STATUS="old",IOSTAT=ios)
   IF(ios /= 0) THEN
   PRINT *,trans_file,"cannot be opened"
   STOP
```

```
  ENDIF
  REWIND dsk
  REWIND dsk_new
  REWIND dsk_tr
  DO
     READ(UNIT=dsk,FMT=50,IOSTAT=ios)roll_no,name,(marks(i),i=1,3)
     50 FORMAT(I4,A25,3I3)
     IF(ios /= 0) EXIT !IF END OF FILE EXIT
     READ(UNIT=dsk_tr,FMT=30,IOSTAT=ios)roll_no_tr,marks(4)
     30 FORMAT(I4,I3)
     IF(roll_no /= roll_no_tr) THEN
        PRINT 60,roll_no,roll_no_tr
        60 FORMAT(1X,"Mistake - transaction file no", I5,"does not match master file roll.no",I5)
        CYCLE
     ELSE
        total_marks = SUM(marks)
     ENDIF
     WRITE(UNIT=dsk_new,FMT=70)roll_no,name,marks,total_marks
     70 FORMAT(I4,A25,5I3)
  END DO
  END FILE dsk_new
  REWIND dsk_new
  REWIND dsk ; REWIND dsk_tr
  CLOSE(dsk);CLOSE(dsk_tr)
  PRINT 80
  80 FORMAT(29X,"STUDENT GRADE REPORT"//1X,"ROLL NO",9X,&
     "NAME",14X,"ENGLISH",2X,"PHYSICS",2X,"CHEMIST", 2X,"MATHS",2X,"TOTAL")
  DO
     READ(UNIT=dsk_new,FMT=70,IOSTAT=ios)roll_no,name,marks,total_marks
     IF(ios /= 0) EXIT
     PRINT 90,roll_no,name,marks,total_marks
     90 FORMAT(3X,I4,2X,A25,2X,4(I3,6X),5X,I3)
     END DO
     REWIND dsk_new; CLOSE(dsk_new)
END PROGRAM update_file
```

In Example Program 17.4 we first read the UNIT numbers to be connected to the ed_stud_file (old master file), new_file (the updated file) and the file with the marks in the fourth subject (the transaction file). The statement is: READ *, dsk, dsk_new,dsk_tr. Appropriate messages are printed if the files cannot be opened. We have assumed that a programmer has stored the data containing the roll_no and marks in the fourth subject in a file using the editor on the terminal and given it a name. In the program the statement:

```
PRINT *, "Give name of file in which marks(4) is entered"
```

types a message on the screen. The file name typed by the user is stored in trans_file. In the statement to OPEN the transaction file observe that in the FILE = specification we have not given the file name but the variable name trans_file which has the file name. Thus it is not enclosed in quotes. The transaction file is now opened. All the files are rewound to start from the first record.

In the DO loop following this we first read a record from the ed_stud_file and a record from the transaction file. For each record read from ed_stud_file there should be a corresponding record in the transaction file containing the marks in the fourth subject. We thus match the roll_no of the record read from ed_stud_file with the corresponding record in the transaction file. If there is no match there is an error and an error message is printed. If the roll numbers match we total the marks in the four subjects and store it in total_marks. The record with roll_no, name, marks in 4 subjects and total_marks is now written in new_file. The DO loop repeats the above steps till the end of ed_stud_file is reached. When the end of file is reached control leaves the DO loop. Observe that an END FILE mark is written in new_file. This is essential as we have created this file. We now REWIND new_file. Other files are also rewound and closed. The contents of new_file is finally printed with a title "STUDENT GRADE REPORT".

This example illustrates the fact that information written on a magnetic file may be read into variable names provided the exact number and order of individual fields of the record are known. Observe that another magnetic file is needed as the new record is longer than the old one and if written back on the old file would overwrite part of the next record.

Assume that there is another section of students who took the same examination and whose Roll Number, Name and marks in 3 subjects are recorded in identical format in another sequential magnetic file in ascending order of roll number. It is required to merge these two files and create a new file with the records of all students in ascending order of roll number. This is known as merging of files. A program to do this is given as Example Program 17.5.

Example Program 17.5 Merging two sequential files

```
!PROGRAM 17.5
!ILLUSTRATES MERGING TWO SEQUENTIAL FILES

PROGRAM merge_files
  IMPLICIT NONE
  INTEGER :: roll_no_1,roll_no_2,roll_no,dsk_1,dsk_2,dsk_3,&
     ios_1,ios_2,ios_3
  CHARACTER(LEN=25) :: name_1,name_2,name
  INTEGER,DIMENSION(3) :: marks_1,marks_2,marks
  LOGICAL :: end_file_1,end_file_2
  READ *,dsk_1,dsk_2,dsk_3
  OPEN(UNIT=dsk_1,FILE="stud_1",IOSTAT=ios_1)
  OPEN(UNIT=dsk_2,FILE="stud_2",IOSTAT=ios_2)
  OPEN(UNIT=dsk_3,FILE="stud_3",IOSTAT=ios_3)
  IF((ios_1 /= 0).OR.(ios_2 /= 0).OR.(ios_3 /= 0)) THEN
     PRINT *,"File opening error"
     STOP
  ENDIF
  REWIND dsk_1;REWIND dsk_2;REWIND dsk_3
  !READ ONE RECORD EACH FROM THE FILES TO BE MERGED
  READ(UNIT=dsk_1,FMT=10)roll_no_1,name_1,marks_1
  READ(UNIT=dsk_2,FMT=10)roll_no_2,name_2,marks_2
  10 FORMAT(I4,A25,3I3)
  DO
     IF(roll_no_1 < roll_no_2) THEN
        WRITE(UNIT=dsk_3,FMT=10)roll_no_1,name_1,marks_1
        READ(UNIT=dsk_1,FMT=10,IOSTAT=ios_1)roll_no_1, name_1,marks_1
        IF(ios_1 < 0) THEN
        end_file_1 = .TRUE.
        EXIT
        ENDIF
```

```
      ELSE IF(roll_no_1 == roll_no_2) THEN
         PRINT *,"Duplicate record in files Roll_no=",roll_no_1
         READ(UNIT=dsk_1,FMT=10,IOSTAT=ios_1)roll_no_1, name_1,marks_1
         READ(UNIT=dsk_2,FMT=10,IOSTAT=ios_2)roll_no_2,name_2,marks_2
         IF(ios_1 < 0) THEN
         end_file_1 = .TRUE.
         EXIT
         ENDIF
         IF(ios_2 < 0) THEN
         end_file_2 = .TRUE.
         EXIT
         ENDIF
      ELSE
         WRITE(UNIT=dsk_3,FMT=10)roll_no_2,name_2,marks_2
         READ(UNIT=dsk_2,FMT=10,IOSTAT=ios_2)roll_no_2,name_2,marks_2
         IF(ios_2 < 0) THEN
         end_file_2 = .TRUE.
         EXIT
         ENDIF
      ENDIF
   END DO
   DO
      IF(end_file_1) THEN
      WRITE(UNIT=dsk_3,FMT=10)roll_no_2,name_2,marks_2
      READ(UNIT=dsk_2,FMT=10,IOSTAT=ios_2)roll_no_2, name_2,marks_2
      IF(ios_2 < 0) EXIT
   ELSE IF(end_file_2) THEN
      WRITE(UNIT=dsk_3,FMT=10)roll_no_1,name_1,marks_1
      READ(UNIT=dsk_1,FMT=10,IOSTAT=ios_1)roll_no_1,name_1,marks_1
      IF(ios_1 < 0) EXIT
   ENDIF
   END DO
   END file dsk_3
   REWIND dsk_1;REWIND dsk_2;REWIND dsk_3
   CLOSE(dsk_1);CLOSE(dsk_2);CLOSE(dsk_3)
END PROGRAM merge_files
```

The program opens two files stud_1 and stud_2 which contain data of the two sections of students. A file named stud_3 is also opened to store the merged file. One record each from the two files stud_1 and stud_2 are read and their keys (namely Roll Numbers) are compared. The record with the smaller key is written on the output file (namely, stud_3). If the two keys happen to be equal then there is obviously an error as the key of each record is unique. In such a case an error message is printed and the next record is read from both the files and compared. As the number of records in the two files being merged may not be equal we have to check the end of file condition of each of the files. When one of the files ends any remaining records in the other file should be copied into the merged file. This is done in Example Program 17.5.

Some more points regarding the use of sequential files are listed below:

i. If a file in UNIT = i is to be backspaced by one record it is achieved by the statement: BACKSPACE i.

ii. When the statement READ (*u, f*) list (where *u* stands for UNIT = unit no., and *f* for FMT = format statement number) is executed once, one record corresponding to all the elements in the list is read. Similarly the statement WRITE (*u, f*) *list* writes one record in which all the individual fields in the list are included.

iii. One or more fields from a record may be read by the READ statement if required. For instance in the following example the READ statement reads only part of the record

```
WRITE (UNIT = 20, FMT = 40) a, b, c
BACKSPACE 20
READ (UNIT = 20, FMT = 40) a, b
```

iv. After reading a record the sequential file is positioned ready to read the next record. If this record is to be re-read the file should be backspaced. The BACKSPACE i statement backspaces the file i by one record whereas the REWIND statement rewinds the file till the beginning is reached. A sequential file should always be rewound.

v. If the READ (*u, f*) statement is executed without a list it moves the file forward by one record.

vi. Individual records in a sequential file may have different lengths.

vii. To avoid reading more information than was actually recorded, the ENDFILE statement is useful. Information beyond the endfile mark cannot be read.

viii. It is possible to write information on sequential files without using a Format specification. For example:

```
WRITE (UNIT = 20) roll_no, name, marks
```

would write the record in the magnetic files in the *internal binary form* used by the computer without any format conversion. The information may be read by using a READ statement without format. Any file recorded in this mode cannot be printed. For example:

```
   READ (UNIT = 20) roll_no, name, marks
   PRINT 30, roll no, name, marks
30 FORMAT (1X, I6, 5A5, 3I3)
```

will not work.

The primary advantage of unformatted READ is its economy in storage and time. When massive quantities of data are manipulated one should investigate the possibility of using unformatted recording. Unformatted files are machine dependent and not portable.

17.4 DIRECT ACCESS FILES

Sequential files are commonly used in Fortran and the corresponding statements are standardized. Direct access files are easy to use. Retrieval of a record is achieved by merely stating the record key. Statements have also been standardized for such files in Fortran 90.

17.4.1 Defining a Direct Access File

The first question we will answer is: How do we specify a file as direct access and what information is to be provided for setting up such a file structure?

A file is specified as a direct access file in the OPEN statement. Besides specifying the unit number and file name it is necessary to specify the file access mode as direct (Code ACCESS = "DIRECT"). If the file is to be formatted then we should specify FORM = "FORMATTED". It is also necessary to give the maximum number of characters in each record. Thus if we want to record student records with roll_no, name and marks with 3 digit roll number, 25 character name and 9 digits for the set of marks the record size (code RECL) should be specified as 37 characters. The direct (or random) access file may be specified by the statement:

```
OPEN (UNIT = 20, FILE = "strand",ACCESS = "DIRECT", RECL = 37, FORM = 'FORMATTED')
```

17.4.2 Creating a Direct Access File

Having defined a random access file "strand" we can store information in this file. Unlike a sequential file a random access file does not require input records to be arranged in ascending or descending order by key. The following statements read information from keyboard and store them in strand.

```
DO
   READ 30, roll_no, name, marks
   IF (roll_no == 0) EXIT
   WRITE (UNIT = 20, FMT = 30, REC = roll_no) roll_no, name, marks
   30 FORMAT (I3, A25, 3I3)
END DO
```

The new statement in the above program segment is:

```
WRITE (UNIT = 20, FMT = 30, REC = roll_no) roll_no, name, marks
```

The statement commands that the record specified be stored in a file connected to unit 20 according to format 30 with roll_no as key. REC = specifies that the file is random access and key variable follows the = sign. The fact that the file connected to unit 20 is a random access file has already been specified in the OPEN statement. Example Program 17.6 reads a file and stores it in the random access file strand.

Example Program 17.6 Program to create a random access file

```
!PROGRAM 17.6
!ILLUSTRATES CREATION OF DIRECT (OR RANDOM) ACCESS FILE

PROGRAM create_rand_file
   IMPLICIT NONE
   INTEGER :: roll_no,marks(3)
   CHARACTER(LEN=25) :: name
   OPEN(UNIT=20,FILE="strand",ACCESS="DIRECT",RECL=37, FORM="FORMATTED")
   DO
      READ 30,roll_no,name,marks
   30 FORMAT(I3,A25,3I3)
      IF(roll_no == 0) EXIT
      WRITE(UNIT=20,FMT=30,REC=roll_no)roll_no,name,marks
   END DO
   CLOSE(20)
END PROGRAM create_rand_file
```

17.4.3 Updating a Direct Access File

A file named strand was created in the last section. In that file each record had a Roll Number, Name and Marks in three subjects. Suppose we have another file with Roll number and marks in one more subject. This file need not be sorted and can be in any order. Example Program 17.7 reads these records and writes in file "strand" the marks in the fourth subject and the total marks for each Roll Number.

Example Program 17.7 Updating a direct access file

```
!PROGRAM 17.7
!ILLUSTRATES UPDATING A DIRECT ACCESS FILE

PROGRAM update_rand_file
   IMPLICIT NONE
   INTEGER :: roll_no,marks(4),i,total_marks
   CHARACTER(LEN=25) :: name
   OPEN(UNIT=20,FILE="strand",ACCESS="DIRECT",RECL=43,FORM="FORMATTED")
!OBSERVE THAT RECORD LENGTH HAS BEEN INCREASED TO 43 AS UPDATED
!RECORD IS LONGER
   DO
   READ 40,roll_no,marks(4)
40 FORMAT(2I3)
   READ(UNIT=20,FMT=50,REC=roll_no,ERR=70)roll_no,name,(marks(i),i=1,3)
50 FORMAT(I3,A25,3I3)
   total_marks=SUM(marks)
   WRITE(UNIT=20,FMT=60,REC=roll_no)roll_no,name,marks,total_marks
60 FORMAT(I3,A25,5I3)
   CYCLE
70 PRINT *,"Record with roll number=",roll_no,"given",&
   "in transaction file is not in master file. This record","has not been used"
   END DO
   CLOSE(20)
END PROGRAM update_rand_file
```

In Example Program 17.7 the file strand is opened first and defined as a direct access file. The records are updated in the DO loop. The roll_no and the marks in the fourth subject are read from the keyboard. These records may be in any order.

Using the roll_no as key the random access READ statement:

```
READ (20, 50, REC = roll_no, ERR = 70) roll_no, name, (marks (j), j = 1, 3)
```

reads the corresponding record from the old file strand. If the roll_no of the record read has no corresponding record in the file strand then there is an error. The READ statement provides an (optional) exit when such errors are detected. This is provided by the entry ERR = 70 in the READ statement which commands that in case of error control should go to statement 70. Statement 70 prints out an error message. Such an error exit can be provided in all generalized READ statements in addition to end of file exit.

If the roll_no is found in the master file strand the marks in the three subjects are extracted and added to the marks in the fourth subject and the updated information is written in the file up_strand. Observe that if a transaction has no corresponding record in strand that record is left unupdated.

17.4.4 Searching a Direct Access File

Retrieving a record with a given key from a direct access file is extremely simple. Example Program 17.8 retrieves a record from the direct access file strand. If the record is not in the file a message is printed. Merging two files is very similar to creating a file as there is no sequence of keys to be maintained.

Example Program 17.8 Searching a direct access file

```
!PROGRAM 17.8
!ILLUSTRATES SEARCHING A RANDOM ACCESS FILE

PROGRAM search_random
   IMPLICIT NONE
   INTEGER :: roll_no,marks(4),total_marks
   CHARACTER(LEN=25) :: name
   OPEN(UNIT=20,FILE="strand",ACCESS="DIRECT",RECL=43,FORM="FORMATTED")
   PRINT *,"Type roll number of record to be retrieved"
   READ *,roll_no
   READ(UNIT=20,FMT=50,REC=roll_no,ERR=70)roll_no,name,marks,total_marks
50 FORMAT(I3,A25,5I3)
!THE ABOVE STATEMENT RETRIEVES RECORD WITH GIVEN roll_no IF IT IS FOUND IN THE FILE 20
!IT IS PRINTED BY THE FOLLOWING STATEMENT
   PRINT *,"Details of retrieved record given below"
   PRINT 60,roll_no,name,marks,total_marks
60 FORMAT(1X,"Roll no=",I3,2X,"NAME=",A25,"marks=",4I5,"total marks=",I5)
   STOP
   CLOSE(20)
70 PRINT *,"Record with roll no =",roll_no,"not in file"
END PROGRAM search_random
```

17.5 THE INQUIRE STATEMENT

The statements already discussed are sufficient to write file oriented programs in Fortran 90. There are situations where one might like to find out the status of a file in a program, particularly if it is a routine written by some other programmer. A statement called INQUIRE is available to achieve this. The general form of the INQUIRE statement is

INQUIRE (list of specifiers)

For example,

INQUIRE (UNIT = 20, OPENED = op_status, NAME = file_name)

will set op_status = .TRUE. if file is opened and will set it FALSE otherwise. The file_name will return the name of the file connected to UNIT = 20 if it exists.

INQUIRE can also be by file name rather than UNIT number (both cannot be specified). For example,

INQUIRE (NAME = "stud_file", NUMBER = p, OPENED = op_status, EXIST = present)

will give UNIT number in p, op_status as TRUE or FALSE and present as TRUE or FALSE.

The statement

INQUIRE (UNIT = "strand", ACCESS = access_type, RECL = length)

will return access_type = DIRECT if "strand" is a direct access file and the record length in length. Many of the other specifiers used in OPEN statement can also be used in the INQUIRE statement.

SUMMARY

1. When large amounts of data are to be processed it is advisable to store them in a file on a magnetic medium (such as disk file) and process these files.
2. Fortran 90 has facilities to create either sequential or direct access files and process them.
3. A file is OPENED with an OPEN statement which specifies the unit number assigned to the file being opened and a number of specifiers which define the nature of the file. In Table 17.1 we summarize various specifications which can be included in an OPEN statement.
4. A file can be read from a sequential file by using the statement:

   READ (UNIT = *file_no*, FMT = *Format statement number*, or *string*, IOSTAT = *iostatus*) *list*

   where *list* is the list of variables to be read. If end of the file is reached *iostatus* has a negative value. If we write:

   READ (20, 30, IOSTAT = ios) a, b, c

   20 is taken by default as unit number and 30 the statement number of format string.
5. A record can be written in a sequential file using the statement:

   WRITE (UNIT = *file_no*, FMT = *Format string or statement no.*, IOSTAT = *iostatus) list.*

   The record specified in the *list* is written in a file connected to the specified unit number.
6. END FILE (*unit_no*) writes an end of file record in the specified *unit_no*.
7. CLOSE (*unit_no*) closes the specified *unit* and releases all computer resources used by it.
8. A direct access file is opened by using the specifications ACCESS = "DIRECT", RECL = *record length* in the OPEN statement. These specifications are compulsory.
9. A record in a direct access file is read by using the statement:

   READ (UNIT = *file_no*, FMT = *Format statement number, or string*, REC = *key field of record to be read) list.*

   To organize a direct access file a unique integer key field in the record should be identified.

10. A WRITE statement writes the record with the specified key field in the slot reserved for it on the disk. The statement is:

    WRITE (UNIT = *file_no*, FMT = *format statement no. or string*, REC = *key field of record to be written*) *list*

EXERCISES

17.1 A student master file was created on disk in Example 17.1. Write a program which will read this file and print out a list of students who have failed in one or more subjects. Assume 40 percent as pass marks.

17.2 An updated record was created in Example Program 17.4. Using this file compute for each student his average marks and class. (Assume that 40 to 49 percent is III class, 50 to 59 II class and ≥ 60 is first class.) Update the file and create a new master file with this additional information.

17.3 Arrange the file in descending order of average marks and create a new file.

17.4 Assume that at the end of the year a set of students join the class and another set leave. Using the roll number and an appropriate code to add or delete a student, update the master file. The updated file should be in ascending order of roll number.

17.5 Repeat Exercise 17.2 with a random access file.

17.6 Repeat Exercise 17.4 with a random access file.

17.7 In Example Program 17.5 two files were merged. It was assumed that each file is in strict ascending order according to roll number. Modify the program to reject records which are out of sequence and print an appropriate error message.

17.8 In Exercise 17.2 a master file was created with average marks and class in addition to other information. Using this file create another file which has only ROLLNO, average marks and class. At the end of the file add a last record which has the total number of records in the file, the number of I class, II class, III class and failing students and the overall class average. Print this summary information.

17.9 Assume that an unsorted file of student's records with the information as in Example Program 17.1 is available. Write a program to create a sorted sequential file with the unsorted file as input.

17.10 Rewrite Example Program 17.7 after storing student information in a random access file.

18. Pointer Data Type and Applications

Learning Objectives

In this chapter we will learn:

1. The concept of pointers in Fortran 90
2. Intrinsic functions available with pointers
3. How to create list data structures using pointers
4. Applications of lists
5. How to create tree data structures
6. Application of trees

The two data structures we have encountered so far for representing collection of similar data items are arrays and files. Retrieval of information from an array is simple. It is, however, necessary to specify the size of an array before it is used. Thus situations could arise where the specified storage is too much or too little. For example, if we have a list of sorted numbers stored in an array and if a new number is to be introduced at the right position of the sorted array, we have to move to the right all numbers appearing after the insertion point. The array size should be sufficient to accommodate the expanded list of numbers. If a set of numbers are to be deleted from the sorted array, the numbers in the array have to be moved around. The numbers stored in the array will be smaller than the array size and consequently space will be wasted. The procedure to delete and insert would also involve fair amount of book keeping of array index to move the numbers.

Files do have the property of growing and shrinking. Insertion and deletion from files, however, are quite time consuming. Thus in applications which require frequent editing of sorted numbers it would be useful to have a data structure in which we can dynamically allocate space as needed and also release unused space.

There are also applications of computers in which it is necessary to have dynamically changing data structures. For example, a list of books issued from a library to a member would grow as new books are issued and shrink when books are returned. Writing programs for such applications is facilitated by using data structure known as a *list structure*. We will define such a structure in this chapter and explain how such lists can be created using an intrinsic data type called a *pointer*.

List structures are also useful in representing a network of roads in a city, piping system in a chemical plant, neural networks, biological systems etc.

The variable names of various types we have encountered so far, namely, integer, real, character etc., store a data item of appropriate type. There is another type of variable known as pointer type which does not store any data but points to a storage location which stores data. Such a data type is very useful in creating a list structure.

A *linear linked* list consists of a number of elements called *nodes*. A node consists of two parts: a part which stores information and a part which gives the identity of the next node in the list. The part which gives the identity of the next node is a *pointer*. Before we discuss how to create a linear linked list in Fortran 90, we will discuss how pointers are declared in Fortran 90 and some of their properties. Fortran 77 did not have a pointer data type.

18.1 THE POINTER DATA TYPE

A variable in Fortran is declared to be a pointer by specifying that it has the POINTER attribute in a type declaration statement. For example, the statement

```
INTEGER, POINTER :: p
```

specifies that the variable p is a pointer that can point to an entity of type INTEGER. A pointer can be declared to point to a REAL, CHARACTER or a derived data type. For example, if we write

```
TYPE (book), POINTER :: pb
```

it states that pb will point to entity of TYPE (book).

A pointer has an *association status* which indicates whether it is pointing to an entity or not. When a pointer is declared it does not point at anything. Thus its association status is *undefined*. Fortran 90 restricts the variables to which a pointer may point to. A pointer can point to only those variables which have an attribute TARGET and are of the same TYPE as the variable name.

For example, if we write

```
INTEGER, POINTER :: p
INTEGER, TARGET :: x
```

then p can point to x. If x is of type REAL then p cannot point to it. We can associate the pointer p with the target x by the pointer assignment statement

```
p => x
```

where => is a composite symbol = followed by >. There should not be any blank between them. The effect of this statement is shown in Fig. 18.1.

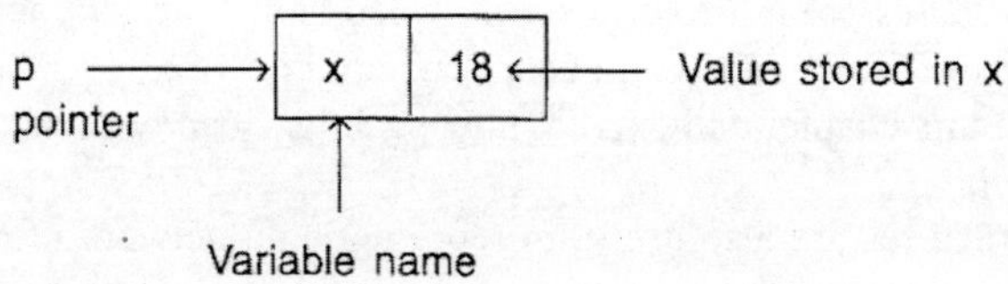

Fig. 18.1 A pointer and its association.

In fact we can look upon p as an alias (or another name) for x. The pointer itself does not store any value but the variable x is a memory location which stores a value as shown in Fig. 18.1.

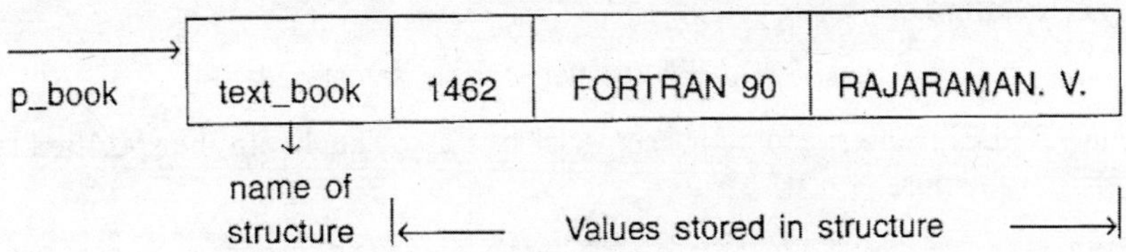

Fig. 18.2 A pointer to a structure.

A pointer can be associated with derived type as shown in Fig. 18.2. It is declared as:

```
TYPE book
    INTEGER :: acc_no
    CHARACTER (LEN = 30) :: book_title
    CHARACTER(LEN = 25) :: author
END TYPE book
TYPE (book), POINTER :: p_book
TYPE (book), TARGET :: text_book
  p_book => text_book
```

A pointer can be associated with an array as shown below:

```
INTEGER, DIMENSION (10), TARGET :: x_arr
INTEGER, DIMENSION (:), POINTER :: p_arr

p_arr => x_arr      ! Associates pointers with target.
```

Observe that in the pointer declaration we have not declared the extent of the array. It should not be specified. It allows p_arr to point to any array which is a one-dimensional array (array of rank 1). When we associate p_arr with x_arr the extent of p_arr is automatically defined as shown in Fig. 18.3.

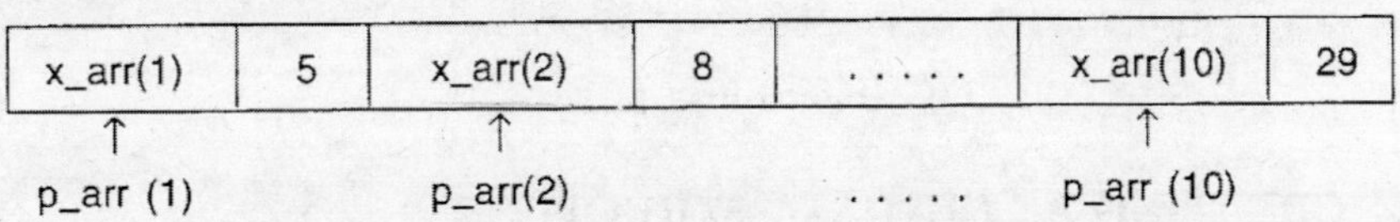

Fig. 18.3 Pointers of an array.

We see that an array of pointers is created with each component of the x_arr(i) being pointed to (or having an alias) by p_arr(i). Pointers for multi-dimensional arrays can also be defined in a similar manner as shown below:

```
REAL, DIMENSION (:, :, :), POINTER :: p_real
REAL, DIMENSION (5, 7, 10), TARGET :: y_arr
```

The statement p_real => y_arr associates the array p_real of pointers with y_arr.

There is an intrinsic function which tests whether a pointer is associated with a target. This function is:

```
ASSOCIATED (pointer_variable)
```

which returns .TRUE. if the pointer_variable is associated with a target and .FALSE. if it is not.

The function:

ASSOCIATED (pointer_variable, target_variable)

will return .TRUE. if the specified pointer variable is associated with the specified target_variable and .FALSE. otherwise.

```
INTEGER, POINTER :: p1, p2, p3, p4
INTEGER, TARGET :: x1, x2, x3, x4
    p1 => x1 ; p2 => x2 ; p3 => x3 ;
    p1 => x4
```

Fig. 18.4 Associating pointers with targets.

In the program segment of Fig. 18.4:

ASSOCIATED (p3) will be .TRUE.
ASSOCIATED (p1, x3) will be .FALSE.
ASSOCIATED (p1, x4) will be .TRUE.

ASSOCIATED (p4) will be undefined as it has been declared and not yet associated. The status of pointer is undefined between the time it is declared to the time it is first associated. To prevent this Fortran 90 has an intrinsic function NULLIFY which sets the association status of a pointer as .FALSE.

Thus if we write

NULLIFY (p4)

and ask ASSOCIATED (p4), a .FALSE. value will be returned.

The effect of NULLIFY. of a pointer is somewhat analogous to initializing a variable to zero. In Fig. 18.5 we illustrate this. The pointer p4 is not pointing to anything.

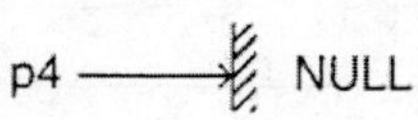

Fig. 18.5 Effect of NULLIFY (p4).

18.2 CREATING A LIST DATA STRUCTURE

A linear linked list consists of a number of elements called *nodes*. A node consists of two fields, a field called the information field and a field called the pointer to the next node. The entire linear linked list is referred to and accessed by a pointer which points to the first node of the list. The pointer is external to the list and is a *list identifier*. The last node in the list has in its pointer field a pointer which is NULLIFIED. (It is a NULL pointer).

The structure of a list is shown in Fig. 18.6.

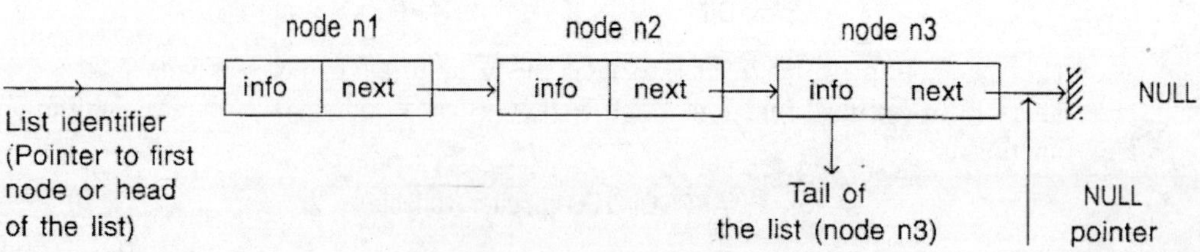

Fig. 18.6 A linear linked list.

A node in a list is declared as follows:

```
TYPE node
      TYPE (rec) :: info
      TYPE (node), POINTER :: next
END TYPE node
TYPE (node), POINTER :: list_name
```

Observe that the pointer next is of TYPE(node) so that its target can be another node. The pointer list_name points to the first node in the list.

Example 18.1

We will illustrate creation of a list of characters. This is shown in Example Program 18.1. Observe that we have first created a derived type ch_node which has an information field to store a character and a pointer field to point to the next character. In this example, we create a list with three nodes similar to that in Fig. 18.6. Thus we declare n1, n2, n3 as three nodes of TYPE ch_node. Next we declare POINTERS ch_list to point to the head of the list, that is, to node n1 and tail_ptr as the pointer at the tail of the list, namely, n3. These two pointers, namely, ch_list and tail_ptr are useful to add new nodes at the head or tail of the list respectively. The next statement reads in values into the information field of the nodes. The next three statements create the list by linking the nodes by pointers.

Example Program 18.1 Creating a list of characters

```
!PROGRAM 18.1
!CREATION OF A LIST OF CHARACTERS

PROGRAM create_list
  IMPLICIT NONE
  TYPE ch_node
    CHARACTER :: letter
    TYPE(ch_node),POINTER :: next
  END TYPE ch_node
  TYPE(ch_node),TARGET :: n1,n2,n3
  TYPE(ch_node),POINTER :: ch_list,tail_ptr
  READ *,n1%letter,n2%letter,n3%letter
  ch_list => n1 !FIRST NODE POINTED BY ch_list
  n1%next => n2 !SECOND NODE CONNECTED TO FIRST NODE
  n2%next => n3 !THIRD NODE CONNECTED TO SECOND NODE
  NULLIFY(n3%next)
  tail_ptr => n3 !TAIL OF LIST POINTS TO LAST NODE n3
  PRINT *,n1%letter,n2%letter,n3%letter
END PROGRAM create_list
```

This program is used to illustrate in a simple way how a list is created. It is, however, not general. It is specific as we have declared only three nodes and linked them together. In general, one should be able to create a list with an arbitrary number of nodes (which is not known ahead of time), insert a node anywhere in the list, delete specified nodes, modify the information in a node, print the contents of the list etc.

Example 18.2

We have written Example Program 18.2 to create a list of characters of arbitrary length. It is assumed that one character is read at a time from the terminal and added to the list. A blank indicates the end of characters. If the very first character typed is a blank the list is a null list. After the creation of the list it is printed.

Example Program 18.2 Creation of list of arbitrary length

```
!PROGRAM 18.2
!CREATION OF A LIST OF CHARACTERS
PROGRAM create_list
   IMPLICIT NONE
   CHARACTER :: data
   TYPE ch_node
      CHARACTER :: letter
      TYPE(ch_node),POINTER :: next
   END TYPE ch_node
   TYPE(ch_node),TARGET :: new_node
   TYPE(ch_node),POINTER :: ch_list,tail_ptr,ptr
   NULLIFY(ch_list,tail_ptr, ptr)
   ch_list => new_node; tail_ptr => new_node
   PRINT *,"Type a letter, blank if no more letters"
   DO
      READ 10 ,data
      10 FORMAT(A1)
      IF(data == " ")EXIT
      tail_ptr%letter = data !STORE LETTER IN NODE
      ALLOCATE(tail_ptr%next)
      tail_ptr=> tail_ptr%next !ADDED NODE IS NOW THE TAIL
   END DO
   NULLIFY(tail_ptr%next) !LIST IS TERMINATED
!PRINT CREATED LIST
   IF(.NOT.ASSOCIATED(ch_list)) THEN
      PRINT *,"List is empty"
   ELSE
   ptr => ch_list !BEGIN AT HEAD OF LIST
      DO
         PRINT *,ptr%letter
         ptr => ptr%next
         IF(.NOT.ASSOCIATED(ptr)) EXIT
      END DO
   ENDIF
END PROGRAM create_list
```

In Example Program 18.2 a TYPE ch_node is declared which is a node storing a character and a pointer to the next node. The head of the list is named ch_list and tail_ptr is intended to indicate the tail, that is, the last node in the list. We first create a target node new_node and at the beginning both the head and tail point to it. In the DO loop we read in a letter and store it in new node. If it is a blank we quit the loop and make the tail_ptr% next NULL. Thus if the very first data read is blank no list is created. If the data is a letter it is stored in the list. Observe the statement:

ALLOCATE (tail_ptr%next)

This statement allocates space for a node whose TYPE has been declared. Sufficient storage space is allocated to store the node. This statement allows us to dynamically create space as required by a program.

In the program when a new node is created, it is linked to the previous node. The tail pointer is moved to point to this new node. Thus the DO loop adds nodes to the list until a blank character is typed. The last part of the program prints the list. Observe that if there are no elements in the list then the head of the list ch_list will be NULL and an appropriate message is printed. Otherwise we start from the head of the list, print its contents and traverse through the list using the next node link until the end of the list is reached.

18.3 MANIPULATING A LINEARLY LINKED LIST

In this section we will illustrate with a running example various manipulations which may be performed on lists.

Example 18.3

A lending library keeps a waiting list of readers who request a specific book. As the number of readers requesting a specific book is a variable we will keep the waiting list as a list structure. The first person who requested the book will be put at the head of the list. Whenever a new request comes for the book it will be put at the tail of the list. When a book is returned the reader at the head of the list will be notified and his name will be removed from the list. If a reader requests that his position in the waiting list for a book is to be given we have to search the wait list using the readers' identification number as key and find the position in the list starting from the head. In case the reader's identification is not found in the wait list, an appropriate message should be printed. If a reader requests that his name be removed from the waiting list, this should also be done.

Example Program 18.3 Processing book requests using a list

```
!PROGRAM 18.3
!WAITING LIST FOR ISSUING OF BOOK
!WE WILL PUT IN A MODULE THE DATA STRUCTURE AND VARIOUS
!OPERATIONS TO BE PERFORMED ON THE LIST
MODULE wait_list_processing
   IMPLICIT NONE
   TYPE request
      INTEGER :: acc_no !ACCESSION NUMBER OF BOOK
      INTEGER :: reader_id !IDENTIFICATION NUMBER OF A USER
      CHARACTER(LEN=30) :: book_name
      CHARACTER(LEN=8) :: date_request
      TYPE (request),POINTER :: next
   END TYPE request
   CONTAINS
      SUBROUTINE add_req(new_req,head,tail)
         !ADD NEW REQUEST TO THE TAIL OF THE LIST
         TYPE(request),POINTER :: new_req,head,tail
         IF(ASSOCIATED(head)) THEN
      !IF LIST NOT EMPTY ADD AT END NEW REQUEST
         tail%next => new_req
         NULLIFY(new_req%next)
         tail =>new_req
         ELSE
```

```
      !IF LIST IS EMPTY PUT AT HEAD OF WAITING LIST
         head => new_req
         tail => new_req
      NULLIFY(tail%next)
      ENDIF
END SUBROUTINE add_req

SUBROUTINE delete_req(first,head,tail)
   !POINT OUT THE FIRST REQUEST IN THE LIST AND REMOVE THAT
   !REQUEST FROM THE LIST
   TYPE(request),POINTER :: head,tail,first
   IF(.NOT.ASSOCIATED(head)) THEN
      !LIST IS EMPTY RETURN NOTHING
      NULLIFY(first)
   ELSE IF(ASSOCIATED(head%next)) THEN
      !THERE IS MORE THAN ONE ELEMENT IN LIST
      first => head !RETURN POINTER TO FIRST
      head => head%next !ELEMENT
   ELSE !ONLY ONE ELEMENT IN THE LIST
      first => head !RETURN ONLY ELEMENT
      NULLIFY(head,tail) !LIST IS EMPTY
   ENDIF
END SUBROUTINE delete_req

SUBROUTINE list_req(head) !PRINT OUT WAIT LIST
   TYPE(request),POINTER :: head
   TYPE(request),POINTER :: ptr !LOCAL VARIABLE
   PRINT *,"Requests in waiting list"
   IF(.NOT.ASSOCIATED(head)) THEN
      PRINT *,"No one in waiting list"
   ELSE
      ptr => head
      DO !LOOP PRINTS WAITING LIST
      PRINT *,ptr%acc_no,ptr%reader_id,ptr%book_name,&
            ptr%date_request
         !ADVANCE TO NEXT ITEM IN LIST
      ptr => ptr%next
      IF(.NOT.ASSOCIATED(ptr)) EXIT
      END DO
   ENDIF
END SUBROUTINE list_req

SUBROUTINE search_req(head,reader,position)
   !TO FIND OUT POSITION IN WAITING LIST OF READER
   TYPE(request),POINTER :: head,ptr !ptr USED TO TRAVERSE LIST
   INTEGER,INTENT(OUT) :: position
   INTEGER,INTENT(IN) :: reader
   position = 1
   IF(.NOT.ASSOCIATED(head)) THEN
      PRINT *,"Wait list is empty"
```

```
   ELSE
      ptr => head
      DO !LOOP SEARCHES LIST
      IF(reader == ptr%reader_id) THEN
         PRINT *,"Position in wait list=",position
         EXIT
         ELSE
         ptr => ptr%next
         IF(.NOT.ASSOCIATED(ptr%next)) THEN
            PRINT *,"Reader id=",reader,"not in the list"
            EXIT
            ENDIF
         position = position + 1
         ENDIF
      END DO
   ENDIF
END SUBROUTINE search_req

SUBROUTINE remove_req(head,tail,reader)
!REMOVES READER FROM WAITING LIST
   TYPE(request),POINTER :: head,tail
!LOCAL VARIABLES
   TYPE(request),POINTER :: ptr,temp
   INTEGER,INTENT(IN) :: reader
!CHECK IF LIST IS EMPTY
   IF(.NOT.ASSOCIATED(head)) THEN
      PRINT *,"Wait list is empty Reader not in the list"
      RETURN
   ENDIF
!CHECK IF READER AT HEAD OF LIST ptr=> head
   IF(reader == head%reader_id) THEN
      head = head%next
   !DELETE NODE AT HEAD
      PRINT *,"Reader with id =",reader,"deleted"
   !CHECK IF THIS WAS THE ONLY NODE
      IF(.NOT.ASSOCIATED(head%next)) THEN
         NULLIFY(head,tail)
      ENDIF
      RETURN
   ELSE
      temp => head
      DO
      ptr => temp%next
      IF(reader == ptr%reader_id) THEN
         !DELETE NODE
            temp%next => ptr%next
               PRINT *,"Reader =",reader,"taken out of list"
         DEALLOCATE(ptr)
               EXIT
      ENDIF
      temp => ptr
```

```
      IF(.NOT.ASSOCIATED(temp)) THEN
            !LIST IS FULLY TRAVERSED
            PRINT *,"Reached end of wait list"
            PRINT *,"Reader =",reader,"not found"
            EXIT
            ENDIF
         END DO
      ENDIF
   END SUBROUTINE remove_req
END MODULE wait_list_processing

PROGRAM book_request
   USE wait_list_processing
   IMPLICIT NONE
   TYPE(request),POINTER :: head,tail
   TYPE(request),POINTER :: book_req,first
   INTEGER :: i,reader_no,pos
   !INITIALISE EMPTY LIST
   NULLIFY(head,tail)
   !CREATE A WAIT LIST WITH 4 REQUESTS
   DO i=1,4
      CALL make_request(book_req)
      !CALL make_request creates one book request
      !ADD THE REQUEST TO THE WAIT LIST
      CALL add_req(book_req,head,tail)
   END DO
   !PRINT WAIT LIST CREATED
   CALL list_req(head)
   !REMOVE REQUEST AT TOP OF LIST
   CALL delete_req(first,head,tail)
   IF(ASSOCIATED(first)) THEN
      !WAIT LIST HAS BOOKS
      PRINT *,"Send notice as follows"
      PRINT *,first%acc_no,first%reader_id,first%book_name&
         ,first%date_request
   ENDIF
   !PRINT REMAINING PART OF WAIT LIST
   CALL list_req(head)
   !TO FIND THE POSITION OF READER_NO'S IN WAIT LIST
   READ *,reader_no
   CALL search_req(head,reader_no,pos)
   CONTAINS !SUBROUTINE TO CREATE TRANSACTION RECORDS
   SUBROUTINE make_request(book_req)
      TYPE(request),POINTER :: book_req
      INTEGER :: error
      ALLOCATE(book_req,STAT=error)
      IF(error /= 0) THEN
         PRINT *,"No space in memory. cannot allocate"
         STOP
      ENDIF
      READ *,book_req%acc_no,book_req%reader_id,&
      book_req%book_name,book_req%date_request
   END SUBROUTINE make_request
END PROGRAM book_request
```

Example Program 18.3 meets all these requirements. We first write a MODULE program wait_list_processing in which we define the structure to store a reader's request for a book. The derived type request describes this. It consists of the accession number (acc_no) which is a unique identification for a book. The other fields are reader_id which identifies a user uniquely, the name of the book, the date the book was requested by the user and a pointer to point to the next request in the list. The module contains SUBROUTINES to add a request which will go to the tail of the list, delete a request when a user gets to the top of the wait list and the book is issued to him and to get the waiting list printed. Observe that in the SUBROUTINE add_req we first find if there are any requests in the wait list. If there are any we add the request to the end of the list, if not we put it at the head of the list. (We have assumed that the book is issued and not in the library.) When a user's request is fulfilled, his/her request is removed from the waiting list by the SUBROUTINE delete_req. This SUBROUTINE removes the request from the head of the wait list. If the wait list becomes empty it is nullified. The SUBROUTINE list_req prints the requests in the waiting list starting from the head of the list to the tail of the list. SUBROUTINE search_req finds out the position in wait list of a request by counting the number in the list starting from the head until the requester's reader_id is reached.

If a user requests that his name be removed from wait list this is done by SUBROUTINE remove_req. The important point to remember while writing this SUBROUTINE is to properly connect the nodes occurring before and after the deleted node. This aspect is shown in Fig. 18.7.

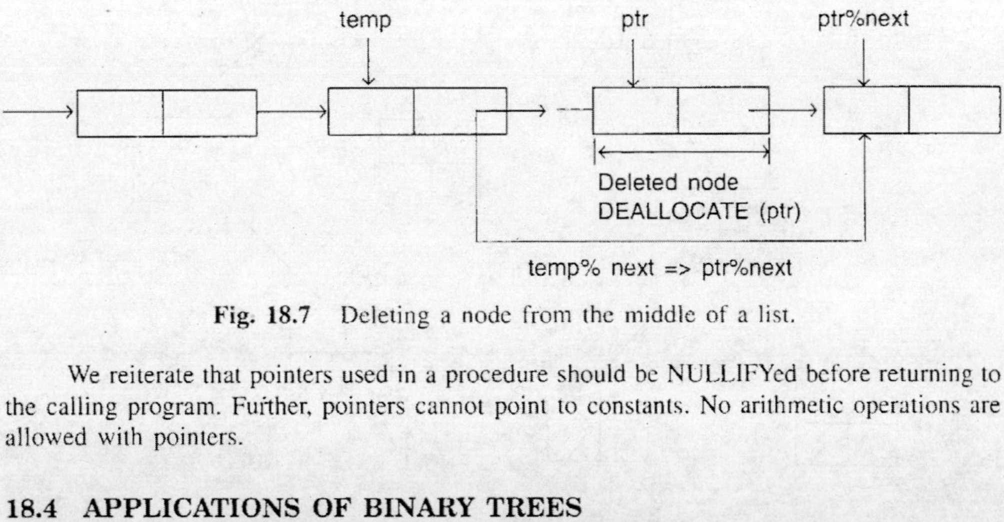

Fig. 18.7 Deleting a node from the middle of a list.

We reiterate that pointers used in a procedure should be NULLIFYed before returning to the calling program. Further, pointers cannot point to constants. No arithmetic operations are allowed with pointers.

18.4 APPLICATIONS OF BINARY TREES

A *binary tree* is a finite set of elements of which one element is called the root of the tree and its remaining elements are partitioned into two disjoint subsets, each of which is itself a binary tree. These two subsets are called the *left subtree* and the *right subtree* of the original tree. Each element of a binary tree is called a *node* of the tree.

Figure 18.8 illustrates a binary tree consisting of 9 elements. In this binary tree, A is the root of the tree. The left subtree consists of the tree with root B. The right subtree is the tree with root C. B has an empty right subtree and its left subtree has root G. C has a left subtree consisting of the single element D. The element which has no further trees emanating from it is known as a *leaf* node. The right subtree of C has E as its root element. E has an empty right subtree and its left subtree is the leaf node F. The node G has a left subtree with a leaf node H and a right subtree with leaf node J. The binary tree of Fig. 18.8 may be represented using pointers as shown in Fig. 18.9.

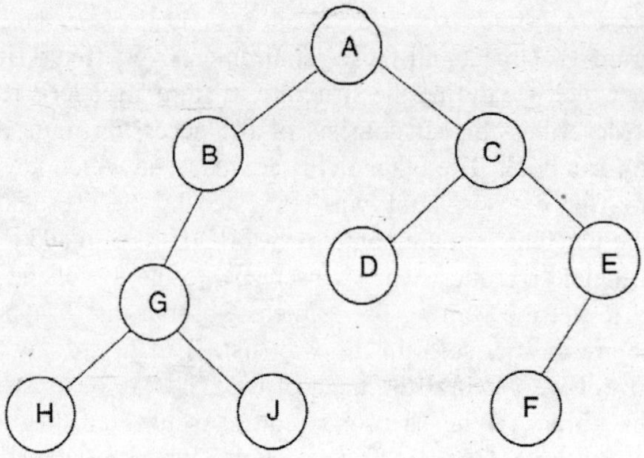

Fig. 18.8 A binary tree.

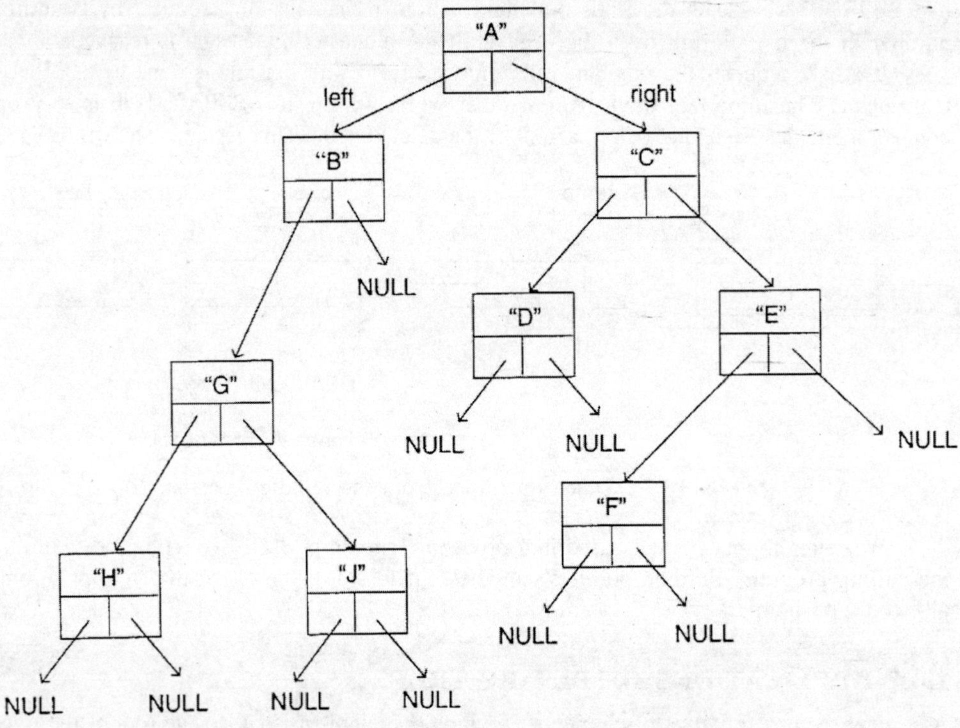

Fig. 18.9 Binary tree representation with pointers.

A node of the tree may be described by the following declaration:

```
TYPE node
    CHARACTER :: letter
    TYPE (node), POINTER :: left_tree
    TYPE (node), POINTER :: right_tree
END TYPE node
```

Binary trees have many applications in programming. They are used to represent arithmetic expressions, moves by opponents in a game, sorting etc.

A binary tree can be recursively defined as follows:

1. A binary tree is a node with a left pointer and a right pointer.
2. A binary tree is a node pointing to two binary trees, a left subtree and a right subtree.

As a binary tree is recursively defined, algorithms which are written using trees are simple to write if they are recursive. We will thus write recursive algorithms and corresponding recursive programs in this section.

Example 18.4

A procedure to pick all duplicate numbers in a set of numbers is to be developed. A straightforward method would be to pick a number and compare it with rest of the numbers in the list. This, however, needs n^2 comparisons for a set of n numbers. A binary tree based algorithm reduces the number of comparisons to a considerable extent. As a by-product it also sorts the numbers. The algorithm is sketched below:

Algorithm 18.1 Algorithm to detect duplicates

```
Read a number
Create a root node for a tree and place the number in it

while data remain in input
   {Read number
   Buildtree (root node, number)}
Buildtree (tree, number)
   {if (number > (value at node))
      then if right branch of tree is empty
         then { create a node
              Place number in it
              Attach node to tree}
         else Buildtree (right branch, number)
   else if (number < (value at node))
      then if left branch of tree is empty
         then {create a node
              Place number in it
              Attach node to tree}
      else Buildtree (left branch, number)
    else Print "number is duplicate"
end of Buildtree
```

This procedure is used in Example Program 18.4. The program has been traced with the following data to illustrate how the tree is built.

Input data: 15 25 30 25 12 22 14 28 – 999999

Example Program 18.4 Picking duplicate numbers from a list

```
!PROGRAM 18.4
!PROGRAM TO REMOVE DUPLICATES USING A TREE ALGORITHM
!THE TREE WHICH IS BUILT CAN ALSO BE USED TO GET SORTED LIST

PROGRAM duplicate_removal
  TYPE node
    INTEGER :: value
    TYPE(node),POINTER :: left,right
  END TYPE node
  IMPLICIT NONE
  TYPE(node),POINTER :: tree
  INTEGER :: number
  NULLIFY(tree) !START WITH EMPTY TREE
  PRINT *,"Type a list of numbers leaving blank between ",&
    "numbers.Indicate end of list by typing -999999"
  DO
    READ *,number
    IF(number == -999999) EXIT
    CALL build_tree(tree,number)
  END DO
  CONTAINS
  RECURSIVE SUBROUTINE build_tree(tree,number)
    IMPLICIT NONE
    TYPE(node),POINTER :: tree
    INTEGER,INTENT(IN) :: number
    !IF TREE EMPTY PLACE NUMBER AT ROOT
    IF(.NOT.ASSOCIATED(tree)) THEN
    ALLOCATE(tree)
    tree%value = number
    NULLIFY(tree%left,tree%right)
    !ELSE PLACE NUMBER IN CORRECT SUBTREE
    ELSE IF(number < tree%value) THEN
      CALL build_tree(tree%left,number)
      ELSE IF(number > tree%value) THEN
      CALL build_tree(tree%right,number)
      ELSE
      PRINT *,"Number =",number,"is a duplicate"
      ENDIF
  END SUBROUTINE build_tree
END PROGRAM duplicate_removal
```

The tree is shown in Fig. 18.10. The student should trace the program and verify the tree building procedure.

The tree was generated by Algorithm 18.1 systematically keeping smaller numbers in a left subtree and larger numbers in a right subtree. The tree has the property that the contents of each node in the left subtree of node x are less than that stored in x. Thus if we trace through all the nodes of the tree in the order of left node, root node, right node starting from the left most node of the tree, we will pass through the numbers in an ascending sequence. This method

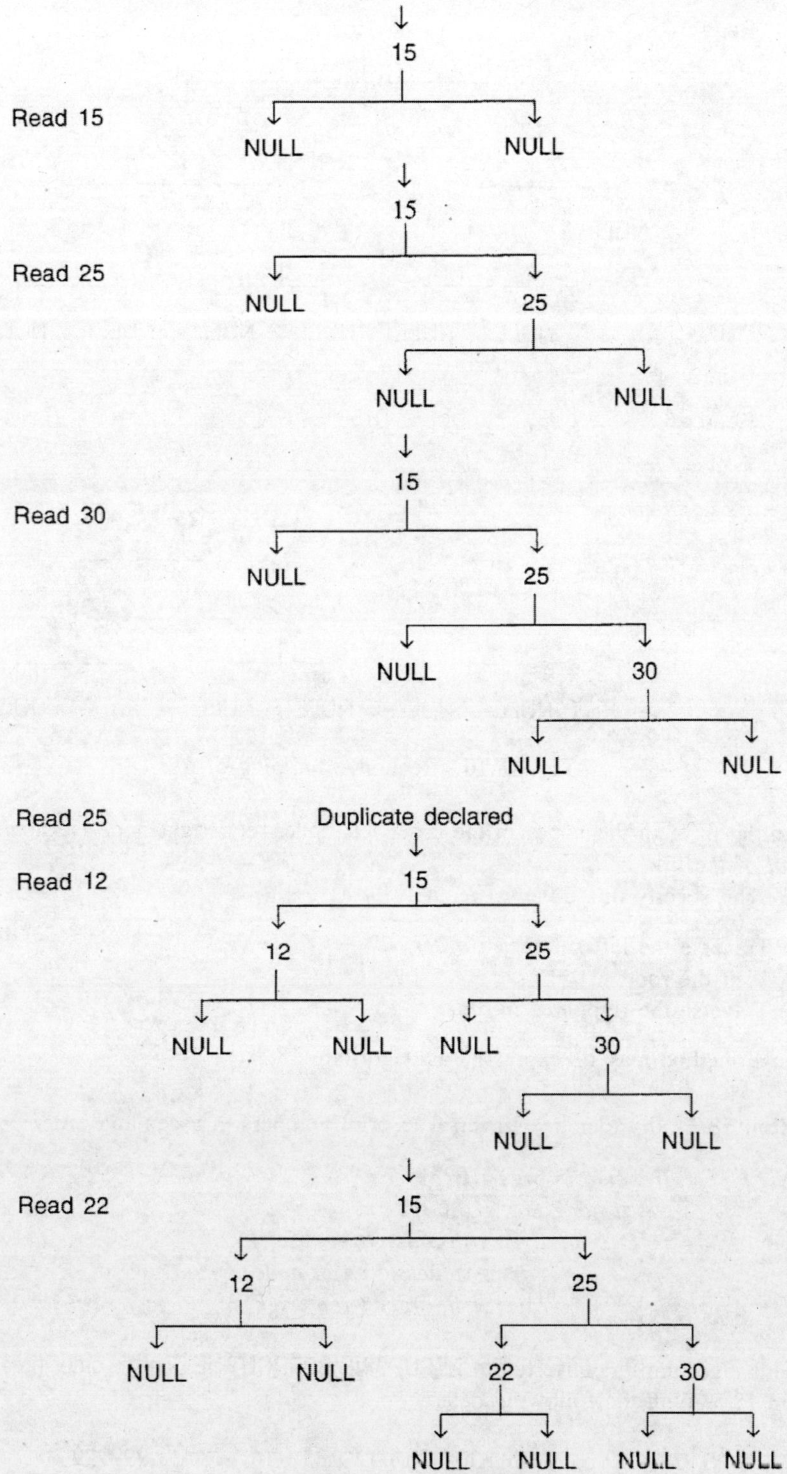

Fig. 18.10 (continued)

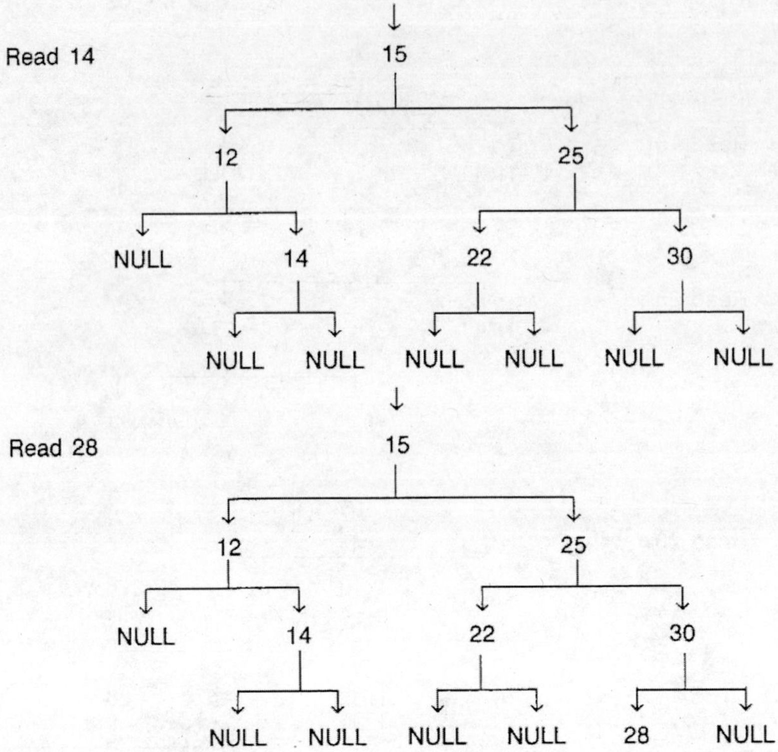

Fig. 18.10 Recursive building of tree.

of travelling through the nodes in the order left node, root, right node is known as *in-order traversal* of the tree.

We can specify this traversal recursively as:

1. Traverse the left subtree *in-order*
2. Visit the root
3. Traverse the right tree *in-order*

The above method may be expressed as Algorithm 18.2.

Algorithm 18.2 In-order tree traversal to print numbers in ascending order

```
Traverse in-order (tree)
    if node not NULL
        {Traverse in-order (tree %left)
            Print value stored in node
        Traverse in-order (tree%right)}
```

This algorithm is converted to RECURSIVE SUBROUTINE print_in_order (tree) in Example Program 18.5. With the following data:

15 25 30 25 12 22 14 28 – 999999

Example Program 18.5 Program to sort integers

```
!PROGRAM 18.5
!TRAVERSING TREE IN ORDER TO PRINT NUMBER IN ASCENDING
!ORDER.THUS CAN BE USED WITH MAIN PROGRAM 18.4
RECURSIVE SUBROUTINE print_in_order(tree)
   !THIS SUBROUTINE TRAVERSES A TREE IN ORDER AND PRINTS
   !VALUES AT NODES IN ORDER. THE OUTPUT IS A SORTED LIST OF
   !NUMBERS
   IMPLICIT NONE
   TYPE(node),POINTER,INTENT(IN) :: tree
   IF(ASSOCIATED(tree)) THEN
      CALL print_in_order(tree%left)
      PRINT *,tree%value
      CALL print_in_order(tree%right)
   ENDIF
END SUBROUTINE print_in_order
```

the order in which nodes will be visited and values printed is shown in Fig. 18.11. If the numbers in the list are to be printed in descending order then we would again traverse the tree in order but from right to left.

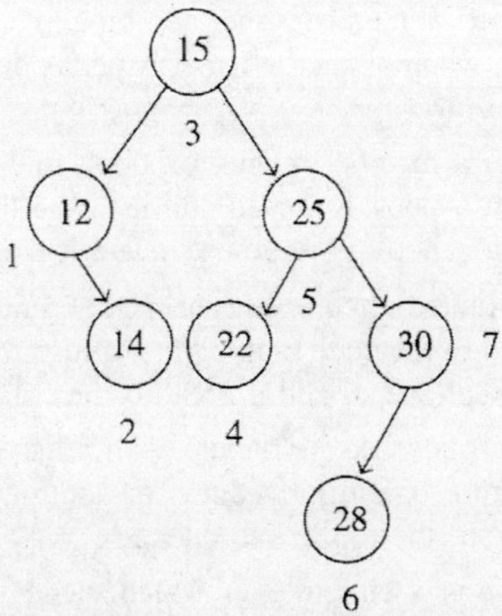

Fig. 18.11 Showing in-order traversal of a tree.

Besides *in-order traversal* in which the root is visited in the middle there are two other methods of systematically visiting the nodes of a tree. They are the *pre-order* and *post-order* traversals. In pre-order we visit the root first and then the left and right subtrees. In post-order we visit the left and right subtrees and the root last.

SUMMARY

1. A variable in Fortran 90 can be declared to have a POINTER attribute.
2. A POINTER variable can point to another variable name which has a TARGET attribute.
3. A POINTER has an association status. It is ASSOCIATED if it is pointing to a target and not associated if it is NULLIFIED by the intrinsic function NULLIFY (pointer variable).

4. When a POINTER variable is pointing to a TARGET, the POINTER is an alias (another name) of the TARGET variable name. Thus the data stored in TARGET variable name can be obtained via the POINTER variable name.
5. The space for a POINTER variable can be dynamically created and released by using ALLOCATE and DEALLOCATE statements.
6. A pointer variable can be a component of a derived data type.
7. A variable with a POINTER attribute which is a component of a derived data type can point to an object of the same type. This allows the creation of linked lists.
8. By traversing the nodes of a linked list using a pointer it is possible to add nodes to a list, delete nodes from a list, search for a specified node in a list and print the nodes of a list.
9. Lists are useful to store groups of objects in which the size of the group is variable.
10. Pointers can be used to build tree data structures. Tree data structures allow formulation of very powerful recursive algorithms.

EXERCISES

18.1 A lending library keeps a list of issued books. Each item in the issue list has the following information. Accession number of the book, issue code which is I, B or L (issued to a member, sent for binding, issued to another library), identity of member to whom issued. A list of issued books is maintained. Write SUBROUTINES to do the following:

   i. When a member requests a book find its status.
   ii. When a book is issued add it to the list of issued books.
   iii. When a book is returned, delete it from the list of issued books.

18.2 A doubly linked circular list consists of a number of nodes where each node is not only linked to the node to its right but also to the node to its left. Write a MODULE to create such a list, add a node to the list and delete a node from the list.

18.3 Simulate a queue data structure with a list structure. A queue is a first-in-first out data structure. Write procedures to add an element to the queue and retrieve an element from the top of the queue.

18.4 A dequeue is a structure in which elements may be inserted at either end and removed from either end. The two ends of the dequeue are called left and right. Use a list structure to simulate a dequeue. Write functions to remove elements from left, remove from right, insert at left, insert at right. The functions should take care of operations when the dequeue becomes empty.

18.5 Write routines to do the following in a sequential list:

   i. Append an element to the tail of the list.
   ii. Concatenate two lists.
   iii. Reverse a list so that the last element becomes the first and vice versa.
   iv. Insert a node as the nth node of the list.
   v. Copy a list into another list.
   vi. Count the number of nodes in a list.
   vii. Delete all even nodes in the list.
   viii. Interchange the nth and k^{th} nodes of a list.

18.6 Create a data structure which would represent the record of each member of a library. The record should contain membership number, name, borrower category and a part which would contain a list of books borrowed by a member.

18.7 Write a function which would scan the member data structure and print out the books borrowed by a specified member

18.8 Write a function which would print out the names of all members who have borrowed more than 6 books.

18.9 Write a function to merge two sorted lists.

18.10 Define a list data structure to facilitate the symbolic manipulation of polynomials. For example a term of the polynomial

$$a_n x^n + a_{n-1} x^{n-1} + a_{n-2} x^{n-2} + \dots + a_1 x^1 + a_o$$

may be represented by the node

Coefficient	Power of x	next

Write a routine to add two polynomials represented by two lists.

Write another routine to symbolically differentiate a polynomial and obtain a list which represents the derivative polynomial.

18.11 A sparse vector is a vector in which more than 80 percent of the components are zero. Represent a sparse vector by a circular list.

18.12 Write a routine to add two sparse vectors represented by two lists.

18.13 Repeat Exercise 18.4 using a doubly linked circular list.

18.14 Design doubly linked circular lists to store the following sparse matrix. Pictorially show the lists to represent this matrix:

$$\begin{matrix} 2 & 0 & 0 & 4 \\ 0 & 0 & 5 & 0 \\ 0 & 7 & 0 & 6 \\ 1 & 4 & 0 & 0 \end{matrix}$$

Each node of the list would have the row and column index of the matrix element and the value of the element.

18.15 Write a program to add two n × n sparse matrices and store the result in a third matrix.

18.16 Write a program to count the number of nodes in a binary tree.

18.17 Write a program to count the number of leaf nodes of a binary tree

18.18 Write a recursive algorithm to search for a key from a list of integer valued keys. (Hint: First place the keys systematically in a tree and then search the tree)

19. Uses of Modules

Learning Objectives

In this chapter we will learn:

1. Use of MODULEs to define abstract data types
2. Extending the meaning of intrinsic operators
3. Use of a stack to evaluate an arithmetic expression

One of the unique new features in Fortran 90 which was not there in earlier versions of Fortran is the program unit called a MODULE. We have seen that a MODULE starts with the initial statement

MODULE *name*

and ends with the statement

END MODULE *name*

We have seen that a MODULE is used in the following situations in programming:

- To define variables and parameters which will be used globally by many subprograms (Refer to Section 14.1).
- To specify derived data types which are to be used as dummy variables of procedures (Refer to Section 15.3).
- To encapsulate a number of procedures in a MODULE so that their interface is explicit. By placing a USE *module name* statement in any procedure the interface of the procedures contained in the module are made explicit to procedure using the MODULE (Refer Sections 16.3 and 16.4).

Besides these, MODULEs are used to create what are known as abstract data types. By the term abstract data type we mean an encapsulation of a user derived data type along with a number of relevant operations on this data type. Such abstract data types can be used very effectively in many applications. We will illustrate this use of MODULEs in this chapter.

19.1 ABSTRACT DATA TYPE WITH MODULES

We will first look at an abstract data type called *vector*. Vectors are extensively used in many applications. A vector is an ordered array of real numbers. The operations on a vector data type we will develop are:

- Create a vector
- Add two vectors
- Find the scalar product of two vectors (also called a dot product)
- Find the magnitude of a vector
- Multiply a vector by a real number

All these will be encapsulated in a MODULE vector_data. We will parametrize the maximum number of components in a vector. A vector will be created from an array. We give the specifications and constraints relating to vectors and operations below:

- A vector is an ordered array of reals. For example V_1 = [1.5 2.5 3.6 7.8 9.4] is a vector with 5 components.
- Two vectors V_1 and V_2 can be added if they have the same number of components. If V_2 = [2.6 3.6 4.2 7.6 2.5] then $V_1 + V_2$ is the vector [4.1 6.1 7.8 15.4 11.9].
- The scalar product or dot product of V_1 and V_2 is V_1 .dot. $V_2 = \sum_{i=1}^{n} V_1(i) * V_2(i)$ where n is the number of components in the vector. The number of components in V_1 should equal that in V_2. For the example being considered

$$V_1 \text{ .dot. } V_2 = 110.8$$

- The magnitude of a vector is defined as

$$\left(\sum_{i=1}^{n} V_i^2\right)^{1/2}$$

The magnitude of V_1 is 13.063.
- The product of a vector by a real is represented by $V * V_1$ where V is a real number and V_1 is a vector

$$\begin{aligned} 2.5 * V_1 &= 2.5 * [1.5\ 2.5\ 3.6\ 7.8\ 9.4] \\ &= [3.75\ 6.25\ 9.0\ 19.5\ 23.5] \end{aligned}$$

We will now develop a MODULE vector_data which will encapsulate all these operations. This is given as Example Program 19.1. Observe the specification PRIVATE in TYPE vector. This restricts accessibility of variable specifications in the derived type to the MODULE. It is also possible to declare some variables in a MODULE as PRIVATE. If a derived type variable is declared PRIVATE then no variable of that type can be declared outside the MODULE. This is an important method of hiding data from entities which do not need them. The rest of the MODULE is straightforward.

Example Program 19.1 A MODULE for abstract data type vector

```
!PROGRAM 19.1
!MODULE DEFINES ABSTRACT DATA TYPE VECTOR

MODULE vector_data
  IMPLICIT NONE
  INTEGER,PARAMETER :: max_comp=12
  !WE SPECIFY 12 AS MAXIMUM NUMBER OF COMPONENTS IN A VECTOR
  PRIVATE
  TYPE vector
    INTEGER :: no_comp
    REAL,DIMENSION(max_comp) :: components
  END TYPE vector
  INTERFACE OPERATOR (.dot.)
    MODULE PROCEDURE scalar_product
  END INTERFACE
```

```
INTERFACE OPERATOR(*)
   MODULE PROCEDURE r_times_vec
END INTERFACE
CONTAINS
   TYPE(vector) FUNCTION create_vec(array,n)
   !THIS FUNCTION TAKES THE FIRST N ELEMENTS OF ARRAY
   !AND MAKES IT INTO A VECTOR
   INTEGER,INTENT(IN) :: n
   REAL,DIMENSION(n),INTENT(IN) :: array
   IF(n > max_comp) THEN !GIVE ERROR MESSAGE
   PRINT *,"No. of components exceeds max_comp"
   PRINT *,"No. of components =",n,"Max_comp =",max_comp
   create_vec%no_comp = 0
   ELSE !CREATE VECTOR FROM GIVEN ARRAY
   create_vec%no_comp = n
   create_vec%components(1:n) = array(1:n)
   ENDIF
END FUNCTION create_vec
INTEGER FUNCTION vector_size(vec)
   !THIS FUNCTION FINDS THE NO. OF COMPONENTS IN A VECTOR
   TYPE(vector),INTENT(IN) :: vec
   vector_size = vec%no_comp
END FUNCTION vector_size
!THE FOLLOWING FUNCTION PUTS THE COMPONENTS OF A VECTOR
!IN AN ARRAY
FUNCTION vec_array(vec)
   TYPE(vector),INTENT(IN) :: vec
   REAL,DIMENSION(vec%no_comp) :: vec_array(vec%no_comp)
   vec_array(1:vec%no_comp) = vec%components(1:vec%no_comp)
END FUNCTION vec_array
REAL FUNCTION scalar_product(v1,v2)
TYPE(vector),INTENT(IN) :: v1,v2
REAL :: dot_prod !LOCAL VARIABLE
INTEGER :: i !LOCAL VARIABLE
!IF THE TWO VECTORS DO NOT HAVE THE SAME NUMBER OF
!COMPONENTS THEIR SCALAR PRODUCT IS UNDEFINED
dot_prod = 0.0
IF(v1%no_comp /= v2%no_comp) THEN !PRINT ERROR MESSAGE
   PRINT *,"v1 and v2 do not have the same no. of components"
   PRINT *,"v1 comp= ",v1%no_comp
   PRINT *,"v2 comp= ",v2%no_comp
   scalar_product = 0.0
ELSE
   DO i=1,v1%no_comp
      dot_prod = dot_prod + v1%components(i) *v2%components(i)
   END DO
   scalar_product = dot_prod
ENDIF
END FUNCTION scalar_product
```

```
  !FUNCTION TO FIND MAGNITUDE OF A VECTOR FOLLOWS
  REAL FUNCTION magnitude(vec)
     TYPE(vector),INTENT(IN) :: vec
     REAL :: sum_sq=0 !LOCAL VARIABLE
     INTEGER :: i !LOCAL VARIABLE
     DO i=1,vec%no_comp
        sum_sq = sum_sq + vec%components(i) ** 2
     END DO
     magnitude = SQRT(sum_sq)
  END FUNCTION magnitude
  TYPE(vector) FUNCTION r_times_vec(r,vec)
     TYPE(vector),INTENT(IN) :: vec
     REAL,INTENT(IN) :: r
     INTEGER :: i !LOCAL VARIABLE
     r_times_vec%no_comp = vec%no_comp
     DO i=1,vec%no_comp
        r_times_vec%components(i) = vec%components(i)*r
     END DO
  END FUNCTION r_times_vec
END MODULE vector_data
!THE FOLLOWING PROGRAM IS WRITTEN TO TEST THE MODULE VECTOR_DATA
PROGRAM test_vector_data
  USE vector_data
  IMPLICIT NONE
  INTEGER :: i
  REAL :: r_t=2.5,prod
  REAL,DIMENSION(5) :: ar_1
  REAL,DIMENSION(8) :: ar_2
  TYPE(vector) :: vec_1,vec_2
  ar_1 = (/1.5, 2.5, 3.6, 7.8, 9.4/)
  ar_2 = (/2.6, 3.6, 4.2, 7.6, 2.5, 4.2, 3.6, 4.7/)
  vec_1 = create_vec(ar_1,5)
  vec_2 = create_vec(ar_2,5)
  PRINT *,"No.of components in vec_1 =",vector_size(vec_1)
  PRINT *,"No.of components in vec_2 =",vector_size(vec_2)
  PRINT *,"Components of vec_1 are=",vec_array(vec_1)
  PRINT *,"Components of vec_2 are=",vec_array(vec_2)
  PRINT *,"Test of operator .dot."
  PRINT *,"Scalar product vec_1 .dot. vec_2 is =",vec_1 .dot. vec_2
  PRINT *,"Scalar product of vec_1 vec_2 is",scalar_product(vec_1,vec_2)
  PRINT *,"Magnitude of vec_1 is =",magnitude(vec_1)
  PRINT *,"Magnitude of vec_2 is =",magnitude(vec_2)
  vec_2 = r_times_vec(2.5,vec_1)
  PRINT *,"2.5 *vec_1 =",vec_array(vec_2)
  PRINT *,"Test of overload operator *"
  vec_2 = r_t * vec_1
  PRINT *,"2.5 *vec_1 =",vec_array(vec_2)
  PRINT *,"Test if vectors are conformable"
  vec_2 = create_vec(ar_2,8)
  prod = vec_1 .dot. vec_2
END PROGRAM test_vector_data
```

19.2 SIMULATION AND APPLICATION OF A STACK

As another example of an abstract data type we will consider a data structure known as a stack and operations on this data structure. A *stack* is a structure with a group of cells in which only the top cell is accessible. Thus only the element at the top of the stack may be retrieved. Any element to be stored is also stored at the top. Figure 19.1 illustrates this.

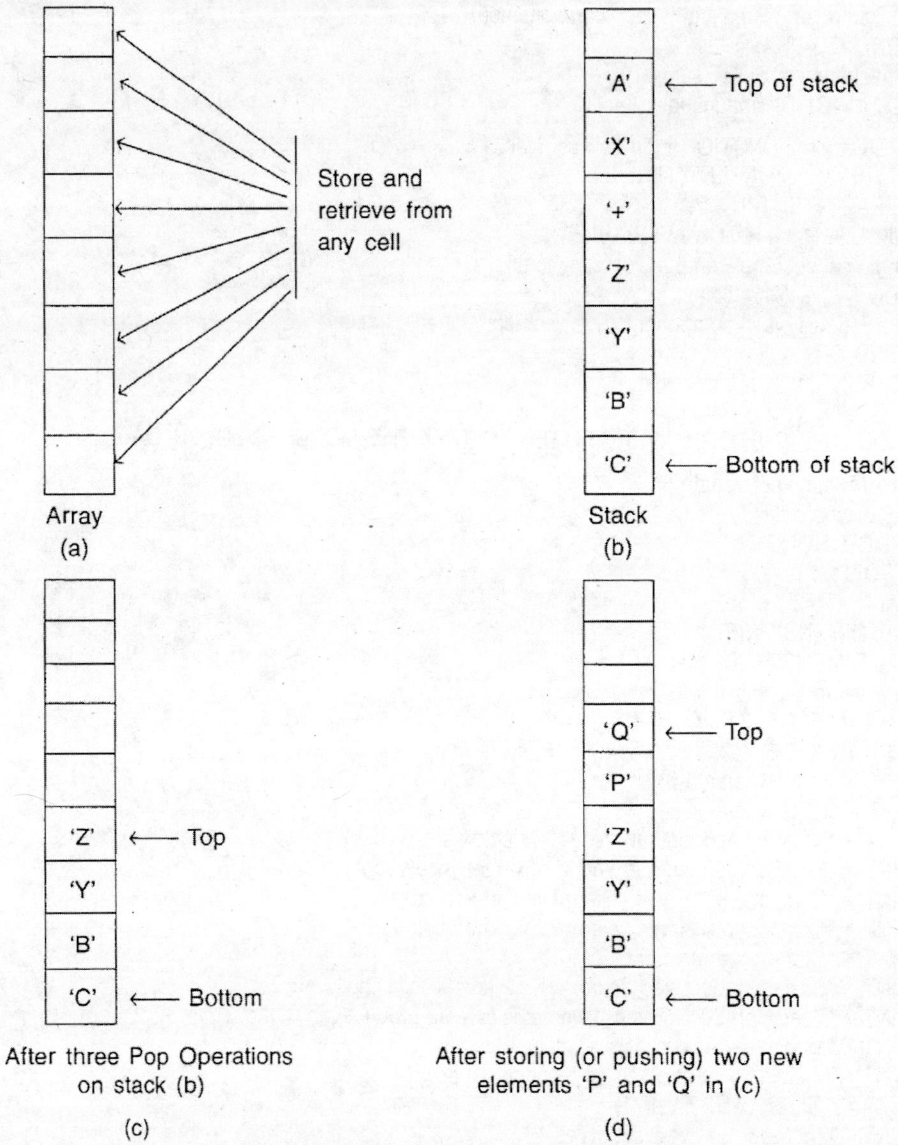

Fig. 19.1 A stack and operations on it.

There are two operations which one can perform with a stack. An operation *Push x* stores the variable *x* at the top of the stack and an operation *Pop y* retrieves the variable *y* from the top of the stack. Given the stack of Fig. 19.1 (b) if we execute 3 POP operations the characters

'A', 'X' and '+' will be removed in the order shown. The stack will be in the state shown in Fig. 19.1(c). If we now carry out the operations PUSH 'P' and PUSH 'Q', the character 'P' will be stored on top of the stack first and 'Q' will be stored on top of 'P'. The status of the stack will be as shown in Fig. 19.1(d). The last_in_first_out (LIFO) retrieval property of a stack is extremely useful in a number of programming situations. These arise in programming language translation such as in evaluating arithmetic expressions using arithmetic operator precedence rules, implementing procedure calls and returns etc. We will first define a MODULE stack. We will simulate a stack using an array. A stack can also be simulated using a list. We leave it as an exercise to the student.

Example Program 19.2 A MODULE to simulate a stack

```
!PROGRAM 19.2
!DESCRIPTION OF A STACK AND OPERATIONS ON IT
MODULE stack_structure
   IMPLICIT NONE
   INTEGER,PARAMETER :: max_size=100
   !THE MAXIMUM SIZE OF THE ABOVE STACK IS 100
   REAL,DIMENSION(1:max_size) :: stack
   INTEGER :: stack_top = 0
   LOGICAL :: stack_full,stack_empty
CONTAINS
   SUBROUTINE push(pushed_no)
      REAL,INTENT(IN) :: pushed_no
      LOGICAL :: stack_full,stack_empty
      IF (stack_full) THEN
      PRINT *,"stack full.cannot push no"
      RETURN
      ENDIF
      stack_top = stack_top + 1
      stack(stack_top) = pushed_no
      stack_empty = .false.
      IF(stack_top == max_size) THEN
      stack_full = .true.
      ENDIF
   END SUBROUTINE push
   SUBROUTINE pop(popped_no)
      REAL,INTENT(OUT) :: popped_no
      IF(stack_empty) THEN
         PRINT *,"Stack empty.cannot pop no"
         RETURN
      ENDIF
      popped_no = stack(stack_top)
      stack_top = stack_top - 1
      stack_full = .false.
      IF(stack_top < 0) THEN
         stack_empty = .true.
      ENDIF
   END SUBROUTINE pop
END MODULE stack_structure
```

We will first examine the MODULE stack_structure of Example Program 19.2. The first part of the MODULE declares a REAL array of size = max_size as stack. The top of the stack is an INTEGER stack_top. The LOGICAL variables stack_full and stack_empty are used to indicate these conditions. The SUBROUTINE push (pushed_no) increments the index indicating top of stack and pushes a number in the array simulating a stack. It is also checked whether the index reaches a value equal to the size of the stack. If it reaches this value then stack_full is set to true.

The SUBROUTINE pop is similar and when it is called, it takes out the number stored at the top of the stack and returns it in the variable name popped_no. This SUBROUTINE also sets LOGICAL variable stack_empty to true if no number is left in the stack.

Observe that we start storing values in the simulated stack from index 1. When index reaches a value max_size the stack is full. Thus index 1 indicates the bottom of the stack.

We will now consider the evaluation of an algebraic expression. Consider, for example, the expression

$$(A - B) * C$$

This is the usual notation and is known as the *infix* notation. In this notation operators appear between the operands on which they operate. Parentheses impose a precedence of operation. The same expression may be written in what is known as *polish postfix* notation shown below:

$$AB - C *$$

In this notation we interpret the expression by scanning it from left to right. The minus sign is applied to the two operands immediately preceding it. After carrying out the subtraction operation we continue scanning till we reach the next operator. When it is found it is applied to the two quantities preceding it. In this case the two quantities are A – B and C to which the multiplication operator * is applied giving (A – B) * C.

Consider the polish postfix expression

$$ABC -/$$

Scanning from left to right, we stop when we reach – and apply it to the two immediately preceding operands obtaining (B – C). Continuing the scan we encounter / and apply it to A and B – C getting A/ (B – C). We give below some more examples of infix and postfix expressions

Infix expression	*Postfix expression*
A + B – C + D	AB + C – D +
(A + B) / (C + D)	AB + CD + /
A + B * (C + D * (E + F))	ABCDEF + * + * +
(A/B) * (C* F + (A – D) * E)	AB/CF * AD – E * + *

The polish postfix form is very important as this form is used by compilers to evaluate expressions. Algorithms are available to convert an expression from infix to postfix form. In this section we will give an algorithm to evaluate the arithmetic expression given in the postfix form. A stack is used to aid the evaluation procedure. An algorithm for evaluation is given as Algorithm 19.1.

Algorithm 19.1 Evaluates value of a postfix arithmetic expression

1. Store in an array values (real numbers) corresponding to each variable name.
Repeat
2. Scan the postfix expression from left to right. If a scanned character is a letter (namely, a variable name) then push its value into a stack.
3. If the scanned character is an arithmetic operator then pop stack. Assign the value popped to operand 2. Pop the stack again and assign the value to operand 1.

   Select *case* (operator)
   $*$: Accumulator ⟵ operand 1 $*$ operand 2
   / : Accumulator ⟵ operand 1 / operand 2
   + : Accumulator ⟵ operand 1 + operand 2
   – : Accumulator ⟵ operand 1 – operand 2
4. Push result in accumulator into stack.
Until the end of postfix string

For example, consider the infix expression (A – B) $*$ C. The corresponding postfix expression is AB – C $*$. If the values of A, B, C are respectively 2.5, 1.4, 3.0 then applying the algorithm we obtain:

1. A = 2.5, B = 1.4, C = 3.0
2. Scanning AB – C$*$ we encounter first A. The value of A, namely, 2.5 is pushed into stack. Next B is encountered and its value 1.4 is pushed into stack
3. The next character scanned is an arithmetic operator, namely, –. The stack is popped and the value is assigned to operand 2. Thus operand 2 ⟵ 1.4. The stack is popped again and the popped value is assigned to operand 1. Thus operand 1 ⟵ 2.5
4. As the operator is – we compute:

   Accumulator ⟵ operand 1 – operand 2 = 2.5 – 1.4 = 1.1

5. 1.1 is pushed into the stack
6. The next character scanned is a letter C. Thus its value 3.0 is pushed into the stack.
7. The next character scanned is $*$. The stack is popped and operand 2 is set equal to 3.0. The stack is popped again and operand 1 ⟵ 1.1
8. As the operand is $*$ we compute:

   Accumulator ⟵ operand 1 $*$ operand 2 = 1.1 $*$ 3.0 = 3.3

9. The algorithm now terminates as there are no more characters in the postfix expression.

Example Program 19.3 Use of stack to evaluate arithmetic expression

```
!PROGRAM 19.3
!Evaluation of arithmetic expression
PROGRAM calculate
  USE stack_structure
  !Local Variables
    INTEGER :: i, m, int_A
    REAL, DIMENSION(0:25) :: memory
    REAL :: opnd_1, opnd_2, acc
    CHARACTER(LEN=80) :: post_fix
```

```
      TYPE var_value
         CHARACTER :: variable
         REAL :: value
      END TYPE var_value
   TYPE(var_value) :: temp
! Read postfix string as first line of input
   READ 40, post_fix
   40 FORMAT (A80)
      m = LEN_TRIM(post_fix)
!Read values of variables from input presented in the form
! < variable name > blank < value > one per line. Last line
! has "*" as first character to indicate end of line.
   int_A = ICHAR("A") ! Integer equivalent of "A"
   DO ! loop stores variable values in memory
      READ 50, temp%variable, temp%value
   50 FORMAT(A1, 1X, F12.4)
      IF(temp%variable == "*") EXIT
      memory(ICHAR(temp%variable) – int_A) = temp%value
   END DO
!Values of variable names "A" to "Z" stored in memory(0) to
! memory(25) respectively.
! The following loop uses stack to calculate arithmetic expression
   DO i = 1,m
      SELECT CASE (post_fix(i:i))
         CASE("A":"Z")
            CALL push(memory(ICHAR(post_fix(i:i)) – int_A))
         CASE("+")
            CALL pop(opnd_2)
            CALL pop(opnd_1)
            acc = opnd_1 + opnd_2
            CALL push(acc)
         CASE("–")
            CALL pop(opnd_2)
            CALL pop(opnd_1)
            acc = opnd_1 – opnd_2
            CALL push(acc)
         CASE("*")
            CALL pop(opnd_2)
            CALL pop(opnd_1)
            acc = opnd_1 * opnd_2
            CALL push(acc)
         CASE("/")
            CALL pop(opnd_2)
            CALL pop(opnd_1)
            acc = opnd_1 / opnd_2
            CALL push(acc)
         CASE DEFAULT
            PRINT *, "Error in post_fix string"
         END SELECT
      END DO
   PRINT *, "The value of the arithmetic expression calculated = ", acc
END PROGRAM calculate
```

The main PROGRAM calculate (Example Program 19.3) uses the MODULE stack_structure. In developing this program we have made the following assumptions:

- The variable names in which values are stored are single upper case letters. Thus A, B, C .... Z are allowed. Variable names a, b, c etc.; are not allowed. The string AB represents two variable names A and B following one another.
- The postfix string is given as input. We assume that this string is in the correct postfix form. Thus AB *, ABC –/ are legal, whereas A – B /C is not legal as the latter one is not a legal postfix string.
- The values of the variables are given one per line. For example,

```
A 2.5
B 3.8
C 6.8
*
```

and the end of input is indicated by a * in the first position. The variable name is separated from its value by 1 blank column.

The main PROGRAM calculate first reads the post_fix string into the character string post_fix. The length of this string is stored in len_postfix. Observe that we have used the intrinsic function LEN_TRIM which finds the length after trimming all the trailing blanks. We next read the values of the variable using a DO loop. Observe that the values of variables are stored in an array named memory which is indexed by the variable name. As we have assumed that the variable names are single characters we can use this method. As the ASCII codes of A, B, C .... Z are in ascending order with A having the least value we have used index 0 in the array memory to store the value of the variable name A and index 25 to store the value of Z.

The next DO loop implements repeat loop (Steps 2 to 5) of Algorithm 19.1. Observe almost the one-to-one correspondence between the algorithm and the program. This has been made possible by using MODULE stack_structure which simulates a stack.

19.3 ABSTRACT DATA TYPE COMPLEX

In this section we develop a MODULE complex_arith which defines a TYPE complex_no and operations of add, subtract, multiply and divide using complex numbers. Observe in Example Program 19.3 that FUNCTIONS comp_add, comp_sub, comp_mult and comp_div contain statements to carry out the respective operations. These are CONTAINED in the MODULE. Observe that we have used a RESULT specification in the FUNCTIONS for clarity. The operators +, –, * and / are overloaded to carry out these operations for complex numbers. The following points must be noted:

- The INTERFACE appears at the beginning of the MODULE along with declarations.
- FUNCTIONs are used as MODULE PROCEDURES to define operators. MODULE Procedure for an operator cannot be a SUBROUTINE.
- The meanings of the operators are extended but not redefined. Fortran 90 allows only extending the meaning of overloaded intrinsic operators.

Example Program 19.4 Module defining abstract data type complex

```
!PROGRAM 19.4
!ABSTRACT DATA TYPE COMPLEX NUMBER
MODULE complex_arith
  IMPLICIT NONE
  TYPE complex_no
    REAL :: real_p,imag_p
  END TYPE complex_no
  INTERFACE OPERATOR(+)
    MODULE PROCEDURE comp_add
  END INTERFACE
  INTERFACE OPERATOR(-)
    MODULE PROCEDURE comp_sub
  END INTERFACE
  INTERFACE OPERATOR(*)
    MODULE PROCEDURE comp_mult
  END INTERFACE
  INTERFACE OPERATOR(/)
    MODULE PROCEDURE comp_div
  END INTERFACE
CONTAINS
  FUNCTION comp_add(x,y) RESULT(z)
    TYPE(complex_no) :: z
    TYPE(complex_no),INTENT(IN) :: x,y
    z%real_p = x%real_p + y%real_p
    z%imag_p = x%imag_p + y%imag_p
  END FUNCTION comp_add
  FUNCTION comp_sub(x,y) RESULT(z)
    TYPE(complex_no) :: z
    TYPE(complex_no),INTENT(IN) :: x,y
    z%real_p = x%real_p - y%real_p
    z%imag_p = x%imag_p - y%imag_p
  END FUNCTION comp_sub
  FUNCTION comp_mult(x,y) RESULT(z)
    TYPE(complex_no) :: z
    TYPE(complex_no),INTENT(IN) :: x,y
    z%real_p = x%real_p * y%real_p - x%imag_p*y%imag_p
    z%imag_p = x%real_p * y%imag_p + x%imag_p*y%real_p
  END FUNCTION comp_mult
  FUNCTION comp_div(x,y) RESULT(z)
    TYPE(complex_no) :: z
    TYPE(complex_no),INTENT(IN) :: x,y
    REAL :: denom
    denom = y%real_p ** 2 + y%imag_p ** 2
    z%real_p = (x%real_p*y%real_p + x%imag_p*y%imag_p)/denom
    z%imag_p = (y%real_p*x%imag_p - x%real_p*y%imag_p)/denom
  END FUNCTION comp_div
END MODULE complex_arith
```

SUMMARY

1. An encapsulation of a user defined data type along with a number of operations of relevance to this derived data type is called an abstract data type. Abstract data types simplify programming of many applications.
2. MODULES are well suited to create abstract data types in Fortran 90.
3. When a data structure is declared PRIVATE in a MODULE it cannot be used outside a MODULE. This is useful to protect data which are internal to a MODULE and not required outside the MODULE.
4. Stack is a memory with a last_in_first_out discipline. In other words, data stored in it last is retrievable first.
5. A MODULE can be designed to simulate a stack.

EXERCISES

19.1 Write a MODULE for implementing arithmetic operations on hexadecimal digits. Use it to perform arithmetic on hexadecimal numbers.

19.2 Write a MODULE to implement a SET of digits. The mathematical definition of SET is to be used. Implement the following operations:

i. Union of two sets
ii. Intersection of two sets
iii. Difference of two sets
iv. Whether an element is a member of a set
v. Whether a set is contained in another set

19.3 Extend 19.2 to a SET of characters.

19.4 Write a program to determine if an input character string is of the form X*a*Y where X is a string of arbitrary length using only characters A and B, and Y is the reverse of string X. The character *a* is any character except A or B. For example, if X is ABB then Y is BBA. An example of X*a*Y is ABBDBBA. An invalid string X*a*Y is ABBBBBA. The program should detect such invalid strings. Use a stack to solve the problem.

19.5 Use Push and Pop operations on a stack to do the following:

i. Assign to a variable name Y the value of the third element from the top of the stack and keep the stack undisturbed.
ii. Given an arbitrary integer n, pop out the top n elements. A message should be printed if an unusual condition is encountered.
iii. Assign to a variable Y the value of the third element from the bottom of the stack and keep the stack undisturbed (You may use a temporary stack if necessary).

19.6 Write a program to convert an infix arithmetic expression to the postfix form. Use stacks. For example the postfix equivalent of (A + B) * (C – D)/(E – F) is

AB + CD – EF –/*

19.7 Write a program to read a postfix string and convert to infix form. The infix string should use parentheses if needed.

19.8 Write a program to read a parenthesised infix expression and do the following:

i. Check if the left and right parentheses match.

ii. If they match then remove all superfluous parentheses and create an infix string with minimum number of parentheses.

19.9 A queue is a data structure in which a new element is inserted at the back of the queue and an element is retrieved from the front (the other end) of the queue. For example, given a queue,

```
A B C D E F X Y Z
↓               ↓
Back          Front
```

a retrieval operation will retrieve Z. An insert operation will insert an element behind A. Write a program to:

i. Define a data structure for a queue of characters. Use an array to simulate a queue.

ii. Write functions to insert a character at the end of a queue and a function to retrieve a character from the head of the queue. Abnormal conditions such as queue empty, queue full etc., must be accounted for.

19.10 A *dequeue* is an ordered set of elements in which elements may be inserted/retrieved from either end. Write a MODULE which will encapsulate a derived type dequeue and perform operations on it. The operations allowed are get_from_left, get_from_right, insert_at_left, insert_at_right. Exceptional conditions should be reported.

20. *Miscellaneous Features of Fortran 90*

Learning Objectives

In this chapter we will learn:

1. The use of KIND specification in declaring REAL, INTEGERS and CHARACTER data types
2. The intrinsic data type COMPLEX in Fortran 90
3. The definition and use of WHERE construct with arrays
4. The definition and use of NAMELIST to describe groups of variables in input/output statements

There are a number of features in Fortran 90 which allow the use of more general data declarations, some new features to manipulate arrays and a facility to allow direct outputs to different units and to input them as input to a program. In the first category Fortran 90 allows the use of INTEGERS with user specified size and real numbers with a large number of significant digits. An intrinsic data type COMPLEX is also available.

In the domain of array manipulation it is possible to selectively manipulate some components of an array using a logical MASK. This is one more feature which enhances Fortran 90's array manipulation capabilities. Finally a flexible formatting for I/O of special relevance to files has been introduced. We will present these features in this chapter.

20.1 KIND SPECIFICATION FOR REALS

Consider Example Program 20.1 and the output of the program. The value of (b – c) we get by long hand calculation is 0.6E – 7. The output d1 = b – c given by the computer is seen to be 0.59604645E – 07. The answer, given by the computer is incorrect. This happens because of the manner in which numbers are stored in a computer and calculations are performed. All decimal numbers are converted to binary and stored in the computer. In doing so there will be a small conversion error which is of the order of 10^{-8} for computers with a word length of 32 bits. As b and c are nearly equal in this example, (b – c) will have many zeros after the decimal point. As these zeros have no significance, the system automatically shifts the result left till the leading digit after the decimal point is non-zero. The exponent is reduced by 1 for every left shift of the number. This is called the *normalized floating point* method of storing numbers. When this is done digits which arise due to the conversion error are also shifted. Thus instead of giving 0.60000000E – 7 as answer the computer gives 0.5960464E – 7. (Observe that the error is less than 0.5×10^{-8}). The computer will carry these digits in all further computations as though they are correct. As a is large a * (b – c) inflates the error in (b – c) and the answer is incorrect. As b and c are almost equal a * b is almost equal to a * c and (a * b – a * c) ≠ a * (b – c). This is due to the fact that both the left and right hand sides have different amounts of rounding errors. Only the first digit of the answer, namely, 7 is significant. Whenever the difference of almost equal numbers occurs in a calculation, significant digits are lost and incorrect digits which arise due to rounding errors are carried in further computations. Loss of significant digits may be partially avoided by using higher precision. Fortran 90 allows specification of higher precision for REAL numbers while declaring them. If we write

```
REAL (KIND = 2) :: a, b, c, d, d1, d2, d3, x1, x2
```

then all the variables in the list will have a precision which is double the normal precision. In other words, if the number of significant digits in single precision in a computer is 7 then when (KIND = 2) is specified it would be 14. Fortran 90 has left the definition of precision to the computer vendor. Thus the number of digits in double precision is processor dependent and one must study the specific manual of the Fortran 90 processor being used.

Example Program 20.1 Use of KIND specification in REALs

```
!Example Program 20.1
!Illustrates loss of significant digits and non associativity of
!arithmetic in floating point calculations.
PROGRAM test_float
   IMPLICIT NONE
   INTEGER, PARAMETER :: real_8_32 = SELECTED_REAL_KIND(P=8, R=32)
   REAL (KIND = real_8_32) :: a, b, c, d1, d2, d3, x1, x2
   a = 0.12e10; b = 0.42467895; c = .42467889
   d1 = b - c; d2 = a*b; d3 = a*c
   x1 = a*d1; x2 = d2 - d3
   PRINT *, "Precision is = ", PRECISION(a),KIND(a)
   PRINT *, "OUTPUT RESULTS"
   PRINT 10, a, b, c, d1, d2, d3, x1, x2
10 FORMAT(1x,"a =", e17.8, "b =", e17.8, "c = ", e17.8 /&
   1x, "d1 = ", e17.8, "d2 = ", e17.8, "d3 = ", e17.8 / 1x, "x1 = ", e17.8, "x2 = ", e17.8)
END PROGRAM test_float
```

```
   Precision is = 15 8

   OUTPUT RESULTS
   a = 0.12000000E+10 b = 0.42467895E+00 c = 0.42467889E+00
   d1 = 0.59604645E-07 d2 = 0.50961474E+09 d3 = 0.50961467E+09
   x1 = 0.71525574E+02 x2 = 0.71525574E+02
```

Precision higher than 2, for example, REAL (KIND = 4) :: a, b, c will use quadruple precision for a, b, c. Real constants may also be specified to have a higher precision. For example, if we write

0.5672E–2_2, 1.5672_2

the constants are taken as double precision. Observe that the precision is specified by using underscore 2 following the constant.

Most processors also have built-in functions which return double precision values. Some examples of such expressions are given below. a, b, c are declared REAL (KIND = 2)

i. a + b ** 2 + 4.52 E–2_2
ii. DSIN (b) + DCOSH (a/c)

The use of (KIND = 2) for double precision may make Fortran 90 programs non-portable as double precision is processor dependent. To make programs portable Fortran 90 provides another specification using an intrinsic function

```
SELECTED_REAL_KIND
```

to allow portability of programs. The declaration of REAL takes the form

```
REAL (KIND = SELECTED_REAL_KIND (P = 8, R = 30)) :: a
```

This declaration specifies that the real variable a must have minimum precision P = 8 for mantissa (that is, the number of significant digits in the mantissa of 8) and a minimum exponent range R = ±30. If precision available in the machine is larger, the value nearest the specified precision is returned. The same holds for the specification of exponent. If the precision specified is not available then the function returns a value –1, if the range is not available it returns –2 and if both are not available it returns –3.

One may use a parameter declaration to make KIND specification easy to change. For example:

```
INTEGER, PARAMETER :: real_16_99 = SELECTED_REAL_KIND (P = 16, R = 99)
REAL (KIND = real_16_99) :: a, b, c
```

An inquiry function KIND may be used to find the actual precision and range allotted by the processor. Thus if we write KIND(a) the precision and range of a will be returned.

20.2 KIND SPECIFICATION FOR INTEGERS AND CHARACTERS

The number of digits that can be stored in an integer variable name depends on the word length of a machine. For a 32-bit word length machine it is -2^{31} to $2^{31} - 1$ which is around 10 digits. If a lesser number of digits is required one may declare

```
INTEGER(KIND = 5) :: i
```

which will allow 5 digits integers to be stored in i (+ 99999 to – 99999).

One may parametrize in this case also by writing

```
INTEGER, PARAMETER :: int_5 = SELECTED_INTEGER_KIND(5)
INTEGER(KIND = int_5) :: i
```

Longer integers may also be declared as shown below:

```
INTEGER(KIND = 16) :: j
```

which defines j to be 16 digits long.

The length specification may also be applied to integer constants. If we write

```
1345_5
```

it will be allocated 5 digits when it takes part in calculation.

Fortran 90 standard allows use of characters other than English in specifying character strings. The types of characters allowed is left to the compiler developer. If Devanagari script is implemented in a particular Fortran 90 processor, one may write

```
CHARACTER(LEN = 30, KIND = DEVANAGARI) :: name
```

in which case Devanagari characters are stored in name. Again such programs will be portable only between processors which have implemented Devanagari script. The intrinsic function

```
KIND(name)
```

will return the KIND of characters used to write name.

20.3 USE OF COMPLEX QUANTITIES

Fortran 90 permits arithmetic computations with complex variables, constants and expressions. In Chapter 19 we defined a MODULE to do complex arithmetic. It was mainly for illustrative purposes. There is an intrinsic data type COMPLEX which can be used to declare complex variables. A number of intrinsic functions with complex arguments are also available.

In mathematics a complex number is defined as x + iy where x and y are real numbers and $i = \sqrt{-1}$. A complex number may also be written as (x, y) where the first component of the pair is taken as the real part. This is the technique used in Fortran 90. Some examples of complex constants are:

i. (2.85, 4.5E2) (This equals 2.85 + i4.5E2)
ii. (0.0, 2.85) (This equals i2.85)
iii. (1.2562E–6, 4.85 E–3)

A complex variable name is one in which a complex number may be stored. The rules used to name variables is the same as that used for any identifier in Fortran 90.

Thus the declaration

```
COMPLEX :: c_number, current, voltage, q
```

defines c_number, current, voltage and q as complex. Complex arrays may also be declared as follows:

```
COMPLEX, DIMENSION (1:10) :: a, b
```

Complex variable names and constants may be connected by arithmetic operators among themselves or with reals to form complex expressions. The relational operators == and /= are the only ones allowed between complex variables or constants. A complex quantity may be raised only to an integer power.

A complex arithmetic statement is defined as:

complex variable name = *complex expression* or *real expression*

One, however, may not set a real variable name equal to a complex expression.

For reading and printing complex numbers no special FORMAT is required. As all complex numbers are pair of reals, E or F format may be used for the pair of numbers. Example Program 20.2 illustrates the use of complex quantities. Observe the use of intrinsic Fortran 90 functions. The function REAL gives the real part of a complex variable and AIMAG the imaginary part. CONJG gives the complex conjugate of a complex variable.

Example Program 20.2 Use of complex data type

```
!Example Program 20.2
!Illustrates use of complex numbers.
PROGRAM comp_calc
   IMPLICIT NONE
   COMPLEX :: a, b, c, sum_a, sum_b, sum_ab, sum_abc
   COMPLEX :: mul_ac, div_ab, conjb
   REAL :: x, y
   PRINT *, "Type values of a and b"
   READ 10, a, b
10 FORMAT (4F4.1)
   c = (1.5, 2.5)
   sum_ab = a + b
   x = REAL(sum_ab)
   y = AIMAG(sum_ab)
   sum_abc = a + b + c
   mul_ac = a*(1.5, 2.5)
   div_ab = a/b
   conjb = CONJG(b)
   PRINT 15
15 FORMAT(20x,"OUTPUT RESULTS"/20X, "——————————")
   PRINT 20, a, b, sum_ab, x, y, sum_abc, mul_ac, div_ab, conjb
20 FORMAT(1X,"a = ", 2F8.2, "b = ", 2F8.2 / "sum_ab = ", 2F8.2/1X, "x = ", F8.2, 8X /&
   "y = ", F8.2/1X, "sum_abc = ", 2F8.2 /&
   1x, "mul_ac = ", 2F8.2, "div_ab = ", 2F8.2 / 1x, "conjb = ", 2F8.2)
END PROGRAM comp_calc
```

```
   Type values of a and b
   1.0 1.0 2.0 2.0

   OUTPUT RESULTS
   ——————————
   a = 1.00   1.00   b = 2.00   2.00
   sum_ab = 3.00   3.00
   x = 3.00
   y = 3.00
   sum_abc = 4.50   5.50
   mul_ac = -1.00   4.00   div_ab = 0.50   0.00
   conjb = 2.00   - 2.00
```

20.4 ARRAY OPERATIONS WITH A MASK

The assignment of an array to another array may be controlled by what is known as a *mask*. A mask is an array of logical values, namely, *true* or *false*. A statement called a WHERE statement is used with a mask. A simple form of WHERE statement is

WHERE *(mask expression) array assignment statement*

In the above statement *mask expression* is a logical expression having the same shape as the array participating in the array assignment statement. The array assignment statement is executed only for the positions of the array for which the mask expression is *true*. Thus if we write

```
WHERE (array /= 0) b_array = 1.5 * array
```

the effect of this statement will be to multiply all the non-zero values of array by 1.5 and store it in b_array. We have assumed that b_array has the same shape as array. The expression array /= 0 is an array logical expression with the same shape as array. For example if array = (1 0 0 0 0 2 0 3) then array /= 0 is : (.T. .F. .F. .F. .F. .T. .F. .T.) where .T. is True and .F. is False.

b_array = (1.5 0 0 0 0 3 0 4.5)

Observe that as array is sparse the multiplication operations are reduced. Another form of the WHERE construct is:

WHERE *(mask expression)*
    array assignment statements – 1
ELSEWHERE
    array assignment statements – 2
END WHERE

In the above form the array assignment statements –1 are performed only at positions where the *mask expression* is *true* and array assignment statements –2 are done in positions where the *mask expression* is *false*. For example in the construct

```
WHERE (array /= 0)
      b_array =1/array
ELSEWHERE
      b_array = 0
END WHERE
```

will make b_array = (1 0 0 0 0 0.50 0 0.3333) when array = (1 0 0 0 0 2 0 3).

The WHERE construct is similar to the IF construct except that WHERE operates on a whole array.

20.5 NAMELIST INPUT/OUTPUT

If a group of variables are to be input together, perhaps many times, we can use one name for this list and use this name instead of specifying the individual variable names. For example, if in a program we have to output the values of following variables:

```
CHARACTER (LEN = 15) :: name
INTEGER, DIMENSION (4) :: marks
INTEGER :: class, position
REAL :: avge_marks
```

We can then write:

```
NAMELIST/student_data/ name, marks, class, position, avge_marks
```

and use the statement

```
WRITE (*, NML = student_data)
```

which will output the values of all the variables specified in the NAMELIST as corresponding to student_data. The output produced will be an ampersand character & followed by the name student_data used to name the group followed by the values of the variables specified in the group. For the example being considered it will be as shown by the output_1 of Example Program 20.3. Observe that the main advantage is in using a briefer name list.

Example Program 20.3 Illustrating use of NAMELIST

```
!Example Program 20.3
!Used to illustrate NAMELIST output

PROGRAM output_name_list
  IMPLICIT NONE
  CHARACTER(LEN = 16) :: name = "V.R. DHARMARAJAN"
  INTEGER, DIMENSION(4) :: marks = (/50, 65, 75, 80/)
  INTEGER :: class = 1, position = 10
  REAL :: avge_marks = 67.5
  NAMELIST /student_data/name, marks, class, position, &
    avge_marks
  PRINT *, "OUTPUT - 1 - STUDENT_DATA"
  WRITE(UNIT = *, NML = student_data)
END PROGRAM output_name_list
```

```
  OUTPUT - 1 - STUDENT_DATA
  &STUDENT_DATA
  NAME = V.R. DHARMARAJAN, MARKS = 50, 65, 75, 80, CLASS = 1, POSITION = 10,
AVGE_MARKS = 67.50000000
  /
```

NAMELIST feature has many restrictions in its use which we have not mentioned. It does not seem to have any overriding advantage. Thus except in very special situations this facility is hardly used.

SUMMARY

1. A KIND specification can be included in the declaration of REAL, INTEGER and CHARACTER data types.
2. KIND in REAL is used to specify the precision of mantissa and the size of exponents. (KIND = 2) specifies that the mantissa precision is double the normal precision.
3. An intrinsic function SELECTED_REAL_KIND is available to specify the number of significant digits in the mantissa and the size of the exponent

   `REAL (KIND = SELECTED_REAL_KIND (p = 16, r = 99)) :: a`

   declares a to have 16 significant mantissa digits and an exponent range of ± 99. If a processor does not have the provision to allow this then such a specification is not effective.
4. The KIND specification in integers declares the number of digits allowed for the integer. For example

   `INTEGER (KIND = 4) :: h`

   will allocate 4 digits for b.

5. The KIND specification for characters allows an implementer to accommodate character sets other than English. If a computer has a provision for Devanagari script and if Fortran 90 is to use Devanagari strings one may declare

```
CHARACTER (LEN = 30, KIND = DEVANAGARI) :: c
```

which specifies that c stores Devanagari strings.

6. An intrinsic data type COMPLEX is available in Fortran 90. Complex variables are declared as

```
COMPLEX :: a, b, c
```

which will allocate storage to store the real and imaginary parts of a, b and c. A complex constant is specified as a tuple

```
(2.5, 3.5)
```

7. A statement called a WHERE statement can be used to control assignments to individual elements of an array taken as an entity. For example if we write

```
WHERE (array < 0) array = – array
```

each of the elements of array will be positive storing its magnitude.

8. A NAMELIST statement is used to name a group of items to be input or output with a single name. It is a declaration and should appear before executable statements.

EXERCISES

20.1 Sine, Cosine and Exponential functions are defined as follows:

$$e^x = 1 + x + \frac{x^2}{2!} + \frac{x^3}{3!} + \ldots$$

$$\sin(x) = x - \frac{x^3}{3!} + \frac{x^5}{5!} - \frac{x^7}{7!} \ldots$$

$$\cos(x) = 1 - \frac{x^2}{2!} + \frac{x^4}{4!} - \frac{x^6}{6!} + \ldots$$

Write a program to compute the above functions to double precision. Find how many terms are required to compute these for x = 0.2 to 14 significant digits. Compare with intrinsic double precision functions.

20.2 Write a program which reads two complex numbers x and z and finds the following:

(i) $x^2 + z^2$ (ii) $\sin(x^2 - z^2)$ (iii) $|x| / |z|$

20.3 Write a program to read an array and output it by replacing all negative values with zeros and all values ≥ 10 by 10.

20.4 Write a function to find the binary equivalent of a decimal integer and display it.

20.5 Write a program to find the octal equivalent of a decimal number.

21. *Additional Features of Fortran 95*

Learning Objectives

In this chapter we will learn:

1. New features introduced in Fortran 95 to facilitate writing programs for parallel computers
2. Some minor new features in Fotran 95 which extend Fortran 90

Soon after the publication of the Fortran 90 standard a group called High Performance Fortran Forum (HPFF) was set up to extend Fortran to the emerging high performance parallel computers. An extension of Fortran 90 called High Performance Fortran (HPF) was proposed by HPFF. The main extensions were directives to Fortran 90 programs on parallelizing opportunities and some additional constructs. As parallel computer architecture is still evolving, parallel constructs in Fortran has not been standardised. In the meanwhile the Fortran standards committee decided on a strategy whereby a minor revision of Fortran 90—Fortran 95—will be prepared in mid 90s and a major revision in the year 2000. The main revisions in Fortran 90 are to include some HPF features to enable writing parallelizable Fortran 90 programs. The other minor revisions are small corrections, clarifications and interpretations of some of the statements made in the Fortran 90 standards document. Fortran 95 is almost completely backward compatible with Fortran 90.

Fortran 95 has officially removed some of the features of Fortran 77 as non-standard and not acceptable by Fortran 95 compilers. A draft of Fortran 95 standard was published in November 1995 and ISO standards documents in October 1996. Compiler for Fortran 95 are not yet widely available in the market. In this chapter we will explain the important new features introduced in Fortran 95.

21.1 FORALL STATEMENT

Fortran 95 has included a statement which generalises the array assignment facility provided by Fortran 90. The statement looks like a DO loop but is quite different in the way it computes. It does not iterate on array indices sequentially like a DO loop. It computes the array expression on the right hand side of an assignment for all the specified indices and then performs the assignment. We give as Example 21.1 a FORALL statement which replaces the four interior elements of a (3 × 3) matrix by the sum of its neighbours.

Example 21.1

```
FORALL (i = 2:3, j = 2:3)
   x (i, j) = x (i, j – 1) + x (i, j + 1) + x (i – 1, j) + x (i + 1, j)
END FORALL
```

The above statement calculates the right hand expressions of the above assignment as shown below:

$$x(2, 1) + x(2, 3) + x(1, 2) + x(3, 2) \quad (1)$$
$$x(2, 2) + x(2, 4) + x(1, 3) + x(3, 3) \quad (2)$$
$$x(3, 1) + x(3, 3) + x(2, 2) + x(4, 2) \quad (3)$$
$$x(3, 2) + x(3, 4) + x(2, 3) + x(4, 3) \quad (4)$$

and assigns the value of expression (1) to x(2, 2), expression (2) to x(2, 3), expression (3) to x(3, 2) and lastly expression (4) to x(3, 3). This is shown using numerical values below:

$$\begin{bmatrix} 1 & 2 & 3 & 4 \\ 5 & 6 & 7 & 8 \\ 9 & 10 & 11 & 12 \\ 13 & 14 & 15 & 16 \end{bmatrix} \qquad \begin{bmatrix} 1 & 2 & 3 & 4 \\ 5 & 24 & 28 & 8 \\ 9 & 40 & 44 & 12 \\ 13 & 14 & 15 & 16 \end{bmatrix}$$

Matrix x before executing FORALL statement — Matrix x after executing FORALL statement

Observe that expressions (1), (2), (3), (4) can be calculated in any order as no sequencing is implied by the FORALL statement. Within the expression also individual terms can be evaluated in any order. The FORALL statement may also be written as:

```
FORALL (i = 2 : 3, j = 2 : 3) x(i, j) = x(i, j – 1) + x(i, j + 1) + x(i – 1, j) + x(i + 1, j)
```

if the FORALL is to be applied to only one statement.

FORALL statements may also be nested as shown with the following example:

Example 21.2

```
FORALL (i = 1 : 4)
      x (i, i) = ABS (x (i, i))
   FORALL (j = i – 2 : i + 2, j /= i .AND. j > = 1 .AND. j < = 4)
      x (i, j) = x (i, i) * x (j, j)
   END FORALL
END FORALL
```

The outer FORALL assigns values to x(1, 1), x(2, 2), x(3, 3) and x(4, 4) as per the statement:

$$x(i, i) = ABS(x(i, i))$$

This is shown with matrix

$$\begin{bmatrix} -1 & 0 & 2 & -3 \\ 2 & -3 & -4 & 5 \\ -6 & 7 & -8 & -9 \\ 0 & -5 & 6 & 5 \end{bmatrix} \qquad \begin{bmatrix} 1 & 0 & 2 & -3 \\ 2 & 3 & -4 & 5 \\ -6 & 7 & 8 & -9 \\ 0 & -5 & 6 & 5 \end{bmatrix}$$

x at start — x after outer FORALL

For each value of i, the inner FORALL computes indices j and the resultant values of (i, j) are:

$$(i, j) = (3, 1), (3, 2), (3, 4), (4, 2) \text{ and } (4, 3)$$

The matrix x after carrying out the statement x(i, j) = x(i, i) * x(j, j) is shown below:

$$\begin{bmatrix} 1 & 0 & 2 & -3 \\ 2 & 3 & -4 & 5 \\ 8 & 24 & 8 & 40 \\ 0 & 15 & 40 & 5 \end{bmatrix}$$

x after inner FORALL

We will now explain formally how FORALL statement is interpreted. The general form of the FORALL statement is:

FORALL (*index* = *lb* : *ub* : *step, scalar-mask-expn*) array variable = expression

or

```
FORALL (index = lb : ub : step, scalar-mask-expn)
   <body of FORALL>
END FORALL
```

If *step* is missing it is taken at 1.

If the scalar mask expression is missing it is taken as .TRUE. The values of the index for which FORALL is executed is calculated as follows:

1. The number of *valid set* of index values is found by first computing $max = \left\lceil \frac{ub - lb + 1}{step} \right\rceil$.

   The set of valid values of *index* are: $lb + (k - 1) * step$, $k = 1, 2, 3.... max$. If $max \le 0$ then FORALL is not executed.
2. The *active set* of index values are the ones for which FORALL will be executed. The active set of index values are those values for which the *scalar-mask-expression* evaluates to .TRUE.
3. For each index value in the active set the right hand side of the body of the FORALL is evaluated. The evaluation for different index values may be done in any order.
4. For each index value in the active set, assign the value of the expression calculated in step 3 to the array variable on the left hand side. It is important to remember that the left hand side is determined from the saved subexpression values. Thus the assignments may be performed in any order.

If there are a set of indices rather than a single index then for each index the valid set is calculated as shown in step 1. The active set of all indices is the Cartesian product of active sets of individual indices.

The indices of FORALL are undefined after the termination of FORALL.

Multi-statement FORALL

A sequence of single-statement FORALLs constitute a multi-statement FORALL. Its interpretation is similar. The steps are:

1. Compute the valid set of index values as done for a single FORALL.
2. Compute the active set of index values.
3. Execute the statements in the FORALL body for all active index values in the order in which they appear.

We conclude this section with a few examples.

Example 21.3

```
FORALL (i = 2 : 5) x(i) = x (i – 1) + x(i) + x(i + 1)
```

Given x = [1 2 3 4 5 6] initially, the value of x after the FORALL statement execution is x = [1 6 9 12 15 6].

Example 21.4

```
FORALL (i = 1 : 3, j = 1:4, y(i, j) /= 0.0) x(i, j) = 1.0/y(i, j)
```

$$\text{Given } y(i, j) = \begin{bmatrix} 1 & 2 & 8 & 0 \\ 4 & 0 & 5 & 8 \\ 2 & 8 & 0 & 10 \end{bmatrix}$$

$$x(i, j) = \begin{bmatrix} 1 & 0.5 & 0.125 & 0 \\ 0.25 & 0 & 0.2 & 0.125 \\ 0.5 & 0.125 & 0 & 0.1 \end{bmatrix}$$

Example 21.5

```
FORALL (j = 1 : 4, i = 1 : 3) a(i, j) = b(j, i)
```

$$\text{Given } b(j, i) = \begin{bmatrix} 1 & 2 & 3 \\ 4 & 5 & 6 \\ 7 & 8 & 9 \\ 10 & 11 & 12 \end{bmatrix}$$

$$a(i, j) = \begin{bmatrix} 1 & 4 & 7 & 10 \\ 2 & 5 & 8 & 11 \\ 3 & 6 & 9 & 12 \end{bmatrix}$$

Observe that this is a simple method of transposing a matrix.

Example 21.6

```
FORALL (i = 1 : 4)
   FORALL (j = 1 : i)
      x(i, j) = SQRT (x (j, i)) * x(j, j)
   END FORALL
END FORALL
```

$$x = \begin{bmatrix} 1 & 4 & 16 & 9 \\ 25 & 36 & 49 & 4 \\ 9 & 25 & 64 & 81 \\ 100 & 1 & 9 & 64 \end{bmatrix}$$

Active index set is (1, 1), (2, 1), (2, 2), (3, 1), (3, 2), (3, 3), (4, 1), (4, 2), (4, 3), (4, 4).

The matrix x(i, j) after assignment is:

$$\begin{bmatrix} 1 & 4 & 16 & 9 \\ 2 & 216 & 49 & 4 \\ 4 & 252 & 512 & 81 \\ 3 & 72 & 576 & 512 \end{bmatrix}$$

Example 21.7

```
FORALL (i = 1 : 4) x(p (i)) = x(i)
```

Given x = [5 6 7 8]
p(i) = [3 1 2 4]

After FORALL execution we have:

x = [6 7 5 8]

Example 21.8

```
FORALL (i = 1 : 2, j = 1 : 3, i >= j)
   FORALL (k = 1 : 3, m = 1 : j, k + m > i)
      x(i, j, k, m) = 2 * j * m + 3 * k
   END FORALL
END FORALL
```

The first FORALL gives active indices

{(1, 1), (2, 1), (2, 2)}

The second FORALL valid indices are:

(1, 1, 1, 1), (2, 1, 1, 1), (2, 1, 2, 1), (2, 1, 3, 1)
(2, 2, 1, 1), (2, 2, 1, 2), (2, 2, 2, 1), (2, 2, 2, 2),
(2, 2, 3, 1), (2, 2, 3, 2)

Out of these the inequality (k + m > i) is not satisfied by (2, 1, 1, 1) and (2, 2, 1, 1). Thus the *active* indices for the inner FORALL are the eight remaining 4 tuples. Thus the elements of x(i, j, k, m) are computed for these indices and replace the earlier values.

We have written Example Program 21.1 which corresponds to Example 21.1. Observe that this program is readable. A program using loops to evaluate the expression (Example Program 21.2) gives a different answer as it uses iterations to update values calculated. The difference in semantics between FORALL statement and DO loop must now be clear.

Example Program 21.1 A program to replace internal elements of a matrix by the sum of its neighbours.

```
!Example Program 21.1
   !Illustrates use of FORALL statement
   PROGRAM sum-internal
   IMPLICIT NONE
   REAL, DIMENSION (5, 10) :: x, y
   INTEGER :: i, j, n, m
   READ *, n, m
   READ *, x
   FORALL (i = 2 : n – 1, j = 2 : m – 1)
      x(i, j) = x(i, j – 1) + x(i, j + 1) + x(i – 1, j) + x(i + 1, j)
      y(i, j) = x(i , j)
   END FORALL
   PRINT *, y
END PROGRAM sum_internal
```

Example Program 21.2 A program to illustrate difference between DO and FORALL statements

```
!Example Program 21.2
   !Illustrates that nested DOs are different from FORALL
   PROGRAM sum_internal – 2
   IMPLICIT NONE
   READ, DIMENSION (5, 10) :: x, y
   INTEGER :: i, j, n, m
   READ *, n, m
   READ *, x
   DO i = 2, n – 1
      DO j = 2, m – 1
         x(i, j) = x(i, j – 1) + x(i, j + 1) + x(i – 1, j) + x(i +1, j)
         y(i, j) = x(i, j)
      END DO
   END DO
   PRINT *, y
END PROGRAM sum_internal – 2
```

21.2 PURE PROCEDURES

A FUNCTION or a SUBROUTINE in Fortran 95 may be declared as PURE, for example:

PURE FUNCTION f(x, y)

When a procedure (i.e., a function or a subroutine) is declared PURE it cannot have any unintended side effects. In other words if it is a FUNCTION it can only return a value as specified in the FUNCTION. If it is a SUBROUTINE it can alter only INTENT(OUT) or (INOUT) parameters. One of the major uses of a PURE function is in FORALL statements.

When a procedure is declared PURE it must satisfy the following rules:

1. All dummy arguments of a FUNCTION must have an INTENT(IN) attribute.

2. All the arguments of SUBROUTINE must be specified with INTENT(IN), INTENT(OUT) or INTENT(INOUT). The INTENT(IN) arguments should not be accidentally modified.
3. No local variables in a procedure may have a SAVE attribute.
4. No local variables in a procedure may be initialized in a type declaration statement as such a declaration implies a SAVE attribute.
5. No global variables may be modified by a procedure.
6. Any procedure called by a PURE procedure must also be PURE.
7. No input/output operations may be performed by a PURE procedure.

The Fortran 95 compiler is expected to check if any PURE procedure has potential side effects and if so give an error message. All intrinsic functions in Fortran 90/95 are PURE.

21.3 ELEMENTAL PROCEDURES

An elemental procedure is one that is specified for scalar arguments but may also be applied to vector arguments. If the arguments are scalar then the result is also a scalar. If the argument(s) are arrays the shape of the result is the same as the shape of the argument(s). If there are two or more arguments they must be conformable. For array arguments, the function is applied to each element of the array and the result is an array. We give an example of an elemental subroutine in Example 21.9. This subroutine may be called with array variables as arguments.

Example 21.9 An elemental SUBROUTINE to interchange vectors

```
ELEMENTAL SUBROUTINE exchange (x, y)
   REAL, INTENT (INOUT) :: x, y
   REAL :: temp
   temp = x
   x = y
   y = temp
END SUBROUTINE exchange
```

Many intrinsic functions in Fortran 90 are elemental and are listed in Appendix A (Table A.1).

21.4 MISCELLANEOUS FEATURES

In Fortran 90 if an allocatable array in a procedure does not have the SAVE attribute it has an undefined allocation status when control is returned to the calling program. This wastes memory. In Fortran 95 such an array is automatically deallocated and memory is thus saved.

Another feature of Fortran 95 is the ability to give pointers a NULL (i.e. disassociated) status in a type declaration statement as shown below:

```
REAL, POINTER, DIMENSION (:) :: a => NULL ( )
```

NULL is a new intrinsic function.

Fortran 95 allows assigning initial values to some components of a derived type. The other changes are minor and we will not discuss them. Fortran 95 has declared certain Fortran 77 features as obsolete. Thus no new Fortran program should use these features. Appendix C lists these features.

21.5 CONCLUSIONS

In this book we have discussed in detail Fortran 90 and Fortran 95. At present it is the most popular high level language for computations in science and engineering. Fortran is continually evolving. In the next standard which will probably become available in 2001, the complete upward compatibility which is assured for Fortran 77 programs by Fortran 90 will not be there. In other words the Fortran compiler will not guarantee that Fortran 77 programs will run without change. However, Fortran 90/95 program will be accepted without change in the next version of Fortran.

Another development which has taken place in Fortran is the emergence of High Performance Fortran (HPF). This is a version which allows efficient use of parallel computers by Fortran programmers. As parallel computers are as yet not widely used we have not discussed HPF in this book.

Besides Fortran, a number of other procedure-oriented languages have been developed for specific purposes. Among them C has found some acceptance. C, however, encourages indisciplined programming. It is extremely difficult to debug. Thus Fortran 90 has an edge over C as it has all the good features of C without its shortcomings.

In 1996, Walt Brainerd and his co-workers defined a language named F. F language is a stricter version of Fortran 90. The language was made simpler by removing the need for upward compatibility with Fortran 77 and reducing the many alternate syntax rules allowed for statements in Fortran 90. It has been designed as a language for beginners in programming and inexpensive compilers are available for most computers. All F programs will run on Fortran 90 compilers as F is a proper subset of Fortran 90. F is a good language for engineers and scientists who want to learn programming.

A generation of computer programmers have been using Fortran. In the process of evolution Fortran 90/95 has become a very well designed language. Fortran 90 compilers are available for almost all general purpose computers including Personal Computers. Fortran 90 compilers are quite efficient. It is thus felt that Fortran 90 and its successors will remain a live language.

SUMMARY

1 Fortran 95 has added some small extensions to Fortran 90 to allow Fortran compilers written for parallel computers to use the features of these computers and to optimize execution of Fortran programs.
2. A statement called FORALL statement is available in Fortran 95 as a generalized array assignment. The FORALL statement computes an array expression on the right hand side of an assignment for all the specified indices and then performs the assignment. The computation of the array expression can be performed in any order.
3. Fortran 95 allows specification of a side effect free procedure as a PURE procedure.
4. Fortran 95 allows specification of elemental procedures in which operations specified on scalars can also be performed on conformable arrays.

EXERCISES

21.1 Write a FORALL statement to add all elements above the diagonal of a 5 × 5 matrix to those below the diagonal.

21.2 Write a FORALL statement to swap neighbouring elements of each row of a n × n matrix.

21.3 Find the values assigned to x(i, j) by the following FORALL statements

```
FORALL (i = 1 : 10)
   FORALL (j = 1 : i)
      a(i, j) = a(j, i) * a(i, i)
   END FORALL
END FORALL
```

21.4 Find out the values assigned to a(i, j) by the following FORALL statements

```
FORALL (i = 1, 4)
   a(i, i) = SQRT (a(i, i))
   FORALL (j = i – 2 : i + 2, j /= i .AND. j > = 1 . AND. j <= 5)
      a(i, j) = a(i, i) * a(j, j)
   END FORALL
END FORALL
```

Assume a(i, j) initially is $\begin{bmatrix} 1 & 0 & 0 & 0 \\ 0 & 2 & 0 & 0 \\ 0 & 0 & 3 & 0 \\ 0 & 0 & 0 & 4 \end{bmatrix}$

21.5 The function given below is not PURE. Pick all the statements which make it not PURE.

```
PURE REAL FUNCTION g(x, y, z)
   REAL, INTENT (IN) :: x
   REAL, INTENT (IN) :: y(10)
   REAL :: z
   REAL, SAVE :: b
   REAL :: a = 20.5
   INTEGER :: i
   DO i = 1, 10
      g = g + y(i) * x + a * b
   END DO
END FUNCTION g
```

21.6 Write an elemental function to find the cube root of elements of an array.

21.7 Write an elemental function to find the square root of the sum of squares of elements of two conformable arrays.

21.8 Write an elemental function to compare element by element the element values of two conformable arrays and give as result array one which has the larger of the two values.

Appendix A—Intrinsic Procedures in FORTRAN 90

There are four classes of intrinsic procedures in Fortran 90:

1. Elemental functions
2. Inquiry functions
3. Transformational functions
4. Subroutines

Elemental Function: An elemental function is one that is specified for scalar arguments but in many cases may be applied to vector arguments. If the arguments are scalar then the result is also a scalar. If the argument(s) are arrays then the shape of the result is the same as the shape of the argument(s). If there are several arguments they must be conformable. For array arguments, the function is applied to each element of the array and the result is an array. The type of the arguments is specified as follows:

i : integer
x, y : real numeric
z : complex
a : any (integer, or real or complex)

All the elemental function names given in Table A1 are generic. In other words, the same name is used regardless of the type of argument. Specific names of intrinsic functions are listed in Table A3. If an intrinsic function is used as an actual argument to a procedure, its specific name (not the generic name) should be used. Only scalar arguments are allowed in this case. If a function has no specific name, it must not be used as an actual argument in a procedure. *Inquiry functions* are those whose result depends on the properties of its principal arguments rather than on the value of the argument. *Transformational* functions have one or more array valued arguments or an array valued result.

Elemental Numeric

A.1 Generic Functions in Fortran 90

Function Name	*Function*
1. ABS (a)	$\lvert a \rvert$ $\sqrt{x^2 + y^2}$ if $a = x + iy$
2. ACOS (x)	arc cos (x), $x < 1$; $0 \le$ ACOS (x) $\le \pi$
3. AIMAG (z)	$z = x + iy$ AIMAG ($x + iy$) $= y$
4. AINT (x)	integer portion of $\lvert x \rvert$. Sign same as sign of x
5. ANINT (x)	Nearest integer to x. If $x > 0$, ANINT (x) = AINT ($x + 0.5$) If $x < 0$, ANINT (x) = AINT ($x - 0.5$)

(*Cont.*)

A.1 (Cont.)

Function Name	*Function*
6. ASIN (*x*)	arc sin (*x*); $\|x\| \le 1$; $0 \le$ ASIN $(x) \le \pi$
7. ATAN (*x*)	arc tan (*x*) ; $-\pi/2 \le$ ATAN $(x) \le \pi/2$
8. ATAN2 (*y*, *x*)	arc tan (*y*/*x*); $-\pi/2 \le$ ATAN $(x) \le \pi$ Both *x* and *y* cannot be 0
9. CEILING (*x*)	Least integer $\ge x$
10. CONJG (*z*)	Complex conjugate of *z*
11. COS (*a*)	cos (*a*); *a* real or complex
12. COSH (*x*)	cosh (*x*) Hyperbolic cosine of *x*
13. DIM (*x*, *y*)	$(x - y)$ if $(x - y) > 0$, else 0 ; *x*, *y* : integer or real
14. DPROD (*x*, *y*)	Double precision product of *x* and *y*
15. EXP (*x*)	exp (*x*), *x* real or complex
16. FLOOR (*x*)	Greatest integer $\le x$
17. FRACTION (*x*)	Fractional part of *x*
18. LOG (*x*)	$\log_e (x)$ *x* real or complex > 0
19. LOG10 (*x*)	$\log_{10} (x)$ *x* real > 0
20. MAX (*a1*, *a2*, *a3* ..)	Maximum value of *a1*, *a2*, *a3* .... *a1*, *a2*, *a3* .... real or integer MAX (5, – 7, 6, 8) = 8 MAX ((/ – 5, 6, 8, 4 /), (/ 3, 6, 7, 6/) = (/ 3, 6, 8, 6/)
21. MIN (*a1*, *a2*, *a3* ..)	Minimum value of *a1*, *a2*, *a3* .... *a1*, *a2*, *a3* .... real or integer.
22. MOD (*a*, *p*)	*a* integer or real. *p* same type as *a* MOD $(a, p) = a - p *$ INT (a/p) ; $p > 0$ MOD (9, 5) = 4, MOD (–9, 5) = – 4, MOD (9, –5) = 4, MOD (–9, –5) = – 4
23. MODULO (*a*, *p*)	*a* integer or real; *p* same type as *a* If *a* integer. MODULO $(a, p) = r$ such that $a = q * p + r$ where *q* is an integer, *p* and *r* have some sign and $0 \ge \|r\| < \|p\|$ For *a* real $r = a -$ FLOOR $(a/p) * p$ MODULO (9, 4) = 5, MODULO (– 9, 4) = 3 MODULO (9, – 4) = –3 MODULO (– 9.0, – 4.0) = – 5.0
24. NEAREST (*x*, *s*)	*x* real, $s > 0$ real Nearest machine representable number different from *x* in the direction of *s*
25. NINT (*x*)	if $x > 0$, NINT (x) = INT $(x + 0.5)$ else NINT (x) = INT $(x - 0.5)$
26. SIGN (*x*, *y*)	sign $(y)\ \|x\|$; *x*, *y* real or integer
27. SIN (*x*)	sin (*x*) ; *x* real or complex
28. SINH (*x*)	Hyperbolic sine of x
29. SQRT (*x*)	$\sqrt{x}$ $x \ge 0$ if *x* real $\sqrt{x + iy}$ if complex. $x \ge 0$. If $x = 0$ $y \ge 0$
30. TAN (*x*)	tan (*x*)
31. TANH (*x*)	Hyperbolic tangent of *x*

A.2 Conversion Numeric Intrinsic Functions

Name	*Explanation*
*1. BIT_SIZE (*i*)	Number of bits in *i*
≠2. CMPLX (*x*)	*x* real. Returns $x + iy$ $y = 0$
≠3. DBLE (*a*)	Returns double precision *a*
*4. DIGITS (*x*)	*x* integer or real. Number of significant digits in *x*
*5. EPSILON (*x*)	A positive number which is almost negligible
≠6. EXPONENT (*x*)	Returns exponent
*7. HUGE (*x*)	*x* integer or real; Largest number of type
≠8. INT (*a*, KIND)	*a* any. Converts to integer of given KIND (KIND optional)
*9. KIND (*a*)	*a* any. Returns KIND of *a* (inquiry function)
≠10. LOGICAL (*l*, KIND)	*l* logical. Returns logical value converted from the kind of *l* to KIND
*11. MAXEXPONENT (*x*)	Returns maximum exponent of type *x* with KIND of *x*
*12. MINEXPONENT (*x*)	Returns minimum exponent of type *x* with KIND of *x*
*13. PRECISION (*x*)	Decimal precision of *x* (inquiry function)
*14. RADIX (*x*)	*x* integer or real. Returns base of *x*
*15. RANGE (*x*)	Returns decimal exponent range of *x*
≠16. REAL (*a*, KIND)	If *a* integer returns real. If *a* real changes KIND
#17. SELECTED_INT_KIND (*i*)	Returns number of digit positions of *i* of specified KIND
#18. SELECTED_REAL_KIND (P, R)	Returns precision P and range R of real
≠19. SET_EXPONENT (*x*, *i*)	Returns in *i* exponent of *x*
*20. TINY (*x*)	Smallest positive number of the same type and KIND as *x*

* Elemental function

≠ Inquiry functions

\# Integer transformation functions

A.3 Specific Names of Functions

Function	*Integer*	*Real*	*Complex*	*Double Precision*
$\lvert x \rvert$	IABS (x)	ABS (x)	CABS (x)	DABS (x)
truncation	–	AINT (x)	–	DINT (x)
nearest integer	–	ANINT (x)	–	DNINT (x)
arc sin x	–	ASIN (x)	–	DASIN (x)
arc tan x	–	ATAN (x)	–	DATAN (x)
arc tan (y/x)	–	ATAN2 (y, x)	–	DTAN2 (y, x)
cos x	–	COS (x)	CCOS (z)	DCOS (x)
cosh x	–	COSH (x)	–	DCOSH (x)
(x – y)	IDM (i, j)	DIM (x, y)	–	DDIM (x, y)
exp (x)	–	EXP (x)	CEXP (z)	DEXP (x)
float (a)	FLOAT (i)	–	–	–
log x	–	ALOG (x)	CLOG (z)	DLOG (x)
$\log_{10}$ x	–	ALOG10 (x)	–	DLOG10 (x)
mod (a, p)	–	AMOD (a, p)	–	DMOD (a, p)
sin x	–	SIN (x)	CSIN (z)	DSIN (x)
sinh x	–	SINH (x)	–	DSINH (x)
sqrt x	–	SQRT (x)	CSQRT (z)	DSQRT (x)
tan x	–	TAN (x)	–	DTAN (x)
tanh x	–	TANH (x)	–	DTANH (x)

A.4 Character Intrinsic Functions in Fortran 90

Function Name	*Explanation of Function*
*1. ACHAR (i)	Returns ASCII character in the ith position in ASCII collating sequence
*2. ADJUSTL (string)	Returns string with leading blanks of string removed and appended as trailing blanks
*3. ADJUSTR (string)	Returns string with trailing blanks of string removed and appended as leading blanks
*4. CHAR (i)	Returns character in the ith position of the processors collating sequence
≠5. IACHR (c)	Returns position of character c in the ASCII collating sequence. If c is not ASCII then returns processor dependent value
≠6. ICHAR (c)	Returns position of c in the processors collating sequence
≠7. INDEX (string, substring)	If LEN(string) < LEN (substring) returns 0 If LEN (substring) = 0 returns 1 If STRING (*i*: *i* + LEN (substring) – 1) = string then return lowest i else return 0

(*Cont.*)

	Function Name	*Explanation of Function*
°8.	LEN (string)	Returns length of string
≠9.	LEN_TRIM (string)	Returns length of string without counting trailing blanks. If blank string returns 0
#10.	LGE (string_a, string_b)	Returns *true* if string_a ≥ string_b in ASCII collating sequence, else *false*. If both 0 length the result is true. The shorter string extended by padding trailing blanks
#11.	LGT (string_a, string_b)	Returns *true* if string_a > string_b in ASCII collating sequence, else *false*. The shorter string extended by padding trailing blanks
#12.	LLE (string_a, string_b)	Returns *true* if string_a ≤ string_b in ASCII collating sequence, else *false*. The shorter string extended by padding
#13.	LLT(string_a, string_b)	Returns true if string_a < string_b in ASCII collating sequence, else *false*. The shorter string extended by padding
♣14.	REPEAT (string, ncopies)	string-a character string ncopies-a non-negative integer Returns a string obtained by concatenating ncopies of string. If either string or ncopies equals zero the result is a zero length string
≠15.	SCAN (string, set, back)	Back is a logical quantity and is optional. String and set are character strings. Returns an integer which is the first instance of a member of the characters in set that appears in string, counting from left. If back is true the search is from the right, but the count is from the left. If no character of string is in set, or if the length of string or set is 0, the result is 0
♣16.	TRIM (string)	Returns string with any trailing blanks removed
≠17.	VERIFY (string, set, back)	Back is a logical quantity and is optional. String and set are character strings. Returns 0 if every character in string is also in set or if string is of 0 length. If a character in string is not in set, the result is its position in string. If back is true, then the search is from right

* Character elemental function
≠ Integer elemental function
° Integer inquiry function
Logical elemental function
♣ Character transformational function

A.5 Bit Intrinsic Procedures

An object consists of s bits numbered from 0 to s–1 from left to right. In most computers s = 32.

	Function	*Explanation of function*
1.	BTEST (i, pos)	Returns *true* if bit in position pos of i is 1, else *false* i, pos integers e.g., BTEST (24, 1) is *false*
2.	IAND (i, j)	Returns an integer which is the logical AND of i and j
3.	IBCLR (i, pos)	Returns i with bit in pos set to 0 e.g., IBCLR (17, 4) = 1
4.	IBITS (i, pos, len)	Returns a right adjusted sequence of bits extracted from i of length len beginning at bit pos. All other bits are 0 e.g. IBITS (343, 6, 3) = 5
5.	IBSET (i, pos)	Returns i with pos bit set to 1 e.g., IBSET (5, 1) = 7
6.	IEOR (i,j)	Returns exclusive OR bit by bit of i and j
7.	IOR (i, j)	Returns OR bit by bit of i and j
8.	ISHFT (i,s)	Returns i logically shifted right (if s < 0) or left (s > 0). Zeros fill up vacated positions
9.	ISHFTC (i, s, size)	Returns value of i with its *size* rightmost bits circularly shifted right (s > 0) or left (s < 0). If *size* is absent, the effect is as though it were present with the value = BIT-SIZE (i). s integer |s| ≤ *size*. *size* > 0, ≤ BIT_SIZE (i)
10.	NOT (i)	Returns logical complements of the bits of i

A.6 Array Intrinsic Functions

In the following definitions

- A scalar is an array of rank 0.
- The optional logical argument *mask* is used by some of the functions to select the elements of one or more of the arguments to be operated on by the function.
- *dim* is an optional argument in many functions and is italicized. If present the result is an array of rank (r – 1).
- In the functions ALL, ANY, LBOUND, MAXVAL, MINVAL, PRODUCT, SUM and UBOUND *dim* when present requires that the corresponding actual argument is not an optional dummy argument of the calling program unit.

Function	Explanation of Function
1. DOT_PRODUCT (vec_a, vec_b)	Returns dot product of two vectors. Vectors are either numeric or logical
2. MATMUL (mat_a, mat_b)	Returns the product of two matrices. Matrices are either numeric or logical
3. ALL (MASK, *dim*)	Returns *true* if all MASK values are true along dimension *dim*, else *false* MASK is logical
4. ANY (MASK, *dim*)	Returns *true* if any MASK value is true along dimension *dim*, else *false*
5. COUNT (MASK, *dim*)	Returns number of *true* elements of MASK along dimension *dim*
6. CSHIFT (array, s, *dim*)	Circular shift of an array by s positions. If *dim* present, s is not scalar. In this case each array section shifted separately based on s
7. EOSHIFT (array, s, *boundary*, *dim*)	Performs an end-off shift of an array expression
8. LBOUND (array, *dim*)	Returns all the lower bounds or a specified lower bound of array
9. MAXLOC (array, *MASK*)	Returns the location of the first element of array having the maximum value of the elements identified by *MASK*. (*MASK* optional)
10. MAXVAL (array, *dim*, *MASK*)	Returns the maximum value of the elements of array along dimension *dim* (if present) corresponding to the true elements of *MASK* (if present)
11. MERGE (tsource, fsource, MASK)	Selects one of two alternative values according to MASK. If MASK (or an element of MASK) is *true* then the result is tsource (or an element of tsource), otherwise it is fsource (or an element of fsource). Example: MERGE ((/1.0, 1.0/), (/2.0 3.0/), (/.true., .false./)) = (/1.0, 3.0 /)
12. MINLOC (array, *MASK*)	Returns the location of the first element of array having the minimum value of the elements identified by *MASK* (*MASK* optional)
13. MINVAL (array, *dim*, *MASK*)	Returns the minimum value of the elements of array along dimension *dim* (if present) corresponding to the *true* elements of MASK (if present)
14. PACK (array, MASK, *vector*)	Packs an array into an array of rank one under the control of MASK. If *vector* is present, the size of the result is the same as the size of *vector*—otherwise the

(Cont.)

A.6 (Cont.)

Function	*Explanation of Function*
	result size is the number of *true* elements in MASK. If MASK is a scalar with value *true*, result size is size of array
15. PRODUCT (array, *dim, MASK*)	Returns product of the elements of array along dimension *dim* (if present) corresponding to the *true* elements of the *MASK* (if present)
16. RESHAPE (source, shape)	Constructs an array of a specified shape from the elements of another array
17. SHAPE (source)	Returns the shape of source as a rank 1 array whose size is *r* and whose elements are the extents of the corresponding dimensions of source
18. SIZE (array, *dim*)	Returns either the extent of array along a specified dimension (if *dim* present) or the total number of elements in the array
19. SPREAD (source, dim, ncopies)	Returns an array of rank *r* + 1 by copying source along a specified dimension.
20. SUM (array, *dim, MASK*)	Returns sum of the elements of array along dimension *dim* (if present) corresponding to the *true* elements of *MASK* (if present)
21. TRANSFER (source, mold, *SIZE*)	Returns either a scalar or rank one array with a physical representation identical to that of source but interpreted with the type and kind of mold source: scalar or array mold: scalar or array *SIZE*: integer If mold is a scalar and *SIZE* is absent, the result is a scalar; if mold is an array and *SIZE* is absent, the result has a size as small as possible such that its physical representation is not shorter than that of source; if *SIZE* is present, the result is a rank one array of size *SIZE*
22. TRANSPOSE (matrix)	Transposes a two dimensional matrix. The (i, j)th element of result is the (j, i)th element of matrix
23. UBOUND (array, *dim*)	Returns all the upper bounds or the specified upper bound of array
24. UNPACK (vector, MASK, field)	Unpacks a rank one array into an array under the control of a mask
25. ALLOCATED (array)	Returns *true* if array is currently allocated, otherwise *false*

A.7 Intrinsic Subroutines

1. DATE_AND_TIME (*date, time, zone, values*)

Returns current date and time

date CHARACTER (LEN = 8) OUT in the form CCYYMMDD

CC	Century
YY	Year
MM	Month
DD	Day

time CHARACTER (LEN = 10) OUT hhmmss.sss

hh	hour
mm	minutes
ss.sss	seconds and milliseconds

zone CHARACTER (LEN = 8) OUT set to + or – hhmm which is the time difference with respect to GMT

values INTEGER (8)

value (1) : year
value (2) : month
value (3) : day
value (4) : minutes difference from GMT
value (5) : Hours in the range 0 to 23
value (6) : Minutes in the range 0 to 59
value (7) : Seconds in the range 0 to 60
value (8) : Milliseconds in the range 0 to 999

2. SYSTEM-CLOCK (*count, count-rate, count-max*)

Returns integer data from a real time clock; the integer is incremented by 1 for each clock count until *count-max* is reached. It is then reset to 0 at the next count; the integer lies in the range 0 to *count-max*.

3. RANDOM_NUMBER (harvest)

Returns pseudo-random number(s) from the uniform distribution over the range 0 ≤ harvest < 1.0. Harvest may be a scalar or an array.

4. RANDOM_SEED (*size, put,* get)

Either restarts the pseudo-random number generator used by RANDOM_NUMBER or returns generator parameters.

size (optional)	set to number of integers the processor uses to hold the value of the seed n (integer)
put (optional)	IN integer *m* m ≥ n; the seed is set to the value of *put*
get (optional)	IN integer m m ≥ n; *get* is set to the current value of the seed

There must either be no arguments in which case the subroutine sets the seed to a processor dependent value or there must be exactly one argument which is used as described above.

A.8 Miscellaneous Inquiry Functions

ASSOCIATED (pointer, *target*): Returns *true* if pointer is associated with a target and *target* is that of the pointer. If *target* not specified then also it returns *true* if pointer is associated with a *target*. Otherwise it returns *false*.

PRESENT (a): Returns *true* if a is present, where a is an optional argument of the procedure in which the reference to PRESENT occurs; otherwise *false*.

Appendix B Statement Order in FORTRAN 90

In Table B.1 we summarize the statement ordering in Fortran 90.

Table B.1 Statement Ordering in Fortran 90

<table>
<tr><td colspan="2">PROGRAM, FUNCTION, SUBROUTINE, or MODULE statement</td></tr>
<tr><td colspan="2">USE statement</td></tr>
<tr><td rowspan="3">FORMAT statement</td><td>IMPLICIT NONE statement</td></tr>
<tr><td>PARAMETER statements, derived type definitions, Interface block, Type declaration statements and specification statements</td></tr>
<tr><td>Executable statements</td></tr>
<tr><td colspan="2">CONTAINS statement</td></tr>
<tr><td colspan="2">Internal subprogram or module subprogram</td></tr>
<tr><td colspan="2">END statement</td></tr>
</table>

Appendix C *Statements of Fortran 77 declared as Obsolete in Fortran 95*

1. Fortran 77 used a fixed format for source statements. The format requires statements to be between columns 7 and 72, comment character C in column 1 etc. This fixed format is obsolete. A statement uses a free format and may be anywhere on a line.
2. Computed GO TO statement available in Fortran 77 is not to be used. It has been replaced by SELECT CASE statement.
3. CHARACTER * form to specify length of strings in CHARACTER specification is obsolete. One should use instead CHARACTER (LEN = n) form.
4. DATA statement used in Fortran 77 (not discussed in this book) should not be used within executable statements.
5. Arithmetic Statement Functions (available in Fortran 77, not discussed in this book) is obsolete.
6. Results of character functions cannot have assumed length.
7. The DO loop indices cannot be reals.
8. Branching to an ENDIF statement from outside an IF block is not allowed.
9. PAUSE statement (not discussed in this book) of Fortran 77 is not allowed.
10. ASSIGN statement and ASSIGNED GO TO statement (available in Fortran 77 and not discussed in this book) are removed from the standard.
11. H edit description in FORMAT statement (not discussed in this book) is removed.
12. ASSIGNED FORMAT (not discussed in this book) is removed.

Appendix D New Fortran 90/95 Features compared with Fortran 77

- Fortran 90/95 programs may be written in a free form and need not adhere to the fixed format imposed in Fortran 77.
- Variable and procedure names may be upto 31 characters long.
- The length of integers and the precision and exponent range of reals need not be fixed. They may be parametrized.
- Use of IMPLICIT NONE statement forces all variables to be declared thereby providing better security to programs.
- User defined data types and operators allows a programmer to define data structures and operations on such structures.
- Data structures and procedures may be encapsulated in a MODULE. This allows definition of abstract data types and language extension.
- Packaging data in MODULEs allows controlled global access to entities within the MODULEs.
- Arrays can be treated as a single object allowing operations on whole arrays without using a DO loop.
- Dynamically allocatable arrays simplifies writing of procedures with arrays.
- Simplified DO loop syntax allows writing error free programs with loops.
- Recursive procedures are allowed in Fortran 90/95.
- Optional arguments in procedures provide greater flexibility in writing programs.
- Fortran 90/95 has a POINTER data type. This allows creation and manipulation of dynamic data structures such as lists and trees.
- FORALL construct in Fortran 95 facilitates optimization of program execution in parallel computers.
- Elemental procedures allow procedures to use operations specified on scalars to be performed on arrays.

References

1. W.S. Brained, C.H. Goldberg and J.C. Adams, *Programmer's Guide to Fortran 90*, McGraw-Hill Book Company, New York, U.S.A., 1992.
2. T.M.R. Ellis, I.R. Philips and T.M. Lahey, *Fortran 90 Programming*, Addison-Wesley Publishing Company, Reading, MA, U.S.A., 1994.
3. M. Metcalf and J. Reid, *Fortran 90/95 Explained*, Oxford University Press, Oxford U.K., 1996.
4. V. Rajaraman, *Computer Programming in Fortran 77*, Prentice-Hall of India, New Delhi, 1984.
5. J.F. Kerrigan, *Migrating to Fortran 90*, Orielly Associates, CA, U.S.A., 1993.
6. I. Chivers and J. Sleightholme, *Introducing Fortran 90*, Springer-Verlag, Germany, 1995.
7. W. Schick and G. Silverman, *Fortran 90 and Engineering Computations*, John Wiley and Sons, New York, U.S.A., 1995.
8. M. Metcalf, *Fortran 95*, Fortran Journal, Vol. 8, No. 3, May/June 1996.
9. C.H. Koelbel, et al., *The High Performance Fortran Handbook*, The MIT Press, Cambridge, MA, U.S.A., 1994.

Index